Against the American Grain

Vera M. Kutzinski

The Johns Hopkins University Press
Baltimore and London

Against the American Grain

Myth and History in
William Carlos Williams,
Jay Wright, and
Nicolás Guillén

1987

This book has been brought to publication with the
generous assistance of the Andrew W. Mellon Foundation.

© 1987 The Johns Hopkins University Press
All rights reserved
Printed in the United States of America

The Johns Hopkins University Press
701 West 40th Street
Baltimore, Maryland 21211
The Johns Hopkins Press Ltd., London

The paper used in this publication meets the minimum
requirements of American National Standard for
Information Sciences—Permanence of Paper for Printed
Library Materials, ANSI Z39.48-1984.

Library of Congress Cataloging-in-Publication Data

Kutzinski, Vera M., 1956–
  Against the American grain.

  Bibliography: p.
  Includes index.
  1. American poetry—20th century—History and
criticism. 2. Myth in literature. 3. History in literature. 4.
Canon (Literature). 5. Williams, William Carlos, 1883–
1963—Criticism and interpretation. 6. Wright, Jay—
Criticism and interpretation. 7. Guillén, Nicolás, 1902–
—Criticism and interpretation. 8. America in literature.
9. Literature, Comparative—American and Cuban. 10.
Literature, Comparative—Cuban and American. I. Title.
PS310.M96K8   1987   811'.52'09   86-18504
ISBN 0-8018-3330-2 (alk. paper)

To my parents and L. L.

Contents

vii

Preface

We are all familiar, I am sure, with those classroom situations in which students respond to certain reading assignments with tenacious silence, suggesting discomfort, skepticism, or sheer indifference. The first time I taught Octavio Paz in an American Studies seminar I was confronted with just such a silence, which was finally broken by a timid, yet somewhat reproachful, voice putting into words what seemed to be written on everybody's face: "Why do we have to read about Mexico? What does this have to do with American Studies?" I was truly perplexed, at least until I realized that these questions were not all that unusual. In fact, they were quite similar in kind to those implicit in the skeptical frowns with which both students and colleagues sometimes still meet the inclusion of Afro-American texts in American literature courses. There clearly seemed to be a problem, but not necessarily with the students in that particular class.

Preface

The real problem is more complex. It has in part to do with the division of academic turf—what some call intellectual ghettoization—and to an even larger extent with the kinds of expectations we as scholars of American cultures and literatures create in our students and our colleagues in other areas of the humanities. That problem is exclusivity, or exclusion, and it has not been solved, one should add, by the presence of Afro-American and Latin American Studies programs even at major universities. To be sure, the existence of those programs has been in many ways a positive development, but it has also indirectly aided the compartmentalization of the study of American literatures and thus facilitated the continued exclusion of so-called marginal authors and texts from our standard curricula. Such compartmentalization does not begin or end with institutional politics; it is a matter of intellectual attitudes and concepts, of cultural ideologies, in short.

Such ideologies enter the study of literature (as well as, of course, any other field) in many more or less subtle ways: for instance, in the form of terminologies and methodologies that define the conditions that make knowledge possible. It is precisely with the ideological underpinnings of Americanist literary criticism that this book takes issue. My thoughts on these matters, which take shape in the form of readings of selected texts by William Carlos Williams, Jay Wright, and Nicolás Guillén, derive their focus from one central question: What is the difference between America and the New World? This difference is not simply a matter of splitting terminological hairs. If we take this question seriously, we will find that it involves a rigorous reassessment of all kinds of familiar critical and literary categories and conventions. It also affords us an opportunity to contemplate other differences, namely, between literature and writing; between a literary canon and literary history; between modernism and postmodernism; and between myth and history. Rather than treating these concerns in a purely theoretical manner (if such a thing were indeed possible), I have attempted to show how they actually affect literary interpretation or what I prefer to call the practice of critical reading.

If my own critical practice is deconstructive, it is so because my readings are inevitably part of the processes of simultaneous dispersion and reassembly of textual fragments in which Williams, Wright, and Guillén engage. My argument is that their deconstructive ventures and the tropes (or textual ideograms) that mediate them are "products" of a very specific cultural and historical environment: that of the New World. Preoccupied with the origins of New World culture, Williams, Wright, and Guillén reinvent American history from a cross-cultural perspective: They assemble in their texts elements from several different cultural and literary traditions (notably African, European, and Amerindian), whose textual interaction generates forms of poetic discourse that challenge the universality of European (and eurocentric) literary models and their metaphysics. That challenge involves, above all, a break with genealogy, which overturns the concept of tradition and the linear view of history on which it is predicated. Freed from genealogical imperatives, tradition can be perceived as a system of elective affinities in which choices regarding literary ancestry are made independent of racial, national, or linguistic criteria. Each writer combines historical with literary revisionism by demonstrating the impact of cultural fragmentation and hybridization on literary production, specifically on questions of literary authority, genre, and canonization. Translating cultural interaction into an exchange of literary forms, Williams, Wright, and Guillén invalidate generic and canonical distinctions and propose their own distinctive mythologies of writing. My aim in exploring these mythologies has been to introduce to the study of American literatures a comparative perspective that would counteract the conceptual segregation and institutional isolation of Anglo-American, Afro-American, and Latin American literary traditions. This book, in other words, is an attempt to formulate what has turned out to be a rather lengthy response to that initial question asked by one of my students and doubtlessly thought by many others.

Like its subject matter, this book is very much the product of many different cultural and academic influences. It is at the same time an opportunity to lay claim and pay tribute to at least some of them. While I received most of my academic training in the United States, some of the most important foundations for my later academic ventures were laid at the University of Hamburg, West Germany, where I first embarked on my studies of American literature and history. Among the many teachers I had during those early years at Hamburg, I would like to single out Professors Rolf Meyn, Reinhard Doerries, and Klaus Oehler, who impressed upon me a lasting sense of intellectual rigor and curiosity. Professor Meyn in particular deserves credit for introducing me to Afro-American literature through the novels of Richard Wright and Ralph Ellison. It was at Smith College, under the guidance of Professors Johnella Butler and Maceo Dailey of the Afro-American Studies Department, that my newly found research interests evolved into a more systematic endeavor, and I decided to pursue the study of Afro-American literature at the graduate level.

This study began to take shape during my years as a graduate student in Yale's Afro-American and American Studies programs. Its beginnings were formulated in my master's thesis on Jay Wright, whose poetry I had first read in a seminar team-taught by Ronald Rassner and Robert Stepto, my dissertation director and adviser. Conversations with Kimberly W. Benston, J. Hillis Miller, Robert L. Caserio, Alan Trachtenberg, R. W. B. Lewis, John W. Blassingame, Harold Bloom, and the late Charles T. Davis gave me many invaluable leads. I cannot thank them enough for their kindness and generosity. Undoubtedly one of my most unrelenting critics, as well as supporters, has been Roberto González Echevarría of Yale's Spanish Department, who made me realize that Spanish was a language I could simply not afford not to know. I owe him special thanks for his unwavering support and for many valuable suggestions concerning my work on Nicolás Guillén and Alejo Carpentier.

Perhaps the most rigorous testing ground for my ideas were continued dialogues with a select group of friends, with whom I was fortunate enough to be able to share most of my years at Yale: Anita Cook, Marcellus Blount, Richard Powell, Raelinda Brown, Dwight Andrews, Judith Wilson, Christopher Healy, Dominic Parisi, Rudolph Byrd, and José Piedra. I also wish to express my deep gratitude to Marion Humbert, Detlev Eggers, and Julia MacKenzie for years of long-distance moral support and encouragement. This book is, in many ways, a tribute to all of them. A very special debt of gratitude I owe to Jay and Lois Wright, whose warm friendship and enthusiasm sustained me through many a period of doubt and frustration. Last but not least, my thanks go to Eric Halpern, my editor, for making the publication of this book possible.

Writing against
the American Grain
William Carlos Williams's
New Language

How to begin to find a shape - to begin to begin again
turning the inside out : to find one phrase that will
lie married beside another for delight . ?
—*seems beyond attainment .*

—WILLIAM CARLOS WILLIAMS, *Paterson*

Although *In the American Grain* is today recognized as one of William Carlos Williams's major literary achievements, it took nothing less than the publication of *Paterson* to rescue this work from oblivion. When *In the American Grain* was first published in 1925, and even when it was reissued fourteen years later, its critical reception was as disappointing as its sales, and Williams quickly abandoned the idea of a second volume.[1] Even critics sympathetic to Williams, like Kenneth Burke, Gorham Munson, and D. H. Lawrence,[2] were puzzled and bewildered by this curious collection of twenty-one "essays" on American history, which seemed to constitute some sort of response not only to Eliot's *Waste Land* and Pound's "archeological" ventures but also to Van Wyck Brooks's clarion call for a "usable past."[3] But nobody, with the possible exception of Lawrence, seemed quite able to grasp the nature and the scope of that response, or if they did, they were offended by it. What Williams considered important, that is, "usable" or useful, about America's past was hardly in agreement with the ideas of Brooks and the other "guardians" of American culture. The main problem with *In the American Grain* was that it went *against* the American grain, at least as those critics defined it.

While there appear to be many similarities between *In the American Grain* and the work of Brooks, Randolph Bourne, Waldo Frank, Paul Rosenfeld, and Lewis Mumford, all of whom embarked on a collective quest for a usable past, these similarities are, as E. P. Bollier has argued, as superficial as they are deceiving.[4] Although Williams, much like Brooks, debunked America's Puritan heritage, he was clearly not interested in rescuing "Thoreau and Whitman and Mark Twain . . . to try to tap through them a certain eternal human tradition of abounding vitality and moral freedom."[5] In fact, the classic nineteenth-century American writers are barely even mentioned in *In the American Grain*. Bollier writes,

Not only does Williams neglect Whitman and elevate Poe, but he devotes chapters to only two other writers who could be considered literary at all—Franklin and Cotton Mather—and condemns them outright as enemies. He slightingly mentions Bryant, Cooper, Hawthorne, James Russell Lowell, and Longfellow in passing; and in a brief sentence dismisses the "New England Eunuchs," presumably

Emerson, Thoreau, and perhaps Melville. Otherwise, he does not even hint that any other American literary men existed. Williams's historic figures, if they were writers at all, were men of action . . . : Eric the Red, Columbus, Montezuma and Cortez, Ponce de Leon, De Soto, Raleigh, Champlain, the early Puritans (and Mather), Père Sebastian Rasles, Daniel Boone, Washington, John Paul Jones (and Franklin), Hamilton, Burr, and Lincoln—and for good measure, Jacataqua, girl Sachem of the Abenaki Indians of Maine. From this litany, it is obvious that Williams in effect rejects the whole American literary tradition.[6]

Even though Bollier's emphasis on Williams's apparent preference for "men of action" over men of letters is somewhat misleading in that it discounts the importance of writing and written texts to *In the American Grain*, his claim that Williams rejects the entire American literary tradition (of course with the exception of Poe) is well founded. However, it must be added that the writers and texts from which Williams distances himself do not, at least to his mind, constitute the entire American literary tradition, but only a small part of it. What they represent is the American literary canon as conceived by Brooks, Lawrence, Mumford, and others. The point is that the formation of literary canons is quite different from the formation of literary traditions, a difference that is already implicit in Williams's choice of Poe as an uncanonical ancestor *par excellence*.[7] For Williams, the origins of American literature, or better, of American writing, were not to be found in the nineteenth century and certainly not in the works of those classic American writers whom he denounced as products of "a field of unrelated culture stuccoed upon [the New World] landscape." "To this latter," he continues, "all the aesthetic adhesions of the present day occur. Through that stratum of obscurity the acute but frail genius of the place must penetrate. The seed is tough but the chances are entirely against a growth. It is possible for every vestige of virtue from the New World to be lost."[8] Canonized American literature to Williams is a "dead layer" that covers "*the* ground" (*IAG*, 213) and smothers the growth of authentic New World writing.

It is significant that Williams, throughout *In the American Grain*, rarely speaks of "America," but mostly of "the New World." This distinction is not simply a matter of substituting one term for another; it is one of the keys to the poetic project of that text: For Williams, *American* Literature is precisely the "dead layer" that must be penetrated, stripped away to make accessible the foundations upon which a New World tradition of writing may be built. Bollier's observation that "Williams's de facto rejection of American literature . . . suggests uncomfortable affinities with, if not a concession to the judgments of Pound and Eliot"[9] is provocative, but again somewhat misleading, because he does not sufficiently explore the precise nature of those affinities. The distinction between canonized American Literature and what I am calling a New World tradition of writing helps clarify Bollier's point. As *In the American Grain*, no less than *Paterson*, demonstrates, the American literary canon was indeed as much a "waste land" to Williams as it was to Eliot and to Pound. But this view is in no way incongruous with Williams's assessment of *The Waste Land* as a poem that "wiped out our world as if an atom bomb had been dropped upon it and our brave sallies into the unknown were turned to dust."[10] For Williams, Eliot was far too obsessed with European letters to take seriously the New World's cultural potential, and Pound's retreat into Renaissance history must have seemed as obsolete to him as it later did to Charles Olson.[11] Williams, in contrast, recognized that while modern America was indeed a waste land, the New World most certainly was not.

Even more than half a century after *In the American Grain* was first published, American Literature remains a problematic concept for both writers and critics alike. It is therefore in order to consider at least some of the ideological and literary dimensions of this problem before turning to Williams's idea of New World writing. Joseph Riddel, although he does not take notice of the crucial conceptual distinction between American Literature and New World writing implicit in Williams's texts, nevertheless states the issues succinctly. For Williams, he writes, "the poet must be a beginner because he can no longer accept the myth of presence, of meaning given from outside one's 'place.' American poetry and American history have been misinterpreted, Williams argues, because of the poets' and the historians' embrace of tradition, their perpetuation of the myth of the idea, whether it is the myth of Western history, of Christianity, or of literature. Every attempt to escape the myth of presence, even Whitman's radical democratization, only reconfirmed it."[12] What is clear from Riddel's assessment of Williams's attitude toward the American literary canon as conceived by his contemporaries is that the difference between American Literature and New World writing has much to do with literature's involvement with myth on the one hand and history on the other.

Myths, in the broadest sense, are storehouses of cultural values and beliefs, which serve as paradigms for the interpretation of historical "facts." Myths, in short, are the foundations of a culture's identity. As is well known, the primary myth from which America as a new world has traditionally derived its cultural identity (or non-identity) is the myth of

American innocence. We shall later see how that myth of America was the product of medieval Europe's desperate, yet futile, attempts to reverse the increasing secularization of its own cultures. In North America, this semireligious myth of American innocence offered fertile grounds for the emergence of the myth of American democracy—after the failure of the French Revolution, the image of the independent United States became that of a social utopia—and of what Sacvan Bercovitch has termed its "consensus rituals." Both myths, which grew out of Europe's perception of the American continent as a "virgin land," gradually evolved into a cultural ideology intended to give meaning and unity to American Literature. Regardless of New World cultural realities, the majority of Anglo–North American writers during the nineteenth and twentieth centuries continued to embrace this cultural mythology. However, with the beginning "incorporation of America" during the mid to late nineteenth century, it became increasingly evident that the founding ideals of freedom and liberty embedded in the pioneer ethics and the idea of democracy were being abused to enforce ideological consensus and to tighten the grip of business and politics on cultural institutions. As the mythical American Adam evolved more and more into the modern technocrat and the financier, using his alleged "innocence" to legitimize his lust for power and his rampant materialism in a society believed to be devoid of traditional cultural and moral values, North American cultural critics finally began to question the reliability of their national founding myths. [13]

Although profoundly troubled by those distortions of their country's founding beliefs, not all North American writers and intellectuals endeavored to expose this mythology and its numerous versions and perversions as fictions designed to smoothe over the violent loss of original unity that lies at the root of all New World cultures. Van Wyck Brooks's *America's Coming of Age* (1915) is an excellent case in point, especially when contrasted to *In the American Grain*. In that book, Brooks envisions American culture as a "ciphered parchment," which must be held up to the fire to reveal its "hidden significances." [14] But what are those hidden significances? The best starting point for a response to this question is Brooks's own title, whose hidden and not-so-hidden significances are most telling. On the one hand, "coming of age" refers specifically to the myth of American innocence as a condition that must be, and presumably was in the process of being, outgrown through the systematic development of a historical consciousness that would replace what Brooks scathingly calls a state of "superannuated boyishness." History, in short, was to replace myth as a vehicle for cultural self-knowledge. On the other hand, Brooks himself remains caught up in the rhetorical threads of the very myth he is attempting to discredit by describing the process that would bring about that historical consciousness as a "quest for a usable past."

The problem with his programmatic formula, which enjoyed tremendous popularity among United Snates intellectuals during the early decades of the twentieth century, is its curious analogy to another, equally popular, formula, employed by the first North American colonists to sanction the idea of American innocence: the Puritan's "errand into the wilderness." Although Brooks engages in a vehement polemic against the Puritan heritage and its intellectual barrenness, he ultimately does little else than redirect the "errant," leaving the myth itself intact.[15] The reasons for this are quite logical: While on the one hand profoundly disturbed by the ways in which their society had corrupted its founding ideals, and, above all, by the ensuing anti-intellectualism, Brooks and his followers did, on the other hand, not aim at a reformulation of fundamental goals and basic social ideals. Confronted with what they perceived as a process of "cultural dissolution," their intention was to offer a stabilizing mechanism that would reaffirm those ideals and generate some sense of cohesion in the face of impending chaos. This stabilizing mechanism was precisely the idea of a "usable past," usable and useful in that it made history perform as myth: History in its pastness became yet another frontier.

The result of this analogy, a brilliant stroke on Brooks's part, was that North America's founding ideals—both the myth of American innocence and the myth of American democracy—remained untouched by this form of cultural criticism, which was largely channeled toward superficial symptoms without ever reaching down to the cultural bases, the "roots," as Williams has it. This is also precisely the reason why Brooks and others like him were so strongly attracted to the writers of the so-called American Renaissance and Whitman in particular. In an effort to clarify these affinities, Sacvan Bercovitch persuasively argues that

none of our classic writers conceived of imaginative perspectives other than those implicit in the vision of America. Their works are characterized by an *unmediated* relation between the facts of American life and the ideals of American free enterprise. Confronted with the inadequacies of their society, they turned for solace and inspiration to its social ideals. It was not that they lacked radical energies, but that they had invested these in a vision which reinforced (because it emanated from them) the values of their culture. Their quarrels with America took the form of intracultural dialogues—as in Thoreau's

7

Walden, where the only "true America" beckons to us as a timeless magic of the country's timebound ideals (minimal government, extravagant economics, endless mobility, unlimited self-aggrandizement); or in Whitman's *Leaves of Grass*, which offers the highest romantic tribute, the process of poetic self-creation, as text-proof of America's errand into the future. In these and other key instances, the autonomous act that might have posed fundamental alternatives, imaginative or actual, became instead a mimesis of cultural norms. [16]

The implications of Bercovitch's study, which traces the historical development of what he terms the rhetoric of the United States' consensus ideology, are most relevant to a discussion of New World writing's double involvement with myth and history. His claim that the major works of Anglo-North American literature since the colonial period have been so deeply entrenched in the rhetoric of the myth (or "vision") of America that they were unable to conceive of any fundamental alternatives to the consensus ideology suggests that as long as American writers continue to subscribe to that myth, be it consciously or unconsciously, they will inevitably remain caught up in a rhetorical and ideological framework that preempts any criticisms directed against it. If that myth of America is indeed, as Bercovitch argues, the foundation of American, or at least United States, culture, then it becomes clear that this concept of culture, by incorporating the element of dissent into its very structure, does not offer any viable basis for effective cultural and social criticism.

Theodor Adorno and Max Horkheimer have warned that "to speak of culture has always been contrary to culture. Culture as a common denominator already contains in embryo the kind of schematization, the process of cataloguing and classification, which brings culture into the realm of administration."[17] As part of a system of social administration, culture is no longer conceived as a process of cultivation or cross-fertilization, as Williams sees it in *In the American Grain*, but becomes a vehicle for social control. In this sense, the institutionalized idea of American Culture can be viewed as an ideological construct designed to control and constrict cultural interaction by postulating the existence of a harmonious whole. Cultural exchange is reduced to a mere ritualistic reaffirmation of that postulated unity or totality, a ritual in which cultural differences between groups and individuals are reduced to a set of preconceived similarities representing a unified, as well as reified, structure.

The concept of American Culture as it is used in the United States—and, by extension, applied to other parts of the New World—may be described as the institutionalization of the myth of America. This formulation assumes greater clarity when one considers with Roland Barthes that "the function of myth is to empty reality" in order to "organize a world which is without contradictions because it is without depth."[18] Precisely because myth "purifies" reality by removing from it everything that would cause contradiction and conflict (that is, history), it surreptitiously evolves into a mechanism for monopolizing historical interpretation in order to project images of cultural unification that justify the existing social order and reinforce traditional values. This is possible only because the language of myth, as Barthes further elaborates, "is not read as a motive, but as a reason."[19] It "naturalizes" its intentions and thus obscures the source from which it derives meaning and authority. This source, clearly, is *not* nature, but society. It is in this sense, and only in this sense, that myth can be defined as "depoliticized speech":[20] it appears to be ideologically neutral—"natural." Myth itself is already a ritual of consensus, which functions as a catalyst between cultural values and social institutions. Brooks's "quest for a usable past," which unabashedly and not all that unintentionally avails itself of the rhetoric of the myth of America, perfectly exemplifies this catalyzing function.

What, then, are the alternatives? How can literary and critical writing in the Americas escape the ideological trappings of the consensus ritual and assert legitimate differences between the various cultural traditions represented in the New World while, at the same time, promoting a sense not of unity (or uniformity) but of coherence? In other words, how can New World writing protect itself against the encroachment of the "tyrannous designs" (*IAG*, 189) of American Culture? How can it evolve forms of effective cultural criticism that would go beyond shallow polemics to show the extraordinary importance of language to the historical development of the United States within the larger context of inter-American relations? Clearly, for the American literary canon to become a New World tradition of writing it has to step outside the consensus ritual that perpetuates the democratic myth of America. It has to unsettle and explode that myth by challenging its reliability as a repository of cultural values and thus its authority as a central, unifying point of origin.[21]

Any revisionary project of New World writing is bound to have a profound impact on literary production: Literature in the traditional sense is itself a mythical system, one that rests on the assumption of "an organizing predesign, of an identifiable or nameable origin which precedes the work and stands outside it."[22] This assumption of an organizing predesign inherent in the very definition of literature may also be called a fiction of the center, of a central consciousness that authors and author-

9

izes the meaning of that structure we call a literary text. This fiction or myth of the center serves the same purpose in relation to the literary text that the myth of America serves in relation to New World culture: It unifies it by controlling the relationships between the individual components. To unsettle the myth of America, New World writing has to begin by subverting the traditional concept of Literature as a mythical system that pretends either to transcend itself into a factual system (as in the case of the novel or other prose) or to contract itself into an essential one (as in the case of poetry).

Barthes suggests that "the best weapon against myth is perhaps to mythify it in its turn, and to produce an *artificial myth*: and this reconstituted myth will in fact be a mythology. Since myth robs language of something, why not rob myth?"[23] Bercovitch, in his turn, argues that the national myth of the United States, that is, the Puritan "errand" as translated into the rhetoric of the continuing revolution implicit in the concept of democracy, has "preempted the growth of a 'conscious mythology,'"[24] a term he borrows from Northrop Frye. Frye's (and Bercovitch's) notion of a "conscious mythology," one that would be independent of the institutionalized mythology produced by society—what I have been calling an ideology—seems analogous to Barthes's concept of an artificial myth. Yet, Frye's term is somewhat misleading: It implies that that ideology (the idea of Culture) is an "unconscious" mythology, which, at least viewed from the perspective of those groups that produce and perpetuate it, is clearly not the case. One could quibble with Barthes's terminology for similar reasons, as his idea of the artificiality of the reconstituted myth seems to suggest that the second-order semiological system, which this new myth takes as a point of departure, is somehow "natural," which, as he himself shows, is not so. It is crucial to understand that the very artificiality of the new myth reveals the seemingly "natural" qualities of any myth as a fiction.

The function of the new myth, which I shall call synthetic, is to demythify the old myth by generating a third-order semiological system to comment on the process of mythmaking. What is made accessible for (re)interpretation as a result of this process are the historical foundations of the old mythology, as well as the ways in which myth de-forms and distorts history by impoverishing the reservoir of meaning it represents.[25] The synthetic myth, then, is a return to and a reconstitution of history, a process in which the confrontation between the old myth and its historical sources yields a new, different kind of mythology which, because of its own self-consciousness, actively subverts the authority of the former.

The formal, "literary" or "poetic," processes that accomplish this subversion are best described as *de-constructive,* a term that, despite its own considerable ideological baggage, still has the advantage of conveying most accurately the idea of simultaneity so crucial to the concept and the mythologies of New World writing that will be elaborated in this study. To speak of New World writing, as opposed to American Literature, is not a matter of simple terminological substitution but of *method* and of displacement. New World writing as a concept already implies a comparative as well as a cross-cultural perspective; it is a system that depends on the differences of its constituents, rather than relying on their similarity.

The extent to which this definition affects critical practice is already suggested by my selection of William Carlos Williams, Jay Wright, and Nicolás Guillén as foci for my discussion. On the one hand, each of these twentieth-century poets is habitually associated with a different literary canon: Anglo-American Literature, Afro-American Literature, and Latin American Literature, respectively. On the other hand, Williams, Wright, and Guillén are also writers of what Wilson Harris calls the cross-cultural imagination.[26] Their texts challenge the institutionalized myths that inform the twin concepts of American Culture and American Literature and thereby question the validity of the canons to which they are assigned. This resistance to traditional Western ideas of order and to conceptual structures that presume to represent a totality of human reality links the works of these seemingly very different authors in more profound ways than strictly thematic considerations could convey. Williams's *In the American Grain,* Wright's *Dimensions of History* (1976), and Guillén's *El diario que a diario* [The Daily Daily] (1972), the three texts on which I shall concentrate, are all literary "experiments in disorder,"[27] whose ultimate goal is to elaborate a logic of possibility and plurality, of diversity and divergence. Concerned with the emplotment of American history from a New World, as opposed to a eurocentric, perspective, these texts offer alternatives to mythologies predicated on the lingering fiction of European cultural supremacy and centrality. Once Europe is no longer assumed to be the nucleus of world society, it becomes possible to contemplate historical processes of cultural interaction without mourning a lost unity and searching for an origin. Although modernism, which, at least in the case of United States literature, involved the "death" of Europe after World War I, is frequently regarded as ahistorical or even antihistorical, *In the American Grain* shows that the "refreshment of values so far as history goes" is not altogether a recent, postmodern development.[28] Without being in the strict sense a precursor of *Dimensions of History* and *El diario, In the American Grain* nevertheless anticipates a postmodern attitude toward history. It asserts the possibility of exploring not only similarities and continuities but also, at the same time, differences and discontinuities in order to emphasize cultural interpenetration rather than assimilation.

At the textual level, cultural exchange becomes an exchange of literary forms. Plays of contrasting grammars and forms, *In the American Grain*, *Dimensions of History*, and *El diario* dissolve traditional generic categories as well as conventional distinctions between literary and nonliterary discourse. They are textual hybrids composed of chaotic admixtures of styles and forms from a variety of different cultural traditions and historical periods. Rejecting the European image of the New World as a "virgin land," Williams, Guillén, and Wright reinvent the American landscape as a vast text, an assemblage of hieroglyphics to be deciphered and ordered by the imagination. But their respective ideas of order are not literary rituals of consensus that simply attempt to reveal unity within diversity, or vice versa. While seeking for some sort of coherence that would not inadvertently reduce cultural differences to similarities, they also seek to unravel the elements of self-deception that always exist within self-revelation.

Because of their resistance to traditional concepts of unity, all three texts pose a challenge to Americanist literary criticism and its own consensus rituals. Most critics, however, have failed to offer constructive responses to this challenge. Their silence or disapproval is reflected unequivocally in the critical reception of each work at the time of its initial publication. Both *Dimensions of History* and *El diario* have so far been virtually ignored,[29] and *In the American Grain*, as mentioned above, did not receive serious critical attention and acclaim until more than twenty years after it had first appeared. The main problem these texts ask readers and critics to confront is this: Can we conceive of a structure, be it a literary text, a literary canon, or a cultural tradition, without a center? If so, how do we approach such a structure, if we can still call it that, without reducing it to a set of fixed meanings or characteristics? As much of my later discussion will be devoted to considering these questions in the context of *In the American Grain*, *Dimensions of History*, and *El diario*, it is appropriate at this point to address a number of concrete terminological and methodological issues relevant to the distinction between American Literature and New World writing.

Williams insists throughout *In the American Grain* that "Americans have never recognized themselves. How can they? It is impossible until someone invent the original terms. As long as we are content to be called by somebody else's terms, we are incapable of being anything but our own dupes" (*IAG*, 226). To invent "original terms" that would make it possible for Americans to "recognize" themselves, their culture, and their literature as something other than an extension of European thought is admittedly a formidable task. For criticism to be able to participate in this process of invention or reinvention, it has to reassess and rearrange traditional literary canons and develop a methodology able to encompass similarities and differences at the same time. The first step toward such a critical revisionism is carefully to consider the current uses (and abuses) of the concept of American Literature with respect to their practical and theoretical implications. Simply to speak of American literature, be it, as is mostly the case, in reference to Anglo–North American Literature or even American literatures as a whole, already poses fundamental problems.

American Literature as a critical category presumes a common ground for all the different groups, styles, and trends that compose the New World literary scene and thus projects onto that vast and diversified body of literature a cultural homogeneity that is but another manifestation of the consensus ideology. Used primarily as a synonym for the Anglo–North American literary canon—or what is called "mainstream" American Literature—the term American Literature poses as a general denominator for a tradition of which it is only a relatively small part. As a critical convention, the idea of American Literature is the product of a liberal ideology that distorts historical realities—namely, the coexistence of several literary and cultural traditions in the New World—to make them conform to the ideal of a cultural democracy. On closer look, however, that all-inclusive cultural democracy is quickly revealed to be a hierarchical structure: By hyphenating all other New World literary and/or cultural traditions, we attempt to assert their differences, while at the same time subordinating them to a category inherently oblivious to those differences. As long as American Literature is used as a general denominator for all New World literatures, while at the same time being implicitly associated with the Anglo–North American literary canon, it preempts the formulation of pluralistic and comparative approaches that would collapse such a hierarchy. Our own critical terminology fails us here.

New World writing appears to be the best terminological alternative to American Literature for a number of reasons: First, it refers to a tradition of writing and not to a literary canon. Second, it is a term that seeks to convey a sense of cultural connectedness without implying a hierarchy. To speak of texts that are currently assigned to the Anglo-American, the Afro-American, or the Latin American literary canons as parts of a New

World tradition of writing is to question the very criteria for canonization: To define a literary canon according to the nationality or presumed genealogy of authors is to confuse political and biological issues with literary ones.[30] To be sure, a strict separation of these areas is not always possible or even desirable. But one has to acknowledge, as John Hollander does with considerable candor, that "much discourse in America today about ethnic origins and searches for meaning in genealogical lineage has degenerated into sleazy cant and travesties of treks toward inner freedom."[31] While Hollander's language might be considered unduly harsh and offensive, his point is well taken: The criteria we use for canonization are, for the most part, highly problematic in that they tend to mistake presumably inescapable genealogical and nationalistic allegiances for literary affinities, which are, as Ralph Ellison emphasizes, *elective* affinities.[32] This deterministic view of canonization is a neopositivistic relic that violates all principles of modern literary investigation by surreptitiously reinstating the notion that literary texts are accurate reflections of sociopolitical circumstances. To reduce literary genealogies to some sort of pseudoscientific determinism—note Ellison's useful distinction between literary "relatives" and literary "ancestors"—is to turn the study of literature into a form of socioanalysis and to render it incapable of evaluating and questioning its own premises. All we accomplish in this way is to widen the already substantial gap between literary interpretation and literary history. As a result of this divorce, literary interpretation is prone to degenerate into gratuitous formalism, while literary history begins to pose as an empirical science, concerned only with the accumulation of data in chronological order. In neither case is it possible to establish meaningful connections between texts, connections that would explain why and how writers choose literary ancestors and what those choices signify.

How do we explain, for instance, the existence of texts such as *In the American Grain, Dimensions of History,* and *El diario,* texts that superimpose upon the conventional schemas of literary canons complex patterns of literary history that are entirely oblivious to geographical, ethnic, or political boundaries? How do we approach texts that appear to belong to several literary canons at the same time? It is precisely this simultaneity that calls for the kind of comparative approach to American literatures implicit in the concept of New World writing. This comparative approach as a form of historical criticism presents a valid alternative to the lingering forms of neopositivism, which in the past have rendered historical criticism (that is, literary history) so sterile. It is an attempt to reconcile historical criticism with formalism, or, put differently, to intertwine literary history with literary interpretation without going to the other, familiar, extreme of simply substituting formalism in its various manifestations for neopositivism and eliminating history in the process.

It is worth interjecting that precisely this kind of substitution has of late caused severe problems, especially for the criticism of Afro–North American and Latin American literatures, which, unlike the criticism of Anglo-American literature and its New Critical heritage, has only recently liberated itself from the grip of positivism in the guise of sociology. Unfortunately, this liberation has, perhaps predictably, taken the form of an overzealous acceptance of European and Euro-American formalism's categories without sufficiently adjusting them to a different historico-cultural setting. As a result, we are now faced with what appears to be yet another version of the consensus ritual, in which important (con)textual differences are systematically leveled under the weight of a seemingly universal language. What this somewhat ironic situation evidences is, above all, criticism's need to return to history, and, furthermore, that this return to history must involve a search for a new "language," for "original" terms.

This search for a new language (literature's and criticism's) is an attempt at self-definition, which, in the work of Williams, Wright, and Guillén, gives rise to a synthetic mythology of writing, in which attitudes toward history are translated into formal attitudes before and within language, and vice versa. Williams, Wright, and Guillén are not concerned with history as a series of past events, but with what the historian Edmundo O'Gorman has termed "process[es] producing historical entities," and particularly the historical entity known as America. These processes, of course, are writing. As is well known, America was a text claiming its territories as a European possession even before the first Spaniards ever set foot on what they believed to be the shores of Asia. [33] An important, though neglected, study of the historical documents connected with the so-called discovery of the New World, O'Gorman's *The Invention of America* (1958) is of vital interest to my present discussion in that it clarifies the origins of those "tyrannous designs" that Williams, Wright, and Guillén endeavor to unsettle. O'Gorman was one of the first historians to assert

the need to focus historical events in the light of an ontological perspective, i.e., as a process producing historical entities instead of a process, as is usually assumed, which takes for granted the being of such entities as something logically prior to it. This conclusion led me to understand . . . that the basic concept for the historian is that of "invention," because the concept of "creation," which assumes that something is produced *ex nihilo,* can have meaning only within the sphere of religious faith. Thus I came to suspect that the clue to the problem of the historical appearance of America lay in considering the event as the result of an *inspired invention of Western thought,* and not as the result of a purely physical discovery, brought about, furthermore, by accident.[34]

What O'Gorman so fittingly calls an "inspired invention of Western thought" was a process of revisionism set in motion as Europe was confronted with the presence of a continent that, in Williams's words, "exist-[ed] in those times beyond the sphere of all things known to history" (*IAG,* 18). The mere physical presence of this *orbis alterius,* this other world, threw medieval Europe into a major spiritual and intellectual crisis by demanding a radical readjustment of the concept of "the island of the world." Although medieval Europe, and Spain in particular, was far from being culturally unified, the existence of another, potentially different, world posed a massive threat to the idea of centrality, both in the sacred as well as in the secular sense, that formed the basis not only for Europe's entire social and economic structure but also for its self-concept.

As Europe conceived of itself as "history's paradigm,"[35] the possibility of a plurality of worlds was an outright heresy. It is thus not very surprising, O'Gorman argues, that certain conceptual and/or ideological mechanisms were developed to circumvent and defer the ultimate acknowledgment of such a potential pluralism: Europe imaged America not as a different world but as a *new* world, or better perhaps, as a new part of the same whole. This distinction is significant because "new" implied, above all else, the inherent potential of this other world for becoming a replica of Europe. O'Gorman explains that "when the *Cosmographiae Introducto* [1507] classified America as a 'continent' on a par with Europe, Asia, and Africa, the implication was not only that these four continents were part of a single whole [the *Orbis Terrarum*], but that they shared the same nature, the same internal structure; that they were all made on the same model, that of the whole itself."[36] It becomes clear, then, how a seemingly innocuous geographical classification had already established the basis for a conceptual framework that allowed Europe to maintain the fiction of its centrality, which would ensure and legitimize its dominant position in world history for centuries to come.

The conclusions O'Gorman attempts to draw from his textual analyses are disputable. Most problematic are those instances when his discussion degenerates to crude polemics and resorts to cultural clichés to prove the superiority of Anglo–North American civilization over that of Latin

America. But even despite such perplexing inconsistencies, *The Invention of America* merits attention as the first systematic interpretation of historical documents such as the *Cosmographiae Introducto* in light of their ideological implications. Octavio Paz's comments on O'Gorman in *The Labyrinth of Solitude* sum up the major points of the study as well as connect the threads of my argument in the formulation of a key question. America, Paz agrees,

is not a geographical region, and it is not a past; perhaps it is not even a present. It is an idea, an invention of the European spirit. America is a utopia, a moment in which the European spirit becomes universal by freeing itself of its historical particulars and conceiving of itself as a universal idea. Almost miraculously, this idea finds its embodiment and home in a specific land and also in a specific time: the future. European culture conceives of itself in America as a superior unity. O'Gorman is correct when he sees our continent as an actualization of the European spirit, but *what happens to America as an autonomous historical entity when it confronts the realities of Europe?*[37]

If I rephrase Paz's question to match my emphasis on literary matters, it reads as follows: What happens to American Literature when its texts confront Europe's mythologies? What happens is a realization of the need for a new language to acknowledge that American Literature, once it is redefined as New World writing, can be neither nationalistic nor universal. It is this realization, namely, as Stevens has it in "The Comedian as the Letter C," that "the relation of each man be clipped,"[38] that engenders texts as different and yet as curiously similar as *In the American Grain, Dimensions of History,* and *El diario.*

II
> *Sólo quedaban huesos*
> *rígidamente colocados*
> *en forma de cruz, para mayor*
> *gloria de Dios y de los hombres.*
>
> [Only bones remained,
> rigidly arranged
> in the shape of a cross, for the greatest
> glory of God and man.]
> — PABLO NERUDA, *Los Conquistadores*

Intent on revising the traditional "script" of American history to fit the new "theater," many twentieth-century New World writers have conducted elaborate literary experiments in disorder, which, like the thunderstorms in Stevens's "Comedian," turn their texts into "a jostling festival." As suggested above, the ultimate goal of such upheavals is to formulate a logic of diversity and plurality, as opposed to a logic of unity and centrality. Those literary experiments in disorder usually start out as critiques of the myth of Literature, that is, of literature as an ordered display of signs that presumes to give a total representation of human reality and history. But, as is well known, such critiques of representation and of available forms of representation are certainly not limited to the New World literary scene. Therefore it is necessary to ask more specifically, What makes those New World literary experiments in disorder as special and distinctive as my previous discussion suggests? In short, what is new and different about New World writing?

To begin with, I wish to propose a fundamental distinction, which has to do with the differences between American Literature and New World writing that I am in the process of elaborating. In twentieth-century American letters, we can distinguish between at least two kinds of literary experiments in disorder and thus between two groups of writers or texts: For the first group, whose major representative is T. S. Eliot, disorder is but a surface phenomenon. [39] It is the result of desperate, yet frustrated, attempts to recover the myth of Literature and to transcend chaos and fragmentation through romantic visions of cosmic totality that bring to mind none other than Whitman. [40] (Ironically, Pound's later enthusiasm for fascism seems to spring from the same source as Whitman's democratic "vistas.") Literature, in this case, becomes a "waste land": the fragments Eliot gathers together remain incapable of representing a unified structure, a totality. The structure a writer like Eliot attempts to restore is that of the *Library*, a homogeneous representational space that would promote textual unity through semantic stability. For him, the Library still is the Universe. [41]

If Eliot can be taken as representative of this kind of involuntary disorder, Williams seems an appropriate contrast. Williams's comments on Eliot, in fact, invite that contrast. Williams's texts, unlike Eliot's and later Hart Crane's, are characterized by a conceptual disorder that evolves into a literary method. This conceptual disorder, which, as we shall see, becomes embodied in the figure of the *Archive*, [42] is best understood as a form of madness—again, Williams's attachment to Poe is symptomatic of such madness, which, it should be added, is quite different from what Crane calls "phonographs of hades in the brain." [43] Let us, then, explore the nature of Williams's madness and its consequences for his (and our) perception of and approach to the possibility of a New World tradition of writing.

Williams's own comments on the peculiarities of his literary endeavors are most revealing. The following lines are the words of the poet's imaginary partner in conversation (presumably Turgenjev) in *The Great American Novel*:

Eh bien mon vieux coco, this stuff that you have been writing today, do you mean that you are attempting to set down the American background? You will go mad. Why? Because you are trying to do nothing at all. The American background? It is Europe. It can be nothing else. Your very method proves what I say. You have no notion what you are going to write from one word to the other. It is madness. You call this the background of American life? Madness?[44]

These lines clearly identify madness as a conceptual disorder resulting from a break with Europe as the presumed center of history and culture. In Williams's case, this break is motivated by the need to "face inland," that is, to develop "inner correctives" to historical documentary and to a literature that envisioned America as a deprived and disadvantaged culture, a virgin land that, by the beginning of the twentieth century, had turned into a waste land.[45] To be sure, from the eurocentric, neoclassical perspective of writers such as T. S. Eliot, rejecting the idea of Europe as history's paradigm, and with it the identity (or pseudoidentity) conferred upon the New World by the mythical constructs of Western Christianity and its logocentrism must indeed appear as an act of madness. For Williams, however, madness is a state of "rich regenerative violence" (*IAG*, 130) that enables him to penetrate the "dead layer" of cultural consensus and touch the very roots of New World history. That "dead layer" is a figure for an American Literature that perpetuates the fiction of the center whose historical embodiment is Europe, a literature, in short, whose sole repository of meaning is Europe's Library.

To rephrase my previous question, what exactly happens to American Literature once it leaves the secure enclosure of that Library? Or, put differently, what shape does the madness of "facing inland" take? A key passage from Carlos Fuentes's monumental novel *Terra Nostra* (1975) will help in formulating an answer. In the following quotation Fuentes's picaresque protagonist, a young sailor who is washed ashore in the New World after a shipwreck, reports his adventures to the Spanish king:

I felt, Sire, as if I were going mad: the compass of my mind had lost its directional needle, my identities were spilling over and multiplying beyond all contact with minimal human reason, I was a prisoner of the most tenebrous magic, the magic represented in stone in this pantheon of all the gods and goddesses I could not conquer in this land, who with fearful grimaces mocked my oneness and imposed upon me their monstrous proliferation, *destroying the arguments of unity I had meant to carry as an offering to this world*, yes, and also the simple unity in which that total unity was to be maintained; my own, the unity of my person. I looked upon the faces of the idols: they did not understand what I was saying.[46]

Like Stevens's Crispin, who "beheld" and "was made new," Fuentes's sailor comes to realize that "the sea / severs not only lands, but also selves."[47] What Fuentes shares with Williams (and with the Stevens of a not-so-harmonious *Harmonium*) is the desire to reinvent and restore to America the history Europe denied it and to use that history as the foundation for a mythology of New World writing. Fuentes, like Williams, endeavors to destroy Europe's "arguments of unity" to make possible a "monstrous" proliferation of identities and meanings that alone would liberate the cultural imagination of the New World writer from the shackles of similarity. Williams and Fuentes call for a literature that would insist on its difference from European paradigms and conventions instead of relying upon them for self-definition.

Derek Walcott's criticisms of Afro-American literature deepen the significance of this point. In his "Overture" to *Dream on Monkey Mountain and Other Plays* (1970), he laments, "Once the New World black had tried to prove that he was as good as his master, when he should have proven not his equality but his difference. It is this distance that could command respect without pleading for respect."[48] Walcott's contention that Afro-American writers cannot hope to attain respect by mimicking white models and pandering to white values parallels Williams's call for New World writing and his emphasis on the "local," the "genius of place" (*IAG*, 216), which he finds embodied in the work of Poe. "The local causes shaping Poe's genius," he declares in *In the American Grain*, "were two in character: the necessity for a fresh beginning, backed by a native vigor of extraordinary proportions,—with the corollary, that all 'colonial imitation' must be swept aside. . . . and, *second* the immediate effect of the locality upon the first, upon his nascent impulses, upon his original thrusts; tormenting the depths into a surface of bizarre designs by which he is known and which are *not at all* the major point in question" (*IAG*, 219). But even though Williams emphatically denies their importance, these "bizarre designs" are of utmost significance as formal manifestations not only of Poe's, but of Williams's own, madness; that is, his resistance to "colonial imitation" and his affirmation of original differences in the act of destroying Europe's tyrannous arguments of unity.

In the American Grain, no less than *Spring and All*, *The Great Ameri-*

can Novel, and particularly *Paterson*, is an exquisite example of Williams's "tormenting the depths into a surface of bizarre designs." It is a "monstrous" disfigurement of the very arguments of unity that most of his contemporaries tried to salvage so unsuccessfully.[49] Joseph Riddel describes Williams's poetry as "a sustained assault on the familiar habits of interpretation and teleological history,"[50] a claim that holds equally true for his "prose" works. The full extent to which Williams sustained that assault is already implicit in the difficulties one encounters upon attempting to draw a clear line between his poetry and his prose. Williams himself was frequently plagued by this distinction, and while he ultimately concluded that all is writing, it is nevertheless useful to consider briefly some of his early comments on the subject in connection with the generic elusiveness of *In the American Grain*.

Given that labels condition the reader's expectations of a text and thus predetermine, at least in part, the course his or her reading will take, it is first of all necessary to question the standard description of *In the American Grain* as a collection of separate historical essays or narratives in order to open fresh critical perspectives on that text. To do so is to pursue the implications of Williams's writing *against* the American grain beyond the usual discussion of theme to the level of literary form: If *In the American Grain* is indeed a text that debunks canonized American culture and literature in an effort to move toward a theory and a practice of New World writing, or what Williams, with reference to Gertrude Stein, called "words in configurations fresh to our senses,"[51] then it is crucial to analyze the formal processes that actually accomplish this transition.

In his prefatory note to *In the American Grain* Williams writes, "In these studies I have sought to re-name the things seen, now lost in chaos of borrowed titles, many of them inappropriate, under which their true character lies hid. In letters, in journals, reports of happenings I have recognized new contours suggested by old words so that new names were constituted. . . . it has been my wish to draw from every source one thing, the strange phosphorus of the life, nameless under an old misappellation." *In the American Grain*, in other words, is a new shape constituted by old words used and arranged in a different fashion; it is a "new form dealt with as a reality in itself" ("Spring and All," in *Imag*, 133).

The latter quotation from "Spring and All" is, interestingly enough, one of Williams's definitions of poetry, and it is even more telling that none of the characteristics he attributes to prose quite seem to fit *In the American Grain*: "Prose: statement of facts concerning emotions, intellectual states, data of all sorts—technical expositions, jargon, of all

sorts—fictional and others. . . . The form of prose is the accuracy of its
subject matter—how best to expose the multiform phases of its material"
(*Imag*, 133). On the other hand, he contends that "the form of poetry is
related to the movements of the imagination revealed in words. . . .
Poetry has to do with the crystallization of the imagination—the perfec-
tion of new forms as addition to nature" (*Imag*, 133, 140). To read *In the
American Grain* simply as a series of factual statements, unified by
historical chronology and theme, would be a gross injustice to the *poetic*
project of Williams's text, a poem disguised as prose. Such an approach
would be insensitive to the "new contours" of Williams's language, a
language concerned with far more than just the accuracy of its subject
matter.

In the American Grain is a text shaped by the movements of Williams's
historical imagination as it reinvents the history of the New World. Much
like *Paterson*, *In the American Grain* is a mythic gathering of historical
fragments scattered by the absence of the center and placed side by side
without connectives. Despite their loose chronological arrangement,
these fragments do not form a continuous historical narrative; rather,
they constitute what is best described as a poetic montage.[52] Riddel's
insightful comments on *Paterson* equally apply to *In the American
Grain*:

> Williams' gathering of local detail does not reveal the priority of things
> to ideas but, on the contrary, unveils the true ground of ideas as the
> undetermined relation of things. Williams seeks a "new measure"
> between things because the old measures have been exposed as
> interpretations, fictions of the center. What he projects as the new
> must escape the fate of the old. It must recognize itself as interpreta-
> tion, as fiction: It therefore must recognize itself as measuring, and
> not as a set measure, as saying and not as the said. The first act of that
> new measuring, then, is to bring into question old measures, to create
> a dissonance.[53]

Williams, to paraphrase the words of Charles Olson's Maximus, mea-
sures his song and the sources of his song, and these new measures or
measurements evolve into a new method.[54] As he puts it in *Paterson*,
Book Four: "Dissonance / (if you are interested) / leads to discovery."[55]

Since the creation of dissonance involves a violation of the idea of
consonance, a harmonious measure that represents the fiction of the
center, it is particularly significant that *In the American Grain* both opens
and closes with an inscription of physical violence: It begins with a
homicide, as the result of which Red Eric was forced into exile, and ends

with Abraham Lincoln's assassination. Barbara Lanati has brilliantly argued this point:

In the inscription of violence are objectified the extremes of the parable Williams uses to define "that period" of history, which is the formative period of the ideological structure underlying American thought. The matrix is a common one: the "past" opens and closes in the inscription of physical violence. Keeping this assumption as his main operative premise, Williams proceeds to analyze what he sees as key moments in the development of American history in two modalities: on the one hand, that of the quotation of historical documents, presented either verbatim or with elaborations; on the other hand, that of commentary and, in some instances, of elabora- tions in the *fictional* mode, the fantastic-imaginary of certain mo- ments in American history. Through this technique, the insertion of history within literature and vice-versa presents a fact alternately in its literalness and its literariness.[56]

This interplay of documentary and fictional modes is crucial to *In the American Grain*. Like partners in a dance, Williams's favorite trope, both forms of discourse join in their separateness to assert the priority of an initial dualism, of an original cleavage. What the assertion of this du- alism accomplishes is a questioning of the authority, that is, the truth- value, generally attributed to historical records. As Williams insists in "The Virtue of History":

No opinion can be trusted, even the facts may be nothing but a printer's error; but if a verdict be unanimous, it is sure to be a wrong one, a crude rush of the herd which has carried its object before it like a helpless condoning image. If we cannot make a man live when he is gone, it is boorish to imprison him dead within some narrow definition, when, were he in his shoes before us, we could not do it. It's lies, such history, and dangerous. Just there may lie our one hope for the future, beneath that stone of prejudice. (*IAG*, 190)

By depriving historical documents of their presumed facticity and thus of their immunity to the rigors of interpretation, Williams creates a defi- ciency in their truth-value. This deficiency breaks the documentary paralysis of the historical texts he uses (their so-called literalness) by opening up a space for (re)interpretation and rewriting (that is, for "liter- ariness" or figuration) as forms of supplementation.[57]

"Red Eric" is the first, and perhaps most obvious, example of the kind of supplementation that serves as a corrective to historical documentary. Although based on two ancient documents known as "The Saga of Eric

23

the Red" and "The Vinland History of the Flat Island Book,"[58] Williams's version of Red Eric is presented as a first-person narrative. By having Red Eric tell his own story, Williams immediately and effectively displaces the original historical narratives. History quite literally becomes "his story"—"his," in this case, referring simultaneously to Red Eric and to Williams himself. The opening lines of "Red Eric" successfully establish that simultaneity and set the tone, not only for this section, but for *In the American Grain* as a whole: "Rather the ice than their way: to take what is mine by single strength, theirs by the crookedness of their law. But they have marked me—even to myself. Because I am not like them, I am evil" *(IAG,* 1). The significance of these utterances goes well beyond the immediate context of Red Eric's historical situation as a rebel and an outcast. At the same time that Williams (re)invents Red Eric as a character who raises his voice to correct the negative image his contemporaries left to posterity, he also uses the words attributed to that character to comment on the nature of his own literary project. In the same way that Red Eric put himself above or outside of the law of Christianity by slaying an offender, Williams violates the "crooked" laws of historical writing by exposing accepted historical facts as distorted truths, as records falsified to serve the ends of those in power:

Because their way is the just way and my way—the way of the kings and my fathers—*crosses* them: weaklings holding together to appear strong. . . . The worst is that weak, still, somehow, they are strong: they in effect have the power, *by hook or by crook.* And because I am not like them—not that I am evil, but more in accord with our own blood than they, eager to lead—*this very part of me, by their trickery must not appear, unless in their jacket.* (IAG, 1; my italics)

For Williams, Red Eric's story is not simply the story of an ordinary murderer, who also happened to be the father of Leif Ericsson, the first European explorer ever to land on American soil. It is also, much more importantly, the story of historical writing's inability to appreciate and measure difference without forcing it into the strait jacket of convention and conformity.

Williams's subversiveness vis-à-vis the objectifying laws of historiography takes a slightly different turn as the narrative of "Red Eric" suddenly shifts to a conventional third-person mode to recount the story of Freydis, Eric's daughter. Drawing heavily on the "Flat Island Book," the second movement of "Red Eric" extends the theme of violence and transgression introduced in the first one: "Eric in Freydis' Bones" *(IAG,* 5). It is significant that Eric's transformation into Freydis should be accompanied by a dramatic change in language, which creates an internal dissonance between the two parts of this section. It may be argued that each part illuminates a different aspect of Red Eric's historical personality. While the first-person narrative mode initially liberates Red Eric from the constraints of his original textual environment and uncovers, through the fictionalization of his character, what Williams perceives as dangerous distortions and narrow definitions, the return to the accepted form of historical discourse gives rise to the figure of Freydis as the very embodiment, and thus the continued victim, of those distortions. The image of Freydis as it emerges from Williams's excerpts of the "Flat Island Book" embodies the kind of historiography Williams seeks to efface. In the same way that Freydis is a reincarnation of her father, her story is a textual reincarnation of the kind of historical writing Williams endeavors to upset: Freydis remains imprisoned in the documentary mode, but only long enough to call attention to that predicament.

Notable about Williams's juxtaposition of fictional and documentary modes in this and other instances is that neither has priority over the other. The respective images of Red Eric and Freydis are products of different forms of discourse which represent two different approaches to history. Since there is no indication in Williams's text that Freydis's story is, for the most part, an almost verbatim reproduction of the "original" historical document,[59] the reader is led to perceive that text as no less a product of Williams's historical imagination than the fictional self-portrait of Red Eric. Distinctions between "original" and "interpretation," as well as between "literal" and "figurative," blur; they are no longer operative. Once the words have been, as Williams himself put it, "broken off from the European mass" (*Imag*, 175) and placed in a different setting— in this case, the setting of *In the American Grain*—they are revealed to be mere fictions of originality.

Williams's version of the Icelandic sagas is no longer part of the mythology of European history. Rather, it marks the beginnings of a different mythology, a mythology of New World writing. But what is the value and validity of such a new mythology, and how does it in effect differ from the old one? Williams explains in *The Embodiment of Knowledge* that

in themselves the tenets of a new mythology would be as useless as the old. But in the making of them words would again be offered a broad sweep through which to assert their power. They would or might be composed as real objects to mold the psyche of peoples over again, . . . by blasting away the stultifying association with the old mythology which has denied them their dynamic potentialities. . . .

But by breaking up formulas would we not merely be losing sight of fixed truths which we need for our continued intellectual existence, would we not be reverting to nonsense without any compensatory gain—even were it possible to break up language to that extent? No. Language is the key to the mind's escape from bondage to the past. There are no "truths" that can be fixed in language. It is by the breakup of the language that the truth can be seen to exist and that it becomes operative again.[60]

For Williams, to "escape from bondage to the past" is to return to history, to reinvent history in language by loosening the grip of a mythology that depends on fixed meanings and fixed truths. To begin *In the American Grain* with "Red Eric," that is, to claim the Icelandic sagas as part of the New World's literary heritage, already tears wide open the classic canon of American Literature as well as explodes the myth of Literature. This is yet another level of dissonance in *In the American Grain*: By using a wide range of so-called nonliterary documents, Williams challenges established notions of "literariness" to assert the difference of New World writing from European literary models and the arguments of unity they impose. But "Red Eric" not only unsettles literary and historiographical conventions by externalizing the theme of violence and turning it into a formal principle. The location of this story at the very beginning of Williams's text also upsets the standard chronology of New World history, which is centered on the figure of Columbus as the discoverer of the Indies and the author of what was later to be codified as the myth of America.

To analyze the extent to which this initial dis-placement of Columbus inaugurates specific textual strategies and ultimately becomes a poetics of New World writing, I shall now compare the literary portraits of Columbus in Williams's *In the American Grain* and in *El arpa y la sombra* [The Harp and the Shadow] (1979), a late work by the Cuban novelist Alejo Carpentier. As mentioned above, *In the American Grain* was rescued from oblivion as critics discovered in it the roots of *Paterson*; yet, discussions of the relationship between these two texts are usually more impressionistic than analytical. By using Carpentier's novel as catalyst between Williams's "The Discovery of the Indies" and the "Library" section in *Paterson*, Book Three, I shall show precisely the extent to which *In the American Grain* anticipates, and perhaps even surpasses, the postmodern poetics of *Paterson*.

Williams's portrait of Columbus in "The Discovery of the Indies," a textual collage of fragments from the admiral's letters and diaries, continues the textual processes of subversion encountered in "Red Eric" in ways that are clarified by a reading of *El arpa y la sombra*, whose protagonist is none other than Columbus himself. Set in the nineteenth century, Carpentier's novel is plotted around a fictive petition submitted to the Vatican's Holy Congregation of Rites by Pope Pius IX and Pope Leo XIII, requesting that Columbus be awarded official sainthood in recognition of his extraordinary achievements and his exemplary life: "The discovery of the New World by Christopher Columbus was the greatest event conceived by man since the advent of Christianity, and thanks to an Unparalleled Feat, he has doubled the space of the known continents and oceans where the word of the Gospel can be spread."[61] The church council, however, is reluctant to grant such a request, "because his [the Admiral's] records lacked certain biographical guarantees which, according to the canon, were necessary if he was to be granted a halo" (El arpa, 17). Columbus, in short, is not considered a legitimate candidate for sainthood because his records lack the necessary evidence of miracles. In the third and final part of the novel, entitled "La sombra" [The Shadow], the council gathers in a "Library of Absences"—Carpentier calls it a "Lipsonoteca," a place where the mortal remains of saints are kept—to examine the admiral's eligibility. After thoroughly scrutinizing and debating over a large number of biographical documents, the members of the council resolve to deny the popes' request on the grounds that Columbus not only had a mistress and an illegitimate son but was also to be held responsible for introducing slavery to the New World (El arpa, 193–94).

But even more interesting than these charges are Columbus's "confessions," presented in the form of an interior monologue that makes up the long middle section of El arpa [La Mano, The Hand]. In this section, Carpentier has the dying admiral admit to his absent confessor—who is, of course, the reader—that his glowing depictions of the New World as an earthly Paradise filled with gold and other riches were mostly lies, visions of wealth fabricated to appease those who had financed his expedition:

But there was the other million to account for: that of the Genovese merchants of Seville who would make my life impossible if I returned empty-handed. . . . Therefore, to buy time, I write: *"This is the most beautiful land that human eyes have ever beheld . . . ,"* and we go on from there, refining the epithalamion. As for the landscape, I do not have to rack my brain: I simply say that the blue mountain ranges that can be made out in the distance are like those in Sicily, although nothing about them makes me think of Sicily. I say that the grass is as tall as in Andalusia in April and May, although nothing here resembles anything Andalusian. I say that nightingales are singing where only some grey little birds were chirping, with large black beaks, which seemed more like sparrows. I speak of the fields of Castile, when here nothing, but nothing, reminds one of Castile. I have not encountered any trees, yet I predict that there must be some sort of trees here. I speak of *gold mines*, when I do not know of a single one. I speak of pearls, many pearls, only because I came across some clams "which are signs of them." Only once did I say something true: that here the dogs do not seem to bark. But with dogs that do not even know how to bark I am hardly going to repay the million I owe the ill-reputed Genovese merchants of Seville, who are capable of sending their own mother to the gallows for fifty *maradevis*. And the worst thing of all is that I have not the slightest idea where we are; this land of Colba or Cuba itself must be the southernmost tip of Vinland. (*El arpa*, 116–17)

As the final sentence of this quotation already suggests, Carpentier's Columbus also confesses that he knew about the earlier voyages of Red Eric and Leif-the-Lucky long before he embarked on his first journey to find not Asia, as he had officially claimed, but in fact the territories of Vinland (*El arpa*, 65–71, 93). In the end, Columbus is not only denied sainthood, he is also completely stripped of his credibility: Historical fact has turned into fabulation.

Both Carpentier's novel and Williams's "The Discovery of the Indies" question the authority of accepted historical truths which, as in the case of Columbus, have reached mythical proportions. Given the centrality of Columbus's writings to the myth of America that informs all of our traditional ideas about American Literature, Williams's and Carpentier's reinterpretations of that founding myth collapse the entire structure of that Library, which is the American literary canon. What becomes visible as a result of the collapse are the historical texts that compose what I am calling the New World writer's *Archive*, a figure that will be explored at greater length in connection with Wright's and Guillén's poetry. Crucial to my discussion is the difference between the concept of the Archive and the figure of the Library as it appears in *Paterson*. As suggested before, this difference is a function of the kinds of texts that compose the Archive. Williams's Archive in *In the American Grain*, like Wright's and Guillén's assemblage of texts in *Dimensions of History and El diario*, respectively, is precisely what Carpentier terms a "Lipsonoteca," a "Library of Absences," a space that houses texts excluded from the official canon of American Literature. The Archive is a collection of uncanonized texts that offer "relief from 'meaning'" (*P*, 111). Given Williams's rejection of the American literary canon in *In the American Grain*, the burning of the Library in *Paterson* can be read as a figure for the destruction—or deconstruction—of precisely that canon. It is an act of liberating or purging language from the fixity of meaning, a razing that creates new spaces for writing as well as establishes the need for a new kind of order to be represented by the Archive. "To write / is a fire and not only of the blood," Williams proclaims as his own writing consumes the old texts and turns them into "burning pages" (*P*, 113, 117). The "burning page" is Williams's master trope in *Paterson* for the deconstructive process of writing: It is a process of erasing old meanings and (re)inscribing new ones.

> Papers
> (consumed) scattered to the winds. Black.
> The ink burned white, metal white. So be it. (*P*, 117)

A figure for the effacement or erasure of old meanings, the white ink comes to represent the Library of American Literature as a voided ("consumed") presence, whose status is rendered most explicit in the well-known quotation from the English poet George Barker that Williams incorporates into his poem: "*American poetry is a very easy subject to discuss for the simple reason that it does not exist*" (*P*, 140). Williams's italics lend a curious emphasis to these lines: They introduce a dramatic visual change that signals the same kind of conceptual disorder brought about by the transformation of black typescript, not into ashes, but into white ink. "American poetry" as representative of the American literary canon has been burned white, that is, transfigured, by the fire of Williams's writing. And it is in this white space that the figure of the Archive begins to take shape, both in *Paterson* and in *In the American Grain*.

In the American Grain is an archival text *par excellence*. In its generic elusiveness, which is the product of its resistance to literary conventions and categories, it calls attention to itself as a "Library of Absences" that houses such texts as the Icelandic Sagas and Columbus's letters and diaries, texts that have been denied literary canonization in the same way and for much the same reasons that Carpentier's Columbus is denied sainthood: They are not "legitimate." Both Columbus's life as reinvented by Carpentier and the texts Williams gathers in *In the American Grain* are imperfect or illegitimate in that they do not fulfill the requirements of moral or aesthetic purity essential to a definition of religious and literary canons alike. In the same way that Columbus's "exceptional life" does not conform to the moral standards of the Catholic church's Invisible Council—which is precisely why it is "exceptional" in the first place—

the texts Williams assembles in *In the American Grain* violate the formal conventions that define the no less sacred realm of Literature: They are not just *un*canonical, but in fact *a*canonical. Those imperfections, those impurities in the design of the various textual fabrics, fuel the "fire" of Williams's writing.

Williams calls attention to those impurities in the immaculate design of the myth of America, as well as in the literary canon founded on that myth, at the very beginning of "The Discovery of the Indies," where he speaks of "a predestined and bitter fruit existing, perversely, before the white flower of its [the New World's] birth. . . . For it is as the achievement of a flower, pure, white, waxlike and fragrant, that Columbus' infatuated course must be depicted, especially when compared with the acrid and poisonous apple which was later by him to be proved" (*IAG*, 7). The "perverse," mad disorder implicit in the notion of the fruit existing, paradoxically, before the flower affects the way in which Williams rearranges the fragments from various accounts of Columbus's four voyages. In defiance of all principles of historical chronology, Columbus's narrative in *In the American Grain* opens with an account of his return to Spain (beginning on 13/14 February 1493) taken from the *Journal of the First Voyage*. It is interesting to note that the text of this journal is not the holograph original of the logbook that Columbus had presented to Ferdinand and Isabella in Barcelona upon his return from the first voyage. That original, as well as the copy Columbus received from the sovereigns shortly before embarking on his second voyage, has disappeared. The only text that has been preserved is an abstract prepared by Friar Bartolomé de las Casas from the transcript of the original, which he probably found in the library of Columbus's son Fernando. Las Casas later included that abstract in his *History of the Indies* (1552).[62] In other words, what we now consider the original text of the *First Voyage* is essentially an amalgam of quotations and paraphrases by Las Casas. It is not an original but already a copy, an interpretation. The lost original can thus only be recovered through fabulation.

The first-person narrative, then, is for the most part Williams's invention, and it invests the portions he takes from that *Journal* (*IAG*, 8–9, 16–26) with the same subjective and confessional tone we encounter in the middle section of *El arpa y la sombra*. The other documents Williams utilizes remain largely unchanged: the "Articles of the Agreement between the Lords the Catholic Sovereigns and Cristóbal Colón" (17 April 1492; *IAG*, 9–10); the "Letter to the Nurse of Prince John" (1500; *IAG*, 11–12); and the few passages from his "Letter of the Fourth Voyage" (1503) are all original first-person narratives. It is significant that all these texts, which precede and further defer Columbus's reported first impression of the West Indies, have very little to do with the actual discovery of America, that is, with the moment of contact, but focus instead on the admiral's precarious relations with the Spanish kings both prior to and after that initial journey. The account of the actual discovery follows almost like an afterthought.

Due to this chronological disorder, "The Discovery of the Indies" closes, quite ironically, with the very same passage that Carpentier's dying Columbus admits to having fabricated by projecting familiar images of Mediterranean beauty onto a land that was radically different. For Williams, as for Carpentier, Columbus's "achievement of a flower, pure, white, waxlike and fragrant," that is, of his image of America as a virgin land, is precisely such an "inspired invention of Western thought." Williams's following comments, which precede the final account of Columbus's discovery and open a frame that closes with the Latin prayer at the end of the section, clarify this beyond doubt:

Storms and men; the very worms of the sea were opposed to him [Columbus]. But if, as he instinctively, but for his insane doggedness, would have done, he had undertaken that holy pilgrimage of which he had spoken [in his "Letter to the Nurse of Prince John"], the flower might again, in that seclusion, often have appeared to him in all its old-time loveliness, as when he himself floated with luck and in sunshine on that tropic sea toward adventure and discovery. (*IAG*, 16)

The "white flower" ultimately appears to be indeed the product of a "bitter fruit": Williams implies that historical reality, like the Aztec idols in "The Destruction of Tenochtitlan" (*IAG*, 34), was sacrificed on the altar of Catholicism so that the New World, stripped of its difference and its radical otherness, could become the immaculate embodiment of European thought: America, El Dorado, a continent gilded by Europe's imagination. America, for Columbus, was not an autonomous historical entity but the divine revelation of a lost Paradise. For Europe, it was a promise of salvation not only from the spiritual confusion and the uncertainties that marked the end of the Middle Ages but also, on a very practical level, from economic bankruptcy. This was particularly true of Spain. Williams inscribes this idea of salvation in the form of a prayer to the Virgin Mary that serves as a coda: "*Eia ergo, advocata nostra, illos tuos misericordes oculos ad nos converte. Et Jesum, benedictum fructum ventris tui, nobis post hoc exsilium ostende. O clemens, o pia, o dulces Maria*" (*IAG*, 26). [Therefore, Our Intercessor, turn to us those merciful eyes of yours. And after this exile, show us Jesus, the blessed fruit of your womb. Oh merciful, pious, sweet Mary.]

Williams's "white flower," then, is a mythical image that initially signifies the absence of history. But once history is restored to that myth in the form of the texts that precede Columbus's final "confessions," those chronicles of the "predestined and bitter fruit," the image of the "white flower" becomes incapable of maintaining its symbolic integrity and thus its truth-value. It can no longer project a unified vision. As we read the accounts of Columbus's various ordeals and misfortunes, the image of the "white flower" as an emblem of his achievement and vision becomes increasingly ambiguous. As "that enormous world . . . [crushes] him among its multiple small disguises" (*IAG*, 10), the "white flower" is gradually emptied of its old meaning. In the end, the myth of America it seeks to uphold is as much of a voided presence as the "blessed fruit" of Mary's womb: The mythical whiteness of the flower literally dissolves in the whiteness of the burned ink; both are figures of the sterility of the imagination.

The fact that Williams ends "The Discovery of the Indies" with a Latin prayer readily identifies the artificial, waxlike image of the "white flower" as part of a Library emblazoned by Williams's writing. Insofar as the Library in *Paterson* is a burned-out structure, a mere skeleton that can no longer shelter language from interpretation and thus from the multiplicity of meaning, the whiteness (of the flower and of the ink) also announces the end of American Literature and the beginning of New World writing. The collapse of the old mythical structure—the fundament of a Library that houses the American literary canon—opens a space for an Archive of acanonical, illegitimate texts. These texts are legitimized, not by being awarded the status of Literature and by being accepted into the fold (or mold) of existing canons, but by being used as repositories of meaning for an alternative system, a tradition or (counter)poetics of New World writing. To reiterate, New World literature is conceived not as a literary canon but as a tradition of writing. This distinction is as crucial to *In the American Grain* as it is to *Paterson* and to *El arpa y la sombra*. It helps us understand that Williams's revisions are a matter not of aesthetics but of literary ideology. He is not interested in elevating so-called nonliterary texts to the lofty heights of Literature in order to protect the "word" from history and from interpretation. On the contrary, his is an attempt to expose literature to history, to turn *doxa* into paradox. By doing so, he calls attention to the fact that the new can only be inscribed as a dynamic process: The kind of writing that is in touch with history, rather than attempting to evade it, does not yield a final product or meaning, lest it be co-opted by myth. Writing, it seems, always wrests away the word.

This pronouncement, of course, is an inverted echo of Hart Crane's *The Bridge*, a poem whose subject matter clearly exhibits the influence of *In the American Grain*. But despite many similarities that superficially appear to link *The Bridge* with its precursor, there are profound differences in the ways in which these two texts approach history. If indeed Williams's text inspired Crane's poem, it may also be argued that Crane, perhaps despite himself, missed his predecessor's main point. Crane's (mis)reading of *In the American Grain*, be it intentional or unintentional, is most conspicuously evident in the "Ave María" section of *The Bridge*, which seems almost like an extension of Columbus's prayer at the end of "The Discovery of the Indies":

Be with me, Luis de San Angel, now—
Witness before the tides can wrest away
the word I bring. (B, 5)

If *The Bridge* as a whole is an attempt "to lend a myth to God" (B, 2), then it is not surprising that Crane's Columbus would be concerned with protecting the "incognizable Word / of Eden"—what Williams calls "the white flower"—from the changes that the tides (or time) may work upon it. The tides, the water, represent Columbus's return voyage to Spain and thus the process of communicating the news of the discovery, of somehow translating the new into the old to render it comprehensible: "For here between two worlds, another, harsh / This third, of water, tests the word" (B, 6).

The anxiety Crane shares with his Columbus is precisely that "the word" may be tested and found incapable of communicating the new. What Crane does not seem to realize is that Columbus's "incognizable Word" communicates not the new in its difference from the old, but the potential of the new to become like the old. Columbus, after all, did not discover the New World; he conquered it by depriving it of its historical autonomy and its otherness, that is, by imposing upon it a familiar biblical myth. In this sense, the "incognizable Word" is an "enchained Sepulchre." Crane may well be said to have committed a similar fatal error: Whatever the new is that he is trying to communicate, the myth he ultimately lends, perhaps not to God but certainly to the New World, is a myth no less familiar and no less confining than Columbus's. Once again, America becomes Atlantis, not a new world, but an old image

33

oddly untouched by the test of water and of time. *The Bridge,* unlike *In the American Grain,* is not a revision of the myth of America. Despite its suggestive "antiphonal whispers," it reinstates everything Williams sets out to destroy.

III   *We are all living on the margin because there is no longer any center.*
                              —OCTAVIO PAZ, *The Labyrinth of Solitude*

In his study of Charles Olson, Robert von Hallberg contends that "after World War II the problem for [American] writers was less how to evade history than how to defeat history's evasion of humanity."[63] While this formulation is quite in keeping with the general tendency among literary historians to designate 1945 as the end of American modernism and the beginning of the postmodern period, it also indirectly addresses the limitations of comprehending modernism and postmodernism as literary periods. But more important than debating the advantages and disadvantages of periodization is taking notice of the fact that von Hallberg's distinction of different attitudes toward history (and toward knowledge) and their implicit respective association with modernism and postmodernism approaches the distinction I have drawn between American Literature and New World writing.[64] If, as I have suggested, the majority of American writers during the first half of this century were preoccupied with evading history as best as possible, then it should come as no surprise that concurrent critical attempts at defining an American literary canon would exhibit similar tendencies: In fact, if literary modernism (in the de Manian sense) is indeed ahistorical, if not outright antihistorical, it may well be argued that the critical endeavor of canonization is a quintessentially modern phenomenon. Since a canon, by definition, only recognizes similarity (or conformity) and not difference or exceptionality—as we have seen in the case of Carpentier's Columbus and the question of his eligibility to sainthood—it is, also by definition, an ahistorical construct. The American literary canon that Williams so adamantly rejects in *In the American Grain* may then, by the same token, be regarded as an attempt to evade history by creating a past that is "usable" only because it is ahistorical and closed. To make that closed past historical, in Williams's sense, is to reintroduce contradictions and thus acknowledge the existence of differences. And it is this reintroduction of contradictions and differences, of exceptions to the canonical rule of representativeness, that produces what I have termed a tradition of writing. The deconstructive processes we have witnessed in both Williams's *In the American Grain* and Carpentier's *El arpa y la sombra* share, not a rejection of the same canon—obviously, Carpentier's literary "relatives" were quite different from Williams's—but a resistance to the very idea of canonization.[65] We have also seen that this resistance is not just a literary theme but a series of formal strategies that may be called, in Paul de Man's terms, postmodern "allegories of reading."

If attitudes toward history (and knowledge) can be employed to mark important differences between American modernism and postmodernism, then it also becomes clear that it is more useful to perceive those two phenomena, not as more or less separate historical periods, but as two simultaneous movements. In that case, New World writing can be grasped more concretely as a postmodern posture that certain American writers such as Williams and Carpentier assume before history, a posture that goes beyond modernism's evasions of history.[66] And it goes beyond modernism, to return to von Hallberg's formulation, precisely to take issue with history's evasion of humanity.

A writer's or a text's resistance to being canonized is, then, not a case of the "anxiety of influence" vis-à-vis those works that already compose the canon, but a resistance to the formal and conceptual limitations represented by the canon and its requirements of conformity to certain aesthetic and/or ideological rules implicit in the notion of literary merit. Williams's inclusion in the American literary canon was certainly a belated response—as, by the way, was Wallace Stevens's—and it is perhaps not all that surprising that his name still remains conspicuously absent from some contemporary versions of that canon, most notably from the Bloomian one. All of this goes to show that Williams's texts, and *In the American Grain* in particular, continue to elicit critical discomfort, as they well should. *In the American Grain* is not, strictly speaking, the property of the Anglo–North American literary canon or even some of its more recent variations, but belongs instead to a tradition of New World writing that deliberately crosses canons and blurs the distinctions between them. In this way, *In the American Grain* enters and shares the cultural and literary space of Carpentier's *El arpa y la sombra*. That these crossings and transgressions are not bloodless formal procedures ought to be sufficiently clear by now: Williams's formal strategies of resistance, like Carpentier's, are directed not so much against individual writers and texts that are part of established literary canons but against the ideology of canonization. Their implications are both cultural and moral in the broadest sense. If we pose the question of what is ultimately to be gained from the kind of deconstructive revisionism both Williams and Carpentier practice, the answer does not lie in the direction of some sort of linguistic nihilism, which has all too frequently been regarded as the trademark of deconstructive ventures. Rather, it lies in their active discontent with history's evasion of humanity and American Literature's refusal to confront that problem by time and again retreating into the safe enclosure of its traditional myths. To elucidate the nature of Williams's discontent with those strategies of evasion (I shall return to Carpentier later), let me retrace my steps and consider his remarks on how he came to write *In the American Grain*. As he explained in a letter to Horace Gregory, who was at the time preparing the preface to the second (1939) edition of that book:

Of mixed ancestry, I felt from earliest childhood that America was the only home I could ever possibly call my own. I felt that it was expressly founded for me, personally, and that it must be my first business in life to possess it; that only by making it my own from the beginning to my own day, in detail, should I ever have a basis for knowing where I stood. I must have a basis for orienting myself formally in the beliefs which activated me from day to day.

Nothing in the school histories interested me, so I decided as far as possible to go to whatever source material I could get a and start my own valuations there: to establish myself from my own reading, in my own way, in the locality which by birthright had become my own.[67]

It was precisely Williams's profound awareness of his mixed ancestry as a peculiarly American or New World condition that put him at odds with most of his contemporaries and their attempts to maintain, for better or for worse, a unified vision of American Culture. In fact, Williams's perspective on American Culture and Literature as elaborated in *In the American Grain* seems to have grown out of the same ambiguous sense of marginality we encounter in the work of many Afro–North American and Latin American writers of that period. Most notable in this respect are James Weldon Johnson's *The Autobiography of an Ex–Colored Man* (1912); Countee Cullen's "Heritage"; Jean Toomer's *Cane*;[68] Claude McKay's autobiography, *Home to Harlem* (1928), as well as his novels *Banjo* (1929) and *Banana Bottom* (1933); Nella Larsen's *Quicksand* (1928) and *Passing* (1929); Nicolás Guillén's *Motivos de son* (1930); Alejo Carpentier's *¡Ecue Yamba-O!* (1933); Adalberto Ortiz's *Juyungo* (1942); and Luis Palés Matos's *Tuntún de pasa y grifería* (1937), to mention only a few.[69] What at the same time distinguishes *In the American Grain* from those texts is that it was a rigorous, systematic attempt at redefining American Culture and Literature from that same postmodern perspective of marginality that would later produce works such as Jay Wright's *Dimensions of History* and Nicolás Guillén's *El diario que a diario*. At a time when writers and critics like Van Wyck Brooks and Waldo Frank almost frantically tried to recapture stale visions of original unity, and when Alain Locke of Howard University triumphantly introduced his "New Negro" to the patrons of the United States cultural establishment, Williams set out, in his own way, to build what Octavio Paz was later to call "a literature of foundations."[70]

Williams's endeavors to find new literary shapes to celebrate the New World's mixed cultural heritage were closely connected with his interest in the Spanish language. As he notes in his *Autobiography*, Spanish, his mother's native tongue, had a strong appeal to him, "temperamentally, as a relief from the classic mood of French and Italian. . . . Spanish is not, in the sense to which I refer, a literary language. It has a place of its own, an independent place very sympathetic to the New World. This independence, this lack of integration with our British past gives us an opportunity, facing Spanish literature, to make new appraisals, especially in attempting translations, which should permit us to use our own language with unlimited freshness."[71] We shall see in Part 2 how this view of the potential of the Spanish language to inspire different uses of English by way of establishing a distance from the British tradition is paralleled in the poems of Jay Wright.

Williams's pronounced interest in Latin American literatures makes Octavio Paz a valuable reference point here, one that deserves more than just a brief mention. Paz and Williams translated some of each other's poetry: Paz, in 1970, translated "Nantucket," "Young Sycamore," "The Red Wheelbarrow," and portions of "Asphodel," while Williams, in his seventies, produced a brilliant English rendition of "Himno entre ruinas" [Hymn among Ruins].[72] In addition, Paz's *The Labyrinth of Solitude* (1950) and Williams's *In the American Grain* share a "search for our own selves, which have been deformed and disguised by alien institutions, and for a form that will express them."[73] Paz's text may well be read as a belated commentary on *In the American Grain* that clarifies some of the major issues with which Williams was grappling as early as the 1920s. As both writers, the Mexican and the North American, penetrate the "dead layers" of institutionalized culture and its respective consensus rituals, shared concerns surface which, in turn, prompt a return to similar sources and founding fables.

Paz begins, in "The Pachuco and Other Extremes," by exploring the cultural differences between Mexicans and Anglo–North Americans. What he arrives at by contemplating the origin of each of these world views is, interestingly enough, a counterpoint quite reminiscent of the dissonant movements of *In the American Grain:*

It seems to me that North Americans consider the world to be something that can be perfected, and we consider it to be something that can be redeemed. Like their Puritan ancestors, we believe that sin and death constitute the ultimate basis of human nature, *but with the difference that the Puritan identifies purity with health.* Therefore he believes in the purifying effects of ascetics and the consequences are his cult of work for work's sake, his serious approach to life, and his conviction that the body does not exist or at least cannot lose—or find—itself in another being. *Every contact is contamination. Foreign races, ideas, customs, and bodies carry within themselves the germs of perdition and impurity.* Social hygiene complements that of the body and soul. Mexicans, however, both ancient and modern, believe in communion and fiestas: *there is no health without contact.* (*Labyrinth*, 24; my italics)

The distinctions Paz draws in this passage loudly echo the contrapuntal movement Williams sets up, most notably, between "Voyage of the Mayflower" and "Père Sebastian Rasles." Purity, for Williams, is equivalent to emptiness and sterility, qualities that translate into a lack or a dwarfing of the imagination and thus into a peculiar form of illiteracy (*IAG*, 65–66). Wilson Harris's concept of the "illiterate imagination"[74] best conveys the moral and intellectual deficiencies Williams associates with purity and Puritanism: "The jargon of God . . . was their dialect by which they kept themselves surrounded as with a palisade" (*IAG*, 64). To be sure, it was quite fashionable at the time to debunk North America's Puritan heritage. But, as Paz correctly points out in anticipation of Bercovitch's argument, it was "a criticism that respects the existing systems and *never touches the roots*" (*Labyrinth*, 21; my italics). Ironically, the very criticism of Puritanism reveals, as we have witnessed in the case of Brooks, the same inability (or unwillingness) "TO MARRY, to *touch*—to *give* because one HAS, not because one has nothing" (*IAG*, 121). Like the Puritans themselves, most of their North American critics shirked the risk of "contamination," be it cultural or social.

Williams is quite different from those self-appointed guardians of American Culture in that he dares commune. Like Père Sebastian Rasles's letter, "a moral source not reckoned with, peculiarly sensitive and daring in its close embrace of native things" (*IAG*, 121), Williams's writings dare make contact with history instead of evading it: "to create, to hybridize, to crosspollenize,—not to sterilize, to draw back, to fear, to dry up, to rot" (*IAG*, 121). This act of making contact, of touching the roots, as it were, is essentially an act of reading. Williams stresses in "Père Sebastian Rasles" that

> we have no conception at all of what is meant by moral, since we recognize no ground our own—and that this rudeness rests all upon the unstudied character of our beginning; and that if we will not pay heed to our own affairs, we are nothing but an unconscious porkyard and oilhole for those, more able, who will fasten themselves upon us. And that we have no defense, lacking intelligent investigation of the changes worked upon the early comers here, to the New World, the books, records, no defense save brute isolation, prohibitions, walls, ships, fortresses—and all the asininities of ignorant fear that forbids us to protect a doubtful freedom by employing it. That unless everything that is, proclaim a ground on which it stand, it has no worth; and that what has been morally, aesthetically worth while in America has rested upon peculiar and discoverable ground. But they think they get it out of the air or the rivers . . . instead of by word of mouth or from records contained for us in books—and that, aesthetically, morally *we are deformed unless we read.* (IAG, 109; my italics)

Williams's own readings are, in effect, allegories of unreading, of undoing ideological deformities and distortions; it is in this sense that they may be called "moral." They are also analogous to the acts of unwriting I shall discuss in connection with Wright's *Dimensions of History* and Guillén's *El diario.*

Even more to the point, Williams's allegories of unreading in *In the American Grain*, inspired by his initial deconstruction of Columbus's "white flower" in "The Discovery of the Indies," are poetic acts of cultural communion strongly suggestive, in both their thematic and their formal aspects, of Paz's *fiestas.* After all, it has to be kept in mind that Williams's master trope for processes of cultural interaction and interpenetration as manifest in the textual exchange of literary (and nonliterary) forms is the figure of the *dance,* which appears most prominently at the end of *Paterson* and in *The Desert Music.* The same kinetic trope lurks just beneath the surface of "The May-Pole at Merry Mount" in " '[Thomas] Morton's inclination to boistrous revelry [that] culminated at last in that proceeding [the May festival] which scandalized the Plymouth elders and passed into history' " (IAG, 78). The processes of transformation and transgression inscribed in Williams's figure of the dance are comparable, in many ways, to those implicit in Stevens's trope of music. The Williams of *In the American Grain* seems very much like Stevens's man with the blue guitar who, twanging the wiry and weary strings of history, plays "a tune beyond us, yet ourselves."[75]

In "The Day of the Dead," Paz describes the fiesta as a ritualistic communion of society with itself" (*Labyrinth*, 52). It is the "advent of the unusual," governed by its own special rules and by a logic that conflicts with, and reverses, everyday norms. He explains that

in certain fiestas the very notion of order disappears. Chaos comes back and license rules. Anything is permitted, the customary hier-archies vanish, along with all social, sex, caste, and trade distinc-tions. . . . Obligatory sacrilege, ritual profanation is committed. . . . Regulations, habits, and customs are violated. . . . Therefore the fiesta is not only an excess, a ritual squandering of the goods painfully accumulated during the rest of the year; it is also a revolt, a sudden immersion in the formless, in pure being. By means of the fiesta society frees itself from the norms it has established. It ridicules its gods, its principles, and its laws: it denies its own self. . . . The fiesta is a cosmic experiment, an *experiment in disorder*, reuniting contradic-tory elements and principles in order to bring about a renascence of life. (*Labyrinth*, 51; my italics)

For Paz, the fiesta as a violent break with society's "arguments of unity," that is, its laws in the broadest sense, is not only an affirmation of creative or re-creative energy but the very source of that energy. The fiesta is a ritualistic subversion of a cultural ideology predicated on unity. It is a ritual of dissent that, for Paz, constitutes a cultural paradigm for acts of intellectual violence that break through the surface of rigidly canonized or institutionalized Culture and clear paths to a tradition of cultural freeplay that poses the constant need for reordering society, for devising what Williams calls "new measures." "However hopeless it may seem," Williams urges in "Descent," "we have no other choice: we must go back to the beginning; it must all be done over; everything that is must be destroyed" (*IAG*, 215). Echoes of the same conviction abound in *The Labyrinth of Solitude:* "Each time we try to express ourselves," Paz observes, "we have to break with ourselves" (*Labyrinth*, 53). This break with oneself (or one's self)—Williams calls it "an agony of self-realiza-tion[76]—is an act of self-revelation that destroys the very concept of a unified self, of which the concept of a unified culture is an extension. Self-realization or self-revelation, then, coincides with self-destruction, and this destruction (or deconstruction) of selfhood leads to a prolifera-tion of identities, cultural identities in this case, all of which are forms of otherness. Paz's fiesta, like Williams's dance, is a ritualization of the "rich regenerative violence" (*IAG*, 130) that characterizes the self's encounter with otherness, or, put differently, man's encounter with himself as other. This encounter is analogous to America's encounter with itself as a New

World. In the poetry of Wright and Guillén, this deconstructive process or agony of cultural self-realization is associated with and embodied in similar rituals, which charge Williams's trope of the dance with more specific cultural meanings: Those rituals or ritualistic grammars are *limbo* and *carnival*.

For Williams, the break with one's self is also equivalent to the burning of the Library. Having voided the myth of America by reinterpreting the texts upon which it was founded, Williams proceeds to reconstruct New World history by further exploring the space of the Archive. In "The Destruction of Tenochtitlan," for instance, he rebuilds from fragments of Hernando Cortés's letters an image of "a spirit mysterious, constructive, independent, puissant with natural wealth; . . . a spirit lost in that soil" (*IAG*, 32). As Williams chronicles the wanton destruction of that magnificent Aztec city in the name of Christianity (and greed)—"because of the awkward names men give their emptiness" (*IAG*, 27)—his "big, square paragraphs like Inca [*sic*: Aztec] masonry"[77] formally reverse the content of Cortés's letters to show "the recreate New unfolding itself miraculously" (*IAG*, 27), not only among the ancient ruins of the city, but within Cortés's own writings. Williams's style in this section reincarnates the very spirit Cortés tried to exorcise by ordering the Aztec idols to be dragged from their places and flung down the stairs and by having the temples cleansed of the blood of human victims, so that they could house images of Our Lady and the Catholic saints. In other words, Williams's textual masonry evolves into a method for *measuring* the cultural differences Cortés fought to level by destroying their external shapes. In its new configuration, Cortés's text, which Williams both quotes and paraphrases, becomes puissant with meaning as the cultural differences it attempts to expunge reinsinuate themselves into the textual fabric. In this way, Cortés's letters, despite themselves, are made to express those differences.

The internal dissonances in "The Destruction of Tenochtitlan" produce an effect quite similar in its subversiveness to Williams's readings (or unreadings) of the Icelandic Sagas and Columbus's letters and journals. These readings also anticipate the more explicit juxtaposition of "Voyage of the Mayflower" and "Père Sebastian Rasles" on which I have commented above. Other sections of *In the American Grain* may be paired in similar ways: for instance, "The May-Pole at Merry Mount" with "Cotton Mather's Wonders of the Invisible World" or "The Discovery of Kentucky" with "George Washington" and "Poor Richard," respectively. More fruitful, however, than tracing every single manifestation of Williams's revisionary paradigm in *In the American Grain* is a closer look at what constitutes potentially the most important contrapuntal movement in that text: the contrast between Cortés and Rasles, which makes me suspect that the ideological differences between Puritanism and Catholicism are not Williams's main concern here. Cortés's *relaciones* and Rasles's letters represent two contrasting approaches to otherness and difference. Cortés's conquest of Mexico was a purging of cultural differences by way of imposing upon Aztec civilization a system of political and religious organization that went against the grain of its cultural traditions. It was not possible to assimilate the Aztec empire into the Spanish body politic without destroying the cultural foundations of that empire. Cortés did not succeed in rebuilding Tenochtitlán because he did not understand the principle on which it had been founded: For him, the dry blood in the temples was simply "human gore," as Charles Olson points out in "The Kingfishers."

Olson's poem, a response to Pound's *Pisan Cantos* and Eliot's *Four Quartets*, is relevant to *In the American Grain* in a number of ways, not all of which I have room to explore here.[78] Suffice it to say that Olson shares with Williams the same attitude toward history.[79] Both writers "hunt among stones," in this case the ruins of the Aztec empire, and their findings are quite similar. After presenting a list of Aztec treasures in the form of a lengthy citation from Prescott's history of Mexico, Olson writes:

(of the two who first came, each a conquistador,
               one healed, the other
tore the eastern idols down, toppled
the temple walls, which, says the excuser
were black from the human gore.

hear
hear, where the dry blood talks
   where the old appetite walks[80]

The two conquistadors here are Alvar Núñez Cabeza de Vaca and Cortés. The significance of this juxtaposition with respect to *In the American Grain* lies in the fact that Cabeza de Vaca—to whom I return in Part 2—represents for Olson what Rasles does for Williams: the willingness to explore cultural differences, the courage to commune with otherness and be transformed as a result of that contact. Although Cabeza de Vaca, unlike Rasles, was a failed conquistador who was forced to live among the North American Indians because of the disastrous events that befell his expedition, his narrative is nevertheless a similar "presentation of the Indian point of view." In Cabeza de Vaca, as in

Rasles, "one feels THE INDIAN emerging from within the pod of his isolation from eastern understanding, he is released AN INDIAN" (*IAG*, 121). The question here is ultimately not one of identification but of the transformation of identity and imagination: that is, of the kind of disfigurement and potential multiplicity of identities that Fuentes's shipwrecked "discoverer" defines as the imprint of the New World upon the European. "No," Williams writes, "we are not Indians but we are men of their world. . . . If men inherit souls this is the color of mine. We are, too, the others" (*IAG*, 39–41). Identity, then, is not a question of unity, of identifying with one culture or another, of conquering or being conquered. It is instead a matter of dialogue between cultures and thus of literacy. For instance, both Rasles and Cabeza de Vaca learned the language of the Indians among whom they lived, while Cortés relied on interpreters, thus keeping his distance and resisting cultural and linguistic "contamination." It is telling that those who did receive the imprint of the New World and were, in that sense, disfigured or contaminated were treated either as outcasts or as traitors: Cabeza de Vaca, held in suspicion by the Spanish soldiers because of his kind treatment of the Indians during later expeditions, was finally returned to Spain in chains and sentenced to eight years of exile in Africa. Rasles, in his turn, was cruelly killed by the English: "They mangled him besides, leaving him disfigured and with his bones all crushed within him" (*IAG*, 127). Having become interpreters themselves, Cabeza de Vaca and Rasles were ultimately treated by the colonial powers, be it the English or the Spanish, little better than Cortés treated his interpreter, La Malinche. For Williams and Olson, they are the shadows that stalk the silences of official histories, silences that signify evasions of humanity.

In the American Grain is an attempt at retrieving such silences or "undersongs" (*IAG*, 59, 193) from the official versions of American history. For Williams, "Père Sebastian Rasles" is exemplary of the kind of "undersong" he restores to Cortés's letters through subtle changes in form, a silence that becomes gradually more articulate as we move through "The Fountain of Eternal Youth" and "De Soto and the New World." It is useful once again to compare Williams's revisionary strategies to those Octavio Paz employs in *The Labyrinth of Solitude*, particularly in "The Sons of La Malinche," which complements Williams's "The Destruction of Tenochtitlan" in that it retrieves from Cortés's letters the silences Williams shapes as big, square paragraphs. These silences constitute a cultural subtext made significant by its absence: the story of La Malinche, or Doña Marina, Cortés's Indian interpreter and mistress.[81] In the context of Mexican cultural history, La Malinche is the concrete historical embodiment of the mythical *La Chingada*, the violated Mother, whose North American counterpart would be the legendary figure of Pocahontas, whom we encounter in Crane's *The Bridge*. "The strange permanence of Cortés and La Malinche in the Mexican's imagination and sensibilities," Paz argues, "reveals that they are something more than historical figures: they are symbols of a secret conflict that we have still not resolved" (*Labyrinth*, 87). This underlying conflict is inevitably bound up in the question of cultural origins. It is inscribed, Paz suggests, in a single word: *chingar*, which, in the broadest sense, means to break, to rip open, to wound.[82]

Chingar and its numerous derivations are prohibited words; they form a sacred language whose magical ambiguities are themselves expressions, as well as results, of the same cultural hybridism they so violently seek to deny. If *chingar*, on the one hand, is used by Mexicans to reject or condemn their violent historical origins, it is also, at the same time, a secret affirmation of the intimate cultural bonds created precisely by that violence. Because of these inherent, unresolved tensions, which cause its meanings to multiply and proliferate, *chingar* is for Paz "living language in a world of anemic vocables" (*Labyrinth*, 74). It is a word whose own semantic structure reenacts the conflictual interpenetration of cultures that characterizes the New World as a historical entity. In the process, the word itself is emptied of its old meaning and its old associations: "The *chingada*, because of constant use, contradictory meanings and the friction of angry or enthusiastic lips, wastes away, loses its contents and disappears. It is a hollow word. It says nothing. It is Nothingness itself" (*Labyrinth*, 79). But, as Paz's essay itself proves, this Nothingness, so reminiscent of Eliot's "waste land," is really a trope for the superabundance of signification, much like "the nothing that is [there]" in Stevens's "The Snow Man."[83] Meanings begin to proliferate almost uncontrollably as the myth of *La Chingada* is reinvested with all its historical and cultural complexities. This transformation is part and parcel of Paz's own discourse: The dissolution of *La Chingada* into various forms of *chingar* is ultimately a process that reinvents history through a deconstruction of that myth. It is a process analogous to Williams's decomposition of the image of the "white flower" and its simultaneous reconstitution in the trope of "white ink." "It is astonishing," Paz concludes, "that a country with such a vivid past—a country so profoundly traditional, so close to its roots, so rich in ancient legends even if poor in modern history—should conceive of itself only as a negation of its origins" (*Labyrinth*, 87). While this may indeed be astonishing to some of his readers, it is certainly not so to Paz himself, who demonstrates, throughout *The Labyrinth of Soli-*

tude, that this negation of the kinds of origins stored in the texts that compose the Library of American Literature is the only way to make accessible to the imagination those ancient legends and traditions. To use words "that cause wounds" and cut traces is to affirm a rupture instead of an origin. It is to separate things so they can join in their separateness instead of becoming one in some ideal union that would reinstate the fiction of original unity.

This idea of joining things, words, cultures, in their separateness, of creating coherence rather than unity, establishes an intimate bond between writers as different as Paz and Williams, or Carpentier and Olson. The very assertion of separateness, of difference, is what makes this bond possible. By unraveling the fictions underlying the myth of America— such as Columbus's "white flower" and the myth of *La Chingada*—all these writers repeat in the double act of reading and writing the original violence glossed over by that myth. For each, that act itself becomes an original rupture that creates an opening through which history can be glimpsed in all its chaotic and fragmented complexity. Writing itself, then, becomes an act of holding irreducible differences in tension, or, as Jay Wright has it, in "limbo."[84]

Williams masterfully sustains these tensions throughout *In the American Grain.* His final section on "Abraham Lincoln" offers neither relief nor resolution, nor closure for that matter, but condenses and reinscribes the very tensions and contradictions that make this text cohere in the figure of Lincoln as "a woman in an old shawl—with a great bearded face and a towering black hat above it, to give unearthly reality"(*IAG*, 234). The male and the female, like Cortés and La Malinche representative of a secret, unresolved conflict, are "married" in these lines, joined in their separateness to produce a third, "a woman, born somehow, aching over it [the place], holding all fearfully together" (*IAG*, 234). By figuring this third, this precarious product of an uneasy yet fertile alliance, as a woman, Williams unsettles the myth of Lincoln as the Father or Savior of the Nation in order to lend final emphasis to the marginality of his own writing. Like Williams's "woman," *In the American Grain* as a text is "born somehow," that is, conceived illegitimately, "aching" over a culture that has indeed tormented itself into the bewilderment and pain we encounter most notably in Eliot's *Waste Land* as well as, for instance, in the novels and stories of Hemingway and Fitzgerald. It is a text holding fearfully together all the different, disparate textual fragments Williams accumulates. It precariously joins them in an agony of textual and cultural self-realization.

In the American Grain is a poetic experiment in disorder, a textual embodiment of the trope of the Archive constituted by the acanonical, marginal texts Williams gathers together. As representative of such social, cultural, and economic marginality, the figure of the woman, a trope that combines previous references and allusions to Jacataqua/Pocahontas/La Malinche, the disembodied female voice in the "De Soto" section, and Freydis, stands for a new "measure" and thus for an alternative approach to American Culture. That alternative takes shape as the image of the last founding father, Abraham Lincoln, is effaced and turned into white ink. Insofar as Williams's "Abraham Lincoln" is also an unreading of Whitman's "When Lilacs Last in the Dooryard Bloom'd," the figure of the woman as representative of cultural subtexts, of silences to be retrieved, compromises Whitman's status as the founding father of modern American Literature. Twisting Whitman's poetic eulogy into a textual surface of most bizarre images, Williams pays a final tribute to Poe's method and madness. With the death of Lincoln, which ultimately becomes a figure for Williams's deconstruction of Whitman's text, America is reborn—or re-dressed—as a new world, a new coherence. "It was the end of THAT period," and the beginning of a new era (and a new method) of writing.[85]

Jay Wright's Mythology of Writing

The Black Limbo

All great poetry is concerned with the true stature of things.
— ERICH HELLER, *The Disinherited Mind*

In an essay entitled "The Place of the Poet in Modern Society" (1966), Wilson Harris declares that "the crucial problem for the modern poet . . . is to visualize a structure which is, at one and the same time, a structure of freedom and a structure of authority."[1] My task in the following pages is to describe such structures of simultaneous freedom and authority as they emerge in the work of the Afro-American poet and playwright Jay Wright, one of the most remarkable contemporary authors in the New World. According to John Hollander, "Jay Wright's poetry is some of the most original and powerful that is being written in America."[2] To date, Wright's poetic canon consists of five books of poetry: *The Homecoming Singer* (1971), *Soothsayers and Omens* (1976), *Explications / Interpretations* (1984), *Dimensions of History* (1976), and *The Double Invention of Komo* (1980), this being the order in which Wright suggests his poetry be read.[3] Of this series, *The Homecoming Singer* is the only book that is properly described as a collection of poems, while the other four texts constitute what Wright calls his first poetic cycle.

At the risk of violating the integrity of that cycle, I have decided to focus on *Dimensions of History*, which, in my view, best exemplifies the literary processes defined above as structures of freedom and authority. Wright frequently envisions those structures as a city, a compound trope that translates specific cultural and historical relationships into spatial configurations, that is, into writing. The trope of the city, quite reminiscent of Williams's *Paterson*, first appears in "Benjamin Banneker Helps to Build a City" (in *Soothsayers and Omens*), a poem I treat as a kind of introduction to *Dimensions of History*, where the city as a locus of transformation plays a dominant role. Frequent excursions, particularly to *The Double Invention of Komo* as well as to some of Wright's other poems, form a necessary and, to my mind, inevitable part of any reading of *Dimensions of History*. A poem best characterized as "contact-high,"[4] *Dimensions* brings into literary contact cultural "geographies" (that is, traditions identified with more or less specific geographical locations) generally conceived as separate entities: Europe, Africa, and the Americas.

Wright's territory is the New World, and I am employing this term very self-consciously to de-emphasize as much as possible the nationalistic connotations the term "America" has acquired as a result of being used as a shorthand expression for the United States. If "America" in any way suggests a potentially unified area of study, it does so, as we have already

49

seen, only by subordinating all cultural elements of a non-European origin to the claims of the so-called Anglo–North American cultural establishment.[5] In contrast, the "New World" is what Auerbach has called a *Sinnganzes*,[6] and this is exactly how Wright perceives it: not as a political entity, but as a "geography" that derives its coherence from a long history of cultural exchange. This coherence liberates it from the need for the kind of false unity imposed by forms of nationalism which are ultimately nothing but feeble disguises for cultural imperialism. Wright would no doubt concur with Auerbach that "our philological homeland is the earth; it cannot be the nation any longer."[7] Consequently Wright's well-charted poetic journeys lead into territories almost completely unfamiliar to most North American readers. Under the careful guidance of his poet (or poetic persona), this "dark and dutiful dyēli," we travel to the most remote corners of European and New World history and mythology and to the even less familiar realms of African religion. This intense unfamiliarity is, at least in part, due to contexts such as Dogon, Bambara, and Akan cosmologies and Ifa divination, but even more so to Wright's poetic method. The language of his poems appears familiar at first, but on closer look we become increasingly doubtful that what we are reading is adequately described as "English." These doubts are justified: Not only does Wright avail himself of a variety of languages, ranging from Spanish and Arabic to the ritual signatures of the Dogon *sigui*. He also interweaves different grammars to enlarge the semantic capacities of the English language.

Yet there is one thing we can be certain about: Wright's poetry is obsessed with history and with the history of the New World in particular. To be more precise, it is motivated by the desire, and in fact the need, to comprehend the complex relations between history, myth, and literature as different forms of self-knowledge. Wright's poet's journeys are set in motion by the search for a language that accommodates both myth and history, that plays off one against the other without submitting to the constraints of either. This interplay of myth and history also offers a key to Wright's use of ritual. *The Double Invention of Komo*, for instance, is explicitly described as a poem that "risks ritual's arrogance."[8] At the same time, it is important for us to understand that poetry, as Wright insists elsewhere, is not ritual.[9] Yet ritual, as we shall see, can be used in poetry, Wright and Harris would agree, "not as something in which we situate ourselves absolutely, but an unravelling of self-deception within self-revelation as we see through the various dogmatic proprietors of the globe within a play of contrasting structures and anti-structures."[10] It is this play of contrasting structures and antistructures (that is, of myth and history) that Wright's poetry seeks to articulate through linguistic and formal rigor. The results are spectacular: Wright is one of the poets in recent literary history who, to use Williams's words, is "making the mass in which some later Eliot will dig."[11] In neglecting his poetry, the criticism of Afro-American (and American) literature(s) has deprived itself of one of the most fascinating and fertile resources for a true critical revisionism.

What form would such a critical revisionism take, and what alternatives can it offer to the established rituals of modern American literary and cultural criticism? Out of a certain protective attitude developed largely in response to those established rituals, Afro-American literary criticism has cultivated its own biases and clichés, which have gradually hardened into an impenetrable crust. But this safe crust of bias is no viable substitute for a critical methodology, one that would duly recognize Afro-American literature's comparative nature instead of attempting to maintain illusions of canonistic purity. Along those lines, a critical revisionism would have to accomplish, to return to Harris's phrase, a rigorous "unravelling of self-deception within self-revelation." The self-deception in this case is the belief in the efficacy of cultural nationalism, manifest in the attempt at defining an Afro-American literary canon in the classical sense. This belief tends to disregard the fact that the Afro-American writer is heir to far more than just the African cultural and literary traditions. Afro-American literature is not simply a matter of certain so-called African retentions. Rather, it is a matter of conscious choices on the part of the writer, choices that enable him or her to compare the different values, aesthetic and moral, embodied by each of the cultural traditions to which he or she has access in the New World. Wright exercises this freedom of choice and comparison rigorously and challenges his readers to do the same.

We witness in Wright's poetry the emergence of a particular kind of literacy out of his perception of the place of Afro-American history within the larger patterns of New World history. Robert Stepto has suggested that the Afro-American literary tradition is governed by a "pregeneric myth," which he defines as the "quest for freedom and literacy."[12] But where does this myth come from? How did it evolve? And, what happens to it once freedom and literacy have been, in some sense, achieved? Although the existence of a substantial body of texts written by Afro-Americans seems to suggest that these objectives have been fulfilled, the quest continues and the question is not only why but also how. It continues mainly because of several vital questions concerning the involvement of Afro-American texts with history, and it is these questions that Wright's poems address: What does it mean for Afro-American literature to have a history, to be able, in other words, to entertain the idea of distinct historical origins?[13] What are those historical origins, and what do they suggest about the nature of Afro-American culture(s) in relation to other New (or Old) World cultures? What does it mean for a writer to take notice of the traces that verify the historical existence of Afro-American culture(s)? And, finally, how does this act of self-realization affect the processes of writing and reading?

The issue at hand is not so much freedom *and* literacy, but freedom *through* literacy, as well as freedom *with* literacy.[14] Literacy, understood at the most elemental level as the ability to read and write, affords a very special kind of freedom, namely the freedom to generate and disseminate knowledge about one's self in the form of written statements, texts. Literacy, in this sense, is a method of gaining self-knowledge, which grants the Afro-American writer the freedom to interpret and to create his or her own myths about history. In short, the quest for freedom-through-literacy is a search for new methodologies. This further implies that the methods and methodologies, that is, the formal strategies Afro-American writers have devised since 1845, have changed substantially. These changes, as manifest in Wright's poems, tell us much about the nature of the self-knowledge that is being generated and thus about the current features of Afro-American writing.

At the risk of stating the obvious, let me briefly recall some of the basic facts about Afro-America, facts that tend to get drowned in most current critical debates. One of those facts is that the vast majority of African slaves imported into various parts of the New World approximately since the beginning of the seventeenth century did not have a written language of their own. A few knew Arabic, as is evident in the case of colonial Brazil, but their number was negligible. In addition, blacks, especially in North America, were systematically denied access to the written language of their white masters, while at the same time being forced to substitute that very language for their own various native tongues. In the North American slave states, more so than in other New World countries, literacy was used to create and reinforce both legitimate and illegitimate cultural differences between blacks and whites.[15] Literacy thus quickly evolved into an ideological vehicle for the perpetuation of white supremacy. The historical link between freedom and literacy is clear: Not only did the ability to read and write afford the black slave intellectual freedom by rendering accessible for interpretation and criticism the texts and documents used to legitimize his or her bondage. Literacy also granted actual physical freedom in those cases where slaves forged free-papers and other legal documents to facilitate their escape. Both instances have been extensively documented by numerous Afro-American slave narratives.[16]

Since it was writing, not the spoken word, that was used as a means of social control and cultural imperialism, Afro-Americans readily resorted to their oral traditions to retain a sense of cultural authenticity and cohesion. They developed forms of expression that actively circumvented writing as a vehicle for self-knowledge. The continued efforts on the part of Afro-American writers to unsettle the authority of writing manifest themselves both thematically and formally in their use of Afro-American folk materials as well as their reliance on dialect, musical forms, and oral modes of composition. As a result, Afro-American writers, in addition to appropriating classic European forms such as the sonnet and the ballad, also developed a substantial number of distinct poetic forms, ranging from the blues poems of Langston Hughes and Sterling Brown and the poetic sermons of James Weldon Johnson to the jazz poetry of Amiri Baraka and Michael Harper, the dozens of Don L. Lee, and the *sones* and *rumbas* of Jay Wright, to name only a few examples.[17]

But things are not as easy and as clear-cut as they may seem, because no matter how strongly indebted to an oral tradition these new forms of poetry are, the fact remains that they are *written* forms. And because they are written forms, the initial idea of subverting the authority of writing becomes a highly contradictory endeavor that raises a number of questions: If Afro-American culture is predominantly oral, how can a writer maintain a dialogue with that culture at the moment of writing? How is it possible to sustain an oral culture in writing? This problem is not resolved by defining literacy or freedom-through-literacy as concepts that somehow go beyond or against writing. Nor does such a definition take into account that the mere existence of an oral tradition is not a unique circumstance. No matter how we turn this argument, the fact remains that literacy is a concept inherently linked with the written, not the spoken, word. Moreover, any attempt to connect literacy with orality implicitly sustains an attitude that Derrida has labeled phonocentrism.[18] To stress Afro-American poetry's indebtedness to an oral tradition is not to emphasize its difference from Western literary discourse and its metaphysics but to situate it squarely within that framework and the metaphors that define it. The frequent claim that Afro-American texts subvert established literary conventions by introducing "oral" elements to written discourse is based upon an argument that unwittingly maintains one of the dearest assumptions of Western thought: the primacy of speech over writing. Afro-American literature's "oral" qualities are regarded as a kind of corrective capable of turning written language into an "authentic" expression of those mental experiences that go by the name of culture. [19] In other words, language that is invested with oral qualities is deemed capable of performing truthfully, or of performing the truth, whereas writing (being secondary and derivative) is the epitome of distortion, inauthenticity, and untruth. This association of speech with truth and authenticity is no doubt a familiar one that has been traced back all the way to Plato and Aristotle. As Derrida has shown quite candidly, Western culture has its own history of problems with, and suspicions of, writing's ability to articulate truth (or reality), and those suspicions seem oddly to coincide with those we attribute to Afro-American literature.

Most Afro-American poets are well aware of this contradiction, as well as of the subversive potential and the inherent unreliability of writing, qualities which, according to Derrida, the West has been at pains either to overlook or to conceal with an anxious and highly ambiguous reverence of the written word. This kind of reverence effectively serves to protect writing from the rigorous questioning that would expose its unreliability. Reverence, like faith, implies distance, and in the case of literature an aesthetic distance that will make us believe in mysterious truths instead of encouraging us to look closely at the language that is supposed to convey them. Reverence and faith render language transparent, invisible.

What this is leading up to is my contention that Afro-American poets have undertaken their own systematic critiques of the sign, not by returning to some notion about re-creating "primary language" through a renewed emphasis on metaphors of voice or speech relating back to an oral tradition, but by exploring the possibilities for subversion that writing itself offers. Consequently, if we argue that the quest for freedom-through-literacy continues in Afro-American writing, as indeed it does, then we have to be very specific about what it is that is being subverted and about the ways in which that subversion takes place. Clearly, what is being subverted is not writing itself but the authority with which Western culture has invested certain forms of writing and certain kinds of texts. For that reason, it is of crucial importance that Afro-American writers frequently claim as part of their tradition texts that are either regarded as "nonliterary" or as the property of other literary canons. To show precisely what those texts are as well as how and why they become part of an Afro-American tradition of writing is one of my main objectives.

Contemporary Afro-American poetry's sustained quest for freedom-through-literacy is best described as a search for a reliable repository of meaning, on the basis of which the Afro-American writer can, in Amiri

Baraka's words, "propose his own symbols, erect his own personal myths"[20]—in short, create his or her own language. This repository of meaning is history, not History as something self-contained and unchangeable in its pastness, but a history that consists of fragments to be assembled and woven together into "new categories for the soul/of those I want to keep."[21]

Wright's work offers one of the most remarkable examples of an Afro-American poet maintaining a very active dialogue with a variety of traditions while at the same time confronting the problems posed by the idea of writing within the specific context of Afro-American culture. Wright is a most skillful weaver of poetic textures that well deserve to be called mythological in that they embrace both the timelessness of mythical discourse and the radical and inevitable historicity induced by the act of writing itself. There is no doubt that Wright is creating a mythology of Afro-American writing, but he is also constantly reminding himself and his readers of the precariousness of such an endeavor. His best poetry emerges from a confrontation—or what Ralph Ellison would call an "antagonistic cooperation"[22]—between history and myth, in which myth is rendered historical and history mythical. Although it is difficult, and at times almost impossible, to separate the two, we nevertheless have to distinguish them as different forms of discourse to be able to experience the effects of their interpenetration and to extract those categories that constitute the methodology (and mythology) of Afro-American writing. I shall begin with what I consider one of Wright's best shorter long poems, "Benjamin Banneker Helps to Build a City." This poem is accompanied, in *Soothsayers and Omens*, by its shorter version, "Benjamin Banneker Sends His 'Almanac' to Thomas Jefferson," a poem that will not be considered separately here but as a kind of double which revoices most of the important aspects of the former poem.

Both "Benjamin Banneker Helps to Build a City" and "Benjamin Banneker Sends His 'Almanac' to Thomas Jefferson" are less concerned with the historical personality of Benjamin Banneker, the first self-trained Afro-American astronomer and doubtlessly one of the numerous grandfather figures which populate twentieth-century Afro-American letters, than with the founding of modern America. The point in American history to which Wright returns in these two poems is the last decade of the eighteenth century, a period that marks North America's transition from colonialism to modern nationhood. This particular historical rite of passage, which is symbolized by the founding of the national capital, the city that Banneker did indeed help to "build," is significant for a number of reasons, all of which have to do with language and with writing.

"Benjamin Banneker Helps to Build a City" is preoccupied with ori-
gins, and more specifically with the controversial origins of the New
World and with the role blacks played in the creation of a cultural (and
textual) space that was more than just an inspired invention of European
thought. This concern for historical origins pervades all of Wright's
poetry and is frequently associated with the figure of the city, not an
unusual connection given the historical significance of the founding of
cities in the New World since the times of Columbus.[23] These early
colonial cities, founded by the conquistadors in the name of the Spanish
crown, were the administrative outposts of the Hapsburg monarchy and
can be viewed as emblems of Spain's desire for political and cultural
totalization (and totalitarianism). But if the colonial cities in the New
World were stony symbols of imperial power, they were also, at the same
time, the first places of intensive cultural interaction of the kind that
eluded official control and surreptitiously undermined the administrative
foundations of the empire.[24] Both of these different historical functions
of the city are relevant to my discussion of the representational dimen-
sions of the particular city Wright evokes at the beginning of "Benjamin
Banneker Helps to Build a City": The future capital of the United States is
to be the seat of political power and thus the nation's new center, the very
embodiment of its autonomy. Although conceived as a monument to
liberty, the national capital is a structure motivated by the same kind of
logocentrism that had produced the cities in the Spanish colonies. The
desire for totalization was equally pervasive in North America, where it
manifested itself in the Puritan concept of the "covenant of grace" and its
secular extensions.[25] Once freed from the British empire, the former
colonies were at liberty to pursue their own imperialistic aspirations. The
construction of the United States capital was a symbolic act of replacing
the old forms of British colonialism with the new forms of North Ameri-
can imperialism.

This view is substantiated especially by Wright's including in the text of
his poem two quotations from Banneker's letter to Thomas Jefferson to
which I shall return shortly. But it would be quite erroneous to presume
that Wright is celebrating the spirit and the achievements of the Ameri-
can Revolution as a potential source of cultural authenticity. In fact, he is
doing quite the opposite, which is rendered evident by the specific histor-
ical date implicit in both the quotations and the references to the found-
ing of the national capital: The survey in which Banneker participated
was launched in 1791 by President George Washington; Banneker's letter
to Thomas Jefferson, then secretary of state, was also written in 1791.[26]
What, then, is the significance of the year 1791 with respect to the origins

of Afro-American cultural (and literary) history? What readily comes to mind, although it is nowhere directly mentioned in the text of this poem, is an event whose significance for Afro-America was vast and whose echoes in Afro-American literature are countless: that event is the Haitian Revolution.[27] By extension, 1791 recalls two other "central" points in New World history, both of which also mark profound historical transitions: The first one happened three centuries earlier in 1492, when Columbus landed in Santo Domingo. The second one occurred a century later in 1892, the official date of the dedication ceremonies for the World's Columbian Exposition in Chicago, the founding of "White City."[28] All of these fragments cluster around the date 1791, which is now no longer simply an isolated point in history, but a historical field.

Although the poem does not invoke the names of Toussaint, Dessalines, or Henri Christophe,[29] the implied date itself is sufficient to shake the foundations of the North American future metropolis and displace the center it aspires to imitate. Even in its absence, the Haitian Revolution provides both an analogy and a contrast to the American Revolution and its future emblem. The contrast is perhaps more obvious than the analogy: Unlike its North American counterpart, the Haitian Revolution was aimed at overthrowing the island's slaveholding society and replacing it with a black government; no such radical changes were ever envisioned for North America. This difference is important in that it substantiates the claim that the American War of Independence was the only revolution in modern times motivated by the desire to prevent drastic social changes, meaning, in this case, the prohibition of the African slave trade and the possible abolition of slavery on "recommendation" of the British crown. But the similarities between the two wars are perhaps even more disturbing: With regard to the black population of both Haiti and the United States, each revolution was, in Alejo Carpentier's words, a veritable "rebirth of shackles," a prelude to reenslavement.[30] In the same way that Haiti's mulatto elite, which replaced the government of the French slaveholders, continued to oppress blacks, slavery in the United States was far from having been abolished by the humanitarian principles of the Declaration of Independence and the federal Constitution.

I cannot resist at this point calling attention to a passage from Carpentier's *The Kingdom of This World*, perhaps the best-known modern novel about the Haitian Revolution, which is all the more relevant to my present discussion for narrating the story from the perspective of a black protagonist. Near the end of the novel in a chapter significantly entitled "The Surveyors," Carpentier's Ti Noel, now an old man, is observing the work of the mulatto surveyors in the Northern Province. At some point he raises his eyes to the old Fortress, sadly musing that "the word of Henri Christophe had become stone and no longer dwelt among us. All of his fabulous person that remained was in Rome, a finger floating in a rock-crystal bottle filled with brandy" (*Kingdom*, 177). Ti Noel's vision of words turned to stone, of idealism stiffened into conservatism, is precisely what Wright associates with the future capital of the United States: He sees it as the epitome of words devoid of any meaning, of empty gestures "with/no sign, of what gave them strength."[31] This last citation is from Baraka's "Poem for Willie Best." Incidentally, Wright uses these lines as an epigraph to his "Variation on a Theme by LeRoi Jones. II," an earlier poem that comments on the plan of transformation, "the alphabet of transformations" as it is called in *Dimensions of History*, now elaborated in "Benjamin Banneker Helps to Build a City."

The image of the city is prefigured in "Variation" in the form of those "massive limestone crosses" that "measure the American continent" (*HS*, 67). They are the stony monuments left by previous "surveyors," whose measure(ment)s almost completely erased all traces of the continent's native civilizations. Their former cities have turned into graveyards. The crosses are emblems of death, of

> a stiff Jesus,
> with his impassive beard,
> driven staunchly on a mountain,
> impervious as well to the babble
> of tongues as to the absurd heights. (*HS*, 67)

But Wright, "would not have him there,/marking some inaccessible point"; instead, "He would have to come down,/and bend his back on the line/. . . /feeling an insatiable desire/to break free and become a sign,/ living gesture, unearthed,/yet rooted in earth, in flesh." Wright literalizes the Christian myth ("the word become flesh") to emphasize the absurdity of worshipping death as an abstract ("stiff") form of salvation, as the measure of all living things. Passivity and imperviousness, the characteristics of sacred immobility, have to yield under the impact of historical experience. Once the "stiff Jesus" begins to take notice of the "babble [or Babel] of tongues" around him, once he is "listening/to the groomed merchants of the soul/bargaining guardedly for every part of him,/letting the echo of exile change him" (*HS*, 68), his poetic features change dramatically as the language of the poem itself breaks free and bursts into a rapid sequence of present participles and unfinished verb forms. The change we witness here is the creation of desire or "uneasiness."

In "Benjamin Banneker Helps to Build a City," this "uneasiness" is a disturbance of the faith, this time not primarily in the myths of Christianity but in the ritual of revolution and specifically the American Revolution. This ritual of revolution, represented by the lining out of the land according to precise mathematical laws, "the language of number," is a self-contained process, a ceremony of imprisoning language by locking it into a definite symbolic shape. This process, in turn, is analogous to the legal rituals involved in the symbolic act of drawing up the Declaration of Independence, the new nation's *charter*, which is reproduced in the form of a *map* or *chart* of the site of the city. But,

These perfect calculations fall apart.
There are silences
that no perfect number can retrieve,
omissions no perfect line could catch. [32]

What are those silences, those omissions, those glaring imperfections in the design? And what language can retrieve them? The most obvious instances of such retrieved silences, examples of which we have previously encountered in Paz's *The Labyrinth of Solitude*, Williams's *In the American Grain*, and Carpentier's *El arpa y la sombra*, are the two passages from Banneker's letter to Jefferson, which cause, within the text of the poem, a disturbance of no small measure. This letter, which was enclosed with the 1792 *Almanac* Banneker sent to Jefferson, was written about six months after the black astronomer had become involved with the survey project for the new capital. It is the only known instance of Banneker's publicly voicing his thoughts about slavery—he himself, it should be noted, was a free man. Jefferson's reply was favorable; he informed Banneker that he had forwarded the manuscript copy of the *Almanac* to the secretary of the Royal Academy of Sciences in Paris as evidence of the talents of the black race. Ironically enough, it was never received there. But Banneker's letter to Jefferson and the latter's reply, first published in pamphlet form and later included with Banneker's other almanacs, were widely circulated by abolitionist societies in the United States and England. Several of Banneker's "abolition almanacs" appeared between 1793 and 1797 in a number of editions, and their great popularity made them some of the most important publications of their times. [33]

All of this is to say that it is hardly an exaggeration to label Banneker's letter to Jefferson one of the founding texts of modern America, one, however, that unsettles the authority of the nation's official charters:

Here was a time, in which your tender feelings for yourselves had engaged you thus to declare, you were then impressed with proper ideas of the great violation of liberty, and the free possession of those blessings, to which you were entitled by nature; but, Sir, how pitiable it is to reflect, that although you were so fully convinced [of the benevolence] of the Father of Mankind, and of his equal and impartial distribution of these rights and privileges, which he hath conferred upon them, that you should at the same time counteract his mercies, in detaining by fraud and violence so numerous a part of my brethren, under groaning captivity, and cruel oppression, that you should at the same time be found guilty of that most criminal act, which you professedly detested in others, with respect to yourselves. (SO, 24)

The contradictions exposed and expounded in this memorable passage are significant beyond their well-known historical implications. Their reverberations are felt throughout the poem as Wright himself is "struggling for a city/free of that criminal act,/free of everything but the small,/imperceptible act, which itself becomes free" (SO, 25), struggling for "different resolutions" and, like Williams, for different *measure(ment)s*.

Documents, Joseph Riddel has pointed out, "decenter the lyrical voice, the centering or narrative subject."[34] In the context of Wright's poem, this decentering or displacement corresponds to the subversiveness of Banneker's letter when viewed not just as an isolated historical datum but as a historical field. I have already examined traces of the historical events which cluster around that date and undermine the centrality of the American Revolution by introducing the notion of multiple origins of New World culture. At the level of textuality, this idea of multiple origins is corroborated by the poem's claim to multiple authorship, a compositional principle that frees it from the singleness of vision associated with a commanding origin or a central consciousness. The title of the poem already anticipates this multiplicity. Not only does the use of the name "Benjamin Banneker" serve to displace the name of the author as it appears on the cover of the book. In addition to that, "helps to build" (instead of "builds") indicates that the city, which is being built here, that is to say, the text of the poem, is not the product of an individual consciousness that alone authorizes its meaning. The poem, in short, is itself off-center. As a result, it becomes a play of originating forces, or what Charles Olson has called a "field" of intersecting lines,[35] of crossing paths, so that it is ultimately an emblem of original and originary multiplicity. Most of Wright's poetry unquestionably partakes of the American tradition of the long poem, whose achievement is, Riddel argues, "essentially a freedom from the commanding origin."[36] Wright is after a "coherence," to borrow another term from Olson,[37] and this coherence is precisely what I have described as a method(ology) that would invest his play of originating traces with culture-specific meanings, although without arresting its motion. So we return again to Afro-America's quest for freedom-through-literacy.

> Free. Free. How will the lines fall
> into that configuration?
> How will you clear this uneasiness,
> posting your calculations and forecasts
> into a world you yourself cannot enter?
> Uneasy, at night,
> you follow the stars and lines to their limit,
> sure of yourself, sure of the harmony
> of everything, and yet you moan
> for the lost harmony, the crack in the universe.
> Your twin, I search it out,
> and call you back;
> your twin, I invoke
> the descent of Nommo. (SO, 25–26)

The link between freedom and writing, and more specifically with writing as (con)figuration, is obvious enough in this citation. But what exactly is that freedom, and how can it be realized in writing? To be sure, it is a freedom from that "most criminal act," from that "great violation of liberty," which is slavery in its numerous guises. But if we want to be rigorous about such a referential reading, we also have to consider that Banneker, unlike Douglass, for instance, was never a slave. Although it could be argued that this difference is merely nominal, given the actual treatment of free blacks in the antebellum South, the implications of Banneker's status as a black man who was not only legally free but also literate in a very special sense (he was a scientist) are nevertheless important to the rhetorical strategies of the poem. It is this seemingly irrelevant difference that enables Wright to charge Banneker's definition of slavery as "criminal act" with a literary and cultural meaning that surpasses historical referentiality in the strict sense. Wright sees the "criminal act" as a slavish submission to the fiction of a single commanding origin, which, in its turn, generates the fiction of "the harmony of everything."

Wright's criticisms here are not simply directed at the monstrous injustices perpetrated in the name of slavery but at those elements in Western thought used to sanction them, incidentally the same conceptual categories later employed to perpetuate slavery in the form of cultural imperialism. Those categories are rooted in the Christian doctrine and the theogonous postulate of a divine consciousness as a single figure of authority (the "Father of Mankind"). This figure had been invented in the image of those who, calling themselves God's prophets, were the interpreters and authors of the biblical myths that served to unify the story of the creation of the world by attributing it to a single source.

However, this particular mythical version of history was, as suggested above, sharply contradicted by the events that led to the "discovery" of the New World. This discovery produced a "crack in the universe" of Western thought by upsetting its previously harmonious, unified image of the world. It is this "lost harmony," this disruptive movement of displacement and transition, to which Wright appeals in order to recapture the fertile turbulence generated by the existence and interweaving of the New World's multiple origins. His text, like Williams's *In the American Grain*, cuts through that image of America projected by its European inventors; it cuts through the New World's superficial newness down to the marrow of history. This deceptive quality of being new is what is represented by the founding of a city that would reinstate the very center from which it seeks to break free. What seems like an autonomous act is really only an imitation of European thought and its desire for centralization. In this sense, "the sight of these lesser gods/lining out the land" (SO, 25) is a figure for historical mimetism. Rather than an act of liberation, it is an act of reproducing and repeating the paradigms of Western culture in the form of its foremost imperial symbol, the city.

How pitiable it is to reflect
upon that god, without grace,
without the sense of that small
beginning movement,
where even the god
becomes another and not himself,
himself and not another. (SO, 25)

What is "pitiable" is the act of imitating, which is all the more "grace"-less for being inauthentic, unaware of the doubleness at the origin of New World history. That double origin is the point at which the "god," who, as we shall see, is a figure for the poem's design, becomes both himself and another. This simultaneity of self and other now generates emblems of doubleness; they condense the essence of Afro-America's historical experience—exile and slavery—and relate that essence to the schism caused by the discovery of the New World. Those figures are "Amma's plan" and the "descent of Nommo." According to Dogon mythology as recorded by Marcel Griaule and Germaine Dieterlen, "Amma's plan" is the design for the creation of the universe, the matrix that eventually becomes Nommo, the first being created by Amma. As Amma's twin, the Nommo embodies the principles of its own creation, that is to say, the process of twinning, of doubling. In this sense, the Nommo is a living design. [38] Its descent, that is, its creation and sacrifice, is a movement from abstraction to representation, from "the lines in your head" to "these lines," which are the lines we are actually reading.

A closer look at the poem's language will clarify this movement from abstraction to representation, which accounts, at least partly, for the difficulty of Wright's poetry. Part of that difficulty is that Wright's language offers very few representational images in the traditional sense for the reader to hold on to. In fact, the only image that can be culled from the text of "Benjamin Banneker Helps to Build a City" is that of Banneker silently contemplating the movement of the stars. But even that picture, which appears at the very beginning of the poem and recurs several times, is semantically highly unstable.

In a morning coat,
hands locked behind your back,
you walk gravely along the lines in your head. (SO, 22)

This is the point where the "vibration" starts. The vibration is an unsettling of language's representational capacities, an effacement of sorts that makes possible the simultaneous projection of another, different image: What we see, yet cannot *see*, as "morning" vibrates into "mo[u]rning" and "gravely" into "*gravely*," is the poet himself traversing a burial ground, which is clearly a figure for the act of memory Wright has to perform to produce an image that appears to be representational. Paul de Man's remarks are helpful here: "All representational poetry," de Man writes, "is always also allegorical whether it be aware of it or not, and the allegorical power of the language undermines and obscures the specific literal meaning of a representation open to understanding. But all allegorical poetry must contain a representational element that invites and allows for understanding, only to discover that the understanding it reaches is necessarily in error." [39]

All that the reader is offered in "Benjamin Banneker Helps to Build a City" are fragments of that representational element, traces of an image as it is prefigured in the poet's mind. The point is that these traces never evolve into a fully graspable representation; instead, they undergo a series of transformations, which culminates in the act of naming at the end of the poem. "And so you, Benjamin Banneker,/walk gravely along these lines" (SO, 26). With the exception of the title of the poem, this is the only other instance where Wright uses Banneker's name. This final baptism is suggestively preceded by the invocation of "the descent of Nommo," which announces the tentative completion of the poetic design. But much happens prior to this apparent closure, so that it is necessary to trace in more detail the development of the poem's initial vibrations into their literate (and literary) configurations.

The second stanza already introduces some important transformations: The grave site is now more fully figured as a field of ruins, and what had previously appeared to be an act of remembrance is revealed to be an act of reading.

Now, I have searched the texts
and forms of cities that burned,
that decayed, or gave their children away. (SO, 22)

The poet now poses as another kind of surveyor, as an archaeologist attempting to decipher the ruins of ancient cities (Rome, perhaps, but more likely cities such as Cuzco, Labná, and Tenochtitlán) in order to recover the cultural origins of the New World. All the while, he is "watching [his] hands move"; they are no longer locked behind his (or Banneker's) back. Their movement, as it produces the very lines we are reading, extends the kinetic trope of *walking* that reappears as "the weight and *shuttle* of my body" (my italics), thus inviting us to apprehend this movement as a kind of *weaving*, one of Wright's main figures of writing.[40]

In the third stanza, the journey back into time, so far figured as a survey of a variety of ancestral sites, leads to "the time/of another ceremony" and to the creation of "another myth." A "familiar tone" enters the poet's voice as the opening of the site, the breaking of the ground, begins to assume the qualities of a *rite de passage*, which is, more specifically, a purification ritual.

A city, like a life,
must be made in purity.

So they call you,
knowing you are intimate with stars,
to create this city, this body.
So they call you,
knowing you must purge the ground. (SO, 23)

It is at this point that we encounter the first quotation from Banneker's
letter to Jefferson. What this document urges us to recall is Afro-Amer-
ica's history of exile and slavery, which now begins to reveal its mythical
dimensions. In the realm of myth, the cut of the umbilical cord connect-
ing Afro-America with Africa ("These people, changed,/but still ours")
becomes an initiation into self-knowledge. However, the connection
itself has not been completely severed, only it is no longer a genealogical
imperative that links Afro-America with Africa. This transformation is
possible because Wright envisions the cut into exile as a sacrificial ges-
ture, an excision that purifies the initiate while at the same time *marking*
him as a member of his community. That the two passages from Ban-
neker's letter should be called upon to serve as purifying agents that
prepare, "exorcise," the ground for the inscriptions of the signs of self-
knowledge is quite telling, and not merely because of this document's
connections with the beginnings of abolitionism in the United States.
We have here another instance of Wright's creating a myth, of turning a
historical context into allegory, only immediately to render that allegory
literal again. Once exile and slavery cease to be viewed as an episode in
Afro-American history that is best forgotten and become part of a larger
historico-mythical pattern that may be described as a ritualistic world
view, then they assume the qualities of communal sacrifices opening old
wounds as new paths toward self-knowledge. History, then, does yield a
myth, which is Afro-America's myth of exile or displacement. This myth
is "the seed vibrating within itself,/moving *as though it knew its end,*
against death" (SO, 22; my italics). It is a secure enclosure, a place where
the fiction of being, that is, of culture, can be entertained. Like any other
myth, it provides a protective shelter from history. But what is it that is
being sheltered here, at least temporarily, from the "harsh winds" of
history? An answer to this question requires a further look at the rhe-
torical nature of myth and its uses in the emplotment of history.

As suggested in Part 1, myth is a culture's storehouse of historical
knowledge. This knowledge is stored by rendering it timeless to protect it
from change. To be even more precise, a myth is a fixed interpretation of
a particular historical event, which is subsequently removed from its

initial historical context so that it may serve as an interpretive model for other, future events. Myth is thus a conceptual device that, in the context of a given culture, promotes a sense of order and continuity. Its function is to bring about cultural unification by not admitting any dissenting interpretations of the past events that generated it in the first place. Myth monopolizes historical interpretation for the sake of establishing ideological consensus. For this reason, the historical knowledge stored in the form of myth is generally apprehended as *truth*, a truth, however, whose origins are not directly accessible to all members of the community.

The epic of Sundiata (or Sun Dyata), King of Mali, alluded to in *Dimensions of History* (27), provides a concrete example of the limited accessibility of the knowledge preserved by myth. A written version of this epic was first published in a French transcription by D. T. Niane in 1960. Most relevant to us are not the intricacies of the story of Sundiata itself but the remarks of the *griot* from which Niane received his version of the epic. These remarks, which frame the actual story, clarify the nature and the function of mythical discourse as a strategic device for sheltering historical knowledge. Here, then, are the introductory words of the Mali storyteller:

I am a griot. It is I, Djeli Mamoudou Kouyate, son of Bintou Kouyate and Djeli Kedian Kouyate, master in the art of eloquence. Since time immemorial the Kouyates have been in the service of the Keita princes of Mali; we are *vessels of speech, we are the repositories which harbour secrets many centuries old*. The art of eloquence has no secrets for us; without us the names of Kings would vanish into oblivion, *we are the memory of mankind*; by the spoken word we bring to life the deeds and exploits of kings for younger generations.

I derive my knowledge from my father Djeli Kedian, who also got it from his father; *history holds no mystery for us*; we teach to the vulgar just as much as we want to teach them for it is we who keep the keys to the twelve doors of Mali [the twelve provinces of which Mali was originally composed].

I teach kings the history of their ancestors so that the lives of the ancients might serve them as an example, for the world is old, but the future springs from the past.

My word is pure and free of all untruth; it is the word of my father; it is the word of my father's father. I will give you my father's words just as I received them; royal griots do not know what lying is. When a quarrel breaks out between tribes it is we who settle the differences, for *we are the depositaries of oaths which the ancestors swore*.

Listen to my word, you who want to know; by my mouth you will learn the history of Mali.[41]

Djeli Mamoudou's prologue is clearly intended to establish his authority as a storyteller by identifying him as a member of an old family of royal *griots*, the traditional teachers of the princes of Mali, as someone, in brief, who has been properly initiated into the secrets of his country's history. He portrays himself as someone who simply passes on the truths he has received from his ancestors without embellishing or distorting them in any way. But at the same time as assuming the role of a mouthpiece of tradition, he also leaves no doubt about the fact that there is a significant difference between the knowledge he has received and that which he is willing to pass on to the "vulgar" in the form of his story. In short, he knows more than he tells. This is most evident at the end of the tale, where he flatly refuses to supply any details of Sundiata's death. In fact, the death is not mentioned at all. Instead, we are told that "Mali is eternal" and that it "keeps its secrets jealously. There are things which the uninitiated will never know, for the griots, their depositaries, will never betray them" (*Sundiata*, 83). Actually, he goes even further by warning his readers or listeners in no uncertain terms: "Never try, wretch, to pierce the mystery which Mali hides from you. Do not go and disturb the spirits in their eternal rest. Do not ever go into the dead cities to question the past, for the spirits never forgive. Do not seek to know what is not to be known" (*Sundiata*, 84).

What, then, is the "truth" we receive from the mouth of the *griot?* The knowledge he transmits as truth has been, as he freely admits, carefully preselected, and it is precisely that ability to select and edit that must arouse our suspicions about those things that are to be known as well as our curiosity about those that are not to be known. It is worth noting here that the *griots*, or *djelis* (*dyēlis* in the spelling Wright adopts in *Dimensions of History*), are the official historians of traditional African societies, and that they, like all official historians, are bound by a set of rules prescribing the treatment of their materials. The decision about what to tell and what to omit is not their own, for it is part of their office to take "an oath to teach only what is to be taught and to conceal what is to be kept concealed" (*Sundiata*, 84). The truth-value of their stories depends on their societies' specific conventions, which determine how history is to be narrated.

The emplotment of history has therefore nothing to do with telling the truth in any absolute sense, because that truth is clearly defined as historical knowledge presented in conformity with social convention. It functions to uphold a society's belief in its conventions and thus guarantees cultural unification and stability. The traditional *griot*, or *djeli*, is a guardian of culture in the strictest sense of the term; he is neither a historian nor an artist in the modern sense, because his office renders him incapable of questioning received truths. He is not free to invent new modes of presentation for the myths he disseminates.

The value of myths as timeless truths can thus be seen to depend entirely and exclusively on an act of faith and obedience. The discourse of myth is not open to internal criticisms; it is not self-reflexive in the sense of being self-critical but rests comfortably in its self-definition as an idealized, sacred (and thus transparent) language, meaningful only to those who are willing to make a leap of faith and regard interpretation as a form of worship. But modern literature does not require faith; it demands methodological rigor.

In the context of Jay Wright's poetry, this rigor of method is best described as an act of disturbing the spirits in their eternal rest, of going into the dead cities to question the past. Wright does not consider myth an end in and of itself. Instead of a permanent shelter from history, it is a transition "from our knowledge to our knowing" (*DH*, 90). Myth as a form of human discourse is transitory or transitional in that it mediates between the objects of knowledge (that is, history as a body of factual events) and the actual experience of that knowledge. To be more precise, myth as a mediation is a formal language that determines the conditions that make knowledge possible, and these conditions, in turn, can themselves become objects of knowledge, which also means that they can be questioned.

This proposition is nothing extravagant or even unusual when placed in its proper context, that of the philosophy of history. It is equivalent to Schelling's (and Hegel's) contention that "as the process of self-knowledge advances, new stages in self-knowledge enrich the knowing mind and thus create new things for it to know. History is a temporal process in which both knowledge and the knowable are progressively coming into existence, and this is expressed by calling history the self-realization of the Absolute."[42] That "Absolute" is apprehended not as a presupposition of the historical process, that is, as a systematic plan or law existing prior to and thus outside of history, but as a dynamic element always in the process of becoming. (The former notion had governed the idea of history from Herder through Kant to Fichte.) Historical knowledge, in this sense, is always self-knowledge, that is, not the knowledge of empirical facts evidencing the workings of some preformulated law (be it natural or scientific), but an understanding of how those facts are (re)created in the mind of the historian. I am not talking about a radically subjective view of historical knowledge—Hegel, as is known, despised subjectivity—but about historical perspectivism and the awareness that historical facts are always conditioned or mediated by language. In de Man's words, "The bases for historical knowledge are not empirical facts, but written texts, even if those texts masquerade in the guise of wars or revolutions."[43]

In keeping with the goals of modern historicism, the emphasis of Wright's poetry is not so much on what we know or can know but on *how* we know, and on how a scrutiny of the conditions that make historical knowledge possible (i.e., forms of language) can lead to a heightened level of self-awareness—Wright calls it "understanding." Wright's poems, in this sense, are studies of what Barthes has termed "ideas-in-form."[44] To the extent that Wright is concerned not simply with the formal presentation of ideas but with questions about how certain ideas are formed and formulated, his poetry must be understood as a mythology in Barthes's sense: as a formal as well as a historical inquiry into the nature and function of myth. Wright's poetry is mythological (as opposed to mythical) in that it generates knowledge *about* myth: it is not the discourse of myth, but a discourse *on* myth. Consequently, it is not sustained by (in the sense of receiving meaning and authority from) the idea of Literature as a mythical system.

Afro-American literature in its perpetual quest for the freedom of literacy has always been at odds with that traditional idea of Literature, and for good reasons. Since the idea of Literature as a mythical system heavily depends on the postulates of Western metaphysics, which invest a literary text with meaning by assuming that these postulates constitute a system of beliefs and values shared by writer and reader alike, it is fairly self-explanatory why writers such as Wright who, for historical, cultural, and ideological reasons, refuse to accept those precepts as an absolute frame of reference would search for other, for them more reliable, repositories of meaning. The result is a systematic breakdown of literary form, the beginnings of which have already been witnessed in "Benjamin Banneker Helps to Build a City." This subversion of established principles of order, such as the aesthetic charters that determine our idea of what constitutes a poem, continues on a much broader scale in *Dimensions of History* and *The Double Invention of Komo*. Perhaps the most obvious indication of the breakdown of literary form in each of these two poems is their conspicuous resistance to poetic closure, which allows for the kind of "freeplay of substitutions" that Derrida has termed "the movement of supplementarity."[45] Conspicuous examples of such supplements evidencing the deferral of poetic closure are the notes in *Dimensions of History* and the afterword in *The Double Invention of Komo*. Both have to be considered not as substitutes for the poems but as parts of the poetic texts themselves. Even if we do not read any farther than the last line of what we regard as the text of each poem, and even if we respect that Wright was explicitly asked by his publishers to supply those annotations,[46] we cannot therefore pretend that those "appendices" do not exist or that they serve no purpose whatsoever with regard to the texts they supplement. It is not acceptable to discard them as useless simply because they do not facilitate the task of reading. But even assuming that the list of sources Wright offers in each instance were complete, which it is not, or that it were at all possible to give an exhaustive account of everything that inspired those two poems, it still would be erroneous to think that the sum total of such references would somehow add up to the poetic text. What, then, do these notes accomplish?

First it ought to be stressed that this practice of annotating one's text is far more common among novelists than among poets.[47] It suggests a dissolution of generic boundaries, or what Mikhail Bakhtin has called the "novelization" of genres,[48] whose most conspicuous manifestions in postmodern New World poetry are Williams's *Paterson*, Charles Olson's *Maximus Poems*, Allen Ginsberg's *The Fall of America*, and Nicolás Guillén's *El diario*. An earlier example that comes to mind even more readily are the notes on "The Waste Land," which Eliot nonchalantly brushed off as a kind of literary joke. Yet, it is not advisable to follow Eliot's lead, because, as we shall see, neither his nor Wright's notes can altogether be passed off as practical jokes at the expense of some perhaps overzealous critics. In short, since such annotations do not appear to help us understand the poetry, their function must lie elsewhere, as in fact it does.

If the notes and the afterword do indeed accentuate the poems' resistance to closure and thus assert the possibility of an infinite number of supplements, of which they themselves are already the first instance, then we have to ask how the absence of closure affects our reading of the poems, which is yet another supplement. *Absence of closure*, of course, does not mean that the poems do not, in the most literal sense of the term, end. What it means is that the tensions upon which the poem is built are not, in the final analysis, resolved or transcended. There is no point that arrests the movement of figuration and conveniently allows us to assign to each individual figure or trope a fixed representational value in the form of a more or less definitive meaning. Consequently, it becomes very difficult to view Wright's poems as anything else but fragments, not fragments of poems, but poems-as-fragments. Yet, how is it possible to read such poetry without submitting to the idea of radical indeterminacy? Does not every reading as an act of communication require a communicator, no matter how ineffable? Regardless of how one defines communication, one cannot answer this last question in the negative; and since that is the case, I must either postulate the existence of such a communicator or else terminate my discussion here and now.

Recall that the point that would arrest the movement of figuration and thus create the possibility of fixed meanings is what I have earlier labeled a "center." In short, the deferral of or resistance to closure as accomplished, albeit involuntarily, by Wright's notes and afterword identifies the movement of supplementarity as a process of decentering. The first thing that is decentered by Wright's annotations is the figure of the author. In the case of "Benjamin Banneker Helps to Build a City," the title of the poem itself already dislocates or effaces the figure of the author. In *Dimensions of History* and *The Double Invention of Komo* the same kind of effacement is achieved by the notes and the afterword: The name of the author seems to be just another bibliographical item. It becomes more and more elusive as other names are added to and superimposed upon it, until it becomes one name and all names. [49] But what are those names that turn Wright's own name into "an interminable name,/made from interminable names" (*HS*, 37)?

In his afterword to *The Double Invention of Komo* Wright mentions as his major sources a series of studies of Dogon and Bambara cosmologies, conducted by a group of French anthropologists associated with Marcel Griaule and Institut d'Ethnologie of the Musée de l'Homme in Paris (*DI*, 109–10). The most important of these anthropological treatises are Marcel Griaule's doctoral dissertation, published in 1938 under the title of *Masques Dogons*, and his *Dieu d'eau: Entretiens avec Ogotemmêli* (1948); Germaine Dieterlen and Marcel Griaule's *Le renard pâle*, vol. 1: *Le mythe cosmogonique* (1965); as well as Germaine Dieterlen's *Essai sur la religion bambara*; and *Les fondements de la societée d'initiation du Komô* (1972), a collaboration of Dieterlen and Youssouf Tata Cissé. Wright further acknowledges his debts to Wande Abimbola's translations of Ifa Divination poetry; Victor Turner's work on the Ndembu; L. O. Sanneh's historical study of the Jakhanke; and, above all, J. B. Danquah's *The Akan Doctrine of God*. [50] No further details are needed here to evidence the major role of anthropology and ethnology in Wright's work.

There is much more to Wright's interest in anthropology than meets the eye. I have earlier described his poetry as discourse on myth, and it does not require any elaborate explanations for us to discern that that is what constitutes the link between cultural anthropology and poems such as *Dimensions of History* and *The Double Invention of Komo*. The anthropological studies listed above are a major part of Jay Wright's *Archive;*

they do not simply supply him with information about various African cultures, raw data of sorts to be transformed into poetry. They suggest, much more importantly, a comparative approach to cultural history that is particularly suitable for Wright's interest in the history of the New World. To a writer, whose cultural heritage does not *per se* constitute a unified whole that could be effectively sustained and mediated by any one mythical system alone, modern anthropology offers an attractive methodological starting point for charting relationships between different cultures and for creating a sense of coherence, in which those vital differences need not be negated or leveled. As proposed above, this kind of coherence is a structure without a center in that it is not founded on, and is thus not reducible to, a single, absolute frame of reference. In Part 1 I presented several decentered or acentric structures in my comparison of Williams, Carpentier, and Paz, whose respective texts dismantle the myth of America by subjecting it to the rigors of (re)interpretation. Anthropology is precisely such a (re)interpretation of myth, and it is therefore appropriate for it to mediate Wright's poetry.

To substantiate this linkage between poetic and social-scientific discourse, it ought to be stressed that the debut of anthropology as a human science tellingly coincided, around the turn of the century, with a rapidly declining faith in Western metaphysics. "One can assume," Derrida contends in one of his early essays, "that ethnology could have been born as a science only at the moment when a de-centering had come about: at the moment when European culture—and, in consequence, the history of metaphysics and of its concepts—has been dislocated, driven from its locus, and forced to stop considering itself as the culture of reference."[51] The philosophical crisis ensuing from that dislocation of Europe as the central cultural reference point is, in many ways, analogous to the crisis brought about, several centuries earlier, by the "discovery" of the New World. This loss of the center, which affected both Europe and the New World in similar ways but with very different results, initiated a "rediscovery" of America, now led by chroniclers of a different kind in search not of gold but of new myths to replace those that had ceased to play the role of secure foundations. For Wright, however, national myths are no longer enough, and in his own search he comes to embrace the "different resolutions" modern anthropology suggests.

What, then, are the "different resolutions" anthropology offers the modern writer? Roberto González Echevarría, with Lévi-Strauss's *Tristes tropiques* in mind, regards "anthropology [as] a way through which Western culture indirectly affixes its own cultural identity. This identity, which the anthropologist struggles to shed, is one that masters nonhistorical cultures through knowledge, by making them the object of its study. Anthropology translates into the language of the West the cultures of the others, and in the process establishes its own form of self-knowledge through a kind of annihilation of the self."[52] We have already witnessed several instances of such a self-effacement (it is not really an annihilation) in Wright's work, and it now becomes clear that the identity he is trying to shed or efface in the process of gaining self-knowledge is the one that has been conceived and formulated on the premise of Europe's central position in world history. The goal of Wright's poetry is to show what, as Octavio Paz has asked, "happens to America as an autonomous historical entity when it confronts the realities of Europe." The traditional concept of the American self, invented by the European spirit at that moment when it "free[d] itself of its historical particulars and conceiv[ed] of itself as a universal idea," becomes an empty shell, a voided presence. The loss of the center renders its mythical identity transparent. It effaces its contours by divesting it of its truth-value, while at the same time preserving it as an instrument.

Wright's poetry is characterized by the attempt to separate truth from method, and this attempt further emphasizes the link between anthropology and literature as parts of the humanities. In much the same way that the separation of truth from method enables the anthropologist tentatively to employ concepts without maintaining their truth-value, it enables the poet to use language—that is, the language(s) of the West—without burdening it with a predetermined set of metaphysical significances. This double intention is essential to Wright's poetics. It characterizes his notion of exile, that principal trope which makes possible the *double invention* of myth and history that links his poetry with the texts of Williams, Carpentier, Paz, and Guillén.

II
> *I take the earth beneath me*
> *as parchment and intention,*
> *memory and project of all*
> *movement it contains.*
>
> —JAY WRIGHT, *Explications/Interpretations*

Wright's poems, as we have seen in the case of "Benjamin Banneker Helps to Build a City," are very much concerned with the problems and possibilities of writing. This concern serves as a point of departure for revising Afro-American literary history by situating it within a tradition of New World writing. Wright's preoccupation with writing leads him to challenge a number of compositional (and critical) clichés that, wittingly

73

or unwittingly, regard the distinctiveness of Afro-American texts as a function of their oral heritage. Perhaps the most pervasive of these clichés is the idea of poetic voice, which, in an Afro-American context, is quite heavily invested with certain cultural significances: more often than not, the gaining of voice is seen as a form of liberation. I need not reiterate here my previous argument concerning the connection between freedom and literacy and the problems resulting from the fallacious association of literacy with orality. Still, it seems necessary to reemphasize that in Wright's poetry voice, as well as freedom, is gained only through writing.

It is well worth noting in this regard that Wright's poet is never cast in the traditional role of the singer of tales; he is a "bookman of the blood," a keeper of records and a chronicler, who becomes a kind of semiotician or grammatologist in his own right. Although Wright obviously uses the phonetic-alphabetic script of the English language, he tempers the metaphysical tradition with which that language is burdened by introducing into his poetry other, formalized languages: In both *Dimensions of History* and *The Double Invention of Komo*, as well as in *Soothsayers and Omens*, he uses a series of nonphonetic ideograms drawn from both Dogon mythology and the Komo initiation ritual of the Bambara. What the presence of those ideograms, some of which will be discussed in detail later on, indicates is that Wright does not treat writing as a more or less faithful transcription of speech. Instead, his poems seek to "translate" one formalized language into another, without assigning priority to either. For Wright, poetic voice is always mediated by writing. Like the ideograms themselves, it has no literal meaning if only because that literal meaning is always already figurative. In this way, Wright's use of ideogrammatic writing becomes an elaborate critique of the authenticity and truth-value associated with literalness and thus of the kind of writing that conceives of itself as secondary to, and derivative of, speech.[53] What happens in Wright's poetry is that figures of voice are systematically decomposed into figures of writing, and these poetic transformations have much to do with his use of ritual.

I have stressed before that Wright is not attempting to turn poetry into ritual. Rather, he is interested in the conceptual structures that underlie specific cultural rituals and in the problem of how to translate those conceptual patterns into linguistic ones. This process is analogous to using one language according to the grammatical rules of another: the outward appearance of the individual words remains unchanged, whereas the ways in which those words combine into meaningful messages are substantially altered. To see more specifically how this applies to poetic practice, we first need to know more about the workings of ritual. As both

Dimensions of History and *The Double Invention of Komo* are based on initiation rituals, it is helpful to consider Lévi-Strauss's observations:

No anthropologist can fail to be struck by the common manner of conceptualizing initiation rites employed by the most diverse societies throughout the world. Whether in Africa, America, Australia or Melanesia, the rites follow the same pattern: first, the novices, taken from their parents, are symbolically "killed" and hidden away in the forest or bush, where they are put to the test by the Beyond; after this, they are "reborn" as members of the society. When they are returned to their natural parents, the latter therefore simulate all the phases of a new delivery.[54]

An important addition must be made to this rather general account. As the anthropologist Michael Houseman points out, initiation rituals are characterized, above all, by a double process: They create at once continuity and discontinuity, sameness and difference.[55] On the one hand, the initiate remains the same individual as before; on the other hand, he undergoes a radical metamorphosis that changes his social identity and thus distinguishes him from the noninitiates. This paradoxical logic—in fact, a "double invention" of the initiate's identity—is one of the keys to Wright's poetics: It is his "alphabet of transformations." This "alphabet" consists of clusters of tropes that translate the language of ritual into the language of poetry. We may say that in this process the English language itself takes the place of the initiate: Its linguistic surface does not change in any noticeable way, but the ways in which its words produce meaning do.

This peculiar logic of the initiation ritual accounts for much of the semantic doubleness (and duplicity) of Wright's language, which seems to be invested with a kind of "double consciousness." The Du Boisian echo here is hardly coincidental.[56] It is particularly obvious in a poem entitled "The Albuquerque Graveyard," which recalls the Benjamin Banneker poems as well as anticipates *Dimensions of History*:

After so many years
of coming here,
passing the sealed mausoleums,
the pretentious brooks and springs,
the white, sturdy limestone crosses,
the pattern of the place is clear to me.
I am going back
to the Black limbo,

an unwritten history
of our own tensions. (*SO*, 38)

The tropological cluster that "double consciousness" generates in these lines immediately invokes the opening of "Benjamin Banneker Helps to Build a City." As in the previous poem, Wright's vision of traversing a burial ground studded with sturdy white limestone crosses is readily identified with the twin activities of reading and writing. The poet's journey is an articulation of the "pattern" inscribed on this place by the marks of time, a pattern quite different from the one represented by a landscape of "sealed mausoleums" and "pretentious brooks and springs." Wright appropriately calls it "an *unwritten* history." It would be erroneous to read that phrase as a reference to the fact that many aspects of Afro-American history have not yet been recorded in written form and are only transmitted orally. While this is doubtlessly true, the idea of walking across graveyards in search of oral histories would be absurd. "Unwritten" does not conveniently translate into "oral"; it is not, as we may initially think, a figure of voice, at least not in this poetic context. The possibility of such an easy equation is already precluded by the figure that directly precedes this line: "the Black limbo." The meaning of "unwritten history" is quite evidently held *in* (Black) *limbo*, suspended but not rendered completely indeterminate. The very act of using one trope to dislocate another is precisely what brings forth another, supplementary meaning of "unwritten": Wright does not perceive Afro-American history (and New World history) as something that has not yet been written, but something that has always yet to be *un-written*, undone through writing in the same way that the meaning of "unwritten" itself is undone by the *limbo*.

The disruptive effect of the trope of the *limbo* on the language in this poem evidences the workings of a different grammar which dislocates conventional meanings. It is in this sense that the *limbo*, which itself inscribes that unwritten history of cultural and linguistic tensions, becomes what Harris has called an "inner corrective": It allows Wright to work within a Western language while at the same time dismantling the underlying conceptual structures—that is, the metaphysics—that govern the way in which meaning is produced in that language.

If we further pursue the *limbo* as a cultural phenomenon, we find that it refers to the Middle Passage and thus implies a journey from an old space (Africa) to a new one (the New World). It is, in other words, closely connected with exile, both as a historical event and as a mental process of dislocation and transformation. Harris's comments on this are most suggestive:

The *limbo* dance is a well-known feature in the Carnival life of the West Indies today though it is still subject to intellectual censorship. . . . The *limbo* dancer moves under a bar which is gradually lowered until a mere slit of space, it seems, remains through which with spread-eagled limbs he passes like a spider. *Limbo* was born, it is said, on the slave ships of the Middle Passage. There was so little space that the slaves contorted themselves into human spiders. *Limbo*, therefore, . . . is related to *anancy* or spider fables. . . . But there is something else in the *limbo-anancy* syndrome, . . . and that is the curious dislocation of a chain of miles reflected in the dance. . . . the *limbo* dance becomes the human gateway which dislocates (and therefore begins to free itself from) a uniform chain of miles across the Atlantic. This dislocation of interior space serves therefore as a corrective to a uniform cloak or documentary stasis of imperialism. The journey across the Atlantic for the forebears of West Indian man involved a new kind of space—inarticulate as this new "spatial" character was at the time—and not simply an unbroken schedule of miles in a log book. Once we perceive this inner corrective to historical documentary and protest literature, which sees the West Indies as utterly deprived . . . , we begin to participate in the genuine possibilities of original change in a people severely disadvantaged (it is true) at a certain point in time. The *limbo* therefore implies . . . a profound art of compensation which seeks to re-play a dismemberment of tribes . . . and to invoke at the same time a curious psychic re-assembly of the parts of the dead muse or god.[57]

One recognizes in these remarks the ritualistic pattern of death/separation/dismemberment and rebirth/reintegration/reassembly. One further notices an emphasis on the simultaneity of those two movements or processes, which is also precisely what occurs in writing. In Wright's poems, writing is always a simultaneous dismemberment and reassembly of meaning. Writing becomes unwriting in that it undoes its own underlying conceptual structures to clear a space for new meanings.

Since both *Dimensions of History* and *The Double Invention of Komo* are preoccupied with ritualistic structures of dismemberment and reassembly, or to use Wright's language, excision and circumcision, it is not very surprising that the *limbo* as a "gateway" should occupy a central place in each poem: "My instruments," Wright declares. "toll you into limbo" (*DI*, 39). In the following quotation the *limbo* is again used to signal the transformation of voice into writing, of sound into space:

I know my double exile in song,
and the way the heel comes down,
   remembering a dance,
on unfamiliar ground.
I have been made serious
by composing
   in the bright afternoons
of reticence and hay,
what I want to say
   without song. (*DI*, 22)

Immediately noticeable in this passage is the movement from knowing exile "in song" to articulating that knowledge "without song," that is, in writing. The difference between these two modes of knowledge is mediated by the figure of the dance, which, given the context established by the word "exile," can easily be read as an allusion to the *limbo*. The knowledge "in song" which, at least initially, appears to be a figure of voice, is significantly predicated on the memory of the dance, a spatial metaphor that evokes the journey implicit in the *limbo*. Voice or song, in other words, depends on a spatial movement (the dance as journey), and spatial movements for Wright are always figures of writing, of speaking, as it were, "without song." As in my previous example, dance or *limbo* dismantles a figure of voice—it "dislocates interior space"— only to reassemble it immediately into a figure of writing.

Wright's poetry emerges from an unwriting of a language that would otherwise not be able to articulate the tensions that characterize the New World as a cultural and historical space. As this formulation may falsely suggest that such an "un-written" language is, in the end, a mere reflection of a particular socio-cultural reality, it is necessary to stress that unwriting is a process that dislocates and supplements that reality as it is presented in historical documentary and protest ("realistic") literature. Wright seeks to demonstrate the process of various levels of conceptual dismemberment and simultaneous reassembly involved in transforming a borrowed language, in this case English, perhaps not into a different language altogether but at least into a different kind of language. His persistent decomposition of figures of voice into figures of writing, which is mediated by the trope of the *limbo*, exemplifies such a transformation. There may not be an Afro-American language in the same way that there is an English or a French language, but that in no way precludes the existence of distinct forms of Afro-American written discourse. Wright would no doubt agree with Octavio Paz that "the language that Spanish

Americans [and Afro-Americans, for that matter] speak is one thing, and the literature they write another."[58] Wright explores in his poetry the tensions between different kinds of language, tensions that arise because each of these languages has its own distinct forms of discourse and its own grammar. These variegated patterns are superimposed upon one another and constitute a sort of master plan, a *design* that we may call the Afro-American concept of New World writing. In my comments on *Dimensions of History* we shall see in detail how Wright enhances the features of his "Black limbo" (that is, the "sea-change" to which he subjects certain aspects of Dogon, Bambara, and Akan-Ashanti cosmologies) with numerous Amerindian and Latin American/Hispanic elements.

Designs play a crucial role in *Dimensions of History*. Each of the three parts of the poem, as well as each of the four subsections in part 2 and, finally, the poem as a whole, has its own distinct ideogrammatic *signatures*, derived from the ritual languages of the Dogon and the Bambara. These signatures are very much part of the poetic text and have to be treated as such. Let us disregard, for the moment, the figure of the Nommo of the Pool which adorns the cover and turn to the ideogram that is reproduced below the title of the first part, entitled "The Second Eye of the World: The Dimension of Rites and Act." This Dogon signature, or *tónú* (schema), represents what Griaule and Dieterlen have translated as "The Separation of the Twins" at the moment of circumcision (see fig. 1), the symbolic cut that marks the transition from childhood to adulthood.[59] This transition is a movement from innocence to knowledge, an initiation into what Wright calls "the clan's knowledge," which is accomplished through the "ennobling" *cut* of the ritual knife. We need not probe the fine details of this circumcision ritual and its complex historical origins to understand why this particular signature appears as a frontispiece in *Dimensions of History*: The entire poem may be described as an initiation into the secrets of an extended Afro-American mythology of writing.

Similarly, the language of the poem must properly be regarded as ritualistic. Not unlike the *sigui* of the Dogon, *Dimensions of History* is presented in a special language, designed specifically as a medium for communicating with one's immortal ancestors.[60] Reading this poem is comparable, in many ways, to learning a new language, one that has relatively little in common with the "borrowed" language in which it is situated. I repeat this analogy to stress that Wright does indeed erode the metaphysical foundations of the English language while still preserving its surface appearance. Simply to equate this process of erosion or subversion with the cliché "literary usage" would be to diminish the actual

Figure 1.
The Separation of the Twins
(Dogon)

effects, as well as the scope, of the dismantling he undertakes. *Dimensions of History* does not offer the kinds of assurances that have always tempted critics into reducing literary texts to a set of supposedly unchanging meanings that serve as stable communicators. I am not suggesting that this cannot be done in the case of Wright's poem(s), but it ought to be done, if at all, with the understanding that such communicators are nothing but tools, grammars of sorts that help us translate this poetry into a language and a form of discourse that are organized very differently.

The problem of translation (and of interpretation-as-translation) indeed looms large in *Dimensions of History*. For instance, the above translation of the Dogon signature as "The Separation of the Twins," a translation already mediated by Griaule and Dieterlen's descriptions, is completely incapable of conveying what the actual shape of this ideogram communicates. The signature itself, consisting of three different circles laid out in the form of an open triangle, prefigures both the triadic structure of the poem as a whole and that of "The Dimensions of Rites and Acts," which is also composed of three parts. In addition, this schema represents, as the title "The Second Eye of the World" and its association with the Southern Cross already suggests, a constellation of stars which includes Sirius, also called "the second eye of Amma" (the other "eye" is the North Star).[61] Since the sign of "The Separation of the Twins" is a ritual figure representing a specific constellation of stars, there evidently exists a connection between initiation rituals and astronomy. This connection informs, either directly or indirectly, all of the poem's fundamental tropes. For example, the general notion that an initiation ritual is a movement from one state of consciousness (innocence) to another (knowledge) gives rise to the kinetic trope of the *journey*, which is not a linear progression but a series of internal transformations. It is further evident that such a journey, lest it be the kind of idle roaming of Whitman's poet, requires a "compass" (*DH*, 7), which also explains the relevance of astronomy and astrology to this initiation ritual: both are navigation aids.[62] All these metaphoric threads come together in the following three lines, which echo not only the Benjamin Banneker poems but also Aimé Césaire's *Cahier d'un retour au pays natal* [Notebook of a Return to My Native Land] (1939).

I travel by the turning of a star
through all the gates that lead me home,
that lead me to my other self. (*DH*, 103)

Wright's poetic travels, like Césaire's, take the form of a *journey home*, a journey toward that "other self," which would represent the final achievement of the freedom accorded by self-knowledge (literacy). But, curiously enough, that journey "home" is also a journey into *exile*, which is already implicit in the association of "home" with the "other self." To explain the nature of and the reasons for this seeming paradox, it is necessary to call attention to the fact that the first line of the above quotation ("I travel by the turning of a star") contains an allusion to how runaway slaves, at least on the North American continent, found their way into freedom. In Wright's own language, running away from slavery may be described as *traveling by the turning of the North Star*, his equivalent of the Césairian neologism *marronner* [to run away like a slave].[63] It is hardly a coincidence that the North Star should have evolved as the foremost emblem of freedom in nineteenth-century Afro-North American writing or that Frederick Douglass should have named his first abolitionist newspaper *The North Star*. Although the direction of Wright's poetic travels is not exclusively determined by the light of the North Star, there is nevertheless an important connection to be found in his invocation of this emblem. Literacy, understood not as the ability to read and write in general but more specifically as the ability to read the stars and thus to navigate, made it possible for the runaway slaves to find their way into freedom and safety, no matter how tenuous that vision of the antebellum North as an abode of freedom and security may have been. In the same way, poetic writing as another, new form of literacy, one that would free literary language from Western metaphysics, now makes it possible for Wright to find his way out of a different kind of bondage. His writing enables him to break out of the "prison house" of the English language and its ideological underpinnings. He thus avoids the trappings of an identity which, because it is cast in and defined by the same language formerly employed to justify and perpetuate slavery, would prevent true self-knowledge.

Wright's journey in *Dimensions of History* is a dynamic resistance to the pull of a language so deeply entrenched in the history of the West that it would inevitably confine and reduce any meaning to that cultural framework and thus to a set system of references unable to account for the broad metaphoric spectrum of Wright's ideogrammatic tropes. There simply are no standard reference points in Western mythology for figures such as "The Separation of the Twins" or "The Second Eye of the World." This becomes quite evident when we consider that these two phrases, themselves only relatively inadequate translations when compared to the actual ideograms, already considerably reduce the semantic range and repertoire these figures are capable of mobilizing. Translation is a tricky business fraught with all kinds of ambiguities. As John Deredita has pointed out, "All translation, considered as the rendering of an original, involves traduction [that is, distortion caused by a reduction of language's disseminating powers]. The parallel text that brings over the original necessarily alters it; difference inscribes itself everywhere as the original is led away from its mother language and its *écriture* points to the difference inherent in that repetition and unsettles the representational myth that traditionally has motivated translation."[64] At the same time as inevitably impoverishing the original, translation also adds something to it, supplements it. As a supplement, a translation is both *a part of* as well as *apart from* the original in the sense that it makes up for a deficiency that it itself has created in the first place. This process best characterizes Wright's poetic method. The paradox of being both a part of something and at the same time being apart, separated from it, corresponds to and illuminates the perplexing relationship between "home" and "exile."

This requires still further clarification, since it would be evasive to designate the relationship between "home" and "exile" an irreducible paradox. Both figures are in fact different configurations of "self," as can be seen in the following citation from "Meta-A and the A of Absolutes."

I am good when I am in motion,
when I think of myself at rest
in the knowledge of my moving,
when I have the vision of my mother at rest,
in moonlight, her lap the cradle of my father's head.
I am good when I grade my shells,
and walk from boundary to boundary,
unarmed and unafraid of another's speech.
I am good when I learn the world
through the touch of my present body.
I am good when I take the cove of a cub,
                    into my care.
I am good when I hear the changes in my body
echo all my changes down the years,
when what I know indeed is what I would
                    know in deed.
I am good when I know the darkness of all light,
and accept the darkness, not as sign, but as my body.
This is the A of absolutes,
the logbook of judgments,
the good sign. (*DH*, 90)

For Wright, to be "in motion" is to think of oneself (one's self) at rest in the knowledge of one's moving, or in other words, to be at home in the knowledge of one's exile. But since "there is no sign to *arrest* us/ from the possible" (*DH*, 90; my italics), "home" is a mere fiction of being created by the mind as a temporary resting place for itself. That resting place is a myth produced by the knowledge of exile. As an idealized locus of self-knowledge, it is a projection of the poet's desire for closure, for the completion of a process of transformation that will not end. That process is history, and its knowledge is the knowledge of exile: It is the process itself of knowing history, of "walk[ing] from boundary to boundary," which promotes exile. The knowledge of being exiled, of being a part of history, is thus a knowledge of the impossibility of returning to one's origins, of becoming one with the source at the moment of perfect (unmediated) self-knowledge. This kind of "homecoming" is possible only in death, a death quite tellingly associated with speech!

And death enters with the word,
the conception of speech. (*DH*, 34)

The crucial question Wright implicitly poses is, How can we *know* death? It has to be taken into account when pondering that question in the context of his poetry that there are two levels on which to consider death: First, the level of the individual, where death is an event that brings about radical discontinuity; second, the level of the community (and ritual), where death establishes the kind of continuity we call tradition. In the latter case, the one that concerns us here, death is not a closure but the point at which life (and experience) are transformed into the knowledge that constitutes tradition. This is the way in which the above citation has to be understood. It is only in this form and at this level that death can be apprehended as a meaningful and knowable event, one that marks not the end of history but a turning point in history. Wright's perhaps most explicit comments on the relationship between death and history can be found in one of his early poems significantly entitled "Death as History." For reasons of economy as well as emphasis, I will quote only the last two parts of that poem.

iv

It is always like the beginning.
It is always having the egg
and seven circles,
always casting about in the wind
on that particular spot;
it is that African myth
we use to challenge death.
What we learn is that
death is not complete in itself,
only the final going from self to self.

v

And death is the reason
to begin again, without letting go.
And who can lament
such historical necessity?
If they are all dying,
the living ones,
they charge us with the improbable. (*HS*, 63)

"Death as History" offers a first, fleeting glimpse of "that African myth" Wright uses in later poems to develop his poetic "categories for the soul/ of those I want to keep." The singular form is somewhat misleading here because what Wright presents as a challenge to death is more than one particular myth. It is a dense admixture of a variety of different African mythologies drawn from Dogon, Bambara, Akan-Ashanti, and Yoruba sources, to mention only the most prominent ones. One of the most important aspects of Wright's own mixed mythology is the element of ritual sacrifice, whose vital link with exile has already been emphasized. Viewed as a sacrifice (a ritual "killing") required to ensure historical continuity, death is not an isolated event, "not complete in itself," but part of an elaborate ritual consisting of the three categories identified above: separation (excision), transition (hibernation), reintegration (circumcision).[65] Translated into my previous terminology, this schema, which recalls the Dogon signature used as a frontispiece in *Dimensions of History*, yields the following: exile—journey—home. We can now clearly see that "home," signifying incorporation or reintegration through circumcision, is not an origin or a center, that is, an ideal point that exists outside of and generates this structure. Instead, it is an integral part of it. "Home" signals the transformation of one self into another, "the *final going* from self to self (my italics)," but can only project that "other self" (or other selves) for a brief moment without being able to arrest the process of transformation as such. The (individual) self is thus never fully figured; it can only know itself *as other* because (self)-knowledge is always mediated by language. The self can only know itself as its own *text*.

Wright's concept of being "at rest/in the knowledge of [one's] moving" articulates the moment when self turns to text, that is, the moment of writing. In the context of the Afro-American literary tradition, this formulation is a variation on, and a tribute to, Robert Hayden's "For a Young Artist" and more specifically the last four lines of that poem:

> . . . Then—
>
>   silken rustling in the air,
> the angle of ascent
>   achieved.[66]

The prominent display of the past participle ("achieved") at the end of the poem seems to suggest that what has indeed been *achieved* here is closure. On closer look, however, we realize that Hayden's "angle of ascent" is precisely a figure for thinking of oneself at rest in the knowledge of one's moving: of being airborne. It is a figure with which Hayden attempts, much like Wright himself, to capture the very moment when self becomes text, or better even, trope. The result of this transformation is not closure but an instance of almost complete self-effacement at the moment of flight, which corresponds to the moment of separation (the "cut") in Jay Wright's poetry. (What Hayden effaces here is the figure of the old man with enormous wings, one of García Márquez's fabulous creations.)[67] We see in Hayden's poem, not the old man trying to lift himself up into the air, but only a line and a space ("Then—") to be immediately supplemented by "the angle of ascent/achieved." This substitution achieves knowledge of the self as other by rendering visible the way in which language, writing, effaces the self in order to make it knowable.

According to the Dogon, each being, as well as what we would consider inanimate objects, has its own "language," which is regarded as a kind of *double* of that being or object.[68] Since knowledge is acquired by decoding the symbolic language of each being or object, it is evident that the world can be known only through its double and, in fact, as its double. For the Dogon, the world is like a book to be read and interpreted. Most importantly, everything is apprehended in terms of the process it embodies, that is, in terms of the process that brought it into being: its history. Since the self participates in the flow of history through language, (self)-knowledge is always historical knowledge; nothing can be known outside of or apart from its history: therefore, "being will speak/ with the tight voice of becoming" (*DI*, 36). And that "tight voice of becoming" is of course a figure of writing. The following passage from *Dimensions of History* readily turns that pronouncement into poetic practice.

Speech is the fact, and the fact is true.
What is moves, and what is moving is.
We cling to these contradictions.
We know we will become our contradictions,
our complex body's own desire. (*DH*, 89)

This poetic manifesto, which is the "Meta-A and the A of Absolutes" of Wright's poetics, exposes as a necessary failure any attempt to divorce the concept of "being" from that of "becoming" (as well as, by the same token, speech from writing) and thus to define self as a static category outside of history. Modernism's often desperate preoccupation with questions such as "How can we know the dancer from the dance?"[69] is indicative of the attempt to achieve a knowledge of the self by stepping outside of time into a conceptual dimension where the self could presumably be contemplated as an unchanging entity, complete in and by itself. Wright, in contrast, is not interested in devising ontological distinctions between "dancer" and "dance." For him, as for Williams, the dance is the language that articulates the dancer, who exists only in the form of his or her dance and has no identity outside of it. The concept of being or self as something that is present, and in fact exists, only in the process of being articulated, finds its equivalent again in the Dogon view of language: For the Dogon, a thought or an idea that does not seek expression simply does not exist.[70] In this sense, speech is the (f)act, or, put differently, language is being.

Wright regards self (or what the Dogon call "personality") as a series of movements in time (history) that can be translated into spatial configurations (poetry), which render visible "our complex body's own desire." The dance (recall the *limbo*) is a trope for history, a structure visualizing the ritualistic pattern of separation, transition, and reintegration. It has to be stressed that these three categories, each of which represents a different aspect or dimension of the self in its steady fluctuation away from and toward its identity, do not constitute an actual sequence in time. Although they can be represented episodically, they nevertheless remain imaginary movements between fictional or fictionalized points. They are not stages in a development, in an evolutionary process that progresses toward an ideal point, but synchronic juxtapositions of different levels of meaning that constitute the complex historical dimensions of Wright's poetic self. These movements are best conceptualized with the help of a visual metaphor: They are like different exposures of the same object, which are superimposed upon one another to form dense clusters of tropes.

In *Dimensions of History* this ritual design or "alphabet of transformations" functions both diachronically and synchronically. While the poem as a whole moves from "The Dimension of Rites and Acts" to "The Aesthetic Dimension" and finally to "The Physical Dimension," or, as it does in the first part, from "The Eye of God" to "The Key That Unlocks Performance" and "The Second Eye of the World," similar triads can be detected in the individual metaphors that simultaneously pull the text in the opposite direction and thus disrupt episodic representation, the poetic narrative, if you will. As a result, the text becomes a vast *field* of signs and references, indeed a "landscape" that is already compressed into the frontispiece. In this poetic landscape, as in the Dogon signature, each of the three dimensions of the initiation ritual forms tropological clusters. Each of these clusters, in turn, emphasizes a different aspect of the whole by temporarily effacing all other aspects that are also latent in it. Consequently, the Dogon signature is a contraction, not a reduction, of the field of the poem.

A look at the poetic posture Wright assumes at various points in the poetic narrative of *Dimensions of History* best conveys the idea of tropological clusters and the relationships between them. One of the first things to notice when reading *Dimensions of History* (as well as Wright's other poetry) is that the narrative voice of Wright's poet is constantly engaged in alternative impersonations of both speaker or listener, or better, writer or reader. At no point is the poetic or narrative "I" ever confined to the space of an individual subject that could neatly be associated with the figure of the author. Instead, it is an intersubject, a figure capable of assuming multiple identities: "I"—"you"—"we." Let us consider the following examples.

Under the tightly bound arms
and the spirit of masks,
I return to you,
    to name,
    to own,

to be possessed and named myself,
following the movement of the eye of God
whose lids will close upon your greater claims. (*DH*, 8)
. . . .

But here alone I sit
    with the tassel and the bell,
holding the celebration of my people's love.
I can hear these bells in the distance,
and hear them shake the child's voice,
singing his ox's name in your womb.
We cut them into peacefulness,
and breed them to witness
our slow coming together,
to bear the burden of the years
in which you will meet me
    again and again,
each death a growth,
a life rising into its clarity of being. (*DH*, 12)
. . . .

Who you are
    and where you are
we teach you to teach us.
So I would wear myself
    the feather of the lourie bird,

and be the hand to cut you
into this special kinship. (*DH*, 13)

Each of these three postures ("I"—"you"—"we") emphasizes a differ-
ent dimension of the poetic self, which is associated with a different
location in time. Their "slow coming together" is represented as a di-
alogue of the "I" with its "other self" (you), a figure that is alternately
situated in the past ("I return to you") and in the future ("in which you
will meet me"). It is not an umbilical cord that links these various man-
ifestations of the poetic self and weaves them together in the figure "we."
The "special kinship" Wright proposes is not a birthright but a matter of
choosing to accept "the claims the living/owe the dead" (*DH*, 7). Wright,
following Ellison here, chooses his ancestors, and this choice is a poetic
gesture that cuts across as well as cuts genealogical lines. This double cut
into exile and kinship is the ultimate configuration of freedom-
through-(and with)-literacy. The cut itself is a figure of writing, which
does not simply represent experience but deepens and purifies it as the
pen cuts the paper. For Wright does not so much seek to create new
experience or new molds for experience; his intention is to create a more
profound understanding of the old ones. After all, the trope of exile is by
no means a novel or even a recent invention in Afro-American literature.
We have only to recall a famous passage from Frederick Douglass's 1845
Narrative: "My feet have been so cracked with the frost," Douglass
writes, "that the pen with which I am writing might be laid in the
gashes."[71] These gashes are marks of exile, wounds inflicted by slavery,
and the Afro-American writer uses these wounds as *molds* for his or her
historical experience. Writing, like Douglass's pen, fills these gashes. It
attempts to heal these wounds by deepening our understanding of what
they signify: "you must learn / the lesson of this sweet dispossession"
(*DH*, 13). In this way, the wounds inflicted by centuries of bondage are
transformed into the insignia of freedom.

The solution is never to yoke,
but to split.
This is the gesture. This is the act.
From every twoness cut from itself,
the scar gives rise to one. (*DH*, 24)

A conjoining of Dogon mythology (again, the sign of "The Separation
of the Twins") and Du Boisian "double consciousness," this brief citation

89

invites us to apprehend and appreciate the poet's quest for literacy, not as a journey toward unified and integrated selfhood, but toward an understanding of the creative potential of his self-divided personality. For Wright, as for Du Bois, to be self-divided and to be conscious of one's doubleness is a "gift," a legacy to be fulfilled, and not a cultural handicap.[72] Wright clarifies this in "The Abstract of Knowledge / the First Test" that appears in *The Double Invention of Komo.*

I now traverse love's dispersal
through your body,
here,
in an exile's scriptorium.
Love itself allows your opposition.
Say that love permits me
to publish my own decline,
to here, where I am pitched up,
waterless, a water spirit compelled
toward a denser wood.
Now, may your necessary injury
guide me to what is true.
What is true is the incision.
What is true is the desire for the incision,
and the signs' flaming in the wound.

I am now your delegate.
I give you order and determination,
and your soul's syntax,
extracted from God's speech. (*DI*, 48–49)

To "traverse love's dispersal / through your body" is to trace an inner geography and thus to translate an external passage into an internal one. The historical event of the Middle Passage, the physical journey into exile, is internalized as a *rite* of passage, something that is infinitely repeated and repeatable in the act of writing. Exile is a form of dispersal and dismemberment, of being cut off from one's community and one's origins. The separation is equivalent to the first stage of the initiation ritual: the ritual "killing," or excision. But this "necessary injury" is also, at the same time, a cut into kinship, a circumcision, in that it transforms the novice into a "delegate," a special member of his community, who is identified as such by the writing on his body: his scars. Writing, once linked with the grammar of the initiation ritual, assumes an explicit double significance: It wounds as well as heals. The scars, which are the signs that flame in the wound, now become the "soul's syntax"; they provide order and determination, but only when read according to that grammar. This syntax, in turn, is "extracted from God's speech," and this process of extraction creates yet another wound, or deepens the old one. Clearly, writing "wounds" speech: It creates a deficiency, an absence, which is represented here as a blank space on the page. This textual incision, the turning point at which the initiate becomes a "delegate," where excision becomes circumcision, and where cultural ritual becomes a linguistic process, again brings to mind the passage from Robert Hayden's "For a Young Artist" discussed above. The blank space equals Hayden's dash: "Then—."

A series of other transformations is occasioned by Wright's ritualistic grammar. The signs "flaming" in the incisive space between the lines consume the "denser wood," turn it into ashes. From these ashes the figure of the delegate arises like a phoenix ("a bennu bird" [DH, 31]),[73] "manuring" the burned place, which Wright elsewhere images as a desert, with his "ashy soul" (DH, 25). This resurrection signals the emergence of a language "to publish" the initiate's "*decline*/to here, where [he is] *pitched up*." My italics here underline two different metaphorical movements—descent and ascent, return and flight—whose simultaneous occurrence follows the logic of the initiation ritual. But this opposition operates only on the surface of the poem. At the level of Wright's poetic grammar, descent or decline is equivalent to being "pitched up," to reaching a higher, but at the same time more profound, pitch. This transformation is also figured as the entering of a state of greater *density* (to be "compelled toward a denser wood"). The notion of density or complexity is, in turn, intensified by the figure of the flaming signs, suggesting the burning of this wood and its transformation into another, even more condensed shape—ashes, or to recall Williams, white ink.[74]

I have suggested earlier that Wright's intention is not to create new experience but rather to purify and deepen the "old" experience of exile, and that this is accomplished through sacrifice, another wounding. This becomes clearer if we engage in yet another reading of the above citation, one that identifies it as a rewriting of the Dogon creation myth mentioned in connection with the Benjamin Banneker poems. At the same time that the poet descends, his other self ascends in the form of Nommo, the "water spirit," who is transformed ("waterless") into a wooden ritual mask and then sacrificed. The sacrificial "burning" of the dense, waterless wood represented by the flaming signs is a figure for the ritual death of Nommo, who, after his necessary injury and because of it, returns to earth to establish a new order out of the chaos of experience.[75] Another important influence on Wright's poetics, J. B. Danquah's *The Akan Doctrine of God*, provides further understanding of the complexities of this new order that Wright labels the "soul's syntax." Danquah explains,

There is the triad—Order, Knowledge, Death. There is also the divine triad, Onyame, the naturally given, Onyankopon, the experience of the given, and Odomankoma, reconciliation of the given and experience of the given, of being and the effort towards non-being, *i.e.*, knowledge. If Odomankoma contains both in himself, then there is no real contradiction, but simply an appearance, what *seemed* merely to be contradiction. . . .
These ideas are not easy of comprehension unless one has made a study of the elementary basis of the Akan conception of life. But, at least, on this level we can feel certain that the first of the given is Order. That is the *thesis*. The *antithesis* is knowledge and experience of that order. Knowledge analyzes, separates, complicates, and, by its own effort, seeks for new adjustments for a new and completed harmony, a striving for development of a whole within which the basis of knowledge, mind, seeks expression.
What then is the *conclusion*, the reconciliation? It is found even in the most simple fact of physical growth. Life is a harmony in which individual experience, the seed that is planted, must first perish, in order to find itself in a new ripened order. . . . The individual dies to himself in order to find himself in a whole that is completely ordered.[76]

This triad, Order-Knowledge-Death, which we have already encountered in the form of exile-journey-home and separation-transition-reintegration, is Jay Wright's "nexus of exchange" (*DI*, 9). It informs both the narrative (episodic or diachronic) and the metaphoric (synchronic) structure of *Dimensions of History*, two movements whose interweaving is most strikingly exemplified in the following lines.

We are born to trade upon and build
the head's intent
    in the river's seed,
    the seed's irruption,
    the milk of the lamb,
    the star's sudden fall,
    the rock's mountain breaking shape,
    the saint bickering with birds,
    the sceptre, flail, and crook,
    the coffin at the neck of things,
    the joker at the soul's bequest,
    the eye,

the key,
the second eye.

This, before you,
    is the life
of a dark and dutiful dyēli,
searching for the understanding of his deeds.

Let my words wound you
into the love of the emblems
    of the soul's intent. (*DH*, 35–36)

When reading this passage, notice that Wright's "emblems of the soul's intent" further qualify the "soul's syntax" and thus the triadic design of the initiation ritual. The assonant sequence "the eye,/the key,/the second eye" is unquestionably indebted to that ritual's logic as well as to the principles of ideogrammatic writing embodied in the Dogon and Bambara signatures on which I have commented. In addition, there is a link with the epilogue in Ellison's *Invisible Man*, which begins, "So there you have all of it that's important. Or at least you *almost* have it."[77] This connection would admittedly seem tenuous were it only predicated on the fact that the above citation appears at the end of the third long section of part 1 of *Dimensions of History* and may thus be regarded as a kind of epilogue. There is, however, more: The Invisible Man's epilogue refers us back to the novel's beginning, the prologue. Both epilogue and prologue are associated with hibernation, and figures of hibernation occur in very interesting, strategic places in Wright's poem. The first one, in fact, opens *Dimensions of History*: "Brightness is a curse upon the day./The light has turned the plain cave dark" (*DH*, 7).

The initial juxtaposition of brightness and darkness yields the image of a cave, "the warm pit of auquénidos," which strongly suggests the Invisible Man's underground residence, which he describes as a "warm hole."[78] The figure of the cave, however, recalls not only the Invisible Man's "hole"; it also alludes to Plato's Allegory of the Cave,[79] so that a parallel can be drawn between Wright's concern for seemingly incompatible relationships and images, in this case the relationship between appearance and reality, and what Plato calls an understanding of the "relation of the shadow to the substance." Wright follows the Platonic notion that the ability to see in darkness, to see the "shadows" projected by the light of the fire—Plato's sun; Wright's star—is a particular kind of blindness.[80] According to Plato, "Blindness is of two kinds, and may be caused either by passing out of darkness into light or out of light into darkness." But while Plato deems the blindness caused by passing from darkness into light "blessed," Wright, in contrast, emphasizes that the descent into the cave is a voyage toward insight (or inner sight), toward "the darkness of all light," in which shadows (doubles) assume their own reality. Wright thus inverts one of the fundamental tenets of the Allegory of the Cave by collapsing the difference between appearance and reality. His poet's ability to see in the darkness of all light is clearly an instance of "double vision": the ability to see both shadow and substance and to identify the shadow, that is, the other self, as substance.

The cave is the first image in a series of transformations set in motion by the Ellisonian trope of hibernation, which recurs, at the very beginning of both "The Key That Unlocks Performance" and "The Second Eye of the World," respectively in the form of images of blindness and sleep: "And, as the god relieved you/of the burden of sight" (*DH*, 17) is a reference to Wright's "Second Conversations" with the blind Dogon sage Ogotemmêli in *Soothsayers and Omens;* "Anochecí enfermo   amanecí bueno" ["I went to bed sick   I woke up well"] (*DH*, 31) will be commented on later in this section. An "exile's scriptorium" for both Wright's poet and Ellison's Invisible Man, the cave is a locus of transformation and as such analogous to the blank spaces representing the incisive power of writing. On the one hand, the cave is a metaphoric space signifying a state of self-imposed exile. On the other hand, the descent into the cave is not simply an act of withdrawal or separation but also a form of immersion, of "understand[ing] the claims the living/owe the dead" (*DH*, 7). This understanding, in turn, becomes the basis for a special kinship, which, as I have noted, is a figure for a new kind of order. In the space of the cave, which is no doubt suggestive of Williams's Archive and particularly Carpentier's "Lipsonoteca," the place where the bones of saints are kept, an old order is suspended, held in limbo, as it were, to make it possible for a new order to emerge. What happens in Wright's cave is a change of his poet's (and our) *angle* of perception, a change represented as the ability to see in the darkness of all light. This "double vision"—to see in the dark as well as see darkness itself—is also a form of internal navigation: the ability to read the contents of the Archive, which is what Wright means by hibernation. This special skill, then, is a state not so much of "double consciousness" but of conscious doubleness. It is best described as "after hibernation," a phrase that signals the extent to which Wright has revised Ellison's trope.[81]

If hibernation, as Ellison defines it, is a "covert preparation for more overt action,"[82] then "after hibernation" is precisely the kind of overt action that not only constitutes a call for a new order but signifies the actual achievement of that order. The difference here is between *indeed* and *in deed*. It must be kept in mind, however, that "after hibernation" by no means designates an actual moment (or period) in a diachrony. Used purely as a metaphor of duration and continuity, "after hibernation" does not announce the end of hibernation and thus closure. Instead, it returns us to the concept of supplementarity, as does Stepto's notion of the "epilogue," which is of course a kind of textual supplement. As Stepto uses "after hibernation" as a trope for postmodernism ("after modernism"), it is instructive to consult his working definition.

> Literary modernism may never end, but there exist in modern literature certain aesthetic as well as historical moments when the modern writer appears to call for a new order. Because it is his call, and because the new set of images demanded is to be in some sense a natural outgrowth of his own figurative language, we may say that the modern writer is prefiguring his epilogue, or at the very least inaugurating a rather specific type of post-modernist expression. . . . "After modernism" may therefore be discussed as a series of incidents in recent literary history wherein a literary exchange (call and response?) between modern writers yields epilogues (or epilogues to epilogues . . .) to the modernist's work. [83]

There is no doubt that *Dimensions of History,* and in fact all of Wright's poetry, constitutes an epilogue to Ellison's novel, an epilogue no less that breaks open the self-confinement of Afro-American literature and literary history represented by the Invisible Man's "hole." It cannot, after all, be overlooked that this kind of self-imposed exile is an evasion of history owing to the reluctance to assert difference that Walcott criticizes in an earlier quotation. The present context of literary modernism and postmodernism brings to mind my initial comments on the relationship between modern literature and anthropology: Wright's poems are to Western literature what anthropology is to Western culture. Put differently, Wright's work is a vast poetic epilogue to the history of Western civilization. Like anthropology, it both voids and supplements the cultural identity and centrality of the West. Wright's concept of New World writing hinges on this idea of supplementarity. The full extent of such poetic supplementation is suggested by the fact that, for Wright, New World writing is not just American and much less United States literature, but a *new* world literature: "Who is my own if not the world?/ Were we not all made at Ife?" (*DH*, 21). Stepto declares with good reason that "Wright's art is neither American nor Afro-American in any familiar, provincial sense. The boundaries of the United States, even in this postmodern era of expansion (military and cultural), cannot contain Wright's poet's 'facts of history,' any more than the rhythmic structures of ballads and blues can fully define that poet's ancient cadences."[84] But if Wright's vision, or better, double vision, and the texts it generates go "beyond geography,"[85] that going beyond cannot be understood simply as an act of transcendence; rather, it is a deepening of vision and a sharpening of focus. Wright's poet's acute angle of perception enables him to see things that cannot be found on ordinary maps but which are none the less real for being invisible.

Now I invoke my map of beads.
I coil the spirit's veins about my wrists.
I kneel at Ocumare to worry
        the saint's bones,
and rise on the walls of Cumaná.
Poco a poco,
I cut my six figures
on another coast, in a western sunrise.
In Carolina darkness, I push
my jaganda into the blessed water.
I ask now:
all the blessed means my journey needs,
the moving past, the lingering shadow
of my body's destination.
I ask my body to be here;
I ask for eyes that can invest
the natural body, the invested land,
the invested star, the natural spire,
landscape of spirit and the spirit's
rise in stone or in the fragile bones
        of the earth's body.
This will be my secular rosary,
my votive map, my guidebook
to the deeper mines of destiny. (*DH*, 93)

The geography mapped here is an inner landscape invested with various manifestations of history and myth, strung together into a "secular rosary." Wright's spiritual landscape recalls Nicolás Guillén's poem "El apellido" with its unmapped "geografía llena de oscuros montes,/de hondos y armagos valles" [geography filled with dark mountains,/with deep and bitter valleys].[86] Guillén's "montes" may be more appropriately rendered as "spaces" or "clearings," since the word also evokes the Afro-Cuban concept of "el monte," a sacred space frequently imaged as a clearing in the forest.[87] There no doubt exists a connection between Guillén's "montes" and Wright's own textual clearings. In addition, Wright's "map of beads" is evidently a metaphoric variation on that "interminable" string of last names Guillén offers at the end of "El apellido" to displace the figure of an umbilical cord and to void, much like Wright himself, the genealogical imperative presumed to connect the Afro-American writer with his or her African origins.

The allusions in the above citation to the poetry of Guillén, as well as Wright's references to the old Venezuelan cities of Ocumare and Cumaná, facilitate the transition from the explicitly African relations of *Dimensions of History* to its elective Latin American/Hispanic affinities. This transition cannot be a complete one, because these two *Kulturkreise* are by no means separate but have a long history of intersection to which the poem appeals throughout. I encounter at this point yet another set of cultural and historical references, which affects the consistency of the poem's texture in ways that make it impossible to conceive of Afro-American literature solely in terms of its African heritage. The figures and images Wright projects become even more aggressively unfamiliar as his "Black limbo" begins to embrace Hispanic American and Amerindian elements. Intent on demonstrating that there is no excuse not to know other cultures, Wright shakes us out of the complacency and indifference that come with familiarity and forces us to experience, in the act of reading, the pain, the anguish, and the restlessness, but also the ecstasy, of knowledge and of the special kinship that knowledge offers. Wright's poems are the reasons of " 'a heart that is stirred/from its foundations, and tormented with its/ceaseless conflagrations' " (*DH*, 9). But that heart is also capable of healing its wounds by recognizing the historical necessity of its ordeal: "Anochecí enfermo   amanecí bueno" [I went to bed sick   I woke up well]. This line is repeated with the first person singular significantly changed into the first person plural to maintain the subject's plurality of identities.

Still, anochecimos enfermo   amanecimos bueno,
learning the dwelling-place of the act,
the spirit holding the understanding
of our life among ourselves. (*DH*, 33)

All this would seem easy enough if it were not for the fact that "the dwelling-place of the act," the locus of the transformation that brings about both rupture and healing, lies precisely in the gap opened up between "anochecimos enfermo" and "amanecimos bueno." Compressed into this space, this opening or clearing that we have already encountered several times, is an entire poetic geography that attempts to *chart* the way from sickness to health, that is, from exile to kinship. Wright's use of *amanecer* (to wake up, to dawn) and *anochecer* (to go to bed, to meet the night, to dusk) is the key to that "geography"; it explains how the "beads" are strung together into a map.

Both verbs are employed, as Wright remarks in his notes (*DH*, 108), to signal a very subtle Arabic influence on the Spanish language and culture. Since both *amanecer* and *anochecer* have unmistakable Latin roots, this influence is evidently not an etymological one, but, as Américo Castro has pointed out, one that has to do with uses of language. What is unusual about these two verbs in the context of the Romance languages is the adoption of a personal conjugation: for instance, *amanezco* (I dawn) or *amanecí* (I dawned), the past tense Wright uses. Castro explains that "the Arabic is grafted not only on objective notions (*hidalgo*, etc.), but also on inner experience, on the manner of behaving inwardly while expressing the existence of an objective reality. Instead of limiting himself to perceiving the existence of a natural phenomenon (it becomes day, it becomes night), the soul of the person transforms what he perceives into its own creation, into something which happens not only outside, but inside, the person: *anochecí*, the night met me, and I met the night."[88] This notion of an intimate intertwinement of the object with the experience of that object is essential to Wright's idea of historical reality, and it is telling that Castro's comments should invoke J. B. Danquah's remarks on the reconciliation of the given with the experience of the given as one of the bases of the Akan concept of life.

Wright offers *anochecer* and *amanecer* as representative examples of how processes of cultural exchange and synthesis manifest themselves in language, of how they affect the "dwelling place" of a people, a phrase Wright directly borrows from Castro.[89] Wright's insistence on using Spanish instead of an English translation is understandable in light of the semantic poverty of "I went to bed sick I woke up well," a line totally incapable of retaining any of the historico-cultural resonances and philological depths of the original. To explore those resonances further, it is worth considering the following lines from Octavio Paz's *Piedra de sol* [Sun Stone] (1957), which stand out because Paz, like Wright, employs *amanecer* in its personal conjugation. I first quote the original Spanish to highlight the turbulences this causes in the English translation.

cada día es nacer, un nacimiento
es cada amanecer y yo *amanezco*,
amanecemos todos, amanece

98

el sol cara de sol, Juan *amanece,*
con su cara de Juan cara de todos,

puerto del ser, despiértame, *amanece,*
déjame ver el rostro de este día,
déjame ver el rostro de esta noche,
todo se comunica y transfigura,
arco de sangre, puente de latidos,
llévame al otro lado de esta noche,
adonde yo soy tú somos nosotros,
al reino de pronombres enlazados.

[Every day is a birth, and every daybreak
another birthplace and *I am the break of day,*
we all dawn on the day, the sun dawns
and daybreak is the face of the sun, John
is the break of day with John's face, face of all

gate of our being, awaken me, *bring dawn,*
grant that I see the face of the living day,
grant that I see the face of this live night,
everything speaks now, everything is transformed,
O arch of blood, bridge of our pulse beating,
carry me through to the far side of this night,
the place where I am You, equals ourselves,
kingdoms of persons and pronouns intertwined].[90]

The italicized words in both the original and the translation convey
some sense of the semantic range of *amanecer.* Yet, to my mind the best
translation of what Paz is trying to accomplish by using *amanecer* in
connection with words and phrases such as "nacimiento," "puerta del
ser," and "todo se comunica y transfigura" is a concise passage from
Wright's *Explications/Interpretations:*

We say each dawn is a bond
of your own beginning,
the ground established for our
movement from dawn to dawn.[91]

For both Paz and Wright, [*to*] *dawn* is a kinetic trope for the process of
bringing together elements from different cultures to form a palpitating
bridge, an arc of intermingling blood or what Wright calls "a bond/of
your own beginning." Dawn is the moment of transformation and trans-
figuration, the point at which the twi[-]light opens the door of being to

become a human gateway. All these figures belong to the tropological cluster building up around that synthetic myth Wright has labeled the "Black limbo."

I have so far been preoccupied with filling the space between "anochecimos enfermo amanecimos bueno." But it is also necessary to take into account that cultural synthesis "does not necessarily mean plenitude, but a void where elements meet and cancel each other to open up the question of being."[92] This comment is helpful insofar as it enables us to ponder the larger theoretical implications of the kind of spacing Wright practices. The gap in the text, which is elsewhere imaged as fertile whiteness (*DH*, 11), is the starting point for Wright's poet's ontological quest, the point at which it becomes necessary for a self or a culture to define (or redefine) its mode of being. This attempt at self-definition becomes necessary because the clash between the different cultures that meet in this space has brought about a deracination. As the result of a process, during which the old values and beliefs of each of the cultures involved have been unsettled and have become floating signifiers in a new commerce, it now becomes inevitable to create a new order into which those signifiers can settle. But since the exchange never really comes to an end, that settling down into a new order is not a permanent achievement but a temporary resting or pausing: The space must remain open for future exchanges.

The poetic "beads" Wright strings together into a map are precisely such places of cultural exchange and deracination. Another, perhaps even more complex "bead" Wright adds to his "secular rosary" right next to medieval Spain is the Hispanic Caribbean and in this instance Cuba.

In Cuba,
Black Melchior caresses the cobra.
Dahomey dance Havana Boa
This Python, sacred serpent of Delphi,
this Pythia, stretching the dark corners,
dark herself, caught in darkness,
sees the fat sin burned on the island.

Upon a Day of Kings,
these women dressed in white
group themselves and pirouette
and become my dawn,
    my sun,
    my dawn,
    my earth,

my lamb,
my buzzard,
my butterfly.
I live this day through them,
counting no clock time
but the blood's time,
the gentle rise and fall
    of a donu bird's wings.
I assert that I am twinned to your light within. (*DH*, 32)

Wright's invocation of the "Día de Reyes" (the Day of Kings) is vital to this passage. Tellingly, a connection with my previous quotation is already established through the conspicuous recurrence of the textual gap: "Dahomey dance   Havana Boa." The significance of the "Día de Reyes" lies in the fact, as Fernando Ortiz has demonstrated, that it was an important ritual during slavery in Cuba, as well as in Brazil.[93] On this day, the black slaves were allowed to act out their desire to be free and symbolically to return to their motherland. Each *cabildo* ("nation," or regional culture group) elected a king for a day and marched, dancing, to their masters' house to request a Christmas bonus. The "Día de Reyes," traditionally celebrated on the day of the Epiphany, was a syncretic ritual, in which the Three Magi (among them, of course, Black Melchior) represented the various groups that make up Cuban culture.[94] The copresence in the above citation of Dahomey, Havana, and Delphi is suggestive of such a syncretism. Commenting on this cultural phenomenon in an essay on Carpentier's *Explosion in a Cathedral*, González Echevarría states that "[the ritual's] force, its movement, is given by inversion, by a kind of *retruécano* in which Blacks assume power, even if only mock power, and freedom, even if only for a day, and a fake freedom at best. Neo-African culture in the Caribbean thus appears as a tropological process akin to the one seen as the language of the islands. African culture is the difference that generates, among many other modifications, the time warp, the whirl of dates and rituals, the new, 'de-formed,' shape of history."[95]

The Afro-Cuban (and Afro-Brazilian) celebration of the "Día de Reyes" is a symbolic ritual of resistance to slavery that stands for the unsettling effects of black culture specifically on Latin America, but also on the New World as a whole. In *Dimensions of History*, as in Carpentier's *Explosion in a Cathedral*, the presence of this ritual creates a time warp: As the women in their white dresses "group themselves and pirouette," history is no longer measured according to "clock time," but

Figure 2.
Doõ (Bambara). The sign is
composed of "God's perma-
nent and immutable knife"
and "the whirlwind's hook."

instead becomes "the blood's time," a whirl(wind) of dates freed from
chronology. This deformation of history brings about a new "dawn"
(*amanecer!*), a fresh beginning at the meeting place of two cultures, the
Spanish and the African.

Instances of this kind of ritual displacement and supplementation,
which is a sort of cultural modulation, abound in *Dimensions of History.*
My following examples are from part 2, "Modulations: The Aesthetic
Dimension," and more particularly from the section entitled "Rhythms,
Charts, and Changes." This section is fittingly introduced by a Bambara
ritual signature announcing the beginning of a new creation (see fig. 2).
This ideogram, which Wright also employs in *The Double Invention of
Komo* (55–56), is composed of "God's" immutable and permanent knife"
and "the whirlwind's hook," whose combination announces the fashion-
ing of a new order after the destruction of the world, from the chaos
produced by the *whirl*wind.[96]

Unlike the first part of *Dimensions of History,* which is divided into
three long sections, "Rhythms, Charts, and Changes" is composed of a
rapid succession of fourteen relatively brief poems, each of which derives
its title (and its cadence) from a particular musical or poetic form. In
some cases, Wright uses the names of individual musical instruments
employed in a specific dance or ceremony: "Teponaztli" is a pre-Colum-
bian wooden drum; "Atabaqué" is a set of drums used in the Afro-
Brazilian ritual of *candomblé*; "Bandola" is a small guitar employed in
Caribbean folk music; "Huehuetl" is a Mexican upright drum, as well as
related to the *huehuetlatolli,* an Aztec form of ritual speech;[97] "Pututu" is

a Quechua shell trumpet; and "Maracas," I believe, is self-explanatory.[98] The important thing is that all these various instruments are peculiar to New World cultures; their origins are, for the most part, Amerindian, Afro-American, or Latin American. The same holds true for "Joropo," a Venezuelan folk dance; "Lundú," a Brazilian folk dance held at harvest celebrations; "Tamborito," a Panamanian-African dance; "Bambuco," a dance form popular in Colombia and Venezuela; "Vela," a Dominican semireligious service; "Son," a Cuban song form written in *romance* or ballad lines;[99] and "Areíto," a *taíno* (Arawak) responsorial chant. "Villancicos" are a form of fifteenth- and sixteenth-century Spanish verse, but Wright's allusion is specifically to Sor Juana Inés de la Cruz, who wrote some *villancicos* in black creole.[100] We need not examine in detail every single one of the above poems to realize that "Rhythms, Charts, and Changes" is a complex admixture of elements gathered together from the different cultures present in the New World in order to "make one music as before/but vaster," to recall the Tennysonian lines Du Bois cites in *The Souls of Black Folk*.[101]

There is, however, one poem that is particularly representative of the mixed cultural congregation evoked in this section of *Dimensions of History*: Wright's version of the "Son de la Ma' Teodora," which appears as the third "tuning" of his "Bandola."

Má lover of god
Má loved by god
Má of the sun
Má of the river
Má of the timber
Má of the wood
Má of the grief
Má Teodora
What source
is in your circle?
Why do you dance
with the *palo codal?*
What itch constrains
your orisha limp?
Who is the simp
to arrange your fall?
Má Má Teodora
fifteen sinners
guide you through the berries
of your own exultation.

Fifteen lines and a stick
make a whip
to remind you of the grave.
Fifteen stones and a star
lift you to a cloud beyond my reach.
Má loved by god
you ride your flesh so surely
the gods within the flat drums
keep a tap
upon the earth. (*DH*, 43)

The original "Son," composed and performed by Teodora Ginés, a black Dominican, during the second half of the sixteenth century, goes like this:

-¿Dónde está la Ma' Teodora?
-Rajando la leña está.
-¿Con su palo y su bandola?
-Rajando la leña está.
-¿Dónde está que no la veo?
-Rajando la leña está.
Rajando la leña está.

[-Where is Ma' Teodora?
-She is splitting logs.
-With her staff and her bandola?
-She is splitting logs.
-Where is she that I can't see her?
-She is splitting logs.
She is splitting logs.][102]

Weaving features from Spanish, African, and *taíno* cultures into a responsorial structure that emphasizes the ritualistic aspect of this performance, the "Son de la Ma' Teodora" is a powerful pretext of Wright's poetic tapestry. González Echevarría's comments are particularly relevant to Wright's rewriting of the "Son de la Ma' Teodora."

The responsorial structure of the "Son" and the ritual that it evokes are not only African, but also *taíno*. The singing and dancing of Teodora's song is an *areíto*, a *taíno* celebration whose name suggestively means "to dance while remembering," or "dancing to remember." Dancing is a way of keeping the past—tradition, heritage, culture—alive. We can assume from the "Ma' " that Teodora is not only a mother, but also old. She embodies tradition. When she asks,

"Where is Ma' Teodora?" she is asking, "Where is tradition?" The mock pursuit of Ma' Teodora is a pursuit of tradition, a spell against its vanishing. Teodora is memory incarnate. The jubilation at the end is the intoxicating recovery of tradition, an immersion in a rhythm that is primordial, that keeps time. [103]

Wright's Má Teodora certainly *keeps time*, and not just by rhythmically *tapping* her African staff (*palo*) on the ground while she dances. More to the point, the rhythm generated by her tapping is an articulation of the thoughts of "the gods within the flat drums," who, like Teodora herself, "keep a tap/upon the earth." Má Teodora is a *keeper* of the rhythm and the music of tradition, of the "language" of those gods in the drums. But this rhythm differs from that of the original "Son." Not only does Wright alter the basic responsorial structure of the *son/areíto* form, he also invests the original figure of Má Teodora with a variety of new, supplementary features, whose enumeration follows the form of Catholic litany. The "constrained orisha limp" associates her with *Eshu-Elegba*, the Yoruba deity who guards the crossroads, while the epitaph "Má of the river" identifies her as Ochún, the Afro-Cuban goddess of the calm waters, who, in turn, is associated with the Virgen de la Caridad del Cobre, the patron saint of Cuba. [104] "Má of the timber" and "Má of the wood," in addition to alluding to "Rajando la leña está," also evokes the image of a carved wooden mask of the kind that is used in a variety of different African divination ceremonies. "Má of the grief," furthermore, stresses that Wright's Teodora, like her original counterpart, is not a "young mother" who has yet to learn "the meaning of another death" (*DH*, 14), but is someone who knows and understands dispossession, that is, the lessons of slavery ("Fifteen lines and a stick/make a whip") as well as the meaning of kinship. Clearly, Má Teodora is the female counterpart of the Dogon sage Ogotemmêli.

Last but not least, we must notice the change from "palo" (staff, stick) to "palo codal," the latter being, as Wright himself explains, a stick hung around the neck as a penance. This alteration is of considerable interest because it evokes a famous figure in Latin American literature: Juan Rodríguez Freyle's Juana García, who appears in *El carnero* (1638). Juana García is the prototype of the black sorceress. At the end of her story, which has been widely anthologized as "Las brujerías de Juana García" or "Un negocio con Juana García," she is punished for her magic transgressions by the Chief Inquisitor of Santafé de Bogotá: Her sentence condemns her to standing on a raised platform with a lighted candle in her hand and a *halter* around her neck. [105] The final image we glimpse of

Juana García is suggestive of Wright's Má Teodora, whose "palo codal" signals the ironic transformation of a sign of bondage (the halter) into an emblem of freedom.[106] The connection between Má Teodora and Juana García adds another dimension to the figure of this dancer: Teodora, like Juana García, is "una negra un poco voladora," a kind of sorceress, or to be more precise, someone who has the power to heal and to "fly," that is, to achieve an "angle of ascent" in Hayden's sense. As the embodiment of tradition, Teodora has the ability to heal the wounds of exile by creating, in the form of her "Son" (her own Black *limbo*), a vital image of a new community, that of the "Orphans of the earth" (*DH*, 52), congregating at the crossroads. These crossroads are a symbolic place of exchange and transformation, which is the inside of Má Teodora's "circle," the "source" of Hispanic Caribbean literature.

My life
is in the middle of this dance.
My heart unfolds
to accept this cross,
the stone of our customary light. (*DH*, 62)

The "Son de la Ma' Teodora," like Benjamin Banneker's letter to Thomas Jefferson, is another founding fable of New World culture and writing, another "bead" to be added to the poet's "rosary."

III   *I felt, Sire, as if I were going mad: the compass of my mind had lost its directional needle, my identities were spilling over and multiplying beyond all contact with minimal human reason.*
      —CARLOS FUENTES, *Terra Nostra*

Symbolic places of cultural exchange and transformation, of simultaneous deracination and supplementation, abound in Wright's poetry, and many other examples could be cited. More important, however, than any diligent accumulation of additional textual evidence is the fact that Wright frequently associates those historico-cultural spaces with a very specific kind of landscape: that of the city. It is not coincidental, for instance, that Afro-Cuban culture, the realm to which both the "Día de Reyes" and the "Son de la Ma' Teodora" belong, is, as Fernando Ortiz and others have shown, a predominantly urban phenomenon.[107] In addition, I have already commented, in my introductory discussion of the Benjamin Banneker poems, on the significance of Wright's trope of

the city with respect to the foundations of New World culture. It is now
necessary to elaborate a broader context for that trope in order to show
how and why the founding of cities plays such a major role in *Dimensions
of History.*

As Albert William Levi has pointed out in his remarks on Goethe's and
Thomas Mann's notion of the *Weltstadt* or *Kulturstadt,* "the city is an
artifact set within nature, but *not of it;* in short, a work of art, mind taking
shape, at once a symbol of physical accommodation and spiritual des-
tiny."[108] In other words, the city is a cultural (as opposed to a natural)
landscape, or what Thomas Mann called a "geistige Lebensform" (Levi
renders it as "spiritual way of life"), whose artful organization of space
suggests a "distinctive metaphysics of order" or disorder, as the case may
be. The city has its own peculiar discourse, a kind of body language,
which is at once historical and mythical. Wright regards the city as a
charged field, constituted by a series of symbolic acts that make up the
ritual of founding. What exactly those symbolic acts are and how they
manifest themselves in a given language can best be observed in the
following quotation from Vico's *The New Science,* which will help us
determine the elements that come together in Wright's concept of the city
as a figure for ritualistic coherence.

Even the philologists say the walls were traced by the founders of the
cities with the plough, the moldboard of which . . . must have been
first called *urbs,* whence the ancient *urbum,* curved. Perhaps *orbis* is
from the same origin, so that at first *orbis terrae* must have meant any
fence made in this way, so low that Remus jumped over it to be killed
by Romulus and thus, as Latin historians narrate, to consecrate with
his blood the first walls of Rome. Such a fence must evidently have
been a hedge (*siepe*) (and among the Greeks *seps* signifies "serpent" in
its heroic meaning of cultivated land), from which origin must come
munere viam, to build a road, which is done by strengthening the
hedges around the fields. Hence walls are called *moenia,* as if for
munia, and certainly *munire* kept the sense of fortifying. The hedges
must have been of those plants the Latin call *sagmina,* bloodwort or
elder, whose use and name still survive. The name *sagmina* as
preserved in the sense of the herbs with which the altars were adorned;
it must have come from the blood (*sanguis*) of the slain, who, like
Remus, had transgressed them. Hence the so-called sanctity of
walls.[109]

This passage contains a cluster of familiar images which make it possible
to establish a clear connection between the ritual of founding a city and
the excision or circumcision ritual. This connection is vital to Wright's

concept of culture and to his perception of the origins of culture in language and in writing.

To found a city is an act of cultivation (from the Latin *colere*) in the sense of cutting the earth with a plough, thus inscribing upon its surface the insignia of human presence. The plough traces the outlines of the city-to-be and thus creates the semblance of a *map* or *charter*, setting down the fundamental laws of the land in accordance with its actual physical boundaries. This initial gesture of breaking the ground already implies, as Vico suggests, an element of ritual sacrifice: The consecration of the first walls of Rome with the blood of Remus is a kind of fortification represented by the bloodwort hedge, whose roots with their red coloring substance penetrate and saturate the soil like the blood of the slain victim. The sacrificial shedding of blood at the very place where the earth has been symbolically and actually "wounded" is an act of cultivation, which also highlights the religious meaning of *colere*: to honor with worship, to protect, which developed etymologically through the Latin *cultus* to the English *cult*. In much the same way that the blood strengthens the foundations of the city, that is, its walls, it reinforces, in another sense, the collective religious beliefs of the community of founders, the "cult." In this sense, the city's walls are like altars, and each symbolic slaying carried out on that spot is a reenactment of that initial ceremonial cut of the plough into the earth. For Wright, as we have seen, the reopening of that fundamental wound is a ritual of kinship.

The link between the cultivation of the land, the founding of ancient cities, and the raising of altars is further supported by Vico's observation that the heroic cities of the Romans were initially "called *arae*, altars, and *acres*, fortresses."[110] To clarify the connection between Vico's philological observations and Wright's poetry, it is necessary at this point to make a leap from *The New Science* to Dogon religious mythology, specifically to Griaule's *Conversations with Ogotemmêli*. Such a leap is justified because Ogotemmêli's remarks about the significance of altars and ritual sacrifice among the Dogon enhance Vico's etymologies in startling ways.

On the altar the virtue of new, fresh, blood combines with what has been left there by a long series of ritual [killings]: for the altar is a storehouse of forces, of which man draws at the appropriate time, and which he keeps constantly fed. It is also the point of contact between man and the Invisible. . . . The Dogon word for sacrifice does in fact come from a root which means to "renew life." . . . "The altar gives something to a man, and a part of what he has received he passes on to others," said Ogotemmêli, "A small part of the sacrifice is for oneself, but the rest is for others. The forces released enter into man, pass through him and out again, and so it is for all. . . ." As each man gives to all the rest, so he also receives from all. A perpetual exchange goes on between men, an unceasing movement of invisible currents.[111]

Seen in relation to Vico's comments, Ogotemmêli's (and Griaule's) explanations help us apprehend the altar as a symbolic locus of cultivation. The place it marks is one characterized by perpetual communal exchange, a process kept alive through sacrifice as reenactment of the breaking of the ground with the ploughshare. The altar is thus a figure that demarcates the point of transition from nature to culture. Ogotemmêli also points out that "the shedding of the blood in circumcision . . . is like the offering of a victim on the altar, and it is the earth that drinks the blood."[112] Like the ritual knife, the altar represents a process of simultaneous destruction and fertilization: The creation of culture requires a violation of nature, and sacrifice is necessary to atone for that violation. But sacrifice is also a form of supplementation: The blood of the slain victim flows back to the wounded earth; it purifies and heals the cut of the ploughshare, which is thus transformed into a kind of scar, signifying the perfection of nature through human grace.

If we recall that this cut-turned-into-scar is a figure of writing, then it may be said that this "perfection" of nature is achieved through the "grace" of language. It follows, then, that culture is the act of perfecting (and supplementing) nature through language, and that the artifact set within nature but not of it, as Levi describes the city, is something created by acts of language. Culture, in short, is a way of imparting language ("the Word," as the Dogon have it) to nature. This idea may be carried even further to reveal the vital connection between culture and *poiêsis*, as Jay Wright himself endeavors in the following citation from "Desire's Design, Vision's Resonance." "*Poiêsis* is not exhausted," he argues, "in the relatively subordinate act of giving a name to some thing. It goes beyond that into real power, that of transformation and action. [Kenneth] Burke clarifies this when he says, there is a sense in which language is *not* just 'natural,' but really *does* add a 'new dimension' to the things of nature (an observation that would be the logological equivalent of the theological statement that grace perfects nature)."[113] Language adds something to nature; it transforms it by first creating a necessary deficiency— the cut that widens into the blank textual space—which is immediately supplemented by the manifestations of that new dimension, those fundamental scars that grow into altars and city walls. This notion of supplementarity as it defines the relationship between nature and culture inevitably returns us to the relationship between myth and history as well as to Roland Barthes's concept of an artificial, or what I have termed synthetic, myth. A synthetic myth in Wright's sense is a founding fable that evolves from the simultaneous decomposition and supplementation of the classical mythologies of the Old Worlds, meaning Africa and Europe, as they meet again in the New World.

But the New World is more than just a setting that frames the renewed encounter of Europe with Africa. Wright does not regard the pre-Columbian Americas as an environment completely untouched by civilization. This is already quite evident in his version of the "Son de la Ma' Teodora." We may even go so far as to say that for Wright the destruction of the ancient civilizations that prospered in the New World long before the first Spaniards landed on its shores is an episode in world history equivalent in significance to the decline of the Roman Empire during the first half of the fifth century. While this analogy is valuable to the extent that it restores to those pre-Columbian cultures their proper status within the context of New World cultural history, it does not form a valid basis for assuming that therefore New World history could be divided into periods roughly corresponding in their historical sequence to European antiquity, the Middle Ages, the Renaissance, and so forth, all compressed into the relatively brief span of approximately five centuries. This is clearly not the case. Moreover, such a linear view of history would remain oblivious to a most decisive factor in New World cultural history, one that clearly distinguishes New World history and culture from its European counterparts: This factor is the time warp, brought about by the copresence of what is generally regarded as separate historical periods. To turn the linear phenomenon we call American history into New World history, it is necessary to transform a diachronic into a synchronic system. We must understand that we are confronted with a historical field, where the Spanish Middle Ages and the Italian Renaissance move side by side, and hand in hand, with the French Enlightenment and the modern age, and where the sounds of the Industrial Revolution mingle freely with Quechua and Náhuatl songs as well as with the compelling rhythms of Yoruba and Ashanti drums, echoes from cultures older than Rome and Greece.

Octavio Paz has argued that "[Spanish Americans] are children of the counter-reformation and the Universal Kingdom; [the Anglo-Saxons] are children of Luther and the Industrial Revolution."[114] This may be true enough, but the value of such an astute observation decreases considerably once it is used to reinstate, albeit surreptitiously, the kind of cultural nationalism Paz himself condemns, in the very same essay, as "a moral aberration" and an "aesthetic fallacy."[115] It seems to have slipped his memory that O'Gorman, in *The Invention of America*, appealed to a similar distinction to explain the alleged superiority of Anglo-American civilization over that of its Latin American neighbors. The point, which both Paz and O'Gorman appear to miss at least in part, is not to substitute different historical origins for some pseudoscientific theory of race (as O'Gorman does) but to realize that the totality of these different historical origins, as well as their peculiar simultaneity, is what constitutes the true cultural legacy of the New World writer. Gabriel García Márquez has made that point brilliantly in *One Hundred Years of Solitude*, and this may well be at least part of the reason for the tremendous success this novel has enjoyed. Jay Wright makes the same point, differently but no less brilliantly, in *Dimensions of History* and offers it as "an initiate's fertile/and uneasy/resolution" (*DI* 56).

If New World history is comprehended not simply as a chronology but instead as a space where all previous historical periods also coexist, then it becomes clear that a New World mythology in Wright's sense can draw from an almost inexhaustible and incredibly diverse reservoir, of which Europe's classical myths are only a relatively small part.[116] For Wright, the most important thing is the way in which different myths interact within the context of New World history and how that process of interaction and transformation gives rise to authentic founding fables. The following long citation from *Dimensions of History*, which returns us to the figure of the city as a cultural landscape, is an excellent case in point.

So Nuño de Guzmán, governor of New Spain,
employs Tejo, the trader,
trader of gold and silver,
bearer of the tales of the Seven Cities.
Weary at Culiacán,
he finds four sailors,
lost in the search for the flowered
end of things.
Now, the friar takes the slave
into the valley, and sends him on above.
Send me a cross as big as my hands,
if the land is good.
If it challenges our new mother,
send a cross larger than that.
A day   two days   four,
and a cross "as tall as a man"
mysteries of Seven Great Cities
under the Black man's eyes.

Following God's candles
further than the friar will go,
your light breaks down at Hawikúh.
Estevan   Stephen
carrying your own stone
into the valley,
victim again of your services,
you lie at the gate of the Seven Cities.
Who will trim your hair and pair your nails
to send your sunsum home?
What sister will shave her hair for your soul?
The friar never approaches the gate.
He stands elevated long enough
to set a cross for Spain.

At that point,
each day, the young priest appears.
He wears the crescent moon embossed
with sun, moon and stars.
He would set the bowl in the friar's tree.
Your 'Nyame dua, father.
Your shrine not anywhere but here.

Friar and the crowned return,
the plumed and mailed blessed ones
search for the gate again.
This is the gate of gold
Gao   Guinea   Hawikúh.
But there is no gold,
only the whisper of the wind
fluting the Black man's liberated bones.

   Into this sound,
   tracking highways, you come.
   Cold morning's return out of the desert.
   Cold metal search in the Golden State
   to return, enchanted again at the gate.
   Not gold. Not the cities' magnificence.
   What the others left at the gate
   you found within, extended,
        "a gateway to the beautiful." (*DH*, 28–29)

   Wright offers in this passage his own poetic version of the history of
Hawikúh, a large Zuñi pueblo whose ruins are located in the northern
region of today's New Mexico. Given that Wright himself was born in

Albuquerque, it is not surprising that the history of New Mexico should hold a special significance for him. But above and beyond any personal memories that may resound in the above lines, it ought to be noted that Hawikúh is an important, though neglected, landmark in early American history. Believed to be one of the so-called "Seven Cities of Cíbola" and reputed to be rich in gold and silver, Hawikúh was the prime motivation behind a series of expeditions organized by various Spanish explorers during the first half of the sixteenth century. Nuño de Guzmán, governor of New Spain from 1528 to 1536, was the first to embark, in 1529, on such an exploratory voyage, inspired by the tales of his Indian slave Tejo. The journey, which lasted for two years, was a failure to the extent that the Spaniard did not succeed in locating the mysterious Seven Cities. It did, however, result in the founding of the city of Culiacán, the present capital of the Mexican province of Sinaloa, which then served as a base for conducting slave raids in that area.[117]

Culiacán was also the place reached in 1536 by four members of another expedition, described in detail in the *Relación que dió Alvar Núñez Cabeza de Vaca de la jornada que hico a la Florida* (1542). Cabeza de Vaca and his three companions, among them the black slave Estevan, were the only survivors of an expedition that had initially consisted of four hundred men, who had landed on the west coast of Florida in 1528, whence they turned north in search of El Dorado, "the flowered end of things." The journey failed miserably, and the disappointed Spaniards returned to the Gulf of Mexico, where they constructed several boats, hoping to sail in them along the coastline toward Mexico. Most were killed in a shipwreck, and the few survivors were enslaved by the Indians. Cabeza de Vaca and his three companions managed to escape and traveled on foot across the continent for six years until they reached the province of Sinaloa. During those years, they lived among various Indian tribes, rendering services as healers, so that by the time they arrived in Culiacán, they had literally been stripped of everything that would distinguish a white man from an Indian.[118] The reports of their impressive voyage across the North American continent reinforced the legend of the Seven Cities of Cíbola, and two other expeditions were outfitted, one in 1538 and the other in 1539. Very little is known of the former, but the second one, headed by Fray Marcos de Niza and including, among others, the black Estevan, is what attracted Wright's attention. Fray Marcos, it may be worth adding, had been in Peru at the time when Pizarro looted the Inca treasure and was thus quite susceptible to tales of gold. Having reached the village of Vapaca, Fray Marcos dispatched Estevan toward the north fifty or sixty leagues to see if by that route he would be able to learn of any great thing such as we sought and I agreed with him that if he received any information of a rich, peopled land that was something great, he should go no farther, but that he return in person or send me Indians with this signal, which we arranged: if the thing was of moderate importance, he send me a white cross the size of a hand; if it was something great, he send me one of two hands; and if it was something bigger and better than New Spain ["our new mother"], he send me a large cross.[119]

Four days later, Estevan's messenger returned with a cross "as tall as a man" and a message that he had secured information about "the greatest thing in the world." After the arrival of messengers with a second cross of the same size as the first one a few days later, the friar hurried after Estevan, who had disobeyed his instructions and proceeded to enter Cíbola. When Fray Marcos finally reached the vicinity of Hawikúh, he was informed that Estevan had been killed by the inhabitants of that city.

The accounts of Estevan's death and the reasons projected for his murder vary substantially. The following is taken for a letter by Hernando de Alarcón, who explored the region of the lower Colorado River in 1540.

Your lordship will remember that the negro who accompanied Fray Marcos had rattles (bells), and feathers on his arms and legs; that he had plates of different colors, and that he came to this country a little more than a year ago. I wished to know why he had been killed. He [the Indian informant] said: "The chief of Cevola having asked him whether he had other brethren, the negro replied that he had an infinite number, that they carried many weapons and were not very far off. Upon this statement a great many chiefs gathered in council, and agreed on killing the negro, so that he might not impart any information to his brethren in regard to the country of Cevola. Such was the cause of his death. His body was cut into a great many pieces, which were distributed among all the chiefs, in order that they might know that he was surely dead."[120]

Having learned of Estevan's violent death, Fray Marcos decided not to enter Hawikúh, as he was not prepared to fight with the resident Indians. Instead, he took possession of the region of Cíbola in the name of Spain by raising a pile of stone and placing on it a wooden cross. He named the new land the "New Kingdom of Saint Francis." Although he claimed in his report to the Spanish emperor that he actually saw Hawikúh, later historians have, for good reason, doubted the truthfulness of that claim.[121] Hawikúh was "officially" discovered and conquered in 1540 by

Francisco Vásquez de Coronado, who named the city Granada. [122] However, no substantial amounts of gold were ever found in that region.

My rather lengthy narrative of the history of Cíbola-Hawikúh-Granada is not intended as a substitute for a reading of the above citation from *Dimensions of History*. It is, however, necessary to be at least somewhat acquainted with the main historical facts and fictions that cluster around the legend of the Seven Cities of Cíbola to understand what exactly Wright is doing in that passage. For what we witness in his poetic version of the history of Hawikúh is a series of displacements and supplementations, whose significance would remain largely incomprehensible outside of this historical context.

To begin with, the conception itself of the Seven Cities of Cíbola is already the result of a displacement brought about by the discovery of the New World. The original legend of the "Septe citate" can be traced back at least as far as the years of the Arabic conquest of the Spanish peninsula, and probably even farther to the ancient tales of the Atlantic isles. Interestingly enough, the contemporary source of that legend is itself a tale of exile and thus of displacement: The "Septe citate," at the time identified with the mysterious islands of Antilia, were presumed to be inhabited by a Portuguese archbishop, six other bishops, and a number of Christians, who had sailed there from Spain in 714 to escape the Moorish invasion. Consequently, the Seven Cities were believed to be a place where Hispanic civilization had been preserved in a state of relative purity. [123] Later on, the Island of the Seven Cities became associated with a variety of unknown Atlantic isles, and the discovery of the New World even inspired cartographers to assign it different places on the maps of the American continent. Ultimately, the elusive Seven Cities became localized as the Seven Cities of Cíbola: The Iberian legend had been transformed into a distinct New World fable, a transformation set in motion largely by the tales of the Indian trader Tejo.

For Wright, this transformation is significant far beyond its contemporary historical context. The fable of the Seven Cities of Cíbola constitutes a syncretism at the meeting place of two cultures; the Spanish, as represented by Nuño de Guzmán, and the Indian, as represented by Tejo. A configuration of ideas generated as the result of the contact and verbal interaction between Guzmán and Tejo, the fable of the Seven Cities of Cíbola is paradigmatic of the kind of cultural exchange and collaboration with which Wright charges the figure of the city. Regardless of its actual existence, Hawikúh in its fabulous manifestation is projected here as a figure for the dwelling-place, in Américo Castro's sense, of New World culture. This notion of syncretism is reinforced by Wright's allusion to

Cabeza de Vaca, whose 1542 travelogue is, next to the Inca Garcilaso de la Vega's tale of Pedro Serrano, perhaps the most notable account of the kinds of visible deracination and denuding some of the conquistadors experienced in the New World. [124] Cabeza de Vaca's *relación* is a remarkable work because at a time when the Spanish were engaged in a large-scale destruction of Indian cultures all over the New World, it admits to the possibility of *mutual* cultural exchange between Europeans and Indians, as well as between Indians and Blacks, as the example of Estevan shows. [125] If we are to believe Alarcón's report, Estevan was actually bearing the marks left by his former life among the Indians in the form of those feathers and rattles that adorned his body and probably identified him as a kind of healer.

It is not too surprising that Wright should consider the story of Estevan's death at Hawikúh as the most significant dimension of the legend of the Seven Cities of Cíbola. To be sure, the mere fact that a black man was to discover the first "city" on the North American continent is quite sufficient to accord his story the status of a founding fable equal in importance to Benjamin Banneker's participation in the founding of the United States capital. But there is more to the "mysteries of Seven Great Cities/under the Black man's eyes." In a way, we are again accompanying Wright's poet on another walk across a graveyard: The cross Estevan sends to the friar, a cross "as tall as a man," is one that comes to mark his own grave, that is, the place of his death. It reappears, in the second stanza, as the cross Fray Marcos set for Spain, only to be even further transfigured into "the friar's tree" and finally into "'Nyame dua" [God's tree], the triadic altar of the Akan. [126] But most compelling about this transfiguration is that the "young priest," who is said to appear at that point every day, wears the insignia of Thoth, the Egyptian god of learning, writing, and medicine: "He wears the crescent moon embossed/with sun, moon and stars." This most curious aggregation of figures in that quotation's third stanza is the key to the founding fable Wright elaborates.

The appearance of Thoth, the Master of the books and the "scribe of truth," in the very place where the friar, according to his own fictionalized narrative, had erected a cross to take possession of the land consecrated with the blood of Estevan openly announces a transition from the realm of history to that of myth. The figure of Thoth opens up another interpretive dimension, which becomes evident once we look more closely at the characteristics ascribed to that god in Egyptian mythology. Derrida has carefully examined Thoth's attributes in "Plato's Pharmacy," and his findings are quite relevant here.

In all the cycles of Egyptian mythology, Thoth presides over the organization of death. The master of writing, numbers, and calculation does not merely write down the weight of the dead souls; he first counts out the days of life, *enumerates* history. His arithmetic thus covers the events of divine biography. He is "the one who measures the length of the lives of gods and men." He behaves like a chief of funeral protocol, charged in particular with the dressing of the dead. . . . This god of resurrection is less interested in life or death than in death as a repetition of life and life as a rehearsal of death, in the awakening of life and in the recommencement of death. This is what *numbers*, of which he is also the inventor and patron, mean. Thoth repeats everything in the addition of the supplement: in adding to and doubling as the sun, he is other than the sun [he is the moon] and the same as it; . . . Always taking a place not his own, a place one could call that of the dead or the dummy, he has neither a proper place nor a proper name. His propriety or property is impropriety or inappropriateness, the floating indetermination that allows for substitution and play. . . . He would be the mediating movement of dialectics if he did not also mimic it, indefinitely preventing it, through his ironic doubling, from reaching some final fulfillment or eschatological reappropriation. Thoth is never present. Nowhere does he appear in person. No being-there can properly be *his own.*[127]

Thoth is a figure for the process of supplementation that Wright engages in this passage. Charged with the dressing of the dead, Thoth is the one who administers Estevan's funeral rites: "Who will trim your hair and pare your nails/to send your sunsum home?" But he also takes the place of Estevan and sets in motion a fascinating play of doublings and substitutions, reincarnating Estevan in a variety of forms and figures and thus preventing his death from bringing about closure. "Estevan Stephen." It is no coincidence that we should once again encounter this textual gap, signifying in this case the presence (or rather, the absence) of Thoth, who occupies the locus of substitution and supplementarity. It is in that spot that Estevan, the discoverer of Hawikúh, is reincarnated as Carpentier's Esteban in *Explosion in a Cathedral*, Miguel Barnet's Esteban Montejo in *The Autobiography of a Runaway Slave* (1966), and, last but not least, as Joyce's Stephen Dedalus in A *Portrait of the Artist as a Young Man*. That Joyce also evokes Thoth in connection with Stephen Dedalus, a character to which especially Carpentier's Esteban is indebted, further strengthens the link between these figures: "A sense of fear of the unknown moved in the heart of his [Stephen Dedalus's] weariness, a fear of symbols and portents, of the hawk-like man whose name he bore soaring out of his captivity on osier-woven wings, of Thoth, the god of writers, writing with a reed upon a tablet and bearing in his narrow ibis head the cusped moon."[128] That Thoth is also the inventor and patron of numbers alerts us to the textual presence of another mythological being, who is equally entrusted with language: Nummo (or Nommo), the seventh ancestor of the Dogon, who, like Thoth, is the master of the Word.[129] In Dogon mythology, Nommo is represented by the number seven, which apears, in the context of *Dimensions of History*, not only in the *Seven* Cities, but also in the line that represents Estevan's journey to Hawikúh: "A day two days four." The number of days mentioned (four) plus the number of phrases that constitute this line (three) yield another seven, while the textual blanks continue to insinuate the ambiguous presence of Thoth, the absent one, who acts as a catalyst for this play of numbers. Incidentally, the stanza in which Thoth appears in the form of a young priest is the only one in this passage that has seven lines.

Let us look more closely at the mythological significance of that number seven as related by Ogotemmêli.

The seventh in a series . . . represents perfection. Though equal in quality with the others, he is the sum of the feminine element, which is four, and the masculine element, which is three. He is thus the completion of the perfect series, symbol of the total unity of male and female. . . . And to this homogeneous whole belongs especially the mastery of words, that is, of language. . . . The others equally possessed the knowledge of these words . . . , but they had not attained the mastery of them nor was it given to them to develop their use. What the seventh ancestor had received, therefore, was the perfect knowledge of a Word—the second Word to be heard on earth, clearer than the first and not, like the first, reserved for particular recipients [the Spirits], but destined for all mankind.[130]

Like Thoth, the seventh Nommo is the author of the second (and secondary) Word. As interpreter of the language of the Spirits (the first Word), he is also the one who introduces difference into language.[131] This difference is the result of the mediation he performs between the realm of the Spirits and that of man, between the living and the dead. Although this Nommo is not directly identified as a scribe, the tale of how he invented the second Word is cast in metaphors strongly suggestive of the act of writing:

At sunrise of the appointed day the seventh ancestor Spirit spat out eighty threads of cotton; these he distributed between his upper teeth which acted as the teeth of a weaver's reed. In this way he made the uneven threads of a warp. He did the same with the lower teeth to make the even threads. By opening and shutting his jaws the Spirit caused the threads of the warp to make the movements required in weaving. The whole face took part in the work, his nose studs serving as the block, while the stud in his lower lip was the shuttle. As the threads crossed and uncrossed, the two tips of the Spirit's forked tongue pushed the thread of the weft to and fro, and the web took shape from his mouth in the breath of the second revealed Word. For the Spirit was speaking while the work proceeded. As did the Nummo in the first revelation, he imparted his word by means of a technical process, so that all men could understand. By doing so he showed the identities of material actions and spiritual forms, or rather the need for their cooperation. [132]

I have mentioned earlier that weaving is one of Wright's foremost figures of writing, one that is of particular significance in his "Second Conversations with Ogotemmêli" in *Soothsayers and Omens*. That there is a close metaphorical resemblance between a woven cloth and a written text is obvious enough, but the link between weaving and writing goes even farther than that and returns us to what I have called the "language" of the city as a cultural landscape. For, as Ogotemmêli also remarks,

The old method of cultivation . . . is like weaving. . . . If a man clears ground and makes a new square plot and builds a dwelling on the plot, his work is like weaving a cloth. Moreover, weaving is a form of speech, which is imparted to the fabric by the to-and-fro movement of the shuttle on the warp; and in the same way the to-and-fro movement of the peasant on his plot imparts the Word of the ancestors . . . to the ground on which he works, and thus rids the earth of impurity and extends the area of cultivation round inhabited places. But, if cultivation is a form of weaving, it is equally true to say that weaving is a form of cultivation. . . . The finished web is the symbol of the cultivated field. [133]

The breaking of the ground, then, is clearly a form of writing. It is a process that transforms the natural landscape into a cultural and cultivated landscape, the city, and thus constitutes an act of founding. With regard to the quotation from *Dimensions of History*, which still remains the focal point of my discussion, it is important that the slaying of Estevan symbolically reenacts that fundamental process of cultivation. Estevan's blood fortifies the gate of the Seven Cities, but, more importantly, it mediates between the history of Hawikúh, the myth of the Seven Cities of Cíbola, and the poet who explores the ruins of both. These traces of blood can be said to render the ruins legible; because of them, the ruins of Hawikúh are "enchanted" by "the whisper of the wind / fluting the Black

man's liberated bones." Wright's figure of the desert wind fluting Es-
tevan's bones stands for a kind of metaphoric symphony, or transference
of spirit, which is also related to the cannibal bone-flute of the Caribs in a
way that Wilson Harris's following remarks elucidate: "In the Bone or
flute [of the Caribs] is implicit the skeleton wall of a cruel age—the
fissures or cracks in the mind or shell of conquest. That shell is no longer
the seat of an absolute proprietorship of the globe but is converted into an
organ of memory through which to sound the invocation of resensitized
perspectives of community as a warning against plastering over afresh the
mind or shell of empire into a recurring monolith or callous."[134] As a
historico-mythical event, Estevan's death produces such fissures or
cracks in the text of the poem, openings that make it possible for both poet
and reader to penetrate the Procrustean surface of American Culture and
sound the mysterious depths of New World (cross-)cultural interaction.

Wright's poet, this postmodern chronicler of the cultural history of the
New World, searches not for gold, as the conquistadors did, but for a
"gateway to the beautiful." This gateway, or threshold, which extends in
the cracks between "Gao Guinea Hawikúh," leads him and us to a
locus of transformation where the black slave Estevan sits, liberated, in
the company not only of his more immediate literary kin, the other
Estebans, but also with Thoth and the seventh Nommo, at the shrine of
the Akan god 'Nyame (or Onyame). According to Danquah, Onyame
embodies "understanding and also . . . extended reality. . . . he is a
unification of all feeling towards being, and in that unity there is a union,
a harmony or fruition of the artistic, a pleasing and articulate placidity,
gateway to the beautiful."[135] As the textual fissures evolve into such a
gateway, Wright's poetic tale of the Seven Cities contracts into an epic
(and epiphanic) moment that loudly echoes a passage from *The Souls of
Black Folk*, where Du Bois writes,

I sit with Shakespeare and he winces not. Across the color line I move
arm in arm with Balzac and Dumas, where smiling men and
welcoming women glide in gilded halls. From out the caves of
evening that swing between the strong-limbed earth and the tracery of
the stars, I summon Aristotle and Aurelius and what soul I will, and
they come all graciously with no scorn nor condescension. So, wed
with truth, I dwell above the Veil. Is this the life you grudge us, O
knightly America? . . . Are you so afraid lest peering from this high
Pisgah . . . we sight the Promised Land?[136]

Wright's poet's "Promised Land," that dwelling place above the Veil,
are the Seven Cities, a place located both within and outside of history, a

place that is at once historical fact and myth. Hawikúh-Cíbola is like the inside of Má Teodora's circle: a place at the crossroads, where historical realities are transformed and extended. It is an "enchanted" place in that it is consecrated with the blood of Estevan in the same way that the walls of Rome were consecrated with the blood of Remus. The parallel between these two deaths lies in their ritual significance. Estevan's blood, like Remus's, nourishes the arid soil of the past; it adds to it another dimension: myth. In this sense, the black man's death may be regarded as another form of cultivation. While Estevan's life can be viewed as a process of turning myth into historical reality (of localizing the Seven Cities as the Seven Cities of Cíbola), his death reverses that process and brings about the transformation of that historical reality into a founding fable. This synthetic myth is both other than and the same as the original or originary myth(s) whose place it takes. Its function is not strictly to replace those myths but to displace them and, in the process, open up a space for itself.

To effect such a displacement is the ultimate purpose of Estevan's death, and this is precisely why Wright associates him with Thoth. Because of this association, Estevan's death itself becomes a figure of writing, of that ambiguous acquisition of literacy that subverts historical chronology and inaugurates a new order in the form of a new set of historical and mythological allegiances. Estevan, like Wright's initiate, is "bled/black, in the space/between the lines" (*DI*, 33) of the official chronicles of the history of New Mexico, the *relaciones* written by Nuño de Guzmán, Cabeza de Vaca, Fray Marcos, and many others. These spaces, representing, as we have seen, deracination as well as plenitude, are the textual dwelling places of cultural exchange and transformation. They localize the play of differences (and of *différances*) on the cutting edge of New World culture.

The textual fissures also ensure the continuation of that play of differences beyond the text in the eyes of the reader and thus prevent the poem from freezing into the shape of an allegedly definitive meaning. The kinetic properties of *Dimensions of History* are best illustrated by the words of another apprentice: the Peruvian novelist and anthropologist José María Arguedas. These are the words of Arguedas's young protagonist as he *beholds* (in Stevens's sense) the remnants of the ancient Inca walls of Cuzco:

The stones of the Inca wall were larger and stranger than I had imagined; they seemed to be bubbling up beneath the whitewashed second story. . . . Then I remembered the Quechua songs which

continually repeat one pathetic phrase: *yawar mayu*, "bloody river";
yawar unu, "bloody water"; *puk'tik yawar k'ocha*, "bloody boiling
lake"; *yawar wek'e*, "bloody tears." Couldn't one say *yawar rumi*,
"bloody stone," or *puk'tik yawar rumi*, "boiling bloody stone"? The
wall was stationary, but all its lines were seething and its surface was as
changeable as that of the flowing summer rivers which have similar
crests near the center, where the current flows the swiftest and is the
most terrifying. The Indians call these muddy rivers *yawar mayu*
because when the sun shines on them they seem to glisten like blood.
They also call the most violent tempo of the war dances, the moment
when the dancers are fighting, *yawar mayu*.[137]

The text(ure) of *Dimensions of History* is, in many respects, like that of
the old Inca wall, whose ruins provided the foundations upon which the
Spaniards rebuilt Cuzco: The poem is stationary like a wall, but the
pattern forming on its surface as the result of Wright's interweaving
bloodlines from so many different sources is ever-changing. *To make a
stone bleed* is an appropriate figure for investing what is generally consid-
ered an inanimate object with its history and to give it, as Lezama Lima
would have it, new metaphorical strength.[138] In this regard, a bleeding
stone is like a germinating seed. Arguedas's "bloody stone" also recalls the
figure of the altar as a place characterized by the commingling of the
blood of the living with that of the dead, that is, as a place of ritual
exchange and revitalization. Wright visualizes the ruins of Hawikúh as
such a place or space, but there are, as we will see shortly, many other
stones on which his poet cuts his time. What Arguedas's protagonist finds
in Cuzco, Wright's poet now experiences among the ruins of the Aztec
city-states in Mexico.

I lay my pyramids wall upon wall.
The walls recall the war of Venus and Mars.
Four days I sat without a sun.
I build that darkness here.
And at the top I place my sun god
and his promise of the years.
Fifty-two serpents wind the years
around my knees. The walls contain me.

And so, in fever, I walk the city's wall.
In the Cathedral, I walk upon
the distinguished dead.
Marble, cal y canto, stone,
cathedral born to Carlos Fifth.
I name you Santa Catalina Alejandrina,

I name you the Cathedral of Cartagena de Indias.
Would the maimed one fill you with light?
Would your Virgin and your Child fall from cedar?
Mozarabic crowns of fragile silver
            would become you. (*DH*, 98)

As Wright points out in the notes, the first stanza of this quotation draws heavily on Aztec (Náhua) mythology. More specifically, it explores the Náhua concept of time and history as manifest in the ancient *Leyenda de los Soles* [Legend of the Suns], which recounts the myth of the creation and subsequent destruction of the world at the end of each of four fifty-two-year cycles. According to Náhua chronology, fifty-two years constitute one century or age in world history.[139] The cataclysm at the end of each cycle is said to be the result of an ongoing struggle for supremacy among the four sons of Ometéotl, the god of duality and principal deity of the Náhuas. The Fifth Cycle of the Sun, presumed to be the present age, is characterized by a harmony between these contending gods, each of whom represents one of the four cosmic forces: earth, water, air, and fire. As long as this balance of forces, in which exactly thirteen years are allotted to each deity, remains undisturbed, the world will not be subject to another apocalypse.

The profound significance the Náhuas attributed to these cycles of creation, destruction, and reconstruction, on which their calendar is based, is also reflected in their architecture. The Aztec temple-pyramids constitute, in Wright's terminology, the "physical dimension" of Náhua historico-mythical thought. "I lay my pyramids wall upon wall" refers specifically to the fact that these temple-pyramids were built by superimposing new levels at the beginning of each fifty-two-year cycle. The same principle underlies Williams's big, square paragraphs in "The Destruction of Tenochtitlan." The best example of that architectural technique is the Pyramid of Tenayuca near Tenochtitlán, the ancient Aztec capital. Archaeologists have suggested that the huge double pyramid of Tenochtitlán, which was almost completely destroyed by Cortés and his men, had been built in the same manner.[140] Wright's allusions to Tenochtitlán are related to the above quotation from *Deep Rivers*: In the same way that modern Cuzco was built upon the ruins of the ancient Inca capital, Mexico City was erected on the former site of Tenochtitlán. Both cities constitute another wall or level superimposed on the previous ones to mark the end of one era and the beginning of another. For Wright, as for Williams, this architectonic phenomenon indicates the superimposition of one culture upon another, a practice whose visible, physical results inadvertently bear witness to the surreptitious, and subversive, continuation of the Náhua tradition in modern Mexico.

That these "walls recall the war of Venus and Mars" opens our view onto another chapter in Náhua history as well as introduces another series of mythological dimensions. This line is not just a general reference to the above-mentioned struggle between the four gods or cosmic forces but points specifically to the conflict between Quetzalcóatl, the plumed serpent, and Huitzilopochtli, the Aztec God of War. The former is associated with Venus, the "Big Star,"[141] while the latter, who came to replace Quetzalcóatl and inaugurated a reign of bloodshed and warfare (the era of the so-called flowered wars), is frequently identified as the "Mexican Mars."[142] Huitzilopochtli was, in that sense, the eagle (the symbol of war) that "swallow[ed] a [plumed] serpent's heart" (*DH*, 99), which is, furthermore, an allusion to the practice of human sacrifice that escalated among the Aztecs during the reign of the War God and constituted the prime motivation behind the warfare with their neighbors. But there is more: It can be said that, after the mysterious disappearance of Quetzalcóatl, Tenochtitlán became the City of Mars, which is also the name for Rome in the *Aeneid*. Romulus and Remus were, of course, the twin sons of Mars whose city, founded by Romulus and consecrated with the blood of his brother, displaced Lavinium, the city founded by Aeneas, son of Venus. The link Wright establishes here between Rome and Tenochtitlán substantiates my earlier argument concerning the analogy between the decline of the Roman Empire and the destruction of the pre-Columbian cultures in the New World. Both events, almost exactly a millennium apart in conventional historical chronology, mark the beginning of a new era, of a new cycle, which is that of the Fifth Sun, figured here as "Carlos Fifth," who is Charles I of Spain, also known as Charles V of the Empire.

Given that Charles V was the emperor in whose name the conquistadors took possession of the overseas territories, Wright's mention of his name as well as his curious association with the cycle of the Fifth Sun is not surprising, particularly since the Aztecs had initially believed the Spaniard to be a reincarnation of Quetzalcóatl, sending his messengers to restore peace. The "cathedral born to Carlos Fifth" is situated in Santafé de Bogotá. The site for this first cathedral in the New Kingdom of Granada was staked out on the same day (6 August 1539) that Jiménez de Quesada, Nicolás Federmann, and Sebastián de Benalcázar founded Santafé de Bogotá in the name of the emperor. Rodríguez Freyle recounts this event in *El carnero*: "The city they baptized Santafé de Bogotá del Nuevo Reino de Granada: the Granada in tribute to the said Jiménez de

Quesada, its first founder, who hailed from Granada in Spain, Santafé because in its setting it resembled the town of that name facing Granada, and Bogotá from its arising on the site of the *cacique's* [the Indian chief's] retreat."[143] *El carnero* is relevant to our reading of Wright's text not only as a source book that details this and other incidents from the history of New Granada, today's Colombia. It is also the first history of New Granada, which was in addition written by an American (a *criollo*)—incidentally, around the same time that the second volume of the *Comentarios reales* appeared in Spain. Both *El carnero* and the *Comentarios* deliberately deviate from the ideal of Renaissance historiography as practiced by the official Spanish court historians. They concentrate on those "spaces" between the lines that were filled, not with heroic deeds, but with stories of everyday events in the colonies; with details, in short, that were either not known to the official chroniclers or considered irrelevant by them. Among these tales in *El carnero* is the story of Juana García discussed earlier. It is this deviant, subversive mode of historiography that Wright's *Dimensions of History* shares with *El carnero*, which may indeed be described, among many other things, as a history of the lives of the "distinguished dead" who are buried in the Cathedral of Bogotá.

It is not without interest, nor entirely without irony, that Wright's poet should dedicate this cathedral to Saint Catherine of Alexandria— "Santa Catalina Alejandrina"—one of the first Christian martyrs decapitated by the Romans and venerated as the patron saint of philosophers, as well as name it "the Cathedral of Cartagena de Indias" in reference to one of the major colonial ports and early commercial centers in the New World. The significance of these names may be sought, and perhaps found, in the fact that the conquest of the New World was a joint venture of church and state, combining the missionary spirit of the Catholic church in Spain with the obsession of the Spanish Empire to enhance its "Mozarabic crowns of fragile silver" with the splendor of "gold and emeralds" from the New World. The "Mozarabic crowns" also evoke the Arabic elements that continued to influence Spanish architecture in the New World, specifically in New Granada (the old Granada with its famous Alhambra was the last Muslim stronghold on the Iberian Peninsula).

But the most remarkable part of the second stanza is the line "Marble, cal y canto, stone," which repeats the Nerudean thrust of "I lay my pyramids wall upon wall": "Piedra en piedra, el hombre, dónde estuve?" [Stone upon stone, and man, where was he?] Neruda exclaims in his *Heights of Macchu Picchu* (1945).[144] The following lines from the same poem constitute a sort of answer to this question, but, more importantly, they help us understand the full significance of the figure of the city as a coherent cultural landscape.

Pero una permanencia de piedra y de palabra,
la ciudad como un vaso se levantó en las manos
de todos, vivos, muertos, callados, sostenidos
de tanta muerte, un muro, de tanta vida un golpe
de pétalos de piedra: la rosa permanente, la morada:
este arrecife andino de colonias glaciales.

Cuando la mano de color de arcilla
se convirtió en arcilla, y cuando los pequeños párpados se cerraron
llenos de ásperos muros, poblado de castillos,
y cuando todo el hombre se enredó en su agujero,
quedó la exactitud enarbolada:
el alto sitio de la aurora humana:
la más alta vasija que contuvo el silencio:
una vida de piedra después de tantas vidas.

[Yet a permanence of stone and word,
the city like a bowl, rose up in the hands
of all, living, dead, silenced, sustained,
a wall out of so much death, out of so much life a shock
of stone petals, the permanent rose, the dwelling place:
the glacial outposts on this Andean reef.

When the clay-colored hand
turned to clay and the eyes' small lids fell shut,
filled with rugged walls, crowded with castles,
and when man lay all tangled in his hole,
there remained an upraised exactitude:
the high site of the human dawn:
the highest vessel that held silence in:
a life of stone after so many lives.][145]

Macchu Picchu, Cuzco, Tenochtitlán—lives of stone, stone petals, bloody stones—are permanent, not because they are monuments frozen in time, but because they continue in silence the movements of the lives they embody. They are solid—"cal y canto"—yet they move. Wright's use of "cal y canto" has the same kinetic effect as Arguedas's "bloody stone." In the same way that the semantic properties of "bloody stone" are deeply entrenched in the Quechua language, "cal y canto," although a Spanish idiom, recaptures one of the most distinctive rhetorical features of the Náhuatl language: the practice of *difrasismo*: "[*Difrasismo*] is a procedure in which a single idea is expressed by two words, which in a way complement one another, either because they are synonymous or because they are placed next to each other. Several examples in Spanish will more suitably illustrate this: 'a tontas y a locas' [recklessly]; 'a sangre y fuego' [by blood and fire]; 'contra viento y marea' [against wind and tide; against all odds]: 'a pan y agua' [on bread and water]; etc. This mode of expression is rare in our languages, but quite common in Náhuatl."[146] Wright's "cal y canto" is a figure for infusing solidity with movement, for creating, as Neruda has it, "a permanence of stone and word," or in other words, a city. *Difrasismo*, according to Garibay a characteristic expression of the fundamental dualism that lies at the heart of Náhua thought, can be described as the art of *thinking in twos* ("We dream in twos,/strict destiny, the two in one" [*DH*, 24]), of making two different things cohere by placing them next to one another and charting the manner in which they interact. This process is at once subversive and supplementary: *Canto* (song), for instance, is clearly not synonymous with *cal* (mortar) but supplements it by creating a deficiency (*cal* alone does not mean "solidly"), a space that has to be filled in order for the idiom to attain its full meaning. But in the process, *canto* also achieves a certain degree of synonymity with *cal*, and vice versa, which is particularly relevant in the context of the above citation from *Dimensions of History*. If mortar is a substance that literally fills the spaces between the individual stones in a wall (or between marble and stone, as the case may be), that joins them together, then "song" accomplishes the same on the metaphoric level. Song, that is to say, poetry (which the Náhuas, in another *difrasismo*, call "flower and song"), is Wright's mortar, that which holds the textual construction together. It is the way in which the "stones" are put together that determines the architecture of Wright's cities and thus the degree of their "enchantment." "Cal y canto" is another one of Wright's figures of writing, which is best translated as "enchanted mortar."

Architecture, like poetry, translates temporal (that is, historical) relations into spatial configurations. This analogy is particularly applicable to the final section of *Dimensions of History*. The most notable formal aspect of "Landscapes: The Physical Dimension" is the way in which the poetic text is strewn with passages that read like encyclopedia entries. Each of these five passages, which vary in length, lists some of the main geographical, economic, and historical features of one particular New World country: Venezuela, Colombia, Panamá, Mexico, and the United States, respectively. Between these block entries, which represent what I have previously termed the Library, the text of the poem winds like a vast stream of images, filling the spaces between these curious "stones" with an intricate web of relationships far beyond the reach of the collections of topographical data they embody. The layout of this section leaves no doubt that these extended spaces between the encyclopedic "stones," frozen into questionable objectivity, are far more important to the poet than the individual "stones" themselves. They belong to a complex whole that is clearly larger than the sum of its parts.

As parts of Wright's poetic landscape, the encyclopedic monoliths formally represent what Wilson Harris has called the "enormous *callouses* and conceits of power in our age*,*" in the midst of which "there continues a complex descent into forces of conscience." Harris continues, "That complex descent into the modern age is less than 500 years old. It scarcely yet possesses criteria of evaluation though I would suggest such criteria must accept the deep fact that all images (or institutions or rituals) are partial, are ceaselessly unfinished in their openness to other partial images from apparently strange cultures within an unfathomable, and a dynamic, spirit of wholeness that sustains all our hopes of the regeneration of far-flung community in an interdependent world."[147] Harris, like Auerbach before him, calls for a mobilization of all the rich tensions each individual is capable of accommodating within the diverse layers of his or her cultural personality. Both Harris and Wright demand that these tensions and frictions be articulated and experienced as something positive, rather than being subjected to, and at least partially leveled by, the kind of intellectual and emotional censorship that comes with the extension of political nationalism to the sphere of culture. Cultural nationalism, as useful and as necessary an ideological tool as it may have been to reinforce the desire for political independence in the Third World, must give way to a vision of cultural interdependence in order to counteract what Harris has aptly termed "illiteracy of the imagination." That illiteracy may be defined as a narcissistic inability (or unwillingness) to experience cultural cross-fertilization through an active probing of the depths of otherness that lie beneath the shallow surfaces of the Ego. Wright's poems, it is safe to say, are figures of a *literate* imagination, taking the form of a language generated by the poet's acute experience of self-division (or hyphenation) as a gift. That gift enables him to remain open to all the different and conflicting aspects of the New World's complex cultural heritage. It also enables him to intuit and articulate mutuality between cultural spaces miles and centuries apart, yet present in the living strata of his exterior and interior geography. In *Dimensions of History,* as well as in *The Double Invention of Komo* and *Explications/Interpretations,* this fundamental openness is manifest in the

ceaseless play of substitutions representing an amazing proliferation of
cultural identities or, again in Harris's words, "a visualization of roots
beyond roots, a visualization of unfathomably rich potential that tor-
ments yet overjoys."[148] To achieve a creative coexistence of those man-
ifold cultural identities, is, for Wright, the major "task in a new land"
(DH, 20). The fulfillment of this momentous task is what liberates him
and his language from the intellectual and emotional strictures of in-
stitutionalized culture. At the same time, this freedom is what lends
authority to his writing.

Dimensions of History shows with utmost clarity that Wright envisions
New World literature as an "accumulation / of all that we have suffered
and won" (DH, 12). Losses and gains figure equally in the articulation of
this new cultural space, opened up by exile as a form of geographical,
historical, and mythological displacement. Since the inevitable result of
such a violent act of displacement is, as we have seen, a kind of deracina-
tion, or razing, it is understandable that, especially in Afro-American
literature, this new space was frequently visualized as a sort of no man's
land, a barren desert and a perilous wilderness. It is this (limbo) area of
uncertainties that Wright sets out to cultivate: "all the powers lying
dead,/with no one to transform them" (DH, 33). His method of cultiva-
tion is a process of threading the fragments of countless myths dispersed
by history into a new tapestry, a map that charts the New World's cultural
and literary tradition of exile. This dynamic construct is a mythological
field constituted by clusters of tropes that merge into, and emanate from,
one master trope: that of the city. Wright's city as a cultural landscape is
"blood given bodily form" (DH, 12), the physical embodiment of tradi-
tion, whose architecture is also an arche-texture: a rainbow arc (as in
Harris) or a palpitating bridge (as in Paz) extending across ideological
divides that segregate so-called cultural majorities from minorities and
one ethnic group from another.

This arc or bridge as a figure for mutuality culminates at the end of
Dimensions of History with the poet's arrival at the ancient Mayan city of
Labná.

And I return now to my city at Labná.
It has been a long march.
I am half-naked.
I retain no more than a band
about my head, and a band about my waist,
my sandals on my feet,
my home-spun mantle and a pouch

for the gods' bones.
But I am victorious.
I march from the humble
to the sacred side of the city.
I enter where I return.
I return again to the land of the star.
There is peace in this elevation.
You come, if not to God,
near to yourself.
It is a star land, a golden land,
our dark and true light,
the image of our life among ourselves. (*DH*, 103–4)

Unlike Tenochtitlán, Cuzco, Macchu Picchu, Cartagena, and Bogotá, Labná is not fortified; it has no walls. Curiously enough, however, it does have a gate in the form of a triumphal arc, which formerly linked the two parts of the city. The Great Gate of Labná synecdochically suggests the existence of a wall that joins rather than divides, and it is this gate that Wright offers as his final "image of our life among ourselves." Redressed as a gateway to the beautiful, this triumphal arc is Wright's ultimate "emblem of the ecstatic connection" (*DH*, 34). Celebrating the triumph of Wright's synthetic approach to New World writing, this emblem embodies a profound poetic dialogue at the crossroads of various Western and non-Western cultures, a dialogue that includes Williams's *In the American Grain* and Guillén's *El diario*. Wright's is a poetic voice that speaks, paradoxically but most effectively, "without song," and in doing so, it brings about "sea-changes" that are "waterless."

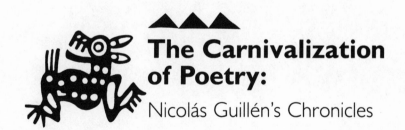

The Carnivalization
of Poetry:
Nicolás Guillén's Chronicles

In Cuba,
Black Melchior caresses the cobra.
— JAY WRIGHT, *Dimensions of History*

Nicolás Guillén has been called the greatest living poet in the Hispanic world. His work, unlike that of Jay Wright, has been read widely, and translations of his poetry have appeared in several languages.[1] At the same time, however, Guillén seems to be one of the most misread and misunderstood poets of our times, and in that respect, his fate has been similar to Wright's. Cuba's *poeta nacional* and president of the National Writers' Union (UNEAC), Guillén has always been closely associated with the ideological movement that prepared the path for the Cuban Revolution in 1959. In fact, many of the collections of poems he wrote and published during the prerevolutionary period, including *Motivos de son* [*Son* Motifs] (1930), *Sóngoro cosongo* (1931), *West Indies, Ltd.* (1934), *Cantos para soldados y sones para turistas* [Songs for Soldiers and Sones for Tourists] (1937), *El son entero* [The Whole Son] (1947), *Elegías* [Elegies] (1948–1958), and *La paloma de vuelo popular* [The Dove of Popular Flight] (1958), have mostly been regarded, by literary critics both within and without Latin America, as sociopolitical prophecies largely fulfilled by the achievements of the Castro regime. Guillén himself celebrates the accomplishments of the revolution, set off against the backdrop of various forms of United States imperialism, in such works as *Tengo* [I Have] (1964), *El gran zoo* [The Great Zoo] (1967), *La rueda dentada* [The Gear] (1972), and *El diario que a diario* [The Daily Daily] (1972). It is not surprising, then, that he has frequently been described as an "avowed Marxist poet" and that, consequently, the majority of critical studies of his poetry have been aimed at "an apprehension of the unified, firm ideological content of his poetry."[2]

The results, especially of the most recent studies, must be disappointing to anyone for whom the step from calling Guillén a bona fide Marxist to subjecting his poetry to the approach known as Marxist literary criticism is not "natural," logical, or inevitable.[3] Traditional Marxist approaches to literature, useful as they are in calling attention to the socioeconomic and political aspects of literary production, have not, for the most part, been very successful in reconciling strictly defined ideological assumptions with the fact that literature frequently mediates between different kinds of realities rather than reflecting any one particular reality. While there is no doubt that Guillén's political commitment to Marxism and to the objectives of the Cuban Revolution lends a certain thematic coherence to his journalistic writings and his poetry, this coherence is as superficial as it is obvious. We need not question the sincerity of Guillén's ideological stance (although one would be quite justified in questioning if the adjective "Marxist" fully captures that stance) to acknowledge that there is also another side to his poetry. This side, which my following readings will explore in detail, eludes categories such as the solid rationality Ellis so readily ascribes to Guillén's work.[4] Almost all aspects of Guillén's poetry are deeply rooted in the cross-cultural imagination of the Caribbean—*mestizaje*, as Guillén himself has called it—and the resistance to any kind of dogmatism is an important part of that historical legacy. At the same time, its exploration requires perhaps even more of a willing suspension of disbelief on the part of an English-speaking North American audience than any of the poet's direct or indirect socialist pronouncements.

Very little attention has been paid to this imaginative dimension of Guillén's poetry and to the way in which it effectively sustains his anti-imperialistic posture by calling for artistic and ideological freedom. It is true that Guillén's poetry is permeated by a keen sense of history, but one must also note that history, for Guillén, as for Wright and Williams, is more than simply the manifestation of a dialectical process underlying a chronology of dates and events. I will argue that this "more" has everything to do with the way in which Guillén embraces the Afro-American elements in Hispanic-Caribbean culture. The following remarks from Lydia Cabrera's introduction to her famous *El monte* (1954) help clarify Guillén's position: "There is no doubt," Cabrera writes, "that 'Cuba is the whitest island in the Caribbean.' But the impact of the African influence on that population which regards itself as white, is nonetheless immeasurable, although a superficial glance may not discern this. You will not be able to understand our people without knowing the blacks. That influence is even more evident today than it was in colonial times. We cannot penetrate much of Cuban life without considering that African presence, which does not manifest itself in skin-color alone."[5] Evidence of the same conviction abounds in Guillén's poetry. As he insists in his "Prólogo" to *Sóngoro cosongo*: "The African injection [*inyección africana*] in this country is so profound and in our well-irrigated social hydrography so many bloodlines [*corrientes capilares*] crisscross that one would have to be a miniaturist to unravel that hieroglyph."[6] In the same vein, the poem "Llegada" [Arrival], which opens *Sóngoro cosongo*, proclaims, "Traemos / nuestro rasgo al perfil definitivo de América" [We bring / our features to the final profile of America] (*OP*, 1:116). Guillén himself has declared on various occasions that Negritude, or *negrismo*, the movement of which especially his first two books of poems are generally considered part, can be explained as a vindication of the artistic, political, cultural, and humanistic values of the Afro-American community and as such as a manifestation of class struggle.[7] We have to be careful, however, to add that this statement is directed primarily against the kind of nostalgia that informs the idea of black culture's superiority put forth by poets like Léopold Sédar Senghor.

René Depestre, in an excellent short essay entitled "Orfeo negro" [Black Orpheus] (1969), addresses the controversial question of Guillén's relationship with Negritude and convincingly suggests that

in order to answer this question in the affirmative, it is necessary, above all, to strip the concept of Negritude of the frequently ambiguous, contradictory character it has in the work of some black poets. If Negritude is understood as the nostalgia for a lost innocence, as a metaphysical feeling similar to that of original sin, then this concept is not applicable to the work of Nicolás Guillén. But if, in contrast, Negritude is regarded as an active state [of consciousness] that integrates itself with the movement of the history of black peoples, then it is legitimate to speak of the exemplary Negritude of Guillén. . . . In Guillén's poetry, the notion of Negritude has lost its metaphysical character to become incorporated into a philosophy of historical initiative [or action].[8]

Guillén's poems, including those written after the Cuban Revolution, clearly indicate a concern for the distinctive features of Afro-American culture and its contributions, not only to Caribbean and Latin American culture, but in fact to all New World cultures. For him as a writer, one of the most important aspects of that contribution are the myths that nourish the historical imagination of Afro-Americans and that have become part of the rich cultural endowment particularly, but not exclusively, of the Caribbean. There would be no disagreement on that issue between Guillén and Wilson Harris, or Jay Wright for that matter. To deprive Guillén's poetry, prerevolutionary or postrevolutionary, of that mythological dimension for the sole purpose of distilling from it the already fairly obvious essence of the poet's political and ideological commitment presents not only a serious disservice to his literary achievements but a gross injustice to Cuba's, and the Hispanic Caribbean's, cultural heritage and potential.

I have earlier quoted Wilson Harris's remarks on the project of reassembling the dead muse or god as a new foundation for New World writing. While it is safe to assume that Guillén would not put it in quite those terms, his poetry is still an attempt to do precisely that: to assemble or reassemble a muse. Hence his keen sense of history. His poetry is neither a prophecy nor an uncritical celebration of the Cuban Revolution but a warning, subtle as it may be, that without such a foundation (or what I have previously termed a reliable repository of meaning), this or any revolution cannot, in the long run, be successfully sustained. If the voluntary exile of Cuban writers such as Severo Sarduy, Guillermo Cabrera Infante, César Leante, Antonio Benítez-Rojo, and Reynaldo Arenas, to mention only a few, is any indication of the failure of Cuba's cultural and political institutions to acknowledge, let alone fulfill, that fundamental need, then Guillén's poems could easily become a prophecy of a very different kind.

To substantiate this claim, which goes very much against the grain of most previous assessments of Guillén's work, I would like to begin with a poem whose treatment at the hands of a variety of critics and reviewers is highly disputable. This poem, "Sensemayá: Canto para matar una culebra" [Chant for Killing a Snake], is one of Guillén's most popular pieces for recital to the drum.[9] It first appeared in *West Indies, Ltd.* (1934), a collection of poems which occupies a central position in the context of Guillén's *oeuvre* because it contains, in embryo, all of the major forms and themes elaborated in his later books.[10] The same is true of "Sensemayá" itself, which is hardly the kind of innocuous and playful folkloristic poem most critics have made it out to be.[11] Keith Ellis is closer to the mark than previous readers when he suggests that "the poem's atmosphere is so charged with emotion . . . that the poem becomes too imposing, and the effort excessively serious, for the mere killing of a snake. This excess suggests that the act has a function of greater significance. It seems to be representative of something, the identity of which has to be sought in the images of the poem."[12] "Sensemayá" is indeed "an allegory of the need for, and the means of, definitive liberation,"[13] but Ellis unfortunately fails to understand what exactly those "means" are. According to him, "The snake in 'Sensemayá' is a symbol of imperialism," which, as I intend to demonstrate, is not the case at all. In fact, quite the opposite is true. In preparation for my argument, it is necessary to examine both the structural and the semantic rhythms of the poem.

¡Mayombe-bombe-mayombé!
¡Mayombe-bombe-mayombé!
¡Mayombe-bombe-mayombé!

La culebra tiene los ojos de vidrio;
la culebra viene y se enreda en un palo;

con sus ojos de vidrio, en un palo,
con sus ojos de vidrio.

La culebra camina sin patas;
la culebra se esconde en la yerba;
caminando se esconde en la yerba,
caminando sin patas.

¡Mayombe-bombe-mayombé!
¡Mayombe-bombe-mayombé!
¡Mayombe-bombe-mayombé! (*OP*, 1: 147–48)

[The snake has eyes of glass;
The snake comes and wraps itself around a pole;
with its glass eyes, around a pole,
with its glass eyes.

The snake walks without legs;
the snake hides in the grass;
walking it hides in the grass;
walking without legs.]

The extent to which this poem relies on the interplay between poetic
imagery and assonant / alliterative drum sequences, which are not, as we
shall see, purely onomatopoeic, is evident from the above citation,
which introduces a familiar responsorial pattern that determines the
relationship between the individual stanzas. This pattern culminates in
the intense antiphonal juxtapositions of drum and chant in the final
stanza:

¡Mayombe-bombe-mayombé!
Sensemayá, la culebra . . .
¡Mayombe-bombe-mayombé!
Sensemayá, no se mueve . . .
¡Mayombe-bombe-mayombé!
Sensemayá, la culebra . . .
¡Mayombe-bombe-mayombé!
Sensemayá, se murió. (*OP*, 1: 148–49)

[Mayombe-bombe-mayombé!
Sensemayá, the snake . . .
Mayombe-bombe-mayombé!
Sensemayá, does not move . . .
Mayombe-bombe-mayombé!

Sensemayá, the snake . . .
Mayombe-bombe-mayombé!
Sensemayá, is dead.]

It ought to be stressed that the poem's phonetic and syntactic rhythms do not merely accompany the "chant"; in other words, its form is not subordinate to its content. Instead, those rhythms have a specific rhetorical function in that they formally establish an already highly referential setting for the poetic narrative, that is, the description of the snake and its death. The particular ways in which this setting, or frame, interacts with, and at appropriate moments interrupts, the poem's narrative flow is essential to the metaphoric processes at work in "Sensemayá." The poem's imagery is generated by the oxymoron of stasis and movement that is prefigured, and, in a sense, rendered visible, by the tensions that determine the poem's formal design. At the same time that the snake's impenetrable and expressionless "eyes of glass" evoke an image of transfixed immobility suggesting death, the poem's compelling rhythmic movements are immediately translated into a kinetic trope, that of the snake "walking without legs," which recalls Wright's speaking "without song." The ambiguities engendered by the contradictory relation between those two images are then inscribed in an emblematic figure: the serpent wrapping itself around a stick. This emblem is the clue to "Sensemayá."

The snake wrapped around a stick is clearly suggestive of the Aesculapian staff, the ideogrammatic signature of the medical profession derived from Aesculapius, the god of medicine and healing in Greek mythology. This reference is crucial to the function of this emblem in the poem. The snake wrapping itself around a stick is a trope for the poetic process itself, that is, for the process of figuration. It is at once sign and referent, self-referential as well as extra-referential, in that it refers to itself as both product and process. Furthermore, its association with healing places this trope in close proximity to the Derridean / Platonic concept of the *pharmakon* as a figure of writing.[14] This connection is substantiated by the fact that the *pharmakon* is fraught with the same kinds of contradictions and ambiguities as the Aesculapian insignia in "Sensemayá," emerging as they do from the tensions between two different kinds of movements that occur simultaneously: One is that of the poetic narrative, moving in linear fashion toward the kind of closure signified by the serpent's death. The other, disrupting and counteracting this linearity, may be called ritualistic and is determined largely by the pounding repetitions of "Mayombe-bombe-mayombé," which resist death and thus

defer poetic closure. In the same way, the *pharmakon* vacillates seman-
tically between negative and positive attributes: It is both poison and
cure. Like Guillén's emblem of the serpent wrapped around a stick, the
pharmakon incorporates both. Finally, Guillén's use of "mayombe,"
derived from the Cuban *mayombero*, which, according to Fernando
Ortiz, is the name for an Afro-Cuban conjurer (*brujo*) from the Congo
region,[15] allows us to establish a link between Greek, West African, and
Afro-American mythologies, as well as to connect the double concepts of
cure and poison with the idea of *magic*. All of these linkages are relevant
to Guillén's poetic ritual of killing a snake.

According to Fernando Ortiz, *matar la culebra* is an Afro-Cuban
dance performed on the "Día de Reyes."[16] I have already commented on
the significance of the "Día de Reyes" in connection with *Dimensions of
History*, however without mentioning the specific ritual to which Wright
also alludes. On the "Día de Reyes" the blacks, in celebration of their
temporary freedom, used to carry through the streets of Havana an enor-
mous artificial snake, several meters in length, stopping at the houses to
request their Christmas bonus (*aguinaldo*). This procession, as Ortiz
further explains, was a kind of ritual pantomime representing the killing
of a snake, a practice suggestive of various snake cults not only in Africa
but also in Asia and Europe (such as, for instance, the cult of the sacred
serpent of Delphi to which Wright refers). It is interesting that the day on
which Guillén wrote "Sensemayá" was, as he reported in a radio talk
quoted by Ángel Augier, incidentally the day on which the "Día de
Reyes" festivities were held in colonial times. Ellis mentions this in
passing, without deeming Guillén's account at all relevant to a reading of
the poem.[17] This dismissal is perplexing, because without being pre-
scriptive in any way, Guillén offers several important clues to "Sen-
semayá."

I remember the day on which I wrote it ["Sensemayá"] without really
intending to, without ever having thought about doing it: It was
January 6, 1932, the "Día de Reyes." I was in bed sick in a Havana
hotel on San Rafael Street where I was staying. Perhaps the enforced
idleness gave wings to my thoughts and took me back to my
childhood. Ever since I had been a child, in my native Camagüey, a
Negro song kept resounding in my mind, a popular song, composed
for killing snakes: "Sámbala, culembe, sámbala culembe, sámbala
culembe. . . ." How, why did this come to my mind then? Perhaps
because I had been reading parts of Fernando Ortiz's work on the
black sorcerers; perhaps because of the prestige of that day, the "Día de
Reyes," evoking events from colonial Cuba. The hoped-for day, the
one, the great, the magnificent day when the black slaves received

from their white masters permission for each one to feel like he was in his home country and to sing and dance in the company of his family and his tribe and worship his gods and be again the vassal of his king.[18]

Treated as a literary document rather than as a purely factual account of the circumstances that led to the composition of "Sensemayá," Guillén's reminiscences legitimize my previous references to Ortiz— what Guillén was reading at the time was *Los negros brujos*—as well as open another dimension of the poem that seems to have eluded previous readers. On the one hand, "Sensemayá" seeks to reenact an ancestral ritual designed to reaffirm and strengthen the slaves' ties with their African heritage. *Matar la culebra*, as Ortiz informs us, is also synonymous with the Spanish expression "matar el tiempo," to kill time. In the ritualistic context of the "Día de Reyes," *killing time* is equivalent to *keeping time*, that is, to keeping alive a tradition in the timeless space of ritual. As I have pointed out in Part 2, ritual performances such as the "Día de Reyes" celebration and the "Son de la Ma' Teodora" open up mythical spaces where the fiction of being and thus of culture can be entertained, if only temporarily. While Wright employs textual gaps to represent such spaces, Guillén in this instance resorts to rhythmic repetition, which systematically breaks up the poetic narrative and thus momentarily arrests the linear flow of time. The result is a synchronization of textual movements that is transferred from the structural level of the poem to the historical, cultural, and political relationships it seeks to articulate. Precisely what those relationships are becomes evident when we recall, again with Ortiz, that the "Día de Reyes" procession in Havana traditionally began and ended in front of the governor's palace, the official seat of the highest local representative of the colonial administration. This set-up immediately suggests a confrontation of the temporarily freed slaves with the colonial authorities responsible for their bondage. Although the "Día de Reyes" is, in a sense, a manifestation of the way in which the clash between the slaves' desire for freedom and oppressive authority had become a carefully controlled, institutionalized game with clearly delineated rules, designed to avert the pending threat of slave insurrections, we cannot altogether ignore the fact that this carnivalesque ritual had distinct subversive undertones, at least from the perspective of the blacks.

This same subversiveness is one of the most significant features of "Sensemayá." The ambiguities of the "Día de Reyes" as a cultural institution, prefigured in the poem's vacillations between motion and stasis, life and death, generate a message similar to the one articulated in the famous execution scene from *The Kingdom of This World*, Alejo Carpentier's most explicit homage to the slave revolts in the Caribbean.

His waist girded by striped pants, bound with ropes and knots, his skin gleaming with recent wounds, Mackandal was moving toward the center of the square. The masters' glances questioned the faces of the slaves. But the Negroes showed spiteful indifference. What did the whites know of Negro matters? In his cycle of metamorphoses, Mackandal had often entered the mysterious world of insects, making up for the lack of his human arm with possession of several feet, four wings, or long antennae. . . . At the decisive moment, the bonds of the Mandingue, no longer having a body to bind, would trace the shape of a man of air for a second before they slipped down the post. And Mackandal, transformed into a buzzing mosquito, would land on the very tricorne of the commander of the troops to laugh at the dismay of the whites. This was what their masters did not know; for that reason they had squandered so much money putting on this useless show, which would prove how completely helpless they were against a man protected by the great Loas.
  Mackandal was now lashed to the post. The executioner had picked up an ember with the tongs. With a gesture rehearsed the evening before in front of the mirror, the Governor unsheathed his dress sword and gave the order for the sentence to be carried out. The fire began to rise toward the One-Armed, licking his legs. At that moment, Mackandal moved the stump of his arm, which they had been unable to tie up, in a threatening gesture which was none the less terrible for being partial, howling unknown spells and violently thrusting his torso forward. His bonds fell off and the body of the Negro rose in the air, flying overhead, until it plunged into the black wave of the sea of slaves. A single cry filled the square:
  "Mackandal saved!"
  Pandemonium followed. The guards fell with rifle butts on the howling blacks, who now seemed to overflow the streets. . . . And the noise and screaming and uproar was such that very few saw that Mackandal, held by ten soldiers, was thrust into the fire, and that a flame fed by his burning hair drowned his last cry.[19]

A curious relationship exists between this passage and Guillén's "Sensemayá." Not only does Mackandal's execution take place on a "Monday in January" (*El reino*, 39), that is, on a date in close proximity to the Epiphany on which the "Día de Reyes" is held. Even more important than that is the way in which Mackandal's being tied to the post reinscribes Guillén's snake ideogram and its semantic (as well as historical) tensions. Without necessarily implying any direct literary influence, these similarities nevertheless lead us to suspect that what we witness in

"Sensemayá" is not just the ritual killing of a snake but in fact the same sort of metamorphosis Carpentier describes in connection with Mackandal's death. [20] Although the black sorcerer, who, as I have argued elsewhere, is yet another manifestation of the *pharmakos*, [21] is indeed burned at the stake, his death is also a moment of triumph to the slaves: "That afternoon the slaves returned to their plantations laughing all the way. Mackandal had kept his word, remaining in the kingdom of this world. Once more the whites had been outwitted by the Mighty Powers of the Other Shore" (*El reino*, 41). By the same token, we could argue that Guillén's "Sensemayá" has succeeded in outwitting most of its readers.

If "Sensemayá" is indeed an allegory of the need for definitive freedom, then we have to take seriously the deceitful duplicity that links the killing of the snake with Mackandal's execution. Clearly, it is not Mackandal's death as such that brings about liberation. If anything, the execution would suggest the defeat of his insurrectionist schemes. Similarly, it is not the death of the serpent in "Sensemayá" that promotes freedom, but rather the slaves' ability to perform this ritual in which the snake is sacrificed to strengthen the religious beliefs of the participants and to ensure the cooperation of the gods, the "great Loas." Mackandal's "flight," a figure embodying the slaves' belief in liberation through metamorphosis, is prefigured in "Sensemayá" by the serpent's elusiveness ("the snake hides in the grass") as well as by the ambiguous properties of the Aesculapian staff. In this sense, the serpent's death at the end of the poem inscribes a figure for metamorphosis similar to that of Mackandal's "flight."

Guillén's poem is a subtle combination of the myth of flying Africans with elements from the Afro-American trickster (Anansi) tales. As such, it is part of what Harris has called the "*limbo* imagination" in New World literature. Both myths associate freedom with metamorphosis and thus emphasize deception and the subversion of oppressive authority over open vigilance. As poetic enactments of the quest for freedom-through-literacy, the liberating metamorphoses in "Sensemayá" and *The Kingdom of This World* depend on referential and semantic ambiguities as a strategy. These ambiguities ultimately reveal the death of the serpent to be as deceptive as the poem's structural and semantic dynamics have already led us to suspect. The conflict of stasis and motion, inscribed in Guillén's imagery throughout "Sensemayá," generates, if anything, more figurative (and emotional) energy and thus openly contradicts the poem's final image of death ("Sensemayá, se murió"). The serpent's death, like Mackandal's, is a transformation that signals the triumph of the poem, not over death in general, but over slavery and cultural imperialism as manifestations of death-in-life. The religio-cultural ritual and its mythological linkages are thus established as the poem's main source of authority. The tenacious ambiguities of "Sensemayá," which articulate the continuous deferral of death (and closure) through the pervasive power of the poem's structural and semantic metamorphoses, combine in the final stanza into a message that is as much of a threatening gesture as Mackandal's moving the stump of his arm, *"which they had been unable to tie up"*! This gesture in "Sensemayá" is no less powerful for being subtle.

Interestingly enough, we witness at the end of "Sensemayá," as well as in the scene of Mackandal's execution, the same kind of effacement at the moment of transformation discussed previously in connection with Hayden's "For a Young Artist" and Wright's textual clearings. While this (self)-effacement inscribed in what appears to be a closure is more obvious in the above passage from *The Kingdom of This World*, where it is directly translated into the flight metaphor, it is equally effective in Guillén's poem, where it indicates the transformation of the snake into a trope. This transfiguration is a transition from *culebra* to *culebrear* (to be evasive or elusive), in the process of which the snake's death at the narrative level confers upon the poetic text properties associated with the serpent in the context of the "Día de Reyes" ritual. This shift or transposition is already announced in the sixth stanza, where the capitalization identifying "Sensemayá" as a proper name dissolves into a lower-case spelling ("sensemayá") signaling the transition from the specific historical context of this particular ritual to a broader field of application.

Sensemayá, la culebra,
sensemayá.
Sensemayá, con sus ojos,
sensemayá.
Sensemayá, con su lengua,
sensemayá.
Sensemayá, con su boca,
sensemayá. (*OP*, 1: 148)

The broader field to which Guillén applies the "Día de Reyes" ritual is determined by the problematic relations between the United States and its Caribbean neighbors, specifically Cuba. Within this extended framework, the tensions between the Caribbean countries— "gente sencilla y tierna, descendientes de esclavos" [simple and tender people, descendants of slaves], as Guillén calls them in "West Indies, Ltd." (*OP*, 1: 159)—and the United States as a modern imperial power are brought into analogy with the historical relationships between black slaves and white masters in colonial Cuba. In this way, the "Día de Reyes" becomes a historical allegory that defines the (Hispanic) Caribbean's position vis-à-vis United States imperialism. Guillén views the "Día de Reyes" ritual as a matrix for such resistance: "Sensemayá" calls attention to the fact that these celebrations, which themselves represent the syncretic nature of Cuba's cultural makeup, constitute a carnivalesque disruption of the colonial society's economic routines as well as an at least momentary suspension of existing power structures. The presence of these subversive, carnivalesque elements below the syntactic surface of the poem is like those "venas misteriosas" [mysterious veins] that flow beneath the "geografía de nieve" [snowy geography] of the mulata's fair skin in "El abuelo" [The Grandfather]. They reveal

la dulce sombra oscura del abuelo que huye,
el que rizó por siempre tu cabeza amarilla. (*OP*, 1: 149)

[the fleeting tender dark shadow of the grandfather,
who put an indelible curl into your yellow hair.]

Like "El abuelo," "Sensemayá" is designed to raise to the level of consciousness that "tender dark shadow" looming large in Cuban (and New World) history.

René Depestre has pointed out that Guillén "is well aware that if art is a form of knowledge, it cannot simply adopt the means of philosophy, and even less those of a political pamphlet."[22] Put differently, art, in this case literature, has to be a form of historical knowledge, a medium in which history is brought to bear on the kinds of ontological questions and issues raised to a position of prominence in situations of social, cultural, and political conflict. For Guillén, as for many other Afro-American and Latin American writers, the most important of these issues is the question of Cuba's and Latin America's cultural identity and historical foundations. He contends that in attempting to resolve that question, Latin America, and in fact all other New World countries, cannot afford to ignore

que en lo hondo de ese ritmo [de su sangre europea] golpea
un negro el parcho duro de roncos atabales. (*OP*, 1: 149)

[that at the bottom of this rhythm (of her European blood), a Negro beats the tough parched skin of hoarse drums.]

It is the sound of those ancestral drums, clearly a metaphor for the figurative potential and potency of Guillén's language, that reverberates not only in "Sensemayá" but throughout *West Indies, Ltd.* to announce the flexibility of a language that may appear to be the product of a single culture (Spain) when it is actually the result of intensive cross-cultural interaction. Guillén's acute sense of history inevitably renders his poetic textures multidimensional and duplicitous, a characteristic feature of his work that manifests itself not only in an abundance of *cubanismos* but also in his ability to combine, and play off against one another, different levels of meaning and forms of discourse. This will be particularly apparent in *El diario*.

We have seen in "Sensemayá" how Guillén mobilizes a broad and intricate historico-cultural context to provide a substantive foundation for the poem's anti-imperialist allegory. This foundation is at once historical and mythical, and these two perspectives or modes of knowledge combine in the poem to create something very similar to what Carpentier has termed "lo real maravilloso," a "marvelous American reality." What is "marvelous" or magical about "Sensemayá" are emblems, such as the snake wrapping itself around a stick, that successfully mediate between history and myth. The results of such mediations are founding fables, and the "Día de Reyes" is clearly one of the most important for both Wright and Guillén.

The subtle subversion of established structures of authority in "Sensemayá" and "El abuelo" is one of the salient features of Guillén's best poems. Not surprisingly, it recurs at the very beginning of "West Indies, Ltd.," the title poem of the collection including both "Sensemayá" and "El abuelo."

¡West Indies! Nueces de coco, tabaco y aguardiente . . .
Éste es un oscuro pueblo sonriente,
conservador y liberal,
ganadero y azucarero,
donde a veces corre mucho dinero,
pero donde siempre se vive muy mal.
(Cierto que éste es un pueblo manso todavía . . .
No obstante, cualquier día
alza de un golpe la cerviz;
rompe por dondequiera con sus calludas manos
y hace como esos árboles urbanos
que arrancan toda una acera con una sola raiz.) (*OP*, 1: 158)

[West Indies! Coconuts, tobacco, and cane liquor . . .
These are dark and smiling people,
conservative and liberal,
cattlemen and sugarcane workers,
where sometimes there flows a lot of money,
but where the living is always very bad.
(No doubt these people are still meek . . .
but some day
they suddenly lift up their heads;
shatter things everywhere with calloused hands,
like those city trees
that tear out an entire sidewalk with a single root.)]

We gather from Augier's notes (*OP*, 1: 501) that the second line, "Éste es
un oscuro pueblo sonriente," which is repeated several times throughout
the poem, initially read "Éste es un oscuro pueblo impotente" in the first
edition of *West Indies, Ltd.* This change is significant especially in con-
nection with the section of the poem that appears in parentheses in the
above citation.[23] The projections in that stanza of violent upheaval, of
the sudden eruption of powers lying latent beneath the smooth surface,
hidden like the roots of a tree, enhance the effect of Guillén's decision to
substitute "sonriente" [smiling] for "impotente" [powerless]. This sub-
stitution considerably changes the tone of the poem: Far from suggesting
acceptance of or resignation to an oppressive situation, the image of
blank smiles at the beginning of "West Indies, Ltd." evokes the impen-
etrable stare of the glass-eyed serpent in "Sensemayá" and, along with it,
the same air of spiteful indifference Carpentier ascribes to the black slaves
who were watching the scene of Mackandal's execution, sure of those
hidden powers their masters could not comprehend. The ambiguity of
"sonriente," reinforced by the simultaneity of "conservador y liberal" in
the next line, recalls the same duplicitousness we encounter in Paul
Laurence Dunbar's famous poem "We Wear the Mask":

We wear the mask that grins and lies,
It hides our cheeks and shades our eyes, —
This debt we pay to human guile;
With torn and bleeding hearts we smile,
And mouth with myriad subtleties.[24]

It is those "myriad subtleties" in Guillén's poetic language that merit our
full attention, so that the "sencillez" of his poems, a concept that links

him with José Martí, not be mistaken for a lack of complexity. Guillén, like the guitar player in "José Ramón Cantaliso,"

canta liso, muy liso
para que lo entiendan bien. (*OP*, 1: 200)

[sings smoothly, very smoothly,
so that they would understand it well.]

"Canta liso" belongs in the same category with the "sonriente" of "West Indies, Ltd.": José Ramón's song to the American tourists in a Havana bar is not just smooth and gentle, pleasing to the ears of his listeners. His words and his tune are also sly and crafty, as smooth, in other words, as they are deceptive to those who do not listen closely enough to hear the singer's "voz de cancerosa entraña, / humo de solar y caña" [voice of cancerous entrails, / smoke of canefields] (*OP*, 1: 199). It is a voice soaring up from the depths of Cuban history, fragrant with the smell of burning canefields, a history that, despite, or perhaps because of, the pain and anguish it still nourishes, also serves as a foundation for the kind of dogged strength imaged as the singer's "duro espinazo insumiso" [hard unbending spine]. This same strength enables Guillén to sing smoothly, as the rhyme of "liso" with "insumiso" confirms. "José Ramón Cantaliso" captures the essence of Guillén's poetics, which is even more clearly and candidly articulated in "Mi patria es dulce por fuera" [My Country is Sweet on the Outside] in *El son entero*:

Bajo tu risa ligera, [Cuba],
yo, que te conozco tanto,
miro la sangre y el llanto,
bajo tu risa ligera. (*OP*, 1: 225)

[Beneath your superficial smile, (Cuba),
I who know you so well,
see the blood and the tears,
below your flippant smile.]

Nancy Morejón has argued that "for Guillén, Africa is neither diaspora nor metaphysical resort: rather, it is a mode of (self)-knowledge through oppression. In this sense, the plane of language becomes fundamental in that there Guillén is also, as Ezequiel Martínez Estrada has called him, 'a *mambí* of letters,' a revolutionary in relation to a language,

Spanish, that he loves and that he has molded until it became transformed into one of the most American discoveries of our times."[25] Morejón is correct in emphasizing the importance Guillén attributes to language as a form of self-knowledge, but she does not, to my mind, sufficiently acknowledge that the attitudes Guillén assumes before and within language cannot fully be grasped in purely dialectical terms. Guillén's rebellion as a poet is one that comes from within language, one that affects the deepest strata of linguistic organization to transform what used to be a vehicle for oppression and intellectual censorship into a means for liberation. That Martínez Estrada should call Guillén a "mambí de las letras" is most telling in this regard: The term *mambí* is a Cubanism referring to the veterans of the War of Independence. According to Ortiz, it probably came to Cuba from Santo Domingo where the Spaniards called *mambís* the *cimarrones* (Indian and black runaway slaves). Carefully tracing the word's African etymology, Ortiz further points out that *mambí*, in addition to being the name of a region in the former French Congo near Mayumbe, or Mayombe, signifies, in its original Congo usage, a "bad person," someone who is cruel, vicious, dangerous, malicious, etc. Slaves from the Congo, he adds, used to call the rebellious maroons *mambí*, thus translating into their own language the slaveholders' hatred for those runaway rebels, whom the slaves themselves regarded as heroes.[26] The step from here to applying the term *mambí* as a general denominator to all those who rebelled against an oppressive situation—first slavery, then Spanish colonial rule, and later United States imperialism—is not hard to follow.

But most interesting about Ortiz's comments is that an African word should have been added to the Spanish lexicon to designate first a particular group, maroons like Mackandal, whose very existence posed a threat to the stability of the slaveholding society, and then a particular attitude toward oppression in general. We encounter in the case of *mambí* an instance of linguistic and cultural supplementation, which is relevant to my discussion mainly because it enables me to establish an important link between the concept of supplementarity on the theoretical level and the struggle for cultural and ideological freedom as it manifests itself in Guillén's poetic practice. Martínez Estrada's assessment of what he perceives to be the essential features of Guillén's poetic method is worth quoting here:

Guillén is at the forefront of the destruction of an aesthetic which . . . has been filtered down to us . . . from Horace to . . . Pablo Neruda. His innovation . . . attacks the roots of a sacrosanct order in poetry. . . . The use of a popular idiom was the minimal basic condition. Even though . . . Guillén scorns the use of demolishing materials, he does not, in his most important poems, preserve the integrity of language as a sign and reduces it to onomatopoeia, to articulated sound, to phonemes into which we can place as much emotional and imaginative substance as we are capable of. Are, then, Guillén's writings poetry? In a very general sense, no; but in a profound sense, yes. It is a poetry of sediments and fluorescences always struggling for articulation. [27]

Although Martínez Estrada is right in calling attention to Guillén's iconoclastic attitude toward classical notions of aesthetics and poetry, his remarks on how Guillén demolishes those notions remain, despite their suggestiveness, rather vague and somewhat misleading as a result. It is true that Guillén does not, strictly speaking, use words as pure signs. But to claim, on the other hand, that he reduces language to onomatopoeia (or *jitanjáfora*) to open up possibilities for new, different kinds of meanings is to simplify and misrepresent his literary achievement. If anything, Guillén's poetic method is not reductive but supplementary. What his poetry supplements and thus dislocates are the formal manifestations of authoritative (and authoritarian) institutions, be they cultural, literary, or political. I am referring to the kinds of formal languages that may be called "legal" in the sense that they are designed to rule out ambiguity to ensure social stability and thus provide a mechanism for protecting the interests of a particular group, class, or political regime. Such systematic inscriptions of power extend into literary writing by way of a formal aesthetic that dictates the criteria a text has to fulfill in order to be admitted to a literary canon (remember the case of Columbus's diaries).

In this context, the question Martínez Estrada raises about the literary status of Guillén's poetry is worthy of some consideration, not in order to revive the popular polemic of literature versus propaganda, but to show that there is another, more serious dimension to it. Guillén's poems are certainly not "poetic" in any conventional sense, which is readily confirmed by a text like *El diario*. While *El diario* most clearly shows the confluence of Guillén's journalistic and poetic activities, this biographical criterion alone is hardly sufficient to account for the poem's rich display of different forms of discourse such as advertisements, public notices, news items, and official decrees as well as a variety of standard poetic forms. All these, to be sure, accentuate the public role of poetry, but they also demonstrate its ability to mediate between the forms of writing employed at various points in history to inscribe and conscribe Cuba's identity. Guillén's poems, like Wright's *Dimensions of History* and

Williams's *In the American Grain*, are engaged in a relentless undoing of those conscriptions of identity by activating all the different semantic levels vibrating below the even, deceptively calm surface of officially documented history.[28]

One of Guillén's later poems that perfectly illustrates this process of semantic decomposition and reassembly of historical and cultural fragments is the above-mentioned "El apellido," one of his famous *Elegías*. This poem will facilitate the leap from "Sensemayá" and "West Indies, Ltd." to *El diario*, because it elucidates the impact of the historic confrontation between African slaves and their Spanish masters, as represented by the "Día de Reyes," on questions of language and writing. "El apellido" anticipates *El diario* in that it dramatizes the transformation of sociohistorical and cultural relationships into linguistic ones. It thus marks the transition in Guillén's work from his initial preoccupation with spoken language—the idiom of the Cuban blacks in *Motivos de son*—to an increasing concern with written forms. Unlike Guillén's earlier works, *El diario* is not a poem for performance. On the contrary, it so heavily depends on the printed medium that it would be completely unsuitable even for a reading. But although this quality seems to make it so different from the rest of Guillén's work, *El diario* does share thematic concerns and formal strategies that are present in his poetic writings almost from the very beginning of his career. As a result, *El diario* makes us wonder, and justly so, if the overemphasis most of Guillén's critics place on the oral and aural properties of his poems did not perhaps blind them to something of which Guillén himself is, I believe, very much aware: the fact that his medium is, above all, writing.

It would seem trivial to raise this issue were it not that the need for rigorous readings of Guillén's poems has frequently been replaced, inadequately, with the kinds of vague, impressionistic remarks that oral composition theory seems to inspire when casually applied to written materials. To contend that a poem approximates the dynamics of an oral performance is, as I have attempted to show in my comments on "Sensemayá," not a valid excuse for disregarding the semantic and rhetorical subtleties such a poem acquires when treated as a written text. These subtleties are precisely the "fluorescence(s)" and "sediments" of which Martínez Estrada speaks. Guillén's poems, even *Motivos de son* and *Sóngoro cosongo*, are not simply transcriptions of a popular idiom into literary language. They are attempts at confronting the conventions and clichés of Peninsular Spanish with a language that, because it is at once the same and different, is capable of sounding the depths of Cuban (and

Latin American) history. While this is generally true of Guillén's poems, it is most immediately obvious in "El apellido."

Desde la escuela
y aún antes . . . Desde el alba, cuando apenas
era una brizna yo de sueños y llanto,
desde entonces,
me dijeron mi nombre. Un santo y seña
para poder hablar con las estrellas.
Tu te llamas, te llamarás . . .
Y luego me entregaron
esto que veis escrito en mi tarjeta,
esto que pongo a pie de mis poemas:
las trece letras
que llevo a cuestas por la calle,
que siempre van conmigo a todas partes. (*OP*, 1: 394–95)

[Ever since school
and even before . . . Since the dawn, when I was
barely a patch of dreams and wailing,
since then,
I have been told my name. A password
for being able to speak with the stars.
Your name is, you shall be called . . .
And then they handed me
what you see written on my card,
what I put at the bottom of my poems;
the thirteen letters
that I carry through the streets on my shoulders,
that are with me always and everywhere.]

The abundance of impersonal passive constructions at the beginning of the poem immediately establishes a distance between the poetic persona and the identity assigned to him in the form of "thirteen letters." The two ellipses reinforce this sense of distance: Like the textual gaps Jay Wright employs in *Dimensions of History*, Guillén's ellipses create a deficiency in the text of the poem, which not only generates an atmosphere of urgency for the quest for identity on which his persona is about to embark, but already defines that quest as a search for a language that would retrieve the same kinds of silences with which Wright grapples in "Benjamin Banneker Helps to Build a City" and which Williams and Carpentier restore to Columbus's diaries. In "El apellido" these elliptical silences or absences signal the inadequacy of the kind of formal writing represented by the process of naming as a vehicle for self-knowledge. Naming is an official legal act in which a notary assigns to an individual an arbitrary set of written characters that has no meaning outside of the bureaucratic system that invests it with the authority of a password. In this sense, names are surrogates for identity, incapable of maintaining the historical relationships within which the individual exists. In fact, they can be said to exist outside of history; their ontological status resembles that of a myth in that they grant only limited access to historical knowledge. To Guillén, names represent official historical records and inventories and as such form part of the vast amount of writing generated by the colonial administration of the Hapsburg empire to ensure social and political stability in the Spanish-American territories. Guillén is attempting to create an awareness of the fact that, although the gradual independence of Cuba and other Latin American colonies had put an end to the workings of that imperial bureaucracy, there remain within the structure of the Spanish language vestiges of precisely the kind of formal discourse used for centuries as a means of social and political control. This legacy of colonialism continues to weigh on Latin American culture, which, despite nominal political independence, is still defined by a language that perpetuates the authority of ideological structures no longer present or functional except as myths.

Those myths, "the freight taken from Europe," to recall Lezama, are further manifestations of an "illiterate imagination," a concept that gives a curious twist to the quest for freedom-through-*literacy* in which both Wright and Guillén (as well as Williams) are engaged. Literacy, for Guillén, is the ability to decompose the rigid mythical structures that determine the concept of Latin American culture and thus continue to lend authority to a language that is as much of a vacuous presence as the crumbled skeletal structure of the old Spanish galleon in *One Hundred Years of Solitude*. The space García Márquez's Spanish galleon occupies is that of myth, precisely of myth driven from its locus, *dislocated* quite literally by some curious twist of history: The enormous ship is found, not on the coast, but inland in the Colombian jungle. This geographical displacement is significant to the extent that it prefigures the conceptual dislocation of the formal structures of conquest the ship represents. In other words, geographical displacement is shown to bring about profound changes in that structure itself, changes that manifest themselves in a paradoxical combination of nautical terms and tropical vegetation: "Tilted slightly to the starboard, it had hanging from its intact masts the dirty rags of its sails in the midst of rigging, which was adorned with orchids. The hull, covered with an armor of petrified barnacles and soft moss, was firmly fastened in a surface of stones."[29] These curious ornaments are symptomatic of the slow disintegration of the rigid mythical structure under the impact of telluric forces associated with a specific geographical location—the New World. But the adornments also have a functional value. They hold together the fragments of the crumbling galleon, however not without considerably altering its appearance in the process. This perfectly illustrates the logic of supplementation we have encountered in Wright's poems: The supplement, much like the tropical vegetation in the above citation, insinuates itself into a formal structure in order to destroy it, while at the same time reassembling the resulting fragments into a new, different kind of coherence. The supplement, in other words, creates a condition (a deficiency or a lack) that makes its presence essential to the very structure it undermines. Without it, the entire structure would collapse.

In "El apellido" those dysfunctional, voided structures of conquest take the shape of a mythology of formal writing (naming) whose fragmentation is evident in the incoherence suggested by the "thirteen letters" as well as by the two ellipses. What emerges from within the spaces between those letters are images that grow out of the fertile soil of the Caribbean and modify not only the texture of received "names" but their very structure and thus the meaning of the process of inscribing identities.

¿Es mi nombre, estáis ciertos?
¿Tenéis todas mis señas?
¿Ya conocéis mi sangre navegable,
mi geografía llena de oscuros montes,
de hondos y amargos valles
que no están en los mapas?
¿Acaso visitasteis mis abismos,
mis galerías subterráneas
con grandes piedras húmedas,
islas sobresaliendo en negras charcas
y donde un puro chorro
siento de antigua aguas
caer desde mi alto corazón
con fresco y hondo estrépito
en un lugar lleno de ardientes árboles,
monos equilibristas,
loros legisladores y culebras?

¿Toda mi piel (debí decir),
toda mi piel viene de aquella estatua
de mármol español? ¿También mi voz de espanto,
el duro grito de mi garganta? ¿Vienen de allá
todos mis huesos? ¿Mis raíces y las raíces
de mis raíces y además
estas ramas oscuras movidas por los sueños
y esta savia que amarga mi corteza?
¿Estáis seguros?
¿No hay nada más que eso que habéis escrito,
que eso que habéis sellado
con un sello de cólera?
(¡Oh, debí haber preguntado!)

Y bien, ahora os pregunto: (*OP*, 1: 395–96)

[Are you sure it is my name?
Have you got all my particulars?
Do you already know my navigable blood,
my geography full of dark mountains,
of deep and bitter valleys
that are not on the maps?
Perhaps you have visited my chasms,
my subterranean galleries
with large moist rocks,
islands jutting out of black puddles,
and where I feel a
pure rush of ancient waters
falling from the heights of my heart
with a fresh and deep sound
of a place filled with flaming trees,
acrobatic monkeys,
legislative parrots and snakes?
Does all my skin (I should have said),
does all my skin come from that statue
of Spanish marble? My frightening voice too,
the harsh cry in my throat? Are all
my bones from there? My roots and the roots
of my roots and also
these dark branches swayed by dreams
and these flowers blooming on my forehead
and this sap that embitters my bark?
Are you certain?
Is there nothing else than this that you have written,
than this that you have stamped

with a seal of anger?
(Oh, I should have asked!)

Well, I am asking you now:]

As these impassioned, anguished lines indicate, there is clearly more than what has been written and sealed in official historical records. "El apellido" is a rewriting, and in fact an "unwriting" in Jay Wright's sense, of such historical documents with the intention of retrieving from the silence of "immemorial ink" [tinta inmemorial] that other name, "el que me viene / de aquella tierra enorme, el apellido / sangriento y capturado, que pasó sobre el mar / entre cadenas" [the one that comes to me / from that enormous land, the captured / and bleeding last name that came across the sea / in chains] (*OP*, 1: 396). It might be interjected here that Guillén's genealogical project in "El apellido" recalls the writings of Garcilaso de la Vega, el Inca, whose bold engravings on the polished "marble" of the Spanish "lengua ideal" appeared to have been as disturbing to Spain's colonial administrators as Mackandal's final gesture was to the French slaveholders. This is confirmed by the fact that the Spanish Royal Council, pressured at the time by 567 petitioners to recognize the royal descent of the Incas, ordered the phrase "Royal Commentaries of the Incas" to be removed from part 2 of the work, which was published seven months after Garcilaso's death under the innocuous title *General History of Peru*.[30]

Guillén's poetic inscriptions of his "last name" are no less unsettling. The statue of Spanish marble in the above citation, which is Guillén's version of García Márquez's Spanish galleon, represents, much like the "pupils of antarctic glass" of the white grandfather in "Balada de los dos abuelos" [Ballad of the Two Grandfathers] and also the glass-eyed snake in "Sensemayá," a myth to be decomposed and invested with new metaphoric strengths: The stony statue is transfigured into, and in a sense effaced by, an image of the human body as a (family) tree, which is a synthesis of the poet's interior geography. Although this image poses as one of the organic metaphors so popular in Romantic poetry, this posture is ultimately deceptive, since the tree's surface, its bark, is embittered by the "sap" of historical knowledge rather than being sweetened by nostalgia. The etymology of "savia" [sap], like "sabio" [sage] and "saber [to know] derived from the Latin *sapere*, infuses with ambiguity the idyllic vision of branches swayed by dreams and flowers blooming on the poet's forehead. This sap surging up from the tree's roots signifies the intrusion of historical knowledge into the mythical New World landscape and thus the awakening of a historical consciousness that invalidates the authority

of Romanticism's organic metaphors in the same way that it voids the
textual presence of the marble statue. It is this historical consciousness
that breaks the seal of colonialism's anger and violence. But what exactly
is being swept to the surface of perception by this "pure rush / of ancient
waters"?

To answer that question it is useful to return to one of Nancy Morejón's
observations. "Any attentive reader of Nicolás Guillén's poetry," she
writes, "cannot but notice . . . the presence of a whole mythology of
images, all of which are part of the ecology of the Antilles. The Tropics
are not ashamed of their condition. Our beautiful and exuberant land-
scape—described as such in Columbus's *Diary* and the countless chroni-
cles of the conquistadores, travelers, and pilgrims—appears in Guillén as
a necessary and suggestive telluric presence."[31] These remarks require
specification: Morejón is no doubt correct in asserting the presence of a
full-fledged mythology in Guillén's poetry, but it must be added that that
mythology is, in many respects, quite different from what we encounter
in the writings of Columbus and the chroniclers of the Indies. "El
apellido" exemplifies this difference. I have argued above that the image
of the (family) tree, which displaces the statue of Spanish marble, also at
the same time subverts and renders most ambiguous the romantic con-
ception of the New World as a "virgin land." That Guillén's projection of
an inner geography, nourished by the sap of historical knowledge, is "a
place filled with flaming trees" sustains this argument in an important
way. In the image of the "flaming trees" the telluric powers of the natural
landscape of the Caribbean merge with the persona's historical con-
sciousness or inner landscape to reassemble the fragments of a body of
mythologies destroyed by the structures of conquest the marble statue
represents. Guillén's flaming trees perhaps intuitively evoke an old *taíno*
(Arawak) and Macusi legend, of which Wilson Harris offers us a version:

The foodbearing tree of the world in Arawak and Macusi legend
reaches to the sky of fiction across forgotten ages, but we become
suddenly aware of it as a creation bridge or myth between sky and
earth at a time of catastrophe when a new genesis or vision has
become necessary.
It is a time of war. The rainbow compression of a tree is set on fire
by the Caribs when the Arawaks seek refuge in its branches, upon
which stand multi-colored birds and fruit overcast in the wake of the
fire by a cloud of smoke. Creation suffers and needs to be re-dressed if
the spirit of the stars is to be discovered again. The fire rages and
ascends even higher to drive the Arawaks up and up until there is no
further escape, they burn and rise into a spark in the sky of fiction.
That spark becomes the seed of the garden of the Pleiades.

The foodbearing tree, therefore, is re-dressed, the blackened fruit unravelled into a garden in the sky of fiction. The most curious enigma of all is the reconciliation that the Caribs and Arawaks appear to achieve, a treaty of sensibility that borders on *coniunctio* between sky and earth.[32]

It has been argued, time and again, that Guillén, unlike Fernando Ortiz, has never attributed any great significance to the Native American influence on Cuban culture.[33] Given that the Indian population, whose numbers rapidly declined after the first arrival of the Spanish in the Caribbean, never constituted a strong cultural presence in Cuba and was even less one after the middle of the eighteenth century during the heyday of the African slave trade, such claims are understandable. But even though Guillén places a premium on the historical impact of slavery on the cultural development of the New World and particularly Cuba and consequently is not interested in using the Amerindian component to fashion, as the *siboneistas* did during the nineteenth century, an autochthonous cultural emblem, he is nevertheless aware that Caribbean culture is an admixture of elements from at least three different groups: Indians, Africans, and Spaniards. This is clear in *El diario* from his allusions to Silvestre de Balboa's "Espejo de paciencia" [Mirror of Patience] (1608), to which I shall return in due time.

In "El apellido" the subtle presence of the Arawak and Macusi creation myth, which unquestionably belongs to the cultural field of the Antilles, establishes the basis for an important analogy that Wilson Harris helps clarify. He asks, "What is the real nature of our involvement with the Amerindian past? It is an involvement . . . in the first place not with these aborigines as such, but with the aboriginal fact of conquest, and through this with the perennial, essentially human or natural fact of obscure, sometimes catastrophic changes, life-in-death, death-in-life. For this aboriginal conquest exists like a ruin of psychological premises and biases in our midst that we are as yet to see as a gateway to a new anthropology, and to a more profound understanding of human nature."[34] As an invocation of Arawak and Macusi legend, Guillén's flaming trees embody a life-in-death and death-in-life situation and articulate the need for a new genesis or vision. If the flaming trees constitute a figure of conquest, they also offer what Harris calls a creation bridge, a myth that makes possible the same kind of magical transformation the figure of Mackandal undergoes when burned at the stake. Mackandal becomes a spark in the sky of the slaves' (and Carpentier's) imagination and thus a seed in the garden of Afro-American mythology inadvertently implanted in the New World by those who attempted to destroy it.

Guillén's flaming trees are not simply images of violence and destruction but emblems of psychological resistance as well as of the phenomenal recuperative powers of the imagination, that is, its ability to reassemble dispersed fragments into new, coherent founding fables. The sparks that rise up from Guillén's flaming trees are the other names with which he supplements his official identity:

¿No tengo pues
un abuelo mandinga, congo, dahomeyano?
¿Cómo se llama? ¡Oh, si, decídmelo!
¿Andrés? ¿Francisco? ¿Amable?
¿Cómo decís Andrés en congo?
¿Cómo habéis dicho siempre
Francisco en dahomeyano?
En mandinga ¿como se dice Amable?
¿O no? ¿Eran, pues, otros nombres?
¡El apellido, entonces!

. . . .
¿Seré Yelofe?
¿Nicolás Yelofe?
¿O Nicolás Bakongo?
¿Tal vez Guillén Banguila?
¿O Kumba?
¿Quizá Guillén Kumba?
¿O Kongué?
¿Pudiera ser Guillén Kongué?
¡Oh, quién lo sabe!
¡Qué enigma entre las aguas! (*OP*, 1: 396–97)

[Don't I have, then,
a Mandingo, Congo, Dahomeyan grandfather?
What is his name? Oh yes, tell me his name!
Andrés? Francisco? Amable?
How do you say Andrés in Congolese?
How have you always said
Francisco in Dahomeyan?
In Mandingo, how do you say Amable?
No? Are there, then, other names?
The last name then!

. . . .
Would I be Yelofe?
Nicolás Yelofe perhaps?
Or Nicolás Bakongo?
Maybe Nicolás Banguila?

Or Kumba?
Perhaps Guillén Kumba?
Or Kongué?
Could I be Guillén Kongué?
Oh, who knows!
What riddle in the waters!]

Important at this point in the poem—the end of part 1—is the persona's realization that it is impossible for him to recover his genealogical origins, that, in fact, these origins are "a riddle in the waters" of the Middle Passage. These waters are like a sea of immemorial ink in which all names dissolve and become fluid. It is the Middle Passage, "voyage through death, / voyage whose chartings are unlove," as Robert Hayden has called it,[35] that come to represent, for Guillén, the very process of deracination and transformation that enables him, in the second part of "El apellido," to embrace an identity that goes beyond the individuation achieved through naming. In this regard, it is telling that the fire motif, employed at the beginning of the poem to signal the need for another genesis, should recur as Guillén moves away from ethnocentrism and toward a "treaty of sensibilities." This treaty of sensibilities, or synthetic myth, now makes it possible for Guillén to invest Amerindian legend with an allegorical meaning drawn from Afro-American culture and history, or, put differently, to extend that legend's allegorical range to encompass Afro-American history or vice versa. This procedure is a familiar one: It finds its parallel in the practices of the Neo-African religions in the Caribbean and elsewhere in the New World, which are based on investing with traditional powers and beliefs objects and concepts the African slaves encountered in the Americas. Guillén does the same with the *taíno* and Macusi legend of the tree of the world in flames by establishing an analogy between the regenerative imagination of the Arawaks and that of the African slaves. Both groups have managed to undermine the historical fact of conquest: They surreptitiously kept intact their traditional beliefs and values by supplementing them with elements from the other cultures present in the New World. The result is a kind of *bricolage* that particularly affects Guillén's metaphors:

De *algun país ardiente*, perforada
por la gran flecha ecuatorial,
sé que vendrán lejanos primos,
remota angustia mía disparada en el viento;
sé que vendrán pedazos de mis venas,
sangre remota mía,

con duro pie aplastando las hierbas asustadas;
sé que vendrán hombres de vidas verdes,
remota selva mía,
con su dolor abierto en cruz y el *pecho rojo en llamas.*
Sin conocernos nos reconoceremos en el hambre,
en la tuberculosis y en la sífilis,
en el sudor comprado en bolsa negra,
en los fragmentos de cadenas
adheridos todavía a la piel;
sin conocernos nos reconoceremos
en los ojos cargados de sueños
y hasta en los insultos como piedras
que nos escupen cada día
los cuadrumanos de tinta y de papel. (*OP*, 1: 398; my italics)

[From some flaming land pierced
by the great equatorial arrow,
I know there will come distant cousins,
my ancestral anguish cast upon the wind,
I know there will come pieces of my veins,
my far-away blood,
with hard feet flattening frightened grass;
I know there will come men with green lives,
my remote forest,
their pain an open cross and their breast red with flames.
Having never met, we will know each other by the hunger,
by the tuberculosis and the syphilis,
by the sweat bought in a slave market,
by the fragments of chains
still clinging to our skin;
having never met, we will know each other
by our dream-filled eyes
and even by the rock-hard insults
that quadrumanes of ink and paper
spit at us every day.]

On the one hand, Guillén's "flaming land" no doubt alludes to Africa, "that enormous continent," as he calls it earlier in the poem. On the other hand, however, the fire motif reinvokes the poet's inner geography, that "place of flaming trees," which is part of the historico-mythical landscape of the Caribbean. Consequently, the "distant cousins" whose reunion he envisions are not just Africans or black Americans, but "los hombres perdidos," the lost men whom Jay Wright has termed "the orphans of the earth." Interestingly enough, this vision of reunion immediately projects a figure of new growth strongly suggestive of the "garden of the Pleiades" in the Arawak and Macusi fable: The "men whose lives are green" constitute the poet's ancestral forest—"ancestral" in Ellison's sense—which grows from the open, inflamed wound on his breast. These are, if we recall *The Double Invention of Komo*, the signs that flame in Guillén's wound. His trees have again become men, in the same way that, according to an old Inca legend, the stones in the field turned into warriors who rushed to the defense of their prince.[36]

The figure of an ancestral "forest" or "jungle" combines references to Amerindian legend with allusions to that mysterious locus of transformation known among Cubans as "el monte." Rather than designating an actual place, "el monte," like the "garden of the Pleiades," ought to be understood as a system of beliefs and values which incorporates elements from different New World cultures into a new, syncretic or synthetic, cultural tradition. Both the "garden of the Pleiades" and "el monte" are spaces or clearings created by the "hunger" for life and for a new kind of humanism. Richard Wright, to whose writings Guillén's poems have been compared on occasion,[37] offers us, at the very end of the second part of his autobiography, entitled *American Hunger* (1944), a brief internal monologue that helps clarify Guillén's concept of "hunger" as it appears in "El apellido."

I picked up a pencil and held it over a sheet of white paper, but my feelings stood in the way of my words. Well, I would wait, day and night, until I knew what to say. Humbly now, with no vaulting dream of achieving a vast unity, I wanted to try to build a bridge of words between me and that world outside, that world which was so distant and elusive that it seemed unreal.

I would hurl words into this darkness and wait for an echo, and if an echo sounded, no matter how faintly, I would send other words to tell, to march, to fight, to create a sense of the hunger for life that gnaws in us all, to keep alive in our hearts a sense of the inexpressibly human.[38]

To be sure, the relationship between "El apellido" and *American Hunger* is not one of literary influence. Rather, it is a manifestation of the kinds of connections Guillén himself describes when he writes "having never met, we will know each other by the hunger." Both Guillén's and Wright's concepts of hunger are figures for that "treaty of sensibilities" that unites Latin American writers with black writers from the United States in their common struggle against cultural and political imperialism. Richard Wright's remarks remind us that this treaty of sensibilities is, in fact, a "bridge of words," something that is achieved by and in language. We have already encountered this idea of language as a bridge between cultures at the end of *Dimensions of History*. In "El apellido," the same idea is articulated in the form of the image of the "fragments of chains / still clinging to our skin," which are the fragments of names Guillén strings together in his "interminable name" at the end of the poem. This new, infinite chain, which strongly resembles Jay Wright's "secular rosary," is Guillén's alternative to an umbilical cord; it consists of an endless number of supplements, made possible, as in the case of Jay Wright's poem, by the conspicuous absence of closure.

¿Qué ha de importar entonces
(¡qué ha de importar ahora!)
¡ay! mi pequeño nombre
de trece letras blancas?
¿Ni el mandinga, bantú,
yoruba, dahomeyano
nombre del triste abuelo ahogado
en tinta de notario?
¿Qué importa, amigos puros?
¡Oh, sí, puros amigos,
venid a ver mi nombre!
Mi nombre interminable,
hecho de interminables nombres;
el nombre mío, ajeno,
libre y mío, ajeno y vuestro,
ajeno y libre como el aire. (*OP*, 1: 398–99)

[What has it mattered then?
(what does it matter now!)
ah, my little name
of thirteen blank letters?
Or the Mandingo, Bantu,
Yoruba, Dahomeyan
name of the sad grandfather drowned
in notary's ink?
What does it matter, my pure friends?
Oh, yes, my pure friends,
come look at my name!
My interminable name
made of interminable names;
My name, foreign,
free and mine, foreign and yours,
foreign and free as the air.]

The absence of closure in "El apellido" results from a process of (self)-effacement which culminates in the figure of the "thirteen blank letters," which is already anticipated by the ellipses at the beginning of the poem. What is being effaced is the symbolic value of the name as an imposed structure of conquest: "blanco," of course, also means white and thus applies to the *peninsulares*, to whom Guillén ironically refers as "pure friends." The "thirteen blank letters" are a figure that marks, in Lévi-Strauss's words, "the necessity of a symbolic content supplementary to that with which the signified is already loaded."[39] As the vestiges of Spanish cultural imperialism (the marble statue, for instance) are emptied of the symbolic content on which their authority is predicated, they are rendered capable of becoming charged with new meanings and functions. This process, as we can see in "El apellido" and also in "Sensemayá," is not strictly one of substitution but one that introduces radical changes to conventional structures of authority, be they political or cultural. The founding fables generated in this way are specific products of the New World cultural landscape, which is quite evident in the subtle tenacity of the Amerindian fire motif in "El apellido." Despite its allegorical properties and functions, the fire motif and the legend with which it is connected remain firmly attached to the historical and cultural geography of the Caribbean. They cannot be separated from this context without losing the metaphorical powers with which Guillén invests them. The same, as we have seen, holds true of the ritual of killing a snake in "Sensemayá." Without their attachment to the specific historico-cultural context of the New World, these fables lose their ability to *radiate* meaning—what Auerbach calls *strahlen*—and become submerged in and reduced to universals.[40]

The important thing to bear in mind with regard to those cultural founding fables is that they are conceived as a part of, as well as apart from, those mythologies that consider themselves universal. By demonstrating that those mythologies can be supplemented, and in fact stand in need of supplementation, Guillén's founding fables invalidate and neutralize the totalizing claims of Western civilization. We may say that Western culture and its mythological foundations are being put in their proper place: They are driven from their central position, so that subordination may give way to equal standing. If in this way equal value is assigned to all cultural elements and influences represented in the New World, then there is a true basis for interaction and exchange, for what Fernando Ortiz has appropriately termed *transculturación* to replace the unfortunate, but popular, concept of acculturation. It is from this interaction that Guillén, like Jay Wright, fashions an identity that makes all the different aspects of his cultural heritage accessible to him. This identity is a structure of freedom in Harris's sense: It derives its authority from its diversity and openness. The only possible form it has is that of the poem itself, insofar at least as the poem is a space for each reader to engage anew the question of, and the quest for, self-knowledge and, in the process, to become part of each poet's endless "name."

II   *Bueno, querido, no todo puede ser coherente en la vida. Un poco de desorden en el orden, ¿no?*

[Well, dear, not everything in life is coherent. A little disorder in order, I always say.]

— S E V E R O S A R D U Y, *De donde son los cantantes* (1967)

In "El apellido," as in "Sensemayá," Guillén is concerned with effacing structures of authority (or better, authoritarianism of various kinds) in an effort to open up a space where ideas of self and culture can be entertained without being subjected to the institutional requirements of an avowed ideology. Such a realization makes it extremely difficult to view Guillén's poetry as an unequivocal defense of the Cuban regime in its present form. This element of doubt is reinforced, more or less subtly, by the fact that most studies of Guillén's poetry—with the possible exception of Ezequiel Martínez Estrada's book—do not allow for the possibility of there being even the slightest discrepancy between the official posture Guillén assumes as a functionary of the revolutionary government and the attitudes he displays in his best poems. It is generally assumed (and accepted) that such discrepancies simply do not exist in his case, and this assumption has made it virtually impossible for most of his critics to approach his poetry on its own terms, that is, without imposing upon it a rigid set of prefabricated ideological categories. This critical disposition may also be the reason for the conspicuous lack of diversity that has characterized Guillén studies, especially for the last twenty years. Given this scholarly stalemate, one is justified to ask, in the poet's own words: Is there really nothing more? The answer is that of course there is much more to Guillén's poems than that which has been written and, one should add, stamped, implicitly or explicitly, with the seal of the Cuban bureaucracy's approval.

To substantiate these suggestions, it is necessary to move from Guillén's prerevolutionary writings to his postrevolutionary poetry, best represented by *El diario que a diario*, written between 1970 and 1972 more than twenty years after "El apellido." The first edition of *El diario*

(UNEAC, 1972) includes an introduction by Guillén, which unfortu-
nately has been omitted from both the reprinted version in *Obra poética*
and the second edition (Editorial Letras Cubanas, 1979), unfortunately
because Guillén's own assessment of his poem is most astute:

> Since the beginning of our history, . . . four centuries have elapsed in
> which Cuba has consecutively been trading post, colony (with two
> rebellions against Spain and the brief period of British rule), republic
> under the Yankees' protectorate, and finally Revolution. In order not
> to write either a *textbook* or an epic poem, I used a series of scenes in
> which this process culminated, alluding to them in a style that seeks to
> be cinematographic, journalistic, vibrant, suggestive. *To suggest* is all
> this little book aspires to. And is not suggestiveness perhaps the most
> direct language poetry has?[41]

What is striking about these lines is not only the absence of any kind of
propagandistic rhetoric but also the cautious tone Guillén employs and
the modesty he appears to display, which clashes with the very am-
bitiousness of the poetic project of *El diario*. Yet it is, on closer look, not
modesty that inspires these remarks, but the poet's urge to convey to his
readers that *El diario* is neither a historical textbook nor an epic singing
the praises of the Cuban Revolution. In fact, the postrevolutionary years
are not included in *El diario*'s historical framework, which stretches from
the sixteenth century roughly to the time when Castro began to reassem-
ble his forces in Oriente Province (1956). The actual revolution and its
aftermath are significant absences in this text.

Yet, *El diario* is unquestionably part of the literature of the Cuban
Revolution, and it is inevitable at this point, that is, before offering any
more commentary on what precisely that means, to take stock of the kind
of literature that has emerged in Cuba during the past twenty-five years.
Roberto González Echevarría's essay "Criticism and Literature in Revo-
lutionary Cuba" is a valuable source of information in this regard. He
summarizes his assessment as follows:

> The literature of the revolution has not been, as the ideologues (and
> bureaucrats) have wished, one that portrayed the process of social
> change, or one dealing with military campaigns. The literature of the
> Cuban revolution has been one created by the sense of self-
> questioning made possible by the countless Cuban texts put in the
> hands of the new writers; the literature that has delved into the opened
> archives of Cuban memory in search of records to assemble them for
> the first time; the literature that has read and reread that record
> relentlessly, constructing a literary past to make it available to this
> generation of Cuban readers and writers. The enduring products of

Cuban literature of the revolution are [Miguel Barnet's] *Biografía de un cimarrón* [Autobiography of a Runaway Slave], [his] *Canción de Rachel* [The Song of Rachel], [Alejo Carpentier's] *El recurso del método* [Reasons of State], [Manuel Moreno Fraginals's] *El ingenio* [The Sugarmill], [Reynaldo Arenas's] *El mundo alucinante* [Hallucinations], and the brilliant new book by Reynaldo González, *La fiesta de los tiburones* [The Feast of the Sharks].[42]

El diario's conspicuous absence from this list of enduring literary products of the Cuban revolution may not be surprising, given that it is the one of Guillén's poems which has received the least attention from literary critics inside and outside Cuba. But the need for including it among these works becomes glaringly obvious once we examine the distinguishing characteristics González Echevarría ascribes to the above texts, characteristics, he adds, that cut across genres and disciplines.

And these characteristics are: 1) all these books involve historical research in the most tangible sense of collecting documents; 2) all assemble those texts in such a way that a political history of Cuban culture emerges, meaning one that emphasizes socioeconomic and political relations other than ethnic; 3) all assemble historical texts in such a way that the reader reads them directly, as if he were the researcher, not through an account that blends them all into a final form (In many cases the texts are not only written ones, but visual: *El ingenio* has not only statistical charts, but also marvelous drawings of old sugar-mill machinery; *Biografía de un cimarrón* has pictures; *La fiesta de los tiburones*, newspaper clippings that include advertisements as well as articles and editorials.); 4) all these books consequently demystify the figure of the author, who is a compiler, a researcher, an investigator who gives his place to the reader, who shares with him his wonder and self-recognition before the texts; 5) all of the books mentioned, then, focus on the very activity of reading as social and political activity, not only as a subjectively creative one; 6) all of these books have been produced by writers who are marginal in relation to the centers of ideological dissemination.[43]

All the above features apply to *El diario*, except one: Guillén, unlike Moreno Fraginals, Carpentier, Barnet, González, and Arenas, is not exactly marginal to Cuba's centers of ideological dissemination. On the contrary, he is one of the most powerful figures in Cuba's present cultural bureaucracy and has been one of the featured writers of *Unión* for quite some time. On his eightieth birthday in 1982, for instance, both *Casa de las Américas* and *Unión* devoted a special issue to Guillén, and the *Revista de Literatura Cubana*, which has Ángel Augier, Roberto Fernández Retamar (who also directs *Casa*), and José Antonio Portuondo on its editorial board, featured Guillén in its inaugural issue.[44] These three tributes alone indicate the popularity Guillén continues to enjoy in Cuba. But even more interesting, and equally telling in a different way, is the fact that none of the contributions to these special issues were devoted to *El diario*. How, then, can we explain this apparent reluctance on the part of Cuban critics to take notice of a work like *El diario*?[45] Does their silence perhaps reveal the same note of uneasiness and the same kind of discomfort that characterized the initial critical responses to *In the American Grain* and that more recently have caused established critics of Afro-American literature in the United States to ignore the work of Jay Wright? Is there, in short, a connection between the fact that *El diario*, much more so than any other of Guillén's poems, is marginal to the official literary trends and requirements in Cuba and the conspicuous silence on the part of most of his colleagues and comrades? I do believe that such a connection exists, mainly because *El diario* does not lend itself to the kinds of one-dimensional, ideology-ridden readings frequently brought to bear on Guillén's other poems. Its complexity eludes the journalistic criticism favored by Cuba's cultural bureaucracy. In addition, if *El diario* is indeed the culmination of Guillén's literary achievements, as I believe it is, then its suggestive marginality vis-à-vis the ideology of the revolutionary establishment is likely to call into question many of the assumptions and generalizations that have been made about his poetry.

How, then, does one account for the literary marginality of a writer as central to the Cuban Revolution as Guillén has always appeared to be? The first step toward answering this question is to look again, this time more closely, at the list of works González Echevarría cites as enduring products of the revolution. The most obvious feature they share is that they are all prose works that incorporate a broad variety of literary and nonliterary materials; in short, none of them has a unilingual stylistic surface. With the exception of *El ingenio*, all are novels in the broadest sense of the term. Without attempting any definition of this most fluid of literary genres, it is necessary, for reasons that will soon become evident, to digress and consider Mikhail Bakhtin's list of characteristics that fundamentally distinguish, so he claims, the novel from other genres:

(1) Its stylistic three-dimensionality, which is linked with the multi-languaged consciousness realized in the novel; (2) the radical change it effects in the temporal coordinates of the literary image; (3) the new zone opened by the novel for structuring literary images, namely, the zone of maximal contact with the present (with contemporary reality) in all its openendedness.[46]

For Bakhtin, the novel, because of its ability to combine a diverse array of "languages" (social, professional, literary, etc.) into a maze of dialogical (*not* dialectical) relationships, is an "intentional hybrid," concerned with the "actual possibility of specific genres coexisting within the living whole of literature in a given era." But this coexistence is not a harmonious one: "The novel parodies other genres (precisely in their role as genres); it exposes the conventionality of their forms and their language; it squeezes out some genres and incorporates others into its own peculiar structure, reformulating and reaccentuating them."[47] One may agree or disagree with Bakhtin's views, but the fact remains that all the texts listed by González Echevarría share these features, even *El ingenio* to a certain extent. But how does *El diario* fit into this?

Given that *El diario* is not, for all intents and purposes, a novel, it is curious that particularly the last citation from Bakhtin seems to be a fitting description of precisely the kinds of literary processes that characterize this poem. This is even more perplexing in light of Bakhtin's claim that "the possibility of employing within a single work words [or texts] of various kinds in their extreme expressions without reducing them to a common denominator is one of the most essential characteristics of prose. Herein lies the most profound distinction between prose style and poetic style."[48] But this distinction, as Bakhtin himself admits, is not an absolute one; it is relativized by what he terms the "novelization" of all other genres at times when the novel becomes the dominant genre. This has certainly been true of the Latin American novel, particularly during the last decade. In this respect, it is no coincidence that the works González Echevarría lists do not include a single work of poetry. Yet, especially with regard to the postrevolutionary development of Cuban literature, the dominant position of the novel raises a number of questions: If processes of sociopolitical and cultural consolidation of the kind we are witnessing in contemporary Cuba are, as Bakhtin has suggested, usually accompanied by literary expressions of forces working toward concrete verbal and ideological unification and centralization, a tendency that conventional poetry as a unitary or monological language epitomizes, then the question arises why the novel, and not poetry, should have emerged as the prime vehicle for the literature of the Cuban Revolution. After all, the novel in its formal disposition is much less suitable, it would seem, for the propagandistic dissemination of an ideologically unified world view, simply because its characteristic heterogeneity makes it unreliable for such a task. While it could be argued that the novels mentioned above are, after all, marginal to the centers of ideological dissemination in Cuba, whereas Guillén's poetry is not, such an argu-

ment still cannot detract from the fact that even Guillén's most can-
onized poems such as "West Indies, Ltd." and the "Elegía a Jesús Me-
néndez," for instance, are unquestionably infused with strong novelistic
features. This is even true of his *Motivos de son*, which uses the black
idiom, neologisms, and wordplay, elements not generally associated with
poetry, be it epic or lyrical. And it is precisely in the poems of *Motivos de
son* that we find the beginnings of the dialogical processes that culminate
in *El diario*. All this is to say that Guillén's work, on closer look, is not
one devoted to linguistic and ideological unification; on the contrary, it is
extremely critical of such practices. This becomes even more evident
when we consider that every single one of what Bakhtin lists as the salient
features of the novelization of other genres is present in Guillén's poems.

They [other genres] become more free and flexible, their language
renews itself by incorporating extraliterary heteroglossia and the
"novelistic" layers of literary language, they become dialogized,
permeated with laughter, irony, humor, elements of self-parody and
finally—this is the most important thing—the novel inserts into these
other genres an indeterminacy, a certain semantic openness, a living
contact with unfinished, still-evolving contemporary reality (the open-
ended present).[49]

To describe in detail the precise nature of those extraliterary hetero-
glossia, the different layers of language and the effects of their dialogic
interaction (or interillumination, as Bakhtin has it) on the poetic texture
of *El diario* is the task on which the remainder of my discussion will
focus. Since *El diario* is a complex textual hybrid, special attention will
be paid to the study of specific images of language as part of the historical
contexts this poem mobilizes, because it is only within those contexts that
the stratification of language with which we are confronted takes on
clarity and meaning. The goal of my investigation is to determine the
extent to which Guillén's literary practice or method in *El diario* and
elsewhere might constitute a reevaluation, as well as a broadening, of the
vision of cultural nationalism with which his work has been so intimately
linked.

To Guillén, poetry is no stagnant reservoir of compositional clichés.
Rather, it is a concerted effort to dismantle such clichés and formulae, to
reveal the existence of a subtext of contradictions in a constant mockery
of those traditional social, political, and literary forms and standards
identified as structures of conquest. This element of mockery or humor is
one of the most important and characteristic aspects of Guillén's poetic
work, ranging from his early *Poemas de transición* (1927–1931) all the

way to *El diario*.[50] I have already stressed the elements of subversive mockery in "Sensemayá," as well as in connection with the process of effacing (or defacing) Romantic metaphors in "El apellido." To summarize what is involved in this kind of mockery, it is useful to consider Adorno and Horkheimer's remarks about the confrontation between a work of art and its tradition.

There is no other way for art to express suffering than in the confrontation with tradition, a process which manifests itself stylistically. The quality of a work of art that enables it to go beyond reality is inseparable from its style; it does not, however, consist in the generated harmony, in the questionable unity of form and content, inside and outside, individual and society, *but in those features which show discrepancy, that is, in the necessary failure of the passionate efforts toward identity*. Weak works of art always rely on their resemblance to others, on the surrogate of an identity, instead of exposing themselves to the risk of that failure, which in all great works of art has always been a moment of stylistic self-abnegation.[51]

The moment when the poet's passionate and anguished attempts at achieving identity fail is precisely what we witness at the end of "El apellido," where the rejection of a surrogate identity (a "name") becomes an act not only of stylistic self-abnegation. "El apellido," "Sensemayá," and also "El abuelo" are exquisite examples of Guillén's confronting the formal structures of the Hispanic tradition, a process in which the superficial harmony that tradition grants collapses under the impact of profound discrepancies between individual and society. By questioning and ultimately rejecting an identity that is cast in those traditional molds, Guillén dismisses as inadequate the very concept of a fixed identity and thus opens a space for the freeplay of substitutions discussed earlier. For Guillén, identity is a kind of magnetic field constituted by a multitude of opposing yet related elements. It is the process of their interpenetration that he renders visible in his poetry. As in Jay Wright's work, manifestations of self in Guillén's poetry immediately dissolve into numerous forms of otherness. These forms of otherness are the different postures the poet assumes before his readers, the strategies he employs to invade our beliefs and evaluative system in order to promote an active, rather than a passive, understanding.

Martínez Estrada avers that Guillén's ideal reader is always a participant, not a spectator. At the same time he also emphasizes that "Guillén's poetry is not popular poetry, but . . . poetry written with care . . . to be read with equal care."[52] The two statements are contradictory only if we reduce the act of reading to passive understanding, as linguistics and the philosophy of language have tended to do by posing the existence of a neutral language shared by author and reader.[53] However, the extent to which *El diario*, like Guillén's other poems, depends on linguistic heterogeneity precludes such passive understanding. To participate in Guillén's poems is to resist the pull of the conceptual categories that shape our thoughts, convictions, and beliefs, of conventions in short that maintain ideological structures and strictures within language. It is from this perspective, and only from this perspective, that we can experience and appreciate any refractions within Guillén's poetic voice, as well as the necessity for an author like Guillén to represent himself in the form of different language-images. This role-play, that is, the persistent transmutation of self into other, culminates in *El diario*, where this refraction is already announced in the "Prologuillo no estrictamente necessario" [Not Absolutely Necessary Little Prologue] entitled "AVISOS, MENSAJES, PREGONES" [Warnings, Messages, Announcements]:

Primero fuí el notario
polvoriento y sin prisa,
que inventó el inventario.
Hoy hago de otra guisa:
soy el diario que a diario
te previene, .te avisa
numeroso y gregario.
¡Vendes una sonrisa?
¡Compras un dromedario?
Mi gran stock[1] es vario.
Doquier[2] mi planta prisa
brota lo extraordinario.

PROBLEMAS DE PURISMO: [1] *Stock*, voz inglesa.
[2] *Doquier*, arcaísmo. Mas para nuestra empresa,
todo es uno y lo mismo.

LA DIRECCIÓN (*OP*, 2: 371)

[At first I was the notary,
dusty and without hurry,
who invented the inventory.
Today I play a different part:
I am the daily newspaper which daily
forewarns you and puts you on guard,
I am numerous and gregarious.
Are you selling a smile?
Are you in the market for a dromedary?

My large stock[1] is full of diversity.
Wheresoever[2] the sole of my foot touches,
it brings to life the extraordinary.

PROBLEMS OF PURITY: [1] *Stock*, Anglicism.
[2] *Wheresoever*, archaic, But in our press, everything
is one and the same.

THE MANAGEMENT]

As we already know from "El apellido," the figure of the notary represents bureaucratic authority; he is the keeper of official records, an administrator bound by the rules and regulations that come with his public office. As inventor of the "inventory," he is a defender of rigid categories that determine what I have earlier termed "legal" discourse. *El diario* seeks to dissolve these formal categories to create a new *exchange* for, in the sense of initiating dialogues between, the various "languages" associated with different areas of social, economic, political, and cultural activity. In order not to blend all these elements into a final form or to predict the results of their interaction, Guillén chooses the format of a newspaper as a frame for *El diario*. This particular format is significant not only because it stresses the important role of periodical literature in Cuban history—in fact, most of Cuba's major literary figures from Martí to Lezama were founders and editors (or both) of newspapers or journals—but also because it enables Guillén to draw attention to the act of reading as an essentially social and political activity. Furthermore, given that *El diario* is concerned with disseminating historical information in the broadest sense under the pretense of presenting the latest news, it brings history into contact with an ever-evolving contemporary reality.

The semantic openness thus inserted into the poetic text also brings into play the historical resonances of the word "diario." A "diario" is not only a daily newspaper but also a diary, a journal, a logbook, as in Columbus's *Diario de navegación*. There is no question that Guillén's title contains an allusion to this chronicle, which many Latin American writer's, as well as North Americans such as Williams, cite as one of the founding texts of their literatures.[54] But *El diario que a diario* is a very different kind of chronicle, as the wordplay in the title itself already suggests. The doubleness of Guillén's title already signals the heterogeneous nature of his text: *El diario* is a poem posing as a newspaper posing as a chronicle. To begin with, a newspaper does not in itself constitute a literary genre; nor does a chronicle, for that matter. Both are, in their own ways, admixtures of genres whose "stock," or stylistic reper-

172

toire, is extremely varied. Since neither form is ultimately able to blend all its constituents into a single unified whole, they both remain fragmented and fragmentary, as Guillén's curious title implies. "El diario que a diario" literally translates as "The daily which daily," a phrase that is not an ellipsis in the proper sense; the missing word is not easily surmised, given the wide range of possibilities. Interestingly enough, the absent verb is clearly one that would specify a function of "to write" (such as informs, warns, announces, etc.), which is also precisely the reason for its conspicuous omission. Guillén, in keeping with the poem's subversive project, refuses to define the exact nature of his discourse; he refuses to supply a label or category for the convenience of his readers, who are thus left with the difficult task of supplementing the title themselves. This task is complicated by the fact that the poet has already shrewdly deprived us of the possibility of attaching any kind of generic label to his text. As in the case of *In the American Grain* and *Dimensions of History*, we are left with the idea of a fragment, in the same way that we are left with a poem that will not close.

But although the title itself of Guillén's poem prohibits generic classification, that very fact allows us to place *El diario* squarely within the context of Latin American literary history: The method reflected in this elliptical title conforms neatly to what Severo Sarduy describes as one of the main features of the Latin American (Neo)baroque. Sarduy contends:

Another mechanism of the artificialization of the Baroque is that which consists of obliterating the signifier of a given signified without replacing it with another, however distant it might be from the first, but rather with a chain of signifiers which progresses metonymically and finally circumscribes the absent signifier, tracing an orbit around it. Through the reading of this orbit—we could call it a *radial* reading—we can infer the absent signifier. Upon being implanted in America and incorporating other linguistic materials—I am referring to all languages, verbal or non-verbal—upon having at its disposal often strange elements . . . from other cultural strata, the workings of the baroque mechanism have become more explicit. Its presence is constant, above all, in nonsensical enumerations, in the accumulation of diverse nodules of meaning, in the juxtaposition of heterogeneous units, and in lists of disparate things and the *collage*.[55]

What Sarduy describes here is an uncontrolled proliferation of meanings in the space of, or around, an absent signifier. In the case of *El diario*, this absent signifier would render explicit the precise nature of Guillén's poetic discourse. But since the whole of *El diario* is, in many ways, a metonymic chain of textual supplements to a fragmentary title, which circumscribes this absent signifier (a form of "to write," as I have noted) by offering a multitude of different facets and features of the process of writing, it is absolutely essential that the signifier remain unnamed and unspecified in order that we be able to experience the complexity of that process. This increasing complexity of writing is specifically due to the incredible diversity of linguistic material available to Guillén as a New World writer. It is a superabundance of forms, styles, and meanings that is irreducible. If it has any common denominator, it is that of the (Neo)baroque,[56] which manifests itself in New World literature as a deliberate and truly "monstrous" proliferation of identities. In *El diario*, this proliferation of identities extends from the level of the sign all the way to the level of genre, including literary as well as nonliterary forms. In this sense, Guillén's text is a veritable *concierto barroco* [baroque concert].[57]

Ellipsis and polyptoton, the phrase "el diario que a diario" plays on words as well as on history: The juxtaposition of different languages or forms of discourse corresponds to the textual coexistence of different historical periods. Because of the title's inherent duplicity, resulting from Guillén's simultaneous and contradictory appeal to the chronological format of a diary or logbook and to the formal irregularities of a newspaper, it would be problematic to view *El diario* simply as a "carefully delineated chronological portrayal of consistently viewed historical reality."[58] To be sure, there is a semblance of chronology in *El diario*: It is roughly divided into five sections, each associated with a specific historical period: (*a*) the Spanish conquest and occupation up to 1762; (*b*) the English occupation of Havana in 1762/63; (*c*) the period of French influence owing to the Bourbon dynasty in Spain itself and also the massive immigration from Haiti during the Haitian Revolution (1791–1805); (*d*) the so-called Ten Years' War, which really lasted for thirty years (1868–1878 and 1895–1898); and (*e*) the final years of the struggle for independence from Spain and the period of United States interventionism until the triumph of the revolution. The transition between each section is marked by a "Paréntesis" [Parenthesis], a short, italicized poem that introduces the theme upon which the following poetic collages improvise. The last of the five "Parentheses," with which the poem ends, is entitled "Final," but instead of bringing about closure, it indicates that the "final" improvisation, whose theme would have to be the postrevolutionary years, is left up to the reader's knowledge and imagination. In this way, "Final" inevitably returns us to the "Prologuillo" and the "Epístola," both of which exist outside of the linear movement charted above. This sudden circular movement cannot but diminish our faith in the reliability of historical chronology in *El diario*. The "Parentheses" infuse *El diario* with the semblance of a chronological structure, which is significantly reinforced by the repetition of phrases such as *"Luego pasó de esta manera"* [Then it happened this way], only to be turned into a parody of the epic poem which Guillén, as we know from his introduction, decided not to write. It is therefore appropriate that he would entitle those short transitions "Parentheses." They are fragmentary reminders of what this poem might have been but is not: a chronicle of the past without any ties to the present. The final line of *El diario*— *"Todo fue así, de esa manera"* [Everything was like this, just like this]—still attempts to maintain this epic mode, but its inability to effect closure reduces it to a flat rhetorical cliché.

It is precisely at this point, the moment when the epic mode falters, that Guillén commences the reorganization of history and of his discourse. The ultimate collapse of the epic format tellingly coincides with the moment of revolution and rupture, which is textually represented by the gap that separates the last line of "Final" from the rest of the poem. The revolution in its absence from the text itself is thus represented as a process that creates new spaces, new possibilities for the writer to explore. Again we are faced with an absent signifier, around which Guillén constructs an orbit of images, which I shall now examine.

The fact that "Final," in sharp incongruity with its title, carries us back to the beginning of the poem already suggests that revolution, for Guillén, is not exclusively a break with the past, as it tends to be defined in modern usage. [59] Retaining part of its older meaning—*revolver*, to turn around, repeat—revolution for him is an event that causes discontinuity by interrupting a strict historical sequence. However, this rupture, this schism, this wound, if you will, is an aperture not only toward the future but also toward the past. Discontinuity thus creates an opportunity for continuity, not in an ideal reconciliation of the old with the new, but in their active and open confrontation. Revolution, in short, is a moment of intellectual violence which clears a space for both remembrance and revision and which, in this case, compels Guillén to return to the historical origins of Cuba and the New World. What we witness at the end of *El diario*, then, is a contraction of all of Cuban history into a single moment about to explode into the multitude of historical fragments Guillén (re)assembles in this poem.

Luego pasó de esta manera:
Su gran frente sombría

sintió arder el Turquino.
La sangre en rudas oleadas vino
a tocar a la puerta de otro día. (OP, 2: 435)

[Then it happened this way:
The Turquino felt its great
somber forehead burn.
In harsh waves the blood was
pounding at the door of a new day.]

Guillén's image of the Pico Turquino, the highest mountain in Cuba, situated in the Sierra Maestra in Oriente where Fidel Castro landed upon his return from Mexico in 1956, is almost like that of a volcano ready to erupt in a tidal wave of blood that would push open the doors to Cuba's future.[60] The fire motif here is reminiscent of the "flaming trees" and the "breasts red with flames" in "El apellido," a connection that accentuates Guillén's vision of a genesis as an event that stirs up and brings to the surface, in the sense of making accessible to the reader, the texts of Cuban history. In this regard, the act of revolution must be understood as the carving out of a space for the reassessment not so much of historical events themselves but of the texts, the images of language in which they have been cast. The crucial question underlying *El diario*, as well as many of Guillén's other poems, is how to establish some sort of coherence in the midst of the turbulence and chaos caused by the break with historical chronology. Guillén's dilemma is similar to that of Williams and Wright: how to visualize a structure that is at once a structure of freedom and a structure of authority.

Authorial control therefore emerges as one of the vital issues in *El diario*. If Guillén, as suggested above, does indeed seek to demystify or displace the figure of the author, then the existence of a prologue at the beginning of the poem must appear incongruous. As is known, the prologue is a standard rhetorical device through which the writer assumes control over his or her text. At the same time, however, prologues, much like the notes discussed earlier, are not very common in poetry, which makes us suspect that Guillén's "Prologuillo" might have a somewhat different function. By introducing a novelistic device at the very beginning of *El diario*, Guillén immediately puts into practice the dissolution of generic distinctions announced by the title. The situation we are forced to confront as a result of this subversive inaugural interdiction is paradoxically one in which the author assumes control over his text in order to prevent the reader from holding on to the traditional concept of authorial control and thus from placing his or her trust in a central consciousness that would authorize (or dictate) the meaning of this peculiar textual assemblage. Guillén does not offer that kind of reassurance. Instead, he intensifies our sense of insecurity by adding a device that is even more unsettling than the intrusion of novelistic strategies: footnotes.

These footnotes, which abound in *El diario*, not only call attention to the "Problems of Purity" at the level of genre but, in fact, add to those problems by even further refracting the authorial voice. The presence of these appendages is even more intrusive in *El diario* than in *Dimensions of History* or *The Double Invention of Komo*, since they are inserted directly into the text of the poem instead of being relegated to a special section at the end. Furthermore, Guillén's footnotes are, for the most part, even less informative or explanatory than Jay Wright's. Their function is evidently not to facilitate interpretation but to supply a formal equivalent to the disturbances in the lexicon caused in the "Prologuillo" by the Anglicism "stock" and the archaic pronoun "doquier." The lexical disturbances and their immediate formal manifestations also carry distinct historical references. They are less the result of Guillén's playfulness than products of a concrete historical situation: "Stock" fittingly represents the impact of Anglo–North American imperialism on all areas of Cuban life, while "doquier" is clearly a relict of Spanish colonialism. In this way, Guillén translates historical conflict into a textual confrontation between different "languages." In this respect, Guillén's approach to Cuban history within the framework of inter-American relations is an extension of the anthropological work particularly of Fernando Ortiz and Lydia Cabrera, whose profound influence especially on Guillén's so-called *poesía negra* has already been noted. It is an extension in that Guillén's collection of texts—his Archive—is much broader in scope than Ortiz's or Cabrera's, being occupied as it is with all the different currents and cross-currents whose presence has left distinctive marks on Cuba's economic, political, social, and cultural profile.

In order for poetry to be able to articulate those variegated levels of historical interaction, it has to affix its identity as a genre to accommodate a wide range of literary and nonliterary forms that are part of such an exchange. It has to become a kind of marketplace for the exchange of textual commodities. This need for supplementation is precisely what these and other footnotes in *El diario* signal; it is a need that motivates Guillén's persistent quest for a poetic method that would serve as a reliable repository of meaning in the absence of a meaningfully defined and conceived identity.

These same issues are elaborated in "Epístola," which, in many respects, qualifies as a second prologue, thus explaining why the initial "Prologuillo" is deemed "no estrictamente necesario." To be more precise, it is a different kind of prologue, whose tone is strongly indebted to the *cartas de relación*, the official reports in which the conquistadors informed the Spanish emperor about their exploits. These *relaciones* were legal documents generally addressed directly to the king. From this tradition of submitting written statements to a superior emerged the literary practice of the "Vuestra Merced" of the picaresque novel, where the *pícaro* addresses the reader presumably in an effort to obtain his or her approval for the truthfulness of his narrative.[61] But since the *pícaro's* entire existence (as well as his narrative) is dedicated to deceit and to undermining the very authority to which he appeals, the "Vuestra Merced" is really a shrewdly concealed mockery: It is less a plea for approval than an invitation to complicity. The posture Guillén adopts in "Epístola" is very similar to that of the author-as-*pícaro*, so that this poem can be described as a mock-*relación*. This is supported by the fact that Eliseo Diego, to whom the poem is dedicated and addressed, is not only a fellow poet but also a bureaucrat: He heads the public relations department of UNEAC's literary section. Unlike Guillén himself, Eliseo Diego was a member of the *Orígenes* group (1945–1954) founded by José Lezama Lima, which was one of the literary centers of ideological dissemination in prerevolutionary Cuba. As Guillén's appeal to Diego is a mock-*relación*, it may well be read as a belated criticism of that particular group of writers.

Estos viejos papeles que te envió,
esta tinta pretérita, Eliseo,
¿no moverán tu cólera o tu hastío? (*OP*, 2: 371)

[These old papers I am sending you,
this ancient ink, Eliseo,
will they not anger or bore you?]

By describing his poem as a collection of old papers and ancient ink, Guillén again diffuses the notion of authorship and assumes the role of a researcher and compiler of historical documents, in this case newspaper clippings of various kinds.[62] In addition, he apologizes profusely for having been unable to exert the "proper" measures of control over his material. Instead of fashioning from these textual fragments a simple, uncomplicated narrative that would flow before the eyes of the reader swiftly and lightly like a pleasant little brook ("como un arroyo fácil"),

Guillén offers us a veritable flood of texts that uncontrollably rises above the embankments of formal literary convention like a swollen stream in the spring: "el arroyo ha inundado la pradera" [the brook has flooded the meadow]. This metaphor of failed intention is not only, as Ellis has suggested, "the concretization of the motive for the apologetic tone in which the collection is offered to the reader."[63] It is also, more importantly, a concretization of the presence of the Baroque in *El diario*. The proliferation of meaning is effectively figured as a flood in anticipation of the harsh waves of blood pushing against the doors to the future in "Final." But at the same time as he thus exposes the shortcomings of traditional historical narrative, whose conventions are, like narrow river-beds, unable to contain the vast flood of materials, Guillén ironically continues to insist on his modesty and good intentions.

Juro por los sinsontes y las flores
que en aquesta ocasión no he pretendido
provocar con mi verso tus furores.

Torpeza y no maldad más bien ha sido.
Mira tú cómo a veces un disparo
medido, bien medido, ultramedido,

al no dar en·el blanco da en el claro,
lo que quiere decir que se va al viento,
hecho por lo demás que en mí no es raro.

Al trote femoral de mi jumento
regreso pues sobre mis propias huellas
hasta dejarlo al fin libre y contento

en campos de zafir paciendo estrellas.
(como Luis el de Góngora decía)
para (me digo yo) eructar centellas. (*OP*, 2: 372)

[I swear in the name of mockingbirds and flowers
that this time I did not try
to provoke your fury with my poetic powers.

Clumsiness rather than malice has caused this.
Look how sometimes a carefully aimed shot,
well-aimed, super-well aimed even,

by missing the target makes a point,
that is to say, it shoots clear through,
which in my case happens frequently.

My donkey's skeletal trot
takes me back over my own footprints
until in the end I leave him, free and content,

in sapphire fields grazing on stars
(as Luis de Góngora used to say)
in order (I tell myself) to burp up embers.]

Given Guillén's well-deserved reputation as a master of poetic styles, clumsiness is not something we would attribute to his poetry. He is, in fact, far from being clumsy in his gentle mockery of the baroque style of Góngora, a poet whose work brilliantly synthesizes the impact of the Greco-Roman tradition introduced to sixteenth- and seventeenth-century Spanish letters by Garcilaso de la Vega (the poet, not the Inca). Garcilaso, it should be added, was the first to popularize in Spain poetic forms such as the Italian tercet, incidentally the same versification Guillén employs in "Epístola."[64] The clash between this traditional poetic form on the one hand and Guillén's often raucously colloquial language on the other—"mear pañales" [to wet diapers]; "culos" [assholes]; "el castrón del Tío" [that ass of an Uncle, meaning, of course, Uncle Sam]; and "maderos" [blockheads]—reveals the irreverence below the unrippled textual surface and the poet's deceptively apologetic tone. This language carries over to the semantic level the dialogic structure of the mock-*relación*. The resulting tensions culminate, at the very center of "Epístola," in the juxtaposition of two language-images, each of which is nourished, albeit in a different way, by the trope of the flood: The first—"en campos de zafir paciendo estrellas"—is a classic Gongorine conceit representing the Spanish Baroque, while the second—"algarabía en lengua de piratas y bozales"—encapsulates Guillén's idea of the Latin American Neobaroque. Both are representations of two different versions of the Baroque, the old and the new, the Spanish and the Latin American, which confront each other in "Epístola" and throughout *El diario*. Góngora's "campos de zafir" exemplify uncontrolled metaphoric exuberance and artificialization owing to the progressive layering over of levels of language. "Algarabía," in contrast, is an expression not of ultimate metaphoric refinement but rather of what Guillén so deprecatingly calls clumsiness. "Algarabía," which may be translated, albeit inadequately, as "noisy chatter," signifies a linguistic heterogeneity so intense that it transforms the normally unilingual stylistic surface of a text into a polyphonic Babel (or babble) of languages. To grasp more fully the complexity this term assumes in the context of *El diario*, let us examine the historico-cultural environment from which it emerged.

As the prefix *al-* indicates, *algarabía* has Arabic roots and goes back in its etymological origins to the time of the Moorish occupation of the Spanish peninsula.[65] It actually means "Arabic" (*al-ᶜarabiyya*), in a way, however, that goes beyond the technical sense to associate that language with everything that is foreign, unintelligible, and disorderly. Perhaps "gibberish" or "jabber" would be the best English approximations. I shall refrain from listing all the semantic nuances this word has acquired over time and instead focus on a definition that allows me to link etymology with cultural history: "Confusing screams of various persons talking at the same time, or a similar noise produced by an individual."[66] Although there is no explicit mention of this, it is likely that *algarabía* was associated with the oriental bazaars that came to be a familiar institution in the large commercial centers of medieval Spain. *Algarabía* probably referred to the tumultuous chaos of those bazaars, which were filled with the loud, insistent cries of street vendors, blending with the buzzing of the excited crowd of customers and spectators into a dense mixture of incomprehensible sounds. *Algarabía*, then, signifies the intense disorder of these markets represented by the confusing simultaneity of voices filling the air.

The same chaos produced by simultaneity inspires the whole of *El diario*, which is a formidable attempt to render visible and intelligible in writing the levels of interaction and interpenetration inherent in the term *algarabía*. The nature of this poetic project becomes even clearer once we remind ourselves that these markets were not simply places for the exchange of material goods. They were also social and cultural institutions, meeting places for all kinds of people which became, in medieval Spain as well as in the New World, the public centers of cultural exchange precisely of the kind that produced a word like *algarabía*. In this sense, *algarabía* is Guillén's master trope for cross-cultural exchange, a figure that replaces and refines terms such as *mestizaje* and *transculturación*. Unlike those earlier terms, *algarabía*, which ultimately serves as a trope for Cuban (and New World) culture, has the advantage of forcing us to include in a definition of the concept of culture *all* levels of human activity which are in some way affected by this process of continuous exchange and transformation, from economics to politics to the arts, without establishing a hierarchy among them.

El diario, then, is a kind of literary marketplace, or, in the words of Balzac, "un bazar de figures, de fortunes et d'opinions."[67] The fact that the poem is also conceived as a historical portrait of Havana, which was a typical New World bazaar, gives Guillén's vision of chaos, or better, his vision of the tensions underlying the pretense of order, a solid historical foundation: As is well known, Havana had been, almost from the very beginning of Spanish rule, the single most important trading post as well as military port in the New World. The city's wealth in the eighteenth century, that is, before the sugar boom, was mostly derived from the supply of provisions for the Spanish royal fleet and a relatively small number of commercial vessels with cargo from Spain. It also had a substantial free mulatto and black population, whose members were well established in a number of professions. All of these factors contributed to the city's special character, which is reflected in the words of Abbé Raynal, who called Havana "the boulevard of the New World."[68] It is this special character of the then largest city in the New World, its diverse "stock" of goods and people, that Guillén aptly conveys with the phrase "algarabía / en lengua de piratas y bozales." When reading these lines, one is also reminded of a remark García Márquez once made in an interview: "Yes, the history of the Caribbean is full of magic, a magic brought here by the black slaves from Africa, but also by the Swedish, Dutch, and English pirates, who could build an opera house in New Orleans as well as they could stud the teeth of their women with diamonds."[69] This magic—"lo extraordinario," as Guillén calls it in the "Prologuillo"—is related to, yet quite different from, that of Góngora's sapphire fields or, for that matter, the colorful tropical tapestries Columbus weaves in his diary.

Guillén's concept of *algarabía* is a revision of the idea of "lo real maravilloso" Alejo Carpentier conceptualized in the 1940s. *Algarabía* is Guillén's trope for the baroque nature of Latin American writing manifest, above all, in its stylelessness, an element Carpentier himself emphasized in the sixties, when he proposed the Baroque as a new metaphor designating that which is peculiarly Latin American. As González Echevarría writes in *The Pilgrim at Home*:

On the one hand, Carpentier maintains that the baroque nature of Latin American literature stems from the necessity to name for the first time realities that are outside of the mainstream of Western culture. On the other, he states that what characterizes Latin American reality is its stylelessness, which results from its being an amalgam of styles from many cultural traditions and epochs: Indian, African, European, Neoclassical, Modern, etc. With the first statement Carpentier is, of course, resurrecting the Blakean and generally Romantic topos of Adam in the Garden after the fall having to give names to the things that surround him. But the second claim runs counter to the first insofar as the reality in question, if it is the product of manifold traditions, would have already been "named" several times, and by different peoples. If what characterizes Latin American reality is that mélange of styles Carpentier discovers in the architecture of Havana . . . then the act of naming that reality is a renaming.[70]

The act of renaming, that is, of supplementing previous names, which has already been discussed especially in connection with "El apellido," is of considerable importance to El diario: It provides the foundation for the heterogeneity of styles that characterizes this poem. Renaming, which achieves the coexistence of different "names" representing different modes of perceiving reality, always implies a kind of doubleness (or tripleness, etc.) and thus the presence of an internal dialogue between the memory of someone else's discourse and one's own. It is this internal dialogue that Guillén exteriorizes in El diario in order to interanimate contexts (social, cultural, literary) commonly regarded as separate. The result is a deformation, a (positive) distortion of the conceptual molds in which the image of the New World, and particularly Latin America, has been cast since the times of the chroniclers of the Indies.

El diario is a large-scale debunking of canonized culture mobilized by the same carnivalistic impulse that underlies a work such as Cabrera Infante's Tres tristes tigres [Three Trapped Tigers] (1967). Like Tres tristes tigres, El diario is characterized "by an extraordinary freedom of composition which manifests itself in a multi-generic or collage texture, by the lack of a finalizing authorial presence which allows characters [or, in Guillén's case, texts or language-images] to evolve their own truth in a Socratic conversation of different voices, and by an apparent shattering of the customary novelesque logic of narrative," which, in this instance, is equivalent to Guillén's subversion of epic chronology.[71] This carnivalistic impulse is not a new or even an unusual feature of Guillén's poetry: We have seen its beginnings in "Sensemayá" in the form of persistent allusions to the "Día de Reyes" as a historico-cultural fundament for the poem's subversive textual activities. It is also present in a different way in the "Elegía a Jesús Menéndez," where Guillén makes extensive use of different styles (such as the language of the stock market) and textual fragments in the form of quoted newspaper clippings.[72] But it is not until El diario that this impulse comes to full fruition.

Since El diario, above all, poses as a kind of documentary history of Cuba, the concept of the Archive (an "inventario" of sorts), which has been regarded as one of the key figures in the modern Latin American narrative, is vital to the poem. The meaning of the Greek etymon arché—"beginning" (from archein, to begin, to rule)—already implies that the Archive is a place of origin, whose heterogeneity, however, precludes any notions of a single origin or center. "The Archive,"

González Echevarría contends in his commentary on Melquíades's study in *One Hundred Years of Solitude,*

is not so much an accumulation of texts as the process whereby texts are written; a process of repeated combinations, of shufflings and re-shufflings ruled by heterogeneity and difference. It is not strictly linear as both continuity and discontinuity [are] held together in uneasy allegiance. This is the reason why the previous mediations through which Latin America was narrated are contained in the Archive as voided presences: they are both erased and a memory of their own demise, keys to filing systems now abandoned, but they retain their archival quality, their power to differentiate, to space. They are not archetypes, but an *arché* of types. [73]

Such voided presences abound in Guillén's Archive: The mock-*relación* in "Epístola," its Italian tercets, and the Gongorine mannerisms are all part of ideological structures (filing systems, as it were) that have been divested of their authority, in this case the Hapsburg empire and its legal as well as literary conventions, influenced as they were by the Greco-Roman tradition. An interesting connection is drawn between these two systems of writing in the brief untitled poem that follows the "Epístola," where Guillén invokes Hermes and Mercury, gods of trade and commerce, only to associate them with "El Gran Ladrón" [The Great Thief], the Spanish king, whose faded authority is subsequently represented by the two "Pregones" [Street Cries].

Both "Pregones" begin with variations on a typical legalistic formula: "Según que lo han de uso y costumbre" [In keeping with custom and habit], a cliché that recurs in the section entitled "Esclavos Europeos" [European Slaves] as "la costumbre general." In the "Pregón primero," concerned with the imposition of property taxes and representative of Spain's "habit" of draining Cuba's economic resources through heavy taxation, the bureaucratic authority inscribed in this formula is effective-ly undermined by the very ridiculousness of the names of the members of the municipal council (the *cabildo*, which at the time was composed almost exclusively of *peninsulares*): Francisco Cartucho, for instance, might be translated as Frank Bigshot, while Pero Caramba (with Pero pretending to be a short form for Pedro) literally means, "What the hell . . . !", perhaps Guillén's own exclamation at what he has earlier described as "un pregón / para saber / lo que a cada uno le puede coger" [a proclamation / to find out / what he (the Great Thief) can steal from each one].

The "Pregón segundo" is more complex, because in this instance a specific historical event provides the basis for the poem's resistance to the formal authority it purports to embody: This event is a pirate attack on the town of Manzanillo in 1604, which is also suggestive of the earlier sacking of Havana by French pirates in 1538. Here, then, is Guillén's version:

Según uso y costumbre,
en reunión del Cabildo fue acordado:
Que las sendas que salen de la playa
se cierren e no haya
habitante ninguno tan osado
de las abrir, pues ha llegado aviso
de que este pueblo e villa
recuestado e robado
de piratas franceses
fue, e que por más de un punto penetraron:
si es español, so pena
de que pague mil pesos
para gastos de guerra,
o recibir azotes hasta cien
si acaso desta plata careciera;
si negra libre fuera,
o mulata tal vez o mero esclavo,
que sea desjarretado
de un pie; si fuese indio, que trabaje
en la obra del Fuerte un año entero.
Así sea pregonado, así se diga
en la plaza e las calles desta villa. (OP, 2: 375)

[In keeping with custom and habit,
it was agreed as the Council reconvened:
that the paths leading up from the beach
be closed and that nobody
should be so bold as
to reopen them, since a warning has been received
that French Pirates are on their way
to invade and sack
this town and its people,
and that they have broken through in several places;
if the transgressor is a Spaniard, the penalty
is a thousand pesos
for the war fund;
or up to one hundred lashes
in case that he does not have enough money;

if it is a free black woman, a mulatto girl perhaps,
or a simple slave, she will have
one foot cut off;
if it is an Indian, he will be sentenced to hard labor
at the Fort for a whole year.
Thus it should be announced, thus it should be said,
in the marketplace and in the streets of this town.]

Pirate attacks on various parts of Cuba were common at the time, so that it is fitting for Guillén to use one such local incident, not simply to represent this particular historical period, but also as the basis for dealing a subtle, but effective, blow to the colonial authority this official proclamation seeks to enforce. Another, "unofficial," document is hidden behind this "Pregón": That literary document is Silvestre de Balboa's "Espejo de paciencia" [Mirror of Patience] (1608), a long epic poem that narrates the above-mentioned attack on the port of Manzanillo by the French pirate Gilberto Girón, who captured Bishop Juan de la Cabezas y Altamirano in order to blackmail the town. Balboa describes how the bishop is heroically rescued by Captain Gregorio Ramos and his twenty-four men, among them the Indian Rodrigo Martín and the black ("criollo") slave Salvador, who is freed as a reward for killing the pirate.[74] Although Balboa's *octavos reales* are no doubt products of Spanish neo-classicism, the "Espejo de paciencia" is also one of the first works of New World literature to include a black character among its protagonists.[75] Not only was Balboa, a native of Gran Canaria, sensitive to the details of the Cuban landscape in a way that prefigures Manuel de Zequeira's famous ode "A la piña," to which Guillén alludes in the section "Últimas novedades en libros cubanos" (*OP*, 2: 408). He was also careful to call attention to the presence in Cuba of three major cultural groups— Spaniards, Indians, and Blacks—whose joining forces against an intruder may be regarded as the first literary projection of a vision of racial cooperation as the mainspring of Cuban nationalism. Balboa's poem is the first literary portrait of colonial Cuba, a text in which exuberant visions of tropical beauty are tempered by images of a violent reality and curious appearances of mythological beings. But most importantly, Balboa assigns to the black slave the role of a savior (*salvador*), a gesture whose symbolic value is particularly relevant to Guillén's emphasis on the black elements in Cuban culture.

The "Espejo de paciencia," then, as it emerges from between the lines of the "Pregón segundo" and effaces it in the process, is the major founding text whose echoes resound throughout this first section of *El diario*. The atmosphere of order and control the "Pregón" is trying to establish with the stiff bureaucratic language in which it meters out different penalties for the same offense, thus legally dividing Cuba's population into three distinct racial groups, stands in vivid contrast to Balboa's heroic vision of racial harmony. But Guillén, while using the "Espejo de paciencia" to undermine the authority of the "Pregón segundo," also exposes the limitations of Balboa's vision: Cuban culture, for Guillén, is a product not of heroic conquests but rather of uncontrollable, violent encounters between different cultures. Guillén's conquistadors are not heroes but "señores en celo" (Lords in heat):

y de las entrepiernas de hembras baratas
caían los frutos de las rudas *cañonas,*
(Cubanismo: bravatas)
que daban los señores en celo
bien repletos de hormonas,
en camas y tarimas, sin olvidar el suelo,
a las esclavas negras y mulatas; (*OP,* 2: 375–76)

[and from the crotches of cheap females
dropped the fruits of cruel *cañonas*
(Cubanism: rapes)
that lords in heat
with an abundance of hormones
forced on enslaved black and mulatto women,
in beds and on low benches, not to say anything about the floors;]

These harsh images of miscegenation invalidate the racial separatism decreed in the "Pregón segundo" to accentuate the actual lack of control on the part of Spain's imperial bureaucracy and its local representatives, not only over the colony's economic affairs, but also over its sociocultural development. Also quite in keeping with custom and habit, royal decrees of whatever sort were, more often than not, successfully ignored: *obedezco pero no cumplo* [I obey, but I do not execute].[76] In addition, such practices of sexual exploitation and abuse as well as other forms of violence remained largely unaffected by the fact that Guillén's "lords in heat" were also devout Catholics. Ironically, such religious beliefs— Guillén's main target in items such as "Aviso contra la culebrilla" [Warning against Hoof-and-Mouth Disease] and "Aviso contra muertes súbitas" [Warning against Sudden Deaths]—were reserved, he implies, for problems of a more concrete and tangible nature (such as epidemics) rather than being extended to humanistic issues. Ultimately, the attempt to contain smallpox and other "diseases" (such as crime and corruption) through public prayers and processions is as absurd as the idea of controlling miscegenation through legal measures.

These contradictions culminate in "Esclavos Europeos" [European Slaves], a section composed of advertisements of the kind that appeared regularly in papers such as *El Papel Periódico de La Habana, El diario de la Marina,* and *El Siglo,*[77] with the difference, however, that the slaves in Guillén's versions are white. Most interesting about this section is the way in which Guillén reverses historical facts along with the color of the human merchandise, which makes these advertisements one of the most obvious examples of the rewriting and unwriting of history in which he engages throughout *El diario.* But it is also worth noting that the kinds of advertisements he mimicks are not contemporaneous with the "Espejo." They represent a different period in Cuban history—the late eighteenth and early to mid-nineteenth centuries—and consequently disrupt historical chronology. This disruption, in turn, places an additional emphasis on Guillén's playfulness and his resistance to the principles of conventional historiography. To be sure, black slaves were introduced to Cuba well before the eighteenth century, but the transatlantic slave trade did not really begin to flourish in the island until the English occupation in 1762–1763, when the severe restrictions the Spanish crown had traditionally imposed on the island's foreign trade were temporarily lifted. Free trade immensely accelerated the influx of slaves into Cuba, given that the companies that controlled the transatlantic trade were, at least initially, almost without exception in the hands of foreigners such as the English, the Dutch, and the Portuguese. In this respect, "Esclavos Europeos" anticipates the second part of *El diario,* which is devoted to the English occupation of Havana (*OP,* 2: 383–85).

To legitimize these conspicuous distortions while at the same time promoting a sense of historical synchronicity, Guillén prefaces his list of advertisements with a brief "editorial statement."

ADVERTENCIA IMPORTANTE

Es sorprendente la semejanza que existe entre el texto de estos anuncios y el lenguaje empleado por los traficantes en esclavos africanos (negreros) para proponer su mercancía. Forzados por la costumbre general aceptamos su publicación, no sin consignar la repugnancia que tan infame comercio produce en nuestro espíritu. (*OP,* 2: 377)

IMPORTANT NOTICE

[The similarity between the text of the following announcements and the language the traffickers in African slaves (slave traders) used to advertise their merchandise is surprising. Compelled by general custom we have consented to print these notices, however not without stating the disgust such infamous commerce produces in our spirit.]

The phrase "Es sorprendente la semejanza" carries even farther the process of authorial self-effacement we have witnessed in the two "Pregones" in order for Guillén to be able to maintain a distance between himself and the "documents" he offers his readers for scrutiny. This distance is an authenticating device employed to assure the truthfulness and historical accuracy of a text that has so ostentatiously been manipulated: The formal similarities between these notices and those found in proslavery newspapers are in no way surprising but of course fully intended.

The discrepancy between the advertisements' formal authenticity and their contents, which completely reverses the actual historical relationships between blacks and whites, creates considerable confusion in the mind of the reader, who has been historically conditioned to think of slaves exclusively as black, and vice versa. But neither the reader nor the fictional newspaper editor can simply dismiss these advertisements as historically inaccurate, if only because they conform stylistically to formal conventions traditionally associated with slavery. They are as much part of the discourse of slavery in the New World as the expression "sacos de carbón" [sacks of coal], which was employed during the nineteenth century as a commercial euphemism for illegally imported slaves.[78] Guillén skillfully breaks the chain of associations which constitutes that discourse by filling the rhetorical shell of these formal conventions with contents that explode their traditional frame of reference and thus render them absurd. This is precisely why special emphasis is given in each item to the color of the human merchandise: "Véndese un blanco joven" [For sale: a white youngster]; "Blanca de cuatros meses de parida" [White girl having given birth four months ago]; "Una pareja de blanquitos" [A pair of white children]; "un blanco libre de tacha" [an unblemished white male]; "un blanco de mediana estatura" [a white man of medium build]. Significant here is not so much the idea of substituting racially the oppressor for the oppressed, but the fact that Guillén forces us to distinguish between slavery as a system of oppression and the question of race. Ellis argues that this "causes the image to picture an oppressed class rather than an oppressed race,"[79] but such a reading, convenient as it may be to prove Guillén's alleged ideological consistency, makes little sense. After all, Guillén could have conveyed the idea of an oppressed class much more effectively by making the slaves in the advertisements both black and white to show that members of both races shared the same predicament, a strategy that he in fact frequently employs in such instances.[80] While there is no question that part of Guillén's message in this section has to do with oppression as something that transcends race, his separation of slavery from racial issues also points to a different set of problems. This distinction forms the basis for his calling attention to the fact that the gradual disintegration of slavery as an economic system during the late nineteenth century did not automatically liquidate race prejudice in Cuba. This is quite obvious in some of the later news items about the Ten Years' War (1868–1878):

El ánimo por otra parte se sorprende ante la
consideración de que un Guillermón, un
Maceo, un Crombet se erijan en paladines de un
país cuya cultura los rechaza.[81]

[*The soul on the other hand is struck by the*
idea that a Guillermón, a Maceo, and a Crombet
would emerge as defenders of a country whose
culture rejects them.]
. . . .

. . . pues los demás jefes de la pasada guerra,
que como es sabido son muchos en aquella
provincia, no sólo no han tomado parte en
el movimiento, sino que lo rechazan, agre-
gando que de los sublevados las siete ocatavas
partes pertenecen a las raza de color.[82]

[. . . for the rest of the leaders of the last war,
who, as is known, are numerous in that province,
have not only not taken part in the movement, but
reject it outright, adding that seven-eighths of
the rebels belong to the colored race.]
. . . .

LA GUERRA   TIENE UN
CARÁCTER RACISTA UN
CARÁCTER RACISTA UN
CARÁCTER RACISTA UN
CARÁCTER RACISTA UN (*OP*, 2: 410)

The same racial prejudice flares up again in an advertisement from the period of the United States protectorate:

Se busca una muchacha para atender a un
niño de dos años. Si no es blanca, o
mestiza adelantada, que no se presente.
Calle X No. 60 (*OP*, 2: 418)

[Wanted: a girl for looking after a two-year-
old boy. Applicants need not inquire unless
they are white or light mestizas.
Street X, No. 60]

Although we are informed in an editorial footnote that "No hemos
podido encontrar la calle X en el Vedado, por lo que suponemos que ya
no existe. Pero existió sin duda antes de la Revolución" [We have not
been able to locate Street X in Vedado; we therefore presume that it no
longer exists. But it no doubt existed before the Revolution], the link
between changed street names and changed attitudes remains ambigu-
ous.[83] This ambiguity is subtly reinforced by the fact that "Street X" is, of
course, anywhere and nowhere. As a floating signifier, it represents
something that has no specific location, that exists but cannot be pin-
pointed or isolated, either before the revolution or afterwards. In brief,
attitudes are not as easily altered as street names.

It is useful, upon returning to the "Esclavos Europeos" section, to
contrast the "Street X" as a floating signifier that exists outside of history
in a kind of mythical timelessness with the *picota* mentioned in the last
item in this series, which bears the ironic title "Acto de justicia" (Act of
Justice).

El blanco Domingo Español será conducido el viernes próximo por
las calles de la Capital llevando una navaja colgada al cuello, misma
con que causó heridas a sus amos, un matrimonio del que era esclavo.
Le darán ciento cincuenta azotes de vergüenza pública, y cincuenta
más en la picota situada en la calle de este nombre. Despues que sane
del látigo será enviado a Ceuta por diez años. (*OP*, 2: 379)

[Next Friday the white man Domingo Español will be dragged
through the streets of the capital carrying around his neck the same
razor with which he wounded his owners, a couple whose slave he
used to be. He will receive a hundred and fifty shameful lashes in
public and fifty more at the whipping post in Picota Street. After his
wounds have healed, he will be sent to Ceuta for ten years.]

The *picota*, or whipping post, a conspicuous presence in the mar-
ketplaces of most of Latin America's colonial cities, was the most tangible
emblem of Spanish imperialism. Its symbolic value may be compared to

that of the guillotine during the French Revolution, an analogy implicit in the second epigraph to Carpentier's *Explosion in the Cathedral*. [84] The *picota* is the ultimate embodiment of the same kind of authoritarianism and oppression represented as language-images in the above advertisements. It is therefore appropriate that Guillén should mention it in the same breath as Ceuta, Spain's ill-famed military prison located at the tip of Gibraltar in Northern Africa. The reference to Ceuta in this context foreshadows many of the later events chronicled in *El diario*: It alludes to Spain's frequently disposing of rebels and political dissidents in the American colonies by shipping them off to Ceuta, thus institutionalizing her own version of a Middle Passage from the New World back to Africa. This curious reversal can be regarded as an extension of the inversion of racial stereotypes in "Acto de Justicia": The mythical razor has suddenly changed hands, a gesture on the part of Guillén which emphasizes the inherent unreliability of symbolic language by suggesting that attitudes commonly associated with blacks may well be adopted by other groups.

The "Soneto," which follows the "Esclavos Europeos" advertisements, transports us from one representation of sanctioned culture to another. The formal clash between the nonliterary advertisements and the stylistic refinement of the sonnet exemplifies the novelistic tendencies at work throughout *El diario*. Their effects are also visible in the "Soneto" itself, where the formal symmetry commonly indicative of monological discourse falls apart under the pressure of colloquialisms and obscenity.

En las calles el pueblo caga y mea
sin que el ojo se ofenda ni el resuello.

[In the streets the people shit and piss
without the eye or the nose taking offense.]

What remains is not a sonnet but the formal image of a sonnet, a structure infested with the same proliferating growth of chaos and violence that characterizes the historical environment it depicts. One of the prominent textual manifestations of that uncontrolled proliferation is the list of images of disease and violence, which is an example of chaotic enumeration. [85]

Moscas, mosquitos, ratas y ratones,
polvo hecho fango, charcas pestilentes,
fiebres malignas, chancros, purgaciones,

contagio son de bestias y de gentes,
bajo un sol de ladrones y gritones
y una luna de dientes relucientes. (*OP*, 2: 380)

[Flies, mosquitoes, rats, and mice,
dust turned to mud, stinking puddles,
malignant fevers, venereal disease, menstrual blood,

contagious for animals and humans alike,
under a sun of gangsters and screaming people,
and a moon with sparkling teeth.]

As Spitzer has shown, chaotic enumeration is a compositional princi-
ple frequently used in modern poetry. Whitman's *Leaves of Grass* may be
cited as perhaps the most prominent example of this technique. But
instead of being an expression of cosmic totality and transcendental unity
(as in Whitman), Guillén's catalogues are intratextual representations of
the turbulent disorder that characterizes *El diario* both as a literary mar-
ketplace and as an Archive. The principle of chaotic enumeration allows
Guillén to maintain a maximum of freeplay both within individual items
and among them. *El diario* as a poetic collage achieves coherence only in
a double reading that would restore to the text the literary and nonliterary
structures it effaces, without, however, simultaneously reinstating their
previous authority or truth-value.

In this respect, the image of the moon in the above citation is of special
interest. It can be traced back to one of Guillén's earliest poems, "Elegía
moderna del motivo cursi" [Modern Elegy on a Ridiculous Motif] in
Poemas de transición. In the first stanza of that poem, Guillén writes:

No sé que tú piensas, hermano, pero creo
que hay que educar la Musa desde pequeña en una
fobia sincera contra las cosas de la Luna,
sátelite cornudo, desprestigiado y feo. (*OP*, 1: 98)

[I don't know what you think, brother, but I believe
that one must teach the Muse very early on
to be seriously afraid of things connected with the Moon,
that cuckolded, discredited, and ugly satellite.]

As in the "Soneto," Guillén mercilessly strips the figure of the moon of its
romantic attributes, connotations without meaning to the modern poet.
The moon with sparkling teeth which emerges from the disfigurement of

Romantic poetry's metaphoric conventions belongs to the same category as the statue of Spanish marble and the (family) tree in "El apellido." Stephanie Davis-Lett has discussed the "Elegía moderna con motivo cursi" as one of the earliest examples of the kinds of literary games that characterize Guillén's poetry.[86] However, Guillén's games are, for the most part, far from being innocuously playful linguistic experiments. In fact, his moon's sparkling teeth are as sharp as the daggers waiting in the dark for those naive enough to take a stroll in the deceptively romantic moonlight: "y quien de noche ingenuo se pasea / a escondido puñal arriesga el cuello" [and anybody naive enough to take a stroll at night / takes the risk of having his throat cut by a hidden dagger]. Guillén's moon with its teeth bared in a posture that is a combination of a laugh and a threat is a figure not only reflecting the violently ambiguous nature of the historical environment itself but also embodying the aggressiveness of Guillén's poetic language.

This literary aggressiveness escalates in the "Interludio," subtitled "Fragmentos de poemas célebres" [Fragments of Famous Poems]. In this fragment, which is based on the first octave of José de Espronceda's popular "Canción del pirata" [Song of the Pirate], Guillén's previous visions of chaos become so intense that the original poem is defaced and deformed almost beyond recognition and to the point of total meaninglessness. In order to render Guillén's devious phonetic distortions more visible, I quote his version side by side with Espronceda's original.[87]

Con diez coñones por bonda	*Con diez cañones por banda,*
vianto en pipa a toda bula,	*Viento en popa a toda vela,*
no carta el mer, sino viula	*No corta el mar, sino vuela,*
un bularo bergantón:	*Un velero bergantín:*
Bajol pireta que lloman	*Bajel pirata que llaman*
por su bravara "El Temodo,"	*Por su bravura el* Temido,
en tido el mer conosodo	*En todo mar conocido,*
del ino al etro confón.	*Del uno al otro confín.*
(*OP*, 2: 380)	

It is almost impossible to duplicate in English (or any other language, for that matter) the kinds of phonetic substitutions with which Guillén reduces this Byronesque poem to incomprehensible babble, or better, to *algarabía*. The following is only one possibility among many.

Ormed with ten connens	*Armed with ten cannons,*
all soils swellen in the wand,	*All sails swollen with the wind,*
she flaus ocress the woters,	*She flies across the waters,*

A swaft braggontan:	*A swift brigantine:*
the Druodful ene they coll her	*The Dreadful One they call her,*
becouse she is so beld,	*Because she is so bold,*
knewn all ocress the ecuon,	*Known all across the ocean,*
from ene to the ether shere.	*From one to the other shore.*

That this outrageous disfigurement is committed under the pretense of creating a new language is evident from the fact that the phonetic distortions are carried over even into the accompanying footnote: "Teda semejonza con Espronzuda es fortuota," which may be translated as "Ony similority with Espronzuda is untirely coinciduntol." This new "language" is Guillén's biting response to the original poem's sentimental glorification of the pirate as a rebel observing no law but his own:

"*Que es mi barco mi tesoro,*
Que es mi Dios la libertad,
Mi ley la fuerza y el viento,
Mi única patria la mar."

[*That my ship be my treasure,*
and liberty by God,
My law the wind and my power,
My only country the sea.]

It is clear from Guillén's nonsensical linguistic permutations that meaning cannot emerge from a text where authorial freedom is total and where, consequently, wordplay becomes an end unto itself. Guillén comes closest here to Cabrera Infante's *Tres tristes tigres.* The following untranslatable "Cantata del café" is an excellent example of Cabrera Infante's employing a technique of phonetic distortion similar to the one we find in Guillén's "Interludio."

Yo to doró
to doró noño hormoso
to doró ono coso
ono coso co yo solo so
COFO
Ye te deré
te deré neñe hermese
te deré ene kese
ene kese ke ye sele se
KEFE[88]

There is an abundance of other, less elaborate wordplays such as the equally untranslatable sequence "El vañe de villales. El llave de nivales. El valle de viñales," "Cristócrates" [a condensation of Cristo and Socrates], or "Popuhilarity" (*TTT*, 343, 429, 333), to mention only a few. Guillén's "Batistafio" (*OP*, 2: 432), a condensation of Batista and *epitafio*, which may be rendered as "Batistaph," as well as his pun on hot dogs— "Perros calientes. Perras en las misma situación" [Hot dogs. Bitches in the same condition"] (*OP*, 2: 413)—belongs in the same category with Cabrera Infante's wordplays. But, as Sarduy has argued, such permutations are not simply invitations to pure play and thus to nonmeaning but are used, in the case of Cabrera Infante, to assert and guard the liberty of the author.[89] The same holds true for Guillén. In *El diario* this play on words, which begins with the title, "El diario que a diario," a phrase whose alliterative powers are akin to those of "Tres tristes tigres," indicates the presence of a structure of both freedom and authority that serves as a controlling mechanism for the textual arrangements. This structure, insofar as we can call it that at all, derives its authority precisely from the freedom to appear in different guises. Authorial control for Guillén is a function of the writer's ability to wear different masks while at the same time calling attention to their status as masks. It is this ability to elude ideological confinement by assuming a multitude of shapes and forms (remember Mackandal) that constitutes the carnival link between poems as superficially different as "Sensemayá" and *El diario*.

This, if anything, is the message encoded in the apparent meaninglessness of the "Interludio," which becomes even clearer when it is read in connection with the adjacent item entitled "Sobre Contrabando" [About Smuggling]. The first part of this "document" consists of fragments from a report (*relación*) addressed to the Spanish king, which may be viewed as a reply to the earlier "Pregones" in that it laments the impossibility of enforcing Spanish legislation in Cuba, ironically because of the corruption that has been imported along with the bureaucratic strictures.

No obstante las providencias que el gobernador ha dado contra el ilícito comercio, no ha conseguido extinguirlo porque abusan de ellas sus adláteres y confidentes, y no tiene de quien fiarse. Y se experimenta en esta cuidad y en toda la Isla una relajación absoluta en la introducción de ropas y todos géneros . . . AL REY.

Distintos almacenes venden a mercaderes y vecinos . . . AL REY

AUN POR LAS CALLES PÚBLICAMENTE

en carretillas, por precios tan baratos como permite su adquisición en
que no se pagan derechos ni se corren riesgos . . . AL REY
Y así. (OP, 2: 381)

[In spite of the legislation the governor has passed against the illegal
trade, he has not succeeded in stopping it because his trusted aids
abuse the laws, and now he cannot trust anyone. And there is in this
city and on the entire island a total laxness about the import of clothes
and other goods . . . TO THE KING.

Certain stores sell to merchants and neighbors . . . TO THE KING.

OPENLY IN THE STREETS

in carts, at prices that are so low because there are no taxes paid to the
King nor risks taken . . . TO THE KING.
And so on.]

Typography plays an important role in this passage; it visually empha-
sizes the counterpoint between smuggling, by definition a covert activity,
and the unabashedly public nature of those operations. Put differently,
smuggling is a kind of masquerade which is gleefully being acted out in
public as an open mockery of the Spanish authorities, whose efforts to
restrict the free exchange of goods parallel the attempted suppression of
literary freeplay through conventional poetic or legalistic forms (the son-
net and the "Pregones"). Guillén elaborates the idea of masquerade in the
second part of this item, after having brushed off the significance of the
official report with an impatient "Y así," which also signals the change in
language we are about to witness.

Si es que vestir pretendes con decencia,
como se viste un mariscal de Francia,
a ley ninguna prestes obediencia,
y acógete a esa amable tolerancia
que en todo contrabando es flor y esencia
lo mismo en Herculano que en Numancia:
Comprar mucho con poco, eso es ser ducho,
y allá quien compre poco y gaste mucho.

    Bando, bando, bando,
    el perrito va meando. (OP, 2: 381)

[If you wish to dress with elegance,
as would a marshal of France,
do not be obedient to any law,
but follow that happy tolerance
that is the essence of all contraband,
be it in Herculaneum or Numancia:
To buy much with little, that's to be skillful,
and let those who buy little spend a lot.

    Decree, decree, decree,
    the doggy goes to pee.]

Far from glorifying smuggling as an act of resistance to economic exploitation on the part of Spain, these lines expose illegal trade to be a way of obtaining the means for imitating the reputed grandeur and glamour of European society, thus reinstating colonial authority in a different form. The pretense of elegance, reflected in the stylistic refinement of the language Guillén employs in this passage, significantly revoices the beginning of the "Soneto": "La aldea es ya ciudad, mas no por ello / se piense que dejó de ser aldea" [The village is already a city, but this should / not make you think that it has ceased being a village]. Greed and corruption are only insufficiently masked by a veil of elegance: "Tanta pechera y pergamino" [All that fancy shirtfront and parchment], as it is called in "Sic Transit . . ." (*OP*, 2: 383). The deceptive front crumbles as the language changes and breaks into a short ditty that instantly destroys all delusions of grandeur. What is accomplished by the ditty is spelled out more clearly in "Sic Transit . . . ," a "soneto con pequeño estrambote" [Sonnet with small irregularities] that appears at the beginning of Guillén's improvisations on the theme of the English occupation of Havana:

Se sabe que una ventolera
soplando a veces levantó
en un gran golpe a Juan Ripiera

Mas cuando el viento se aquietó
guay pergamino y guay pechera
y guay señor Comendador
qué honor. (*OP*, 2: 383)

[A gust of wind, as we know
can at times sweep away
John the Vulgar with a single blow

But after the wind has settled down
gone were the parchment and fancy gown
and gone was even the Commander
lo and behold what honor.]

Guillén's reference to France in the previous quotation is significant
not only in that it anticipates the section chronicling the French influ-
ence on Cuba. It also alludes to the alliance between France and Spain
which led England to declare war on Spain in January 1762, resulting in
the attack of the British fleet on Havana shortly thereafter. The fact that
Havana was completely unprepared for such an attack broadens the
semantic range of phrases such as "relajación absoluta" and "amable
tolerancia" and invests them with historical concreteness as well as irony:
The lack of political stability owing to greed and corruption is seen in
direct correlation with the lack of military defense that made Havana an
easy target for the British. It took indeed little more than a gust of wind to
blow away Captain-General Portocarrero, who, after Spain had lost the
battle, was tried as a scapegoat for the negligence of the colonial admin-
istration.[90]

Se acabó Don Juan Prado
Portocarrero;
manchado está su nombre,
roto su acero.

Los ingleses lo hallaron durmiendo a la bartola,
o por mejor decir, roncando a la española. (OP, 2: 382)

[Finished is Don Juan Prado
Portocarrero;
tarnished is his name,
broken his steel.

The English found him sleeping like a sloth,
or better even, snoring like a Spaniard.]

The English occupation of Havana lasted for eleven months, a period
characterized by increasing tensions between the Cuban *criollos*, who
collaborated with the invaders, and the loyal *peninsulares*. Guillén estab-
lishes an effective counterpoint between the "most faithful servants" who
bemoan the "terrible tragedy," while ironically longing for "the gentle
yoke of serfdom / under which we were born" (Llanto de las habaneras),
and those who regarded the occupation as a "fruitful experience." This

counterpoint is partly visible in the juxtaposition of the formal poetic mode of the "Lament of the Women of Havana" and the random assembly of news items that follows it. But the relationship between those two subsections is far from being strictly dialectical, if only because the news items themselves do not constitute a unified whole expressing a single opinion. Each item illuminates a different aspect of that complex historical situation. The result is a textual kaleidoscope, a constantly changing picture dominated again by the principle of chaotic enumeration. The imprisonment and subsequent deportation of the historian Bishop Pedro Agustín Morell de Santa Cruz, who protested against the British invasion,[91] is reported side by side with the slaying of fifty blacks, who had probably fought under Juan Prado Portocarrero,[92] the importation of thousands of African slaves for work in the canefields, the extraordinary number of commercial embarcations owing to the temporary free trade,[93] the flourishing of prostitution, the repressive measures of the Protestant "heretics" against the Catholic church, and the vengeful cruelties of Lord Albemarle, the commander of the British fleet. All these fragments yield another image of *algarabía*, which best embodies the dynamics of the entire section:

han pedido . . . tenemos no obstante que para inde . . . su conducta se dibuje . . . con perspectiva . . . algún denigrante . . . concepto los havaneros . . . y su impericia y . . . los lances de una en (*OP*, 2: 385)

[they have requested . . . we held, however, that for inde . . . his behavior shows . . . with perspective . . . something belittling . . . conception of the people of Havana . . . and his lack of skill . . . the adventures of a]

This complicated freeplay of textual fragments comes to an abrupt halt in the last item of this section, "Aviso a la Población" [Warning to the Population], announcing the reinstatement of Spanish rule in Cuba. It is sufficient to quote the first sentence of this lengthy "press release" to convey a sense of the return to monologic discourse that appropriately accompanies these political changes.

Para el 6 del presente mes de julio, en la tarde, está prevista la entrada a esta noble y siempre fiel ciudad del nuevo Capitán General Excmo. Señor Condo de Tecla. (*OP*, 2: 386)

[The solemn entry into this noble and always faithful city by the new Captain-General, His Excellency the Count of Tecla, is planned for the afternoon of the 6th of the current month of July.]

Despite the official nature of this "document," Guillén manages to sustain a high level of irony, which becomes evident once this text is played off against its historical background, which it distorts or masks in substantial ways. This distortion or fictionalization of history is signaled by Guillén's changing the name of the new Captain-General: The Conde de Ricla becomes the Conde de Tecla. This simple act of masking alerts us to the fact that the very formal language of this document (for instance, "de acuerdo con lo que sé" [according to the information released]) covers up more than it reveals. What it hides is that the *cabildo* of this "always loyal city" had previously received Lord Albemarle with the same show of enthusiasm it now displays upon the arrival of the Spanish Captain-General. Furthermore, the "congratulatory speech to praise especially the city justices and the regiment for their honorable conduct during the siege" conceals the fact that a number of local officials were charged with treason and shipped off to Ceuta. Ironically, but perhaps not surprisingly, the only members of the council who were ennobled for their "valiant service against the English" were four sugar barons who had reaped the full benefits of that occupation.[94] It is interesting to note that the phrase "siempre fiel" with all its inherent irony should recur in another alleged press release, this time announcing the measures adopted by Captain-General Lersundi in 1868 to suppress, unsuccessfully, the uprisings in Oriente Province which marked the beginning of the Ten Years' War.[95] As we have ample opportunity to observe throughout *El diario*, Cuba was as loyal to Spain as Guillén is faithful to the literary conventions of the Hispanic tradition.

III

¡imposible armonía! ¡Nunca se hubiese visto semejante
disparate, pues mal pueden amaridarse las viejas y nobles
melodías del romance, las sutiles mudanzas y diferencias de
los buenos maestros, con la bárbara algarabía que arman
los negros cuando se hacen de sonajas, marugas y tambores!

[Impossible harmony! Has one ever seen such nonsense!
One can hardly marry the old and noble melodies of the
ballad, the subtle nuances and differences of the great
masters with the barbaric noise the blacks make on their
rattles and drums!]
— ALEJO CARPENTIER, *Concierto barroco*

I have so far examined several aspects of linguistic freeplay and intertextuality through a close reading of the first two sections of *El diario* in order to show the different textual manifestations of *algarabía* as Guillén's trope for the Latin American Neobaroque. Moreover, I have argued that *El diario*, as a prime example of the novelization of poetry under the overall impact of the modern Latin American narrative (as represented by *Tres tristes tigres*) cannot be regarded as an ideologically unified, unilingual text precisely because of its generic and stylistic heterogeneity and the resulting proliferation of conflicting meanings and identities. Yet, the chaos in *El diario* is not the product of authorial carelessness or incompetence, as I have demonstrated in connection with Guillén's wordplays that indicate the underlying presence of a controlling consciousness whose main motivation is freedom from literary and ideological constraints. I have further suggested that *El diario* derives coherence from the various historical contexts it evokes in the form of images of language which constitute a vast Archive. At this point, it is necessary to return to the figure of the Archive in its concrete textual manifestations. While the whole of *El diario* is an archive transfigured into a newspaper to illustrate the process of making accessible for public scrutiny texts usually stored away in special locations (such as Melquíades's study in *One Hundred Years of Solitude*), there are a number of items in this poetic collage that are either explicitly or implicitly bibliographical.

The first is a random list of "Latest Books from France" [Novedades francesas], supplemented by a footnote politely asking the reader to overlook possible anachronisms.

Dictionaire [sic] *de la Musique*, 2 tomos. *Histoire de France*, 1 tomo. *Oeuvres* de Molière, con preciosos grabados, 1 tomo. *Lettres* de Leoni, 1 tomo. Chopin, *Etudes;* los dos tomos de la *Anatomía de Bayle; Lettres de Mon Moulin*, de Alphonse Daudet, 1 tomo, Lamerre editeur, París; tomo V de *Les Contemplations*, de Victor Hugo con viñetas; *Etudes sur la littérature et les moeurs angloméricains* [sic] *au XXme siècle*, par Philarete Chasles, Amyot, Rue de la Paix; *Biographie de Béranger*, Perrotin, París. (OP, 2: 392)

Except for the *Etudes sur la littérature et les moeurs angloméricains* [sic] *au XXme siècle*, a title in which the nineteenth century has surreptitiously been replaced by the twentieth,[96] these works are not in the least anachronistic within the historical context Guillén evokes in this section.[97] Anachronism, in fact, only comes into play because these works are classified as the "latest novelties" rather than as historical documents.

Perhaps the most interesting aspect of this bibliography is Guillén's parodic treatment of the French influence on Cuban culture, manifest here in the development of a kind of "Fragnol," a linguistic hybridization that dominates the advertisements in this section and later on recurs in the "Notas de sociedad" (*OP*, 2: 423–27). Combinations such as the tautological "La Grenouille / La Rana Restaurant" (both "grenouille" and "rana" mean frog), "Chez Gamboa" or "todo très chic," as well as, of course, the mixture of Spanish and French in the "Novedades francesas" itself, are presented as negative products of Cuba's cultural "barroquismo," which, in all of these instances, creates an atmosphere of pomposity and cultural inauthenticity. This atmosphere is already evoked in the "Paréntesis" at the beginning of this section in the substitution of Paris for Havana: *"Paris c'est une grande ville / que también place mucho a l'espagnol"* (*OP*, 2: 387). Another indication of the meaninglessness of this layer of "french dressing" ("aliños franceses" in the original [*OP*, 2: 388]) is the conspicuous suppression in the entire section of references to specific historico-political events such as the French and the Haitian revolutions and their effects on Cuba. One of those effects was the 1826 royal decree prohibiting the importation of books which opposed "the Catholic religion, monarchy, or which in any other way advocated the rebellion of vassals or nations,"[98] which may well account for the politically innocuous titles in Guillén's "Novedades francesas." On the whole, the few scattered allusions, for instance to Robespierre (in "Cólera" [*OP*, 2: 389]), General Tacón[99] ("Gran Teatro Tacón [*OP*, 2: 396]), the illegal slave trade[100] ("Ayer en el puerto" [*OP*, 2: 399]), Cuba's increasing commerce with the United States[101] ("El Fido" and "Desgracia" [*OP*, 2: 399–400]), and the importation of Chinese laborers[102] ("Coolies" [*OP*, 2: 401]), scarcely interrupt the overall picture of affluence and social refinement. Yet these fleeting allusions do serve as reminders of significant omissions such as the slave conspiracy of "La Escalera" [The Ladder] in Matanzas in 1844, in connection with which 4,000 people were arrested, 78 executed, and about 100 whipped to death. Among the victims was the famous mulatto poet Plácido (Gabriel de la Concepción Valdés).

All this is to say that the "Novedades francesas," in a manner indicative of the nature of this entire section, are far more revealing with regard to what they omit. The same is true of the advertisement for a "Diccionario de la rima" [Rhyme Dictionary] (*OP*, 2: 395), which articulates the discrepancies between appearance and reality on which this part of *El diario* thrives.

Se vende un diccionario de la rima (editorial Fallières) con una rima en *olmo* (colmo) en buen estado, y tres en *uvia* (alubia, lluvia, rubia).

Se puede ver todas las tardes (hábiles) de 3 a 6. Conejos, 15.
Preguntar por Inés.[1]

[1] Hemos visto este léxico. No se trata de un diccionario de la rima,
sino de un diccionario normal—un PALLAS—que tiene, eso sí, uno
de la rima al final de sus páginas (1485–1593).

[For sale: a rhyme dictionary (Edition Fallières) with a rhyme on *olmo*
(colmo), in good condition, and three rhymes on *uvia* (alubia, lluvia,
rubia). Can be looked at in the afternoons (working days) from 3 to 6.
Conejos, 15. Ask for Inés.[1]

[1] We have seen this lexicon. It is not a rhyme dictionary, but an
ordinary dictionary—a PALLAS—which has, it is true, one of the
rhymes on its final pages (1485–1593).

Another advertisement that merits our attention is the "Gran funerario
'Berceo'" [Great Funeral Home "Berceo"] (*OP*, 2: 403) at the end of this
section. The thirteenth-century Spanish poet Gonzalo de Berceo, whose
Milagros de Nuestra Señora are cited in the footnote to the advertise-
ment, occupies a prominent place in Guillén's Archive: The first Spanish
poet to insist on writing in the language of the people ("romanz pal-
adino"),[103] he embodies an important aspect of Guillén's own work and
of his understanding of the Latin American Neobaroque as "al-
garabía / en lengua de piratas y bozales." In Guillén's Antillean version,
the Baroque is a kind of literary argot, a written language alive with the
same heterogeneity and playfulness that characterizes colloquial speech.
In this sense, the reference to Berceo indirectly illuminates the positive
aspects of Cuba's cultural *barroquismo* and sets them off against the
pretentious stylishness (or stylelessness) of the "Fragnol" used in the
previous advertisements. What Berceo stands for in this context is the
development of an authentic literary idiom beneath the false glamour of
official cultural imports such as the "Novedades francesas." It is justified
to regard this as a continuation of the picaresque strain that surfaces in the
"Epístola" and that again insinuates itself into this section in the form of a
seemingly innocuous advertisement (*OP*, 2: 402):

CARPINTERO DE VIEJO

Se reparan vírgenes

Todos los días (excepto los domingos) a lado de la catedral.

[REPAIRMAN FOR OLD THINGS

Virgins restored

Every day (except Sundays) right next to the Church.]

Guillén's explicit reference to Berceo establishes the context within which this brief text is revealed as another important archival item: By far the most famous restorer of virgins in all of Spanish literature is Fernando de Rojas's Celestina, crafty conjurewoman (like Rodríguez Freyle's Juana García[104] and, in many ways, mother of the picaresque. *The Celestina*, published in 1499, is the first European novel, even though it is written in dialogue and divided into acts. What links this seminal text with Gonzalo de Berceo's *Milagros* is a similar concern for incorporating into Spanish letters the dynamics of colloquial speech and for achieving the kind of heterogeneous linguistic texture that has since come to be a salient characteristic of novelistic discourse. The dialogic confrontations in *Celestina* between different strata of language, which are invariably tied to the social status of the characters, lead to exchanges suggestive of the frequent juxtapositions in *El diario* of poetic elegance and colloquial "clumsiness." The following scene, extracted from a conversation between the nobleman Calisto and his servant Sempronio,[105] shall suffice to illustrate this point:

Calisto: I'll not eat till then, even though Apollo's horses have been put out to pasture after their daily run.

Sempronio: Leave off these high-flown phrases, sir, this poetizing. Speech that is not common to all, or shared by all, is not good speech. Just say "until sunset" and we'll know what you mean.

What distinguishes Celestina from both Calisto and Sempronio is her ability to mediate between "high-flown" phrases and "plain" language, that is, to play one off against the other and in the process create a maze of meanings in which all the other characters get hopelessly entangled. Celestina, as she herself admits, "live[s] on words" (*Celestina*, 21); hers is a special kind of poetic consciousness nourished by the freedom of multi-languagedness that is rooted in the deceptive plainness of popular speech. This same novelistic consciousness, as distinct from the kind of "poetizing" for which Sempronio reproaches Calisto, is what controls *El diario* as well as poems such as "Sensemayá." Especially with regard to the latter text, it is worth noting that Fuentes's Celestina in *Terra Nostra* bears on her lips an indelible tattoo of snakes, "which formed a separate mouth, a second mouth, a unique mouth, perfected and enriched by the contrasting colors exaggerating and underlying every glimmer of saliva and every line inscribed on those full lips."[106] Fuentes's image of the duplicity that characterizes Celestinesque discourse is indeed suggestive when connected with Guillén's own attitude about language. As *El diario* clearly conveys, Guillén lives as much on words as Celestina, who is the patroness of the breakdown of both genealogical and generic purity that lies at the beginning of modern writing. This breakdown is the real origin of *El diario*, a legacy that places Guillén's text in the direct line of succession of works such as *Don Quijote, Finnegans Wake*, and of course *Three Trapped Tigers*.[107]

But let us continue our exploratory voyage through the recesses of Guillén's Archive. The historical battlefield of the Ten Years' War is textually reconstituted in the dialogic confrontation between the "Autoridad pública," represented by Captain-General Francisco Lersundi on the one hand and a chorus of dissenters assembled in "Últimas novedades de libros cubanos" [Latest Cuban Books] on the other. Lersundi's outline of legal measures against the revolutionary movement that had been organized in Oriente under the leadership of Manuel de Céspedes in 1867–1868 is ironically prefaced by an elaborate rhetorical defense of national progress and prosperity.

Turbando el orden público en algunas localidades del departamento oriental de esta isla, pretendiendo trastornar insurreccional y violentamente la manera social de existir de los honrados habitantes de Cuba, que con laboriosidad y a la sombra de la nacionalidad española la han sabido conducir al grado envidiable de prosperidad en que se encuentra, he considerado como el primero y más alto de mis deberes acudir enérgicamente al restablecimiento de la paz. (*OP*, 2: 405)

[As in some parts of the eastern province of this island the public order has been disrupted by the attempt to overturn, through insurrection and violence, the way of life that the honorable citizens of Cuba, through hard work and under the protection of the Spanish government, have turned into its present enviable state of prosperity, I have considered it as the first and highest of my duties to reestablish the peace rigorously.]

To be sure, these "honorable citizens" were a relatively small group of West Cuba's leading businessmen, who unsuccessfully tried to pressure Lersundi into taking military action against the rebels, and who, it might be added, had accumulated their fortunes not because of, but rather in spite of, the "protection" of the Spanish government.

Set off against the Captain-General's pseudonationalist rhetoric are the works of several Cuban poets and essayists representative of what José Enrique Varona called "la nueva era." The works Guillén includes in his bibliographical catalogue—Rafael María Mendive's *Poesías* (1883),[108] Varona's *Conferencias filosóficas* (1880), Antonio López Prieto's *Parnaso cubano* (1881), and *Arpas amigas* (1879), as well as the reference to Victor Patricio de Landaluze's paintings, which were part of Antonio Bachiller y Morales's *Tipos y costumbres de la isla de Cuba*—may be regarded as echoes of Maceo's Protest of Baraguá, in which he emphatically rejected the terms of the "Peace" of Zanjón in favor of a continued fight for both the abolition of slavery and Cuban independence.[109] In a way, all these different texts (literary or visual, as in the case of Landaluze) trace an orbit around a conspicuously absent "signifier": the name of José Martí, "la cabeza pensante y delirante de la revolución cubana" [the thinking, delirious head of the Cuban revolution] (*OP*, 2: 411). These words are from a brief headline that appears in the last section of *El diario* announcing Martí's death on 19 May 1895. Curiously enough, this is the only direct reference to Martí in connection with the revolutionary activities both during and after the Ten Years' War. Yet the writings of Martí are an important subtext of *El diario*. The following lines from his famous essay "Nuestra América" in particular give coherence to the "Últimas novedades en libros cubanos." Martí writes,

Knowledge holds the key. To know one's country, and to govern it with that knowledge, is the only alternative to tyranny. The European university must give way to the American university. The history of America, from the Incas to the present, must be taught until it is known by heart, even if the Archons of the Greek go by the board. Our Greece must take priority over the Greece that is not ours. . . . *Let the world be grafted on our republics; but the trunk must be our own.*[110]

Above and beyond noting the strong nationalistic sentiment that most of the writers listed in the "Últimas novedades" shared with Martí, it is in order to be more specific with regard to their individual contributions to Cuban arts and letters. To begin with, Rafael María Mendive (1821–1886), high-school teacher, poet, and separatist—he was deported to Spain in 1869, and from there he went to New York—was a powerful intellectual influence on the young Martí, whom he also supported financially throughout his high-school years.[111] Enrique José Varona, best known as a poet for his *Paisajes cubanos* (1879) and influenced as a philosopher by the utilitarianism of John Stuart Mill and the Spencerian brand of positivism, was also exiled owing to his political radicalism. Like Mendive, he was a separatist who also ended up in New York, where, in 1895, he became editor of *Patria*, a newspaper that Martí had founded three years earlier. Also in 1895, the year of Martí's death, Varona published *Cuba contra España*, an essay that the Partido Revolucionario Cubano adopted as its manifesto.[112] Varona also collaborated with the brothers Francisco and Antonio Sellén, Luis Victoriano Betancourt, Diego Vicente Tejera, Esteban Borrero Echeverría, and José Varela Zequeira in the production of *Arpas amigas*, one of the first collections of Cuban poetry (the other one was *Arpas cubanas*), soon followed by López Prieto's anthology *Parnaso cubano*.[113]

Guillén's reference to the painter Landaluze (1827?–1889) is of special interest, not only in the context of late nineteenth-century Cuban nationalism, but also with respect to Guillén's early *poesía negra* and the Afro-Antillean movement. A Spaniard from Bilbao who had arrived in Cuba in 1863, Landaluze has been called, not without a hint of irony, "the most Cuban painter of his times."[114] Although he was a loyalist and as such hostile to the movement for Cuban independence, Landaluze's paintings, in which he portrayed Spanish and Creole noblemen side by side with scenes from the "Día de Reyes" (such as the famous "Diablitos"), slaves working in the canefields, and *cimarrones* chased by bloodhounds,[115] were unique expressions of Cuba's national spirit and varied cultural heritage. According to Loló de la Torriente, Landaluze supplied Cuban historiography with invaluable documents that were to become indispensable pictographical resources for writers like Fernando Ortiz,[116] Alejo Carpentier, and also Nicolás Guillén. Landaluze's preferred subjects were the same blacks and mulattoes we find in Cirilo Villaverde's *costumbrista* novel *Cecilia Valdés* (1882), characters who would return to life, half a century later, in Guillén's *Motivos de son*.

Upon returning to the text of *El diario*, we find that the "Últimas novedades de libros cubanos" reads like a select bibliography to the comprehensive study advertised on the preceding page:

ANÁLISIS CRÍTICO HISTÓRICO
Y FILOSÓFICO
de la
GUERRA LLAMADA DE LOS DIEZ
AÑOS

DEBIDO A UN GRUPO DE ESCRITORES
CUBANOS, CON EL TEXTO DEL PACTO
DEL ZANJÓN Y TODO LO RELATIVO
A LA PROTESTA DE BARAGUÁ.

SEPARE SU EJEMPLAR CON TIEMPO. (*OP*, 2: 407)

[CRITICAL, HISTORICAL, AND PHILOSOPHICAL
ANALYSIS
of the
SO-CALLED TEN YEARS'
WAR

BY A GROUP OF CUBAN WRITERS
WITH THE TEXT OF THE PACT OF
ZANJÓN AND ALL THAT IS
RELATED TO THE PROTEST OF BARAGUÁ.

RESERVE YOUR COPY IN TIME.]

Unlike the items examined so far, this advertisement appears to be a reference without a referent: The work whose publication it announces does not, to my knowledge, exist, or it does not *yet* exist. To understand its purpose within this section of *El diario*, it is advantageous to compare it to the blank pages at the beginning of "Algunas revelaciones" (pp. 261–63) in *Tres tristes tigres*, as well as to the use of textual clearings in the poetry of Jay Wright. In neither case do the blanks indicate an omission from the text; instead, they supply an opening for future texts to be generated by the reader. These future texts function as supplements to the novel, or in this case, the poem. As a projection of such a supplement, Guillen's advertisement presents what Wright has called an "unwritten history," not only in the sense of being an image of a text that has not yet been written, but also in the sense of "unwriting" previous official documents (such as Lersundi's legislation) by bringing them into contact with texts like the ones included in the "Últimas novedades." Because these different texts exist side by side in *El diario*, it is possible to see that Lersundi's postulate of "la integridad nacional" is as much of a rhetorical smokescreen as the notion of an "always loyal" Cuba.

Given the social, political, and cultural tensions in Cuba during the second half of the nineteenth century, it seems absurd, in retrospect, even to speak of the destruction of national unity. On the contrary, it was the desire for national unity in an independent Cuba that had motivated the Ten Years' War as well as the continuation of revolutionary activities in the form of the *Guerra Chiquita* [the Little War] of 1879–1880.

Although the failure of the *Guerra Chiquita* dealt a severe blow to the separatist movement headed by José Martí, Antonio Maceo, Juan Gualberto Gómez, and other exiled veterans of previous revolutionary struggles, they persisted for more than a decade to enlist the support of other Cubans in the United States and to prepare for another battle for independence. The movement gained increasing support within Cuba herself as the *autonomistas* were faced with Spain's unwillingness to fulfill the constitutional changes guaranteed in the Pact of Zanjón. In addition, the Cuban economy during the 1880s was in a state of crisis, aggravated by the formal abolition of slavery per royal decree, which raised the cost of sugar production at a time when beet sugar already dominated the European market. As a result, the Cuban sugar industry went through a phase of drastic reorganization, a process during which many of the estates fell into the hands of United States investors.[117] The United States' concern for protecting American investments in Cuba as well as securing a permanent market for exports was paralleled by an increasing interest in the island's strategic value. By the late 1800s, Martí was fully aware of the United States' growing imperialistic aspiration and of Cuba's need to gain independence to avoid annexation. "I have lived inside the monster and know its insides," he wrote in 1895 shortly before being ambushed and shot to death by the Spaniards in the recently launched Second War of Independence.[118] Three years later, however, the rebel leader Máximo Gómez rejected the armistice proposed by Spain to welcome United States interventionism in what was about to turn into the Spanish-American War.[119]

If the Spanish-American War did free Cuba from Spain, it was at the same time a realization of Martí's worst fear: Goliath had finally swallowed David, to use his own analogy. Guillén picks up on Martí's figure of the "monster" in the "Paréntesis" that prefaces the final and longest section of *El diario*:

El cielo azul se abrió rasgado
por la uña extranjera.
Espeso inglés de maquinaria
el rostro de la patria detenía. (OP, 2: 409)

[The blue heavens were scratched open
by the foreign fingernail.
Thick English of machines
froze the face of the fatherland.]

Striking indeed is the resemblance of the synecdochic "foreign finger-nail" to the claws of the American eagle "that flew sixty years ago over the 'Maine,' in Havana" [voló sesenta años sobre el Maine, en la Habana] (*OP*, 2: 240), the figure Guillén used in *El gran zoo* ("Las águilas") to commemorate the beginning of the Spanish-American War.[120] Also part of this metaphoric cluster is the "ala del pájaro sangriento / que desde el alto Norte desparama / muerte" [the wing of the bloodthirsty bird / that from the high North brings / death] (*OP*, 1: 393). These lines from the "Elegía cubana" are a fitting introduction to *El diario*'s final section. It may in fact be argued that this last section, in which Guillén explores various aspects of the relationship between Cuba and the United States, is a rewriting of the "Elegía cubana," published more than a decade earlier.

To be sure, United States imperialism is a theme that underlies amost all of Guillén's poems.[121] It makes its first significant appearance in "Tú no sabe inglé" [Don' Know No English] in *Motivos de son*. Few indeed are the poems in which Guillén's anti-imperialistic sentiments do not surface. But in no other instance is his indictment of United States imperialism as poignant as in *El diario*. The reason for this is the consistently dialogical textual environment of *El diario* and the resulting freeplay both among and within individual items, which permits Guillén to produce irony not only at the level of semantics but also at the level of form. This free exchange between different forms of discourse is still restricted in the monologic environment provided by the more conventional poetic forms and structures employed in "Elegía cubana." By comparing and contrasting the following passage from that poem with several textual items from the final section of *El diario*, we shall be able to see how Guillén's concept of the Neobaroque as elaborated in *El diario* affects his poetic treatment of the theme of United States imperialism.

Afuera está el vecino.
Tiene el teléfono y el submarino.
Tiene una flota bárbara, una flota
bárbara . . . Tiene una montaña de oro
y un mirador y un coro
de águilas y una nube de soldados
ciegos, sordos, armados
por el miedo y el odio. (Sus banderas
empastadas en sangre, un fisiológico
hedor esparcen que demora el vuelo
de las moscas.) Afuera está el vecino,

rodeado de fieras
nocturnas, enviando embajadores,
carne de buey en latas, pugilistas,
convoyes, balas, tuercas, armadores,
efebos onanistas,
ruedas para centrales, chimeneas
con humo ya, zapatos de piel dura,
chicle, tabaco rubio, gasolina,
ciclones, cambios de temperatura,
y también desde luego,
tropas de infantería de marina,
porque es útil (a veces) hacer fuego . . .
¿Que más, que más? El campo roto y ciego
vomitando sus sombras al camino
bajo la fusta de los mayorales,
y la ciudad caída, sin destino
de smoking en el club, o sumergida,
lenta, viscosa, en fiebres y hospitales,
donde mueren soñando con la vida
gentes ya de projectos animales . . . (*OP*, 1: 391–92)

[Right outside there is our neighbor.
He has the telephone and the submarine.
He has a barbaric fleet, a barbaric
fleet . . . He has a mountain of gold,
a penthouse and a chorus
of eagles and a cloud of soldiers,
blind, deaf, armed
with fear and hate. (Their flags
caulked with blood, spread a physiological
stench that stops even the flies
dead in their tracks.) Right outside is our neighbor,
surrounded by nocturnal
demons, sending ambassadors,
corned beef in cans, pugilists,
convoys, bullets, screws, shipbuilders,
onanistic ephebes,
wheels for sugarmills, chimneys
already filled with smoke, leather shoes,
chewing gum, blond tobacco, gasoline,
changes in temperature,
and also, of course,
Marine infantry troops,
because it is (at times) useful to let arms speak.
What else, what else? The torn and blind countryside

vomits its shadows on the road
under the lash of the overseers,
and the fallen city, without destiny,
of smokings in clubs, or submerged,
slow, viscous, delirious, and hospitals
where people already turned into animals
die, dreaming of life . . .]

The difference between this passage and the radical revisions it under-
goes in the process of becoming the final section of *El diario* can best be
understood by recalling some of Walter Benjamin's comments on the
nature of baroque language. In *The Origin of German Tragic Drama*
Benjamin contends that "the language of the Baroque is constantly con-
vulsed [*erschüttert*] by the rebellion of its elements"; and he adds, "lan-
guage is broken apart [*zerbrochen*] in such a way that, in its fragments, it
may assume a changed and more intense meaning."[122] It would be idle,
in this instance, to argue either for or against the applicability of Ben-
jamin's aesthetic theories to Guillén's poetry. Much more to the point
than any general theoretical discussion is the fact that Benjamin's com-
ments on the Baroque are very helpful in explaining the literary processes
at work in *El diario*. We glean from the above citation from the "Elegía
cubana" the beginnings of the process of fragmentation that Benjamin
describes: Guillén's use of chaotic enumeration clearly indicates the
rebellion of the poem's individual elements against the formal unity the
poem as a structure seeks to impose. This internal rebellion shatters
dreams of formal unity, of a possible harmony between form and content,
as it broadens the gap between reality and appearance. Life is crushed
under the weight of useless excess; reality suffocates in the vacuum that
forms at the center of this incoherent assembly of seemingly concrete, yet
insubstantial, images, a vacuum whose presence is signaled by the nag-
ging question "What else, what else?" This vision of emptiness and
inauthenticity is an elaboration of the images presented at the beginning
of the "Elegía cubana":

Cuba, palmar vendido,
sueño descuartizado,
duro mapa de azúcar y de olvido . . . (*OP*, 1: 389)

[Cuba, sold-out palm grove,
quartered dream,
tough map of sugar and neglect . . .]

These lines might have served as an epigraph to the final section of *El diario*, where the internal rebellion that challenges the poetic unity of Guillén's "Elegía cubana" is exteriorized in such a fashion that the textual surface of the poem is broken up into what appear to be completely separate, unrelated fragments, no longer bound by the requirements of formal unity. By liberating himself from such formal poetic conventions, Guillén is now able to intensify his vision of chaos. The principle of chaotic enumeration takes over the entire poem, and individual items from the previous catalogue of imported rubble are radically stripped of their seeming concreteness and realism as they enter the word-world of advertising, where the distance between language and object is rendered absolute. What is being advertised here and throughout *El diario* are not concrete objects, but *attitudes* before and in language. This is particularly obvious in the item that advertises motor oil as "The King of Smoothness" [El rey de la suavidad]:

Dadme, oh Musas, el cándido deleite
de cantar al aceite
que llaman "Essolube,"
en el techo subido de una nube.
La Standard soberana,
que procesa este oil,
lo brinda a la república cubana.
HIGHER AND HIGHER EVERY DAY
    Standard Oil Co. (*OP*, 2: 413)

[Grant me, oh Muses, the simple pleasure
of singing to the oily treasure
they call "Essolube,"
from a cloud's lofty altitude.
The Standard so majestic,
which processes this oil,
toasts with it to the health of the Cuban republic.
HIGHER AND HIGHER EVERY DAY
    Standard Oil Co.]

These lines expose the intimate ties between the language of advertising and the language of the Baroque suggested by Spitzer. "If we ask ourselves," he writes, "with which historical literary climate we should associate this playful language of advertisement, which is satisfied with feigning gratuitously an ideal *word-world* in empty space, the kinship with certain baroque or *précieux* ways of speech becomes evident: 'sunkist' for 'oranges' [or 'the King of Smoothness' for 'motor oil'] belongs to a poetic 'as-if' speech, no different essentially from *conseiller des graces* for *miroir*."[123] The language of advertising, like the language of the Baroque, creates an illusion absolutely unwarranted by reality. "Essolube," which Guillén insists on rhyming with "nube" [cloud] to emphasize its loftiness and thus extend the atmosphere of artificiality generated by the poem's style to the semantic level, assumes the qualities of an intoxicating substance, which dulls the senses to divert attention from ugly realities, such as the fact that the Standard Oil Co. does not drink to Cuba's health but to its own profits, which rise "Higher and higher every day." "Smoothness," therefore, cannot simply be read as a literal reference to the quality of motor oil; it also refers to the quality of the language used in this advertisement, to the way in which baroque rhetoric creates an appealing linguistic veneer to conceal the fundamental tensions between individual language elements—tensions that, in this case, represent the actual historical relationship between Cuba and the United States. At the level of textuality, these political and cultural tensions are manifest in the corruption of the Spanish language by English words and phrases ("este oil," for instance), as well as in the juxtaposition of "La Standard soberana" and "la república cubana," where the harmony feigned by the endrhymes clashes with the semantic values to produce bitter irony. Guillén effectively appeals to the inherently contradictory language of the Baroque, which, in the very process of destroying reality through exaggerated stylization, also heightens our perception of the very tensions it seeks to conceal. Baroque language, precisely because of its excessive artificiality, accentuates the deceptive nature of all literary language and in fact of all writing.

The point Guillén makes is an important one: Not only does he alert us to the fact that he himself is well aware of the distance between word and object, between language and reality, and of the inevitable interference of language itself in the process of representation. He also demands that we as readers be conscious of and sensitive to that distance so that we may perceive what appears to be a harmonious relationship between form and content also, at the same time, as a necessary discrepancy. To be sure, Guillén is not a baroque poet in the same way that Góngora and Lope de Vega were baroque poets. However, his use of baroque language in *El diario*, both in individual items and as a compositional principle that underlies the entire poetic project, as a strategy for exposing modern Cuban culture as an outrageous artifice is a comment on the deceptive quality of all language, and in particular of the kind of language that purports to be concrete, direct, and unproblematic.

Concrete, direct, and unproblematic (in the sense of "sencillo," un-complicated) are all qualities that, for better or for worse, have elicited the praise of many of Guillén's critics. I suggested at the beginning of my discussion of *El diario* that this poem poses a profound challenge to such popular views, and we are now, I believe, in a position to grasp the full extent of such a claim. Ellis, for instance, has argued that Guillén's poetry favors metonymy over metaphor as a vehicle for clarity and di-rectness of expression, which, according to him, makes metonymy the most salient characteristic of all "social poetry." But, as Sarduy has noted, metonymy is also one of the principal vehicles of the Baroque, where it is employed to achieve precisely the opposite effect. The fact that neither Ellis nor Sarduy is right or wrong in any absolute sense helps us com-prehend that metonymy works at two or more different levels at the same time. By projecting a superficial unity of form and content, of language and reality, metonymy ensures that the discord and disunity that are revealed once we probe more deeply into the text are intensified by the surprise at the deception. Metonymy, in other words, is a set-up, and the more subtle the set-up, the greater the effect. Let us consider the follow-ing advertisement in this regard.

UNA OBRA QUE HARÁ EPOCA

Querido señor o señora:
Invitamos a usted oficialmente a facilitarnos los datos sobre su persona, que se incluirán en el presente modelo, destinados a la confección de uno nuevo diccionario biográfico de un prestigio y de una calidad excepcionales, a saber:

WHO'S NOT

Su colaboración sera altamente apreciada por todos los interesados. ¡Veinte mil hombres y mujeres famosos y eminentes presentados con elegancia insuperable en un solo volumen! (*OP*, 2: 414)

[AN EPOCH-MAKING WORK

Dear Sir or Madam:
We officially invite you to provide us with your personal data by filling out the present questionnaire, for the purpose of compiling a new biographical dictionary of exceptional prestige and quality, entitled:

WHO'S NOT

Your cooperation will be much appreciated by all who have an interest in this project. Twenty thousand famous and eminent men and women presented in a single volume of insuperable elegance!]

In this text, Guillén achieves a maximum of semantic disruption through very simple means: By changing "Who's Who" into "Who's Not," he effectively undermines the pretentious rhetoric of the rest of the advertisement. The "epochal" social register, an attempt at canonizing Cuban culture by limiting it to a selective inventory of twenty thousand names, represents yet another structure, a filing system, whose lack of authority is exposed by the erasure of the pronoun "who" and the appearance of "not" in its stead: "Who's Not" could also be represented as "Who's ~~Who~~." What is being erased and negated is the identity of those whose names are to be included in this biographical dictionary. As a result, the adjectives "famous" and "eminent" lose their old meaning, their semantic identity, if you will, in a process of inversion that turns them into representations of nonidentity. Similarly, phrases such as "exceptional prestige and quality" become mere images of language testifying to their own representational limitations. The bold(faced) presence of the "NOT," in short, makes it impossible for the language in this advertisement to represent anything but a hermetic world of words: Language here only serves to project an elegant illusion totally unwarranted and unaffected by a reality where "people . . . die, dreaming of life." "Who's Not" is a powerful recasting of that line from the "Elegía cubana": As in "El rey de la suavidad," language has become a dream of life and of identity signifying death. To be more precise, what prevents language, that is, the Spanish language, from generating meaning in any positive sense is the drastic interference of English words and phrases embodying the presence of the United States' imperialistic authority.

In the above advertisement, the English phrase "Who's Not" has already replaced any possible Spanish equivalent (such as "Quién es quién") that might have served as a title for such a biographical dictionary. This suppression of Spanish in favor of English, which significantly occurs in a place that is the visual center of this textual item, is also what motivates the "Not," whose presence intensifies this act of linguistic suppression. Since "Who's Who" does not really have an equivalent in Spanish, it is meaningless in the context of that language and its cultural origins. The cultural institution to which it refers in its original Anglo–North American context, the social register, is equally meaningless when transferred to Latin America. In other words, "Who's Who," when used as a formal system for the representation of Cuba's cultural realities, is inevitably transformed into "Who's Not" in order to call attention to the kinds of distortions that would result from such a transposition. To Guillén, "Who's Not" is Cuba's distorted reflection in the mirror of imposed North American cultural and linguistic conventions, a mirror that filters out cultural differences and thus destroys the basis for a distinctive cultural identity. This mirror, of course, is language itself, and more specifically, the language of North American advertising as a vehicle for both economic and cultural imperialism.

A similar linguistic defacement occurs in the advertisement entitled "Tiperrita" [Typist]:

Se ofrece como mecanógrafa señorita cubana de buena familia, educada en Boston, U.S.A. Ardiente como un crisol de la cabeza a los pies. Habla muy bien el inglés y no mal el español. En esta imprenta informan. (*OP*, 2: 418)

[Cuban girl from good family, educated in Boston, U.S.A., is seeking employment as a stenographer. Hot all over like a furnace. Speaks English very well. Her Spanish is not bad either. Information available at the press.]

Like the linguistic hybrid "tiperrita," which, strictly speaking, belongs neither to the Spanish nor to the English lexicon, this "Cuban girl from a good family" suffers from an acute loss of cultural identity: Her bilingualism testifies, above all, to the fact that she is a native speaker of neither language. She is the product of a "melting pot" [un crisol], which, given the erosion of her native Spanish, is clearly a figure for the same deculturation that underlies the construct "Who's Not."

Symbolic of this process of deculturation (or cultural defacement) in an even more direct sense is the slogan "Bosques hasta se acaben" [Forests until they last] from the advertisement of the Cuban Railroad Company ("Transporte" [*OP*, 2: 417]). The destruction of Cuba's magnificent forests—"los mejores árboles y finas maderas al servicio de la seguridad y elegancia ferroviaria nacional" [the best trees and finest woods for the safety and elegance of the national railroads]—is used as an allegory about the disintegration of national cultural values in the name of progress. The defacement of Cuba's natural landscape is analogous to the erosion of the country's cultural foundations: Again, what is left are beautiful images of language—"majagua, ácana, granadillo, jiquí, ebano real"—representing objects no longer in existence, representing, as Guillén puts it in the "Elegía cubana," a "sold-out palm grove." In the process of being transformed into marketable commodities, in this case, beams and cross-beams for railroad tracks, these natural objects have lost their former symbolic value; they have become disfigured almost beyond recognition in order to signify superficial elegance.

Nothing, it seems, remains unaffected by this process of disfigurement. Even Maceo's machete, the very emblem of Cuba's desire for national independence, is transfigured into an elegant dress sword ("el artístico machete") resting in "a magnificent case made of the country's most precious woods" ("Curiosidades" [*OP*, 2: 412]). It is no longer a lethal weapon but an artifice, a "curiosity," exhibited to the public in a glass vitrine. But Guillén goes even further: The veterans of the War of Independence, the same men who fought at Maceo's side, now exchange his cane knife for an equally fancy hardbound copy of the Platt Amendment, presented by General Leonard Wood, who took over the Cuban government on 20 December 1899. The occasion for this symbolic exchange is, of course, the inauguration of the republic, an event tellingly represented as an act of the Cuban soldiers surrendering their arms to an ally all too ready to spread its "protective" wings over its Caribbean neighbor. Needless to say, the cover of the Platt Amendment is adorned with the American eagle "con alas abiertas en todo su envergadura" [with its wings spread open all the way].

The fact that "Curiosidades" directly precedes the above-mentioned advertisements for all kinds of North American imports, ranging from hot dogs, chewing gum, vitamin pills, and condoms to cars and engine parts, already suggests the precise nature of that foreign "protection." Havana has once again become "the boulevard of the New World," with the difference, however, that hardly any of the merchandise sold in this new market place is domestic: Names like Purdy and Henderson ("Maquinaria"), Ford ("Autos, Tractores y Camiones") and the National Bank ("Dinero en Hipoteca") dominate the scene along with strange products such as "Sanitube" and "Syrgosol." In the same way that the Cuban economy is flooded with such imports, the social life of Havana is dominated by North American customs and institutions, all of which are further manifestations of "Who's Not." The following advertisement for the "Miami Club," an item that would not have been out of place in Cabrera Infante's *Tres tristes tigres*, is explicit about North American attitudes toward Cuban culture.

Diviértase cada noche bailando con las mejores orquestas de la Habana. Estrictamente privado. Clientela distinguida en su mayoría norteamericana. Aviso importante: la Administración o su delegado a la entrada del local se reservan el derecho de admisión, sin explicaciones. Buffet frío y platos criollos. Show especial a las 12, con la negra Rufina y el negrito Cocoliso, los mejores bailadores de la rumba cubana. (OP, 2: 416)

[*Have fun every night dancing with the best orchestras of Havana. Strictly private. Distinguished clientele, mostly North Americans. Important warning: The Management or its representative at the gate to the premises reserves the right to deny admission, without explanations. Cold buffet and creole dishes. Special show at 12, with the negress Rufina and the little negro Cocoliso, the best performers of the Cuban rumba.*]

"Miami Club" is of particular interest here because it adds another dimension to the theme of United States imperialism, one that Guillén had previously denounced in *Sones para turistas*. Cuban culture, represented by the black dancers Rufina and Cocoliso, figures drawn directly from the repertoire of characters of Guillén's own *Motivos de son*, has become a vast "show especial," staged, it seems, exclusively for the benefit and amusement of the distinguished North American clientele, "our Good Neighbors," as Cabrera Infante calls them.

Cabrera Infante is an unexpected, but important, literary presence in *El diario*. In fact, "Miami Club," viewed within the context of Cuban literary history, may well be read as an allusion to *Tres tristes tigres*. This is particularly evident if we recall the novel's "Prólogo," which introduces Cabrera Infante's version and vision of modern Cuba in the same way that his aggressively playful pun "casinos"—"casi no" literally means "almost nothing"[124]—is a possible source of Guillén's "Who's Not." Here, then, is the beginning of Cabrera Infante's prologue:

Showtime! Señoras y señores, *Ladies and Gentlemen. Muy* buenas noches, dames y caballeros, tengan todos ustedes. *Good evening, ladies and gentlemen. Tropicana,* el cabaret MÁS fabuloso del mundo . . . *"Tropicana," the most fabulous night-club in the* WORLD . . . presenta . . . *presents* . . . su *nuevo* espectáculo . . . *its new show* . . . en el que artistas de fama continental . . . *where performers of continental fame* . . . se encargan de transportarlos a ustedes al mundo maravilloso . . . *They will take you all to the wonderful world* . . . y extraordinario . . . *of supernatural beauty* . . . y hermoso . . . *of the Tropics.*[125]

What interests me most about this quotation with regard to the final section of *El diario* are the tensions issuing from the simultaneity of Spanish phrases and their English translations, tensions which are visualized by the ellipses. The pair particularly worthy of attention is "mundo maravilloso" and "wonderful world." Given his insidious parodies of Carpentier, Lydia Cabrera, and even Guillén in *Tres tristes tigres,*[126] it is safe to assume that Cabrera Infante is not using the term "maravilloso" as innocently as the accompanying translation "wonderful" may suggest. The English adjective "wonderful" is clearly a distortion of "maravilloso," a trivialization on the linguistic level whose implications are similar to those I discussed in connection with the transformation of Maceo's deathly machete into a tame dress sword. The same process of disfiguration to which Cabrera Infante's "Prólogo" calls special attention is at work in "Miami Club": The performance of Rufina and Cocoliso is at once a representation of "el mundo maravilloso" in Carpentier's sense as well as of "the wonderful world" of the Tropics, which is a veritable parody of Cuban culture resulting from the North American influence. In the "mundo maravilloso," which is the realm of Cuba's own distinct cross-cultural imagination as associated with "lo real maravilloso," the performance of the rumba is, much like the "Son de la Ma' Teodora," an indigenous cultural ritual redolent with meaning. But as "maravilloso" is distorted into "wonderful," with all its implications of superficiality, this ritual is reduced to a mere "show," a word that already indicates the loss of semantic and cultural depth and the substitution of appearances for reality. Translation itself thus already becomes a form of deculturation, of purging language of its culture-specific meanings. This process is represented in "Miami Club" by dislocating the performance of Rufina and Cocoliso from its original cultural context, the streets of Havana—the "hampa afrocubana"—to the hermetic environment of a prestigious nightclub. The cultural setting that would invest this performance with meaning, that is, the Afro-Cuban community, is literally closed out: Blacks (a category which, by United States standards, would also include mulattoes) are not admitted to the "Miami Club."

"Miami Club," "Who's Not," and "Tiperrita" are all manifestations of the trivialization of Cuban cultural values as a result of the presence of the United States. This process of erasing cultural differences in the name of creating elegant surfaces—"elegance," of course, being a trope for the kind of cultural refinement that Matthew Arnold would call "sweetness and light"—culminates in the "Notas de Sociedad" [Society Notes], a section that owes much to *Tres tristes tigres*. The following lines are representative:

Todavía resuena en nuestros oídos el eco de tan brillante fiesta.

Una noche de "charme," come decía Verlaine.
Era de esperar, tratándose de la opulenta familia Siguanea.

Que desde hace varios años ha establecido su residencia en nuestra turbulenta "city."

Con general beneplácito.

Fue la boda de Cusita, la monísima hija mayor de los esposos Siguanea, que contrajó quintas nupcias, esta vez con el correcto joven Walter Rice Taylor y Pimienta, de la mejor sociedad del Histórico Cayo, como llamamos cariñosamente a Cayo Hueso.

Bajo una iluminación "a giorno," que hacía resaltar sus naturales encantos, se presentó la novia.

Vestida iba con un hermoso traje de "moaré," de color verde-nilo-desmayado.

El velo amarillo huevo (nos referimos a la yema) caía como un sutil niágara de seda sobre las ebúrneas espaldas de la gentil "fiancée."

Tanto el vestido—elegantísimo—como el velo, debidos fueron a las manos del modisto del momento.

Tito Tato, el gran "desinateur" femenino.

Que se ha anotado un triunfo más.

El joven Walter, naturalmente emocionado, iba del brazo de la feliz mamá, la señora de Siguanea.

Vestía un elegante "smoking" cortado por el simpático Juancho Rizoto, el sastre de los que están a la moda.

La novia, resplandeciente en su delicadísima virginidad, daba el brazo a su señor padre, Don Sinecuro.

Párrafo aparte. (*OP*, 2: 424–25)

[Today our ears are filled with the echo of a most brilliant party.

A night of "charme," as Verlaine used to say. It was to be expected, given that it was held by the opulent Siguanea family.

They became residents of our turbulent "cité" several years ago.

With general pleasure.

It was the wedding of Cusita, the cute oldest daughter of the Siguanea couple, who married for the fifth time, this time the proper young gentleman Walter Rice Taylor y Pimienta, of the best circles of the historical Key, as they tenderly call Key West.

The bride was presented under lights as bright as the day, which brought out her natural charm.

She was wearing a beautiful gown of "moiré," whose color was a faint nile-green.

The egg-yellow veil (we are of course referring to the yoke) fell like a subtle silken Niagara over the chalk-white shoulders of the graceful "fiancée."

222

The entire outfit—like the veil, very elegant—must have been created by the most fashionable designer of the day.

Tito Tato, the great "desinateur" of women's fashions.

He has scored another victory.

The young Walter, naturally overcome with emotion, was guided by the arm of the happy mama, Mrs. Siguanea.

He wore an elegant "smoking," made by the well-liked Juancho Rizoto, the tailor for those who go with the times.

The bride, aglow with the splendor of her very delicate virginity, extended her arm to her father, Don Sinecuro.

New paragraph.]

A few brief examples from *Tres tristes tigres* will suffice to reveal basic rhetorical as well as lexical similarities:

Saludamos a la encantada jeune-fille, como dicen nuestros cronistas sociales, señorita Vivian Smith Corona Alvarez de Real, que celebra esta noche sus quince . . . *Happy, happy birthday!* . . . es nuestro gran fotografo de las estrellas. *Yes, the Photographer of the Stars. Not a great astronomer but our friend, the Official Photographer of Cuban Beauties. Let's greet him as he deserves:* ¡un aplauso para el Gran Códac![127]

There is no doubt that Cabrera Infante's Vivian Smith Corona and the photographer Códac are models for Guillén's Walter Rice Taylor y Pimienta, Tito Tato, and Don Sinecuro. These and other characters with equally ridiculous names, including that of the social column's fictitious editor, Fradique Fontanals, are the protagonists in what is yet another "special show," a masquerade of sorts which is strongly suggestive of the soap opera scenes in Mario Vargas Llosa's novel *Aunt Julia and the Scriptwriter.* The desperate attempts of Havana's "high society" to fashion their identity from an admixture of the most trivial foreign-language phrases show their profound alienation from Cuba's true cultural foundations. As a result of their painstaking efforts to duplicate the social ambience and the way of life represented by establishments like the "Miami Club," they become parodies of themselves, fictional characters whose only reality is that of a show. They themselves become as trivial and as hollow as the platitudes posing as quotations from famous authors: "nos sentimos 'enchantés,' como decía el famoso Baudelaire"; "Una noche de 'charme,' como decía Verlaine"; " 'entourage,' . . . Como decía Montesquieu"; and "Descanse en paz, como decía Walter Johnson."

The fact that Walter Johnson, who was hardly a famous writer but an American baseball pitcher, is quoted in the same breath with Baudelaire, Verlaine, and Montesquieu exposes the falseness of the images of social and cultural refinement assembled in the "Notas." As in the case of the epoch-making social register, the substitution of trendy phrases from various languages for their Spanish equivalents has the effect of trivializing that language by making it equally unreliable and vacuous. As a result, the entire section is reduced to a random assortment of meaningless formulae, images of language whose exaggerated metaphoric splendor increases in proportion to their loss of meaning. For instance, the fact that the bride in the above citation has already been married five times completely voids the image of her being "aglow with the splendor of her very delicate virginity" and renders that image as meaningless as the interjection "New paragraph," which signifies precisely the absence of a new paragraph.

We need not continue. Far more interesting than citing additional examples from the "Society Notes" is the way in which the "press release" from the National Police Headquarters ("Jefatura de la Policía Nacional" [OP, 2: 428]), which immediately follows the "Notas," applies the same method of distortion to the realm of political history. This news clipping announces President Calvin Coolidge's visit to Havana to confirm "las relaciones amistosas que tradicionalmente han existido entre nuestra pequeña isla y el coloso del Norte" [the amiable relations that have traditionally existed between our small island and the colossus of the North]. But in order to maintain this convenient fiction, which is as much of a distortion of historical realities as "Calvino Cooleridge" is a disfigurement of the president's name, it is necessary to suppress any reference to historical facts that would bespeak the real nature of this allegedly untroubled friendship between the two countries:

Queda terminantemente prohibido cualquier demostración hostil al ilustre huésped, gran amigo de Cuba, así como toda alusión a la Enmienda Platt, a la Estación Naval de Guantánamo, a la zafra azucarera, o en general a las inversiones de ciudadanos de Estados Unidos en nuestro país.

[All demonstrations of hostility to our illustrious guest, the great friend of Cuba, are strictly prohibited, as well as any allusions to the Platt Amendment, the Guantánamo Naval Base, the sugar crop, or in general to the investments of United States citizens in our country.][128]

This "wonderful world" of amiable Cuban-American relations is as much of a fraud as is the splendid virginity of the bride in "Notas." Both are rhetorical constructs, images of a world that exists only in words. But, as is typical of *El diario*, important is what is *not* said, what lies behind the eloquent façade set up by the advertisements, the official press releases, and gossip columns. This "negative space," as Stephanie Merrim calls it, is as important in *El diario* as it is in *Tres tristes tigres*.[129] It is a space in which the elegant rhetoric representing canonized culture is exploded and broken up into small particles, into fragments that can now be reinvested with meaning. Fragmentation liberates language from the constraints of a rhetoric that seeks to reduce its semantic complexity by isolating it from its cultural context, by sterilizing it. While fragmentation and freeplay are compositional principles underlying all of *El diario*, the vast importance of these literary processes is best revealed in "La quincalla del ñato" [The Flat-Nosed Man's Drugstore], where Guillén completely forgoes literary convention to create a text that is styleless in the most literal sense.

LA QUINCALLA DEL ÑATO agujas de coser y de máquina papalotes bolas de cáñamo para los mismos alfileres de cabecita alfileres de criandera botones cintas de variado ancho chancletas de palo para el baño frazadas de piso cepillo y pasta de dientes chicles chambelonas brillantina sólida y líquida hilo blanco y de color salfumán y creolina perfumes de siete potencias flores de papel mejores que las legítimas postales iluminadas sellos de correos peinetas tijeritas peines antina para zapatos blancos esponjas grandes y pequeñas torticas de Morón serpentinas y confetis esmalte de uñas ojetes palos de trapear oraciones entre ellas la de San Luis Beltrán para el mal do ojo la de San Judas Tadeo la del Justo Juez bombillas eléctricas velitas de Santa Teresa la oración del Ánima Sola redecillas para el pelo. . . . (*OP*, 2: 429)

[THE FLAT-NOSED MAN'S DRUGSTORE needles for sewing and sewing machines kites string for those kites pins safety pins buttons ribbons of various widths wooden clogs for the bath mops tooth brushes and toothpaste chewing gum lollipops hair grease paste and liquid white fabric disinfectant perfumes of seven potencies paper flowers better than the real ones picture postcards stamps decorative combs scissors combs polish for white shoes large and small sponges little Moran pancakes streamers and confetti nailpolish mop handles snap buttons prayers including the one to San Luis Beltrán against the evil eye the one to San Judas Tadeo the one to Just Judge lightbulbs Santa Teresa candles Ánima Sola prayers hairnets. . . .]

"La quincalla del ñato" is the most spectacular textual outburst of Guillén's master trope, "algarabía en lengua de piratas y bozales." In contrast to the excessive rhetorical flourishes of the "Notas de Sociedad," this text is totally formless; it disregards even the most basic rules of punctuation. One phrase effortlessly flows into the next, and individual words playfully begin to enter entirely nonsensical allegiances such as "cabecita alfileres" [little head needles] or "ancho chancletas" [width slippers]. We are, in short, confronted with linguistic freeplay, or *caotismo*, in one of its most radical manifestations. At first glance, the result is a blur of words that resembles neither prose nor poetry, that simply refuses to be discursive in any conventional sense. It does not, to recall one of Guillén's earlier metaphors, "run" [*discurrir*] effortlessly across the page to create a recognizable pattern. "La quincalla del ñato" is precisely what Derrida calls a structure without a center. Yet it is more than just an incoherent, random collection of words and phrases. It is a text that forces us to abandon, completely and without reserve, the safety or even the most elemental formal conventions that govern literary and nonliterary discourse in order to create a radical awareness of the extent to which form is capable of obstructing meaning. But how is it possible to create meaning in a formless and styleless environment? Given my previous comments on stylelessness in connection with the Neobaroque and Guillén's concept of "algarabía," it is obvious that the value and the importance of this question are far from being purely theoretical. Given also that the Latin American Neobaroque, for Carpentier as well as for Guillén, is a revision or reformulation of the concept of "lo real maravilloso," it is furthermore possible to see the radical stylelessness of "La quincalla del ñato" as a bold attempt at reconstructing "el mundo maravilloso," that is, a true image of Cuban culture, from the scattered fragments of its distorted, official image, that exotic, Hollywood-like "wonderful world" of the Tropics.

To perceive the way in which Guillén subtly recovers the "marvelous" essence of Cuban (and Latin American) culture from the ruins of a fiction that he himself exposes as such and explodes in the "Jefatura de la Policía Nacional," it is useful to identify "La quincalla" as a textual mosaic. Walter Benjamin's comments on the value of fragments in relation to a mosaic whole deserve careful consideration in this regard. "The value of fragments of thought," he writes, "is all the greater the less direct their relationship to the underlying idea, and the brilliance of the representation depends as much on this value as the brilliance of the mosaic does on the quality of the glass paste. The relationship between the minute precision of the work and the proportions of the sculptural or intellectual whole demonstrates that truth-content is only to be grasped through immersion in the most minute details of subject matter."[130] To begin with, "la quincalla del ñato," which literally translates into "the flat-nosed man's drugstore" or, as Ellis suggests, "the snub-nosed man's hardware store," is a familiar Cuban idiom: To get something in the "quincalla (or bodega) del ñato" means to take something from the place where one works without paying for it like a regular customer. In other words, the employee momentarily affords himself the same privileges as the owner to justify what is in effect a theft, facilitated by the employer's trust. The phrase "la quincalla del ñato" is already a trope for subversion which, in the context particularly of the final section of *El diario*, works in two different ways: On the one hand, Guillén's "Quincalla del ñato" is yet another revision of his image of Cuba as a "sold-out palm grove" and as such places additional emphasis on historical processes of economic and cultural exploitation disguised as "protection." On the other hand, the fact that Guillén suddenly introduces a familiar idiomatic expression into a textual environment contaminated by stylish foreign phrases has as much of a disruptive effect as Cabrera Infante's emcee's sudden exclamation "¡coño!" [Fuck!] has among the false glitter of rhetorical eloquence that characterizes the prologue in *Tres tristes tigres*. Like "coño," "la quincalla del ñato" is a linguistic act of debunking and subverting the false images of canonized culture that dominate this section of *El diario*.

The subversive effects of this trope are enhanced even further by the linguistic syncretism from which the idiom evolved: "Ñato" is a familiar pejorative reference to blacks, and, as Ortiz suggests, probably of African origin.[131] Although this is nowhere documented, it is possible that the phrase "la quincalla del ñato" derived its idiomatic meaning from the general conviction that it was not a crime to steal from a black man. But if "Ñato," on the one hand, serves as a reminder of racial prejudice underlying the United States' attitude toward Cuba, it is also, at the same time, a vehicle for self-assertion in that it calls attention to the luminous presence of African elements in Cuban language. To Guillén, this "inyección africana" was as important in 1972 as it was forty years earlier when he wrote his *Motivos de son*. "La quincalla del ñato," for him, is a storehouse of Cuban culture.

Let us consider some of the items that make up this chaotic catalogue. At first it seems as if Guillén gives us nothing but the usual list of imported junk: Toothpaste, hair grease, and shoelaces are not exactly objects invested with any special cultural significance. But if we patiently continue to read, we suddenly encounter several items that stick out from the piles of combs, buttons, and scouring pads: "prayers including the one to San Luis Beltrán against the evil eye the one to San Judas Tadeo the one to the Just Judge . . . Santa Teresa candles Anima Sola prayers." To anyone familiar with the work of Fernando Ortiz and Alejo Carpentier, it is instantly clear that we have moved from the "wonderful world" of fancy clubs and exotic shows down into the vortex of Cuban culture: the "hampa afrocubana," the world of *brujos* [sorcerers], of *embos* and *contre-embos* [spells and counter-spells]. We have returned to the "mundo maravilloso" of "Sensemayá" and the Great Loas.

All the prayers, as well as the Santa Teresa candles, are, like the "Día de Reyes" festivities, authentic products of Cuba's cross-cultural imagination. More specifically, they represent processes of cultural exchange in which Catholic beliefs and values are assimilated into African religions and infused with new meanings. To use Carpentier's words, the Catholic divinities are invested with "secret lives"; they are "ennobled" by black identities.[132] Miguel Barnet explains that "faced with the flimsy Christianization campaign on the [sugar] plantations during the nineteenth century, faced with the imposition of gods unknown to him, the black man responded by working out his own models; he substituted, established exact or approximate equivalences, worked with parallel concepts, related matching features, associated colors and symbols."[133] In this sense, the "Prayer to the Just Judge" [Oración al Justo Juez], for instance, is not simply an act of worshipping the Christian God but a specific appeal for protection directed at the highest Yoruba deity, *Oloruñ*, also known as *Olodumare* (the One Who Is Always Just).[134] Carpentier's transcription of this particular prayer, which, he reports, was once given to him as a gift by an old black sorcerer at Regla, is a good example of this kind of religio-cultural syncretism:

There are lions and lionesses pursuing me. May they stop, as our Lord Jesus Christ stopped before the Just Judge, when he said to him: I see my enemies arriving. May they have hands, but may they not touch me; may they have eyes, but may they not see me; may they have feet, but may they not reach me. I drink their blood; and I crush their hearts. Because I wear the holy garment in which your son was wrapped, and through it I will set myself free from prisons, evil tongues, sorceries, and witchcraft. I put my trust in the Holy Trinity and in the milk that blessed the breast of the very holy Holy Mary. Deliver me, Lord, from my enemies, as you delivered Jonas from the belly of the whale. Mr. Saint-John, I ask you, in the name of the bitter saliva that you swallowed at the crucifixion. God with me; I with him; God before me; I behind him. Jesus, Mary, and Joseph. Note—He who carries this prayer with him will be saved from the persecution of justice, and will triumph over his enemies. His sleep will not be troubled by the bites of scorpions, spiders, and similar animals. If he has a wife, she will bear children without difficulty. It may be useful to know this prayer by heart for unexpected cases.[135]

The fetichistic use of Christian phraseology serves to concretize this plea for deliverance from evil; evil is not an abstract category but is directly embodied, in this case, in certain animals.

Even more detailed instructions as to how to avert a specific kind of danger are contained in the "Prayer to the Damned Soul" [Oración al Anima Sola]:

Sad and Lonely Soul: Nobody calls you, I call you; nobody needs you, I need you; nobody loves you, I love you. Since I suppose that you cannot enter into heaven, because you are in hell, you will get on the best horse, race to the Mount of Olives, cut off three branches from a tree, and rub the abdomen of Mr. N., so that he may no longer be able to stop anywhere, to sit down, to eat, or to sleep, and so that no negress or mulatta [nor a white or a Chinese woman] may be with him, and so that he will run after me like a wild dog.

This prayer must be said every day, at noon and at midnight, while a lamp is being lighted and placed on the ground behind the door.[136]

The "Anima Sola prayer," designed specifically for "the jealous woman whose lover is about to leave on a voyage," is addressed to the Yoruba deity *Elegbara* (or *Eshu-Elegua*), who is associated with the "Blessed Souls of the Purgatory."[137] Elegbara, the guardian of the crossroads, already encountered in my discussion of Jay Wright's version of the "Son de la Ma' Teodora," is frequently believed to sit at the door of a house to protect its inhabitants against the intrusion of evil spirits. In this prayer, he is embodied in the lighted lamp that is placed behind the door at the time the prayer is recited. Another interesting aspect of this prayer is the allusion of voodoo and *ñañiguismo* rituals: The best way to get to the Mount of Olives is "to mount a horse" ("montarás el caballo" in the original). In the context of those rituals, a "mount" is an initiate possessed ("ridden") by a loa, so that the pilgrimage to the Mount of Olives is symbolically re-dressed as a ritualistic transfiguration and thus assumes distinct Afro-Caribbean features. In this way, the "Monte Oliva" as a ritual ground becomes indirectly associated with the symbolic space of "el monte."[138]

The "velitas de Santa Teresa" evoke a similar encounter between African religious beliefs and Catholicism: the altar. We read in *Ecue*, for instance, that "[a]quella noche, para preservar al rorro de nuevos peligros, la madre encendió una velita de Santa Teresa ante la imagen de San Lazaro que presidia el altar" [That night, in order to protect the infant from new dangers, the mother lighted a Santa Teresa candle in front of the image of Saint Lazarus, who was the patron of the altar].[139] It can be said that the Santa Teresa candles illuminate Saint Lazarus's other identity, which is that of *Babayu-ayé*, a deity requiring a special reward or tribute in exchange for his medicinal powers.[140] While I have been unable to locate specific details about the prayers to San Luis Beltrán and San Judas Tadeo, it is safe to assume that they are employed for protective or preventive purposes similar to the ones discussed above.

It is evident, then, that these seemingly innocuous references Guillén includes in "La quincalla del ñato" are, in fact, invocations of Afro-Cuban divinities. Like the prayers themselves, these divinities are invoked by Guillén as protection against specific evils, in this case the concrete threat United States imperialism poses to Cuban culture. In this sense, "La quincalla del ñato" is a textual ritual designed to exorcise those dangerous influences. As in "Sensemayá," Afro-Cuban religio-cultural beliefs acquire the status of founding fables that provide a reliable repository of meaning and thus offer an alternative to the impending danger of deculturation and corruption resulting from white Cubans embracing both European and United States cultural values. As Barnet explains, "The world of the white offers nothing but contradiction and an obsession with everything non-Cuban, first with the European mecca, and later with the capitalist one." But, he continues, "in the world of the black, we find general laws and a philosophy."[141] This is also precisely the world to which Guillén returns in *El diario* in order to contrast what Barnet calls "the *culture* that sugar created" to the *society* that sugar created.

I have suggested earlier that "La quincalla del ñato" is the single most striking textual manifestation of "algarabía," Guillén's master trope for continuous cultural cross-fertilization. It is now possible to mobilize the full semantic range of this trope by connecting it with the specific context already implicit in the phrase "en lengua de piratas y bozales." Upon entering a Caribbean setting, "algarabía," itself already representative of syncretisms between Spanish and Arabic cultures, is invested with the qualities of Afro-Cuban ritual and thus becomes a figure for transculturation. In its new context, "algarabía" signifies the freeplay between African and European cultural beliefs and values, whose literary image is that of a text generated by the kind of chaotic enumeration that renders visible the idea of a marketplace. It was precisely through this interaction with African cultural elements that Spanish culture was transformed into Cuban culture. The various forms of cultural and literary freeplay that we encounter throughout *El diario* all come together in "La quincalla del ñato" in a vast ritual of cultural (and textual) regeneration: As we already know from "Sensemayá," Guillén's trope for that kind of intertextual ritual is *carnival*.

In *El diario*, carnival as an enactment of the historico-cultural processes that created Cuban culture is envisioned as a profound cultural fiction, indeed a major foundation fable that voids the hollow social fictions of the "Notas de Sociedad" and the advertisements in this section. For Guillén, carnival signifies the ritualization of "algarabía en lengua de piratas y bozales." This ritualization is achieved, at the formal level, by employing chaotic enumeration to create a space for the kind of double(d) discourse represented by the Afro-Cuban prayers. Furthermore, other items on this list acquire different semantic values as a result of the textual presence of these prayers: They become ritualistic objects of sorts. This is particularly evident in the case of "serpentinas y confetis" [streamers and confetti], paraphernalia connected with carnival activities. "Serpentina," of course, is also a kind of snake (from the French *serpentin*, snake, and the Latin *sepere*, to creep), which, in this context, recalls the "Día de Reyes" celebrations and their connection with voodoo and *ñañiguismo*, both of which are snake cults. In the same way, "almanaques" [calendars] alerts us to the fact that carnival is a ritual celebrated at the beginning of the new year. In order to see how these seemingly insignificant references combine to evoke the "Día de Reyes," we have to consider that different cultures have different liturgical years and thus different calendars. As Ortiz points out, the fact that carnival is a universal phenomenon does not mean that it is celebrated at the same time by all cultures. With respect to Cuba, he continues:

The whites in Cuba, who derived their ancient carnival tradition from the European religions, hold their *mystical* celebrations prior to the equinox of Spring [March 21]: the blacks, who in this country perform their carnival rites in accordance with the solstice of Winter [December 22], have chosen Christmas Eve and the Epiphany for the festivities. In ancient Rome, the Saturnalian rites were held either in December or in March; accordingly, the solar year would begin on either one of the two astrological dates. This is, however, not to say that the Epiphany, so profoundly important to the Afro-Cubans, did not also have an important folkloric meaning since remote times. Just as Christmas Day, corresponding roughly to the day of the solstice of Winter, is the first day of the period of "the twelve days," as Fraser called it, which, since antiquity and since the times of the Arians, has been considered the augural period of the new year, so the Epiphany is the last day of that symbolic twelve-day year.[142]

Thus, Afro-Cuban liturgy as represented by the above prayers charge words like "serpentinas" and "almanaques" with culture-specific meanings that ground the carnivalesque formal properties of "La quincalla del ñato" in a distinct historico-cultural environment. This fact assumes an even larger significance in connection with the strategic position of this text in *El diario*. "La quincalla del ñato" marks the end of the rhetorical distortions that dominate *El diario* and that culminate in the poem's final section; it celebrates the end of conventional literary discourse in much the same way that the "Día de Reyes" announces the end of the old year and ushers in the new one. As a consequence of this analogy, "La quincalla del ñato" becomes the textual equivalent of the "Día de Reyes" ritual: Writing creates a simulacrum of a cultural ritual ground where the black and the white worlds meet. "La quincalla del ñato" may be viewed as a literary rite of collective purification, performed, like the agrarian rites that underlie carnival, to expel evil spirits.

In this way, "La quincalla" anticipates the "Teatro Republicano" advertisement (*OP*, 2: 431), which announces the demise of the Machado dictatorship: "De Leonardo a Gerardo"; "Entrada gratis—salida a trompadas, trompetas y trompetillas" [From Leonardo to Gerardo; admission free—tumultuous exit, with trumpets and farting sounds]. It also prefigures "Batistafio" (432), the swan song for the Batista regime:

el general (¡salud!) que todo era,
a ser nada volvió como cualquiera.

[the General (Health!) who was everything,
has become nothing like nothing again.]

With the literary exorcism of these malevolent "spirits" Guillén has also cleared the ground for the resurrection of Martí. The symbolic value of the announcement of a lecture by Martí is intensified by the fact that January 28 [1853] is Martí's actual birth date.

28 DE ENERO

DESFILE POPULAR Y GRAN ACTO
DE MASAS
A LAS 9 DE LA NOCHE

¡ASISTA!   ¡ASISTA!

Sepa cómo impedir a tiempo, con la independencia de Cuba, que se extiendan por las Antillas los Estados Unidos y caigan con esa fuerza más sobre nuestras tierras de América.

HABLARÁ JOSÉ MARTÍ. (*OP*, 2: 433)

[28th OF JANUARY

PUBLIC PARADE AND GREAT DEMONSTRATION
OF THE MASSES
AT 9 P.M.

BE THERE!   BE THERE!

Learn through the independence of Cuba how to prevent in time the
United States from taking over the Antilles and from forcibly
subjecting to their rule our countries in the Americas.

JOSÉ MARTÍ WILL SPEAK]

Martí's textual presence in the form of a quotation from his last,
unfinished letter[143] marks the beginning not only of a new year but of a
new era in Cuban history. As Guillén writes in "Elegía cubana": "Alto
Martí, tu azul estrella enciende. / Tu lengua principal corta la bru-
ma. / El fuego sacro en la montaña prende" [Great Martí, your blue star
blazes yet. / Your mighty word divides the mist. / The sacred fire glows
on the mountain]. Echoes of these earlier lines resound particularly in
the phrase "Hablará José Martí" as well as in Mount Turquino's burn-
ing forehead in "Final." In El diario, Martí's call for Cuban indepen-
dence is immediately answered by another advertisement announcing
the publication of Fidel Castro's famous attack on the Batista regime,
History Will Absolve Me.[144]

Acaba de aparecer "La Historia me absolverá." Un volumen en
cuarto, artísticamente impreso, con fotos y documentos inéditos.

HAY UN EXEMPLAR PARA USTED

Editorial Moncada (OP, 2: 434)

[The text of "History Will Absolve Me" has just appeared. One
quarto volume, artistically printed, with photographs and un-
published documents.

THERE IS A COPY FOR YOU

Moncada Publishers]

The link between Martí and Castro, who proclaimed that "the Revo-
lution . . . recognizes and bases itself in the ideals of Martí,"[145] is
underscored by the fact that the attack on the Moncada Barracks in
1953 coincided with the first centennial of Martí's birth. Interesting
about Guillén's advertisement is that History Will Absolve Me, first
printed as a pamphlet in June 1954, was, of course, circulated clan-

233

destinely.[146] It was hardly the kind of publication that would have been officially announced in any Cuban newspaper at the time. Furthermore, Guillén omits Castro's name from the text of the announcement, an omission that separates the author from his text and thus suggests the possibility for investing the personal pronoun "Me" with larger, collective connotations.[147] This implicit notion of collective authorship of a revolutionary text is reinforced by the fact that "Editorial Moncada" also contains yet another veiled reference to carnival: The attack on the Moncada Barracks on 26 July 1953 had been planned to coincide with the carnival festivities in Santiago de Cuba, for obvious strategic reasons.[148] The subtle symbolism with which Guillén imbues this military decision should not be dismissed: It is important because it establishes a metaphoric connection between a momentous event in recent Cuban history and the cluster of textual references in "La quincalla del ñato." In this way, the revolution against the Cuban-American establishment embodied in Batista is intimately associated in its subversiveness with Afro-Cuban carnival. Given that, at the time, Castro's followers were denouncing blacks and mulattoes as supporters of Batista,[149] this is indeed a curious twist, which could be read as an indirect criticism of Castro's initial failure to perceive a historical connection between his own struggle and that of the Afro-Cuban community.

Guillén's recourse, at the end of *El diario*, to the "marvelous" imaginative resources of traditional Afro-Cuban ritual is significant for a variety of reasons. To begin with, the trope of carnival, which thematizes the function of Guillén's poetic language by reinserting his intricate play with literary masks into its proper historico-cultural context, bridges the thirty-five-year gap between the poem "Sensemayá" and *El diario*. This trope lends to Guillén's poetic canon a coherence far more profound than any superficial unity created by the presumed ideological content of his poetry. What underlies Guillén's carnival is not a Marxist dialectic but an irreducible intercultural dialogue, a dynamic ritual of transculturation that represents the very foundations of Cuban (and New World) culture. All this demonstrates that Guillén, in spite of what most of his critics would like to believe, has never ceased being an Afro-American poet. That the poetry he wrote after the *poesía negra* of *Motivos de son*, *Sóngoro cosongo*, and *West Indies, Ltd.* does not fit the conventional, predominantly thematic molds that have been devised for Afro-American texts is indicative not of Guillén's attributing less significance to the role of black culture. It testifies, if anything, to the radical reorganization of the Afro-American literary canon. Guillén's work, like Jay Wright's, shows that Afro-American writers, both in North

234

America and in the Caribbean, have moved from their quest for free-dom-through-literacy to an assertion of freedom *with* literacy. For Guillén, as for Wright, Afro-American writing is an ever-changing historical process, at once a gathering of diverse elements and a system of indissoluble and irreducible differences. It is the very irreducibility of these differences which feeds the cultural and literary cross-fertilization characteristic of New World writing. Afro-American literature is the product of a long historical tradition of resistance to authority in all its different manifestations, and it is this posture of resistance that con-stitutes Guillén's most profound legacy.

The Writing
on the Wall

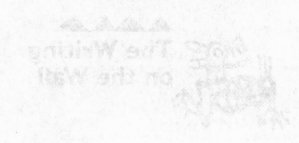

—WILLIAM CARLOS WILLIAMS, *Paterson*

Throughout my discussion I have spoken in detail about walls—the walls of cities such as Cuzco, Tenochtitlán, Labná, Hawikúh, Cartagena de Indias, and Havana—whose ruins come alive again under the poet's touch. Like the cities themselves, these walls or ruins of walls are places of cultural communion, altars of sorts, where the blood of the living mixes, miraculously and marvelously, with the blood of the dead. They are *genii loci* and "gateways to the beautiful," reconstructed by the historical imagination of writers like William Carlos Williams, Jay Wright, and Nicolás Guillén. As such, they are visible manifestations of peculiar rites of passage, of those processes of transformation through which the New World writer is (re)initiated into cultural self-knowledge.

The walls of which I want to speak now, both in order to close the present discussion and to suggest possibilities for future openings, are not city walls; yet they are places of communion, meeting places of history and myth. What makes those walls fascinating with regard to Williams, Wright, and Guillén (as well as Carpentier, Paz, Neruda, Fuentes, and Arguedas) is the fact that they are located inside a library. They are, in fact, representations of what I have been calling the Archive within the actual structure of a library: I am referring to the Orozco Frescoes in the Baker Library at Dartmouth College.

I first saw these magnificent murals, which were painted by the Mexican artist José Clemente Orozco between 1932 and 1934, during a Visiting Professorship in Dartmouth's Art Department, when I went to see Jay and Lois Wright in Piermont, New Hampshire, in the summer of 1984, shortly after having completed what was to become the second part of this study. When entering the corridor connecting the Baker Library with the Carpenter Art Building, I could not believe my eyes: It was as if everything I had been writing about had suddenly come to life, both in the images on the walls of the corridor and in the mental images the paintings inspired my imagination to project. I had walked, it seemed, not into a room, but into one of the poems on which I had been meditating for the past months. As I stood silently, surrounded by Orozco's *Epic of American Civilization*, the words of Carlos Fuentes's lone sailor began to resonate in my mind:

Above the orient of my simultaneous vision of all things, Venus was gleaming within reach of my hand, near my extended hand, and as at the beginning of my story, I called her morning star, night's last glimmer, but also its perpetuation in the dawn's clear light, the sailor's guide: I repeated that name, the same name, the only name, the name of my destination, go where I go, sailing away from port or in return, embarked victorious or vanquished, Venus, Venus; Vésperes—evening; Vísperas—eve; Víspero—evening star; Héspero—Venus; Hesperia—the Western land; Hespérides—daughter of the West; España, Spain; España/Hespaña/Vespaña, name of the double star, twin of itself, constant dusk and dawn, silver stele that joins the old and the new worlds and carried me from one to the other borne on her fiery train, star of evening, star of dawn, Plumed Serpent, my name in the New World was the name of the old world; Quetzalcóatl, Venus, Hesperia, Spain, identical stars, dawn and dusk, mysterious union, indecipherable enigma, but cipher for two bodies, two lands, cipher for a terrible encounter.[1]

Here it was, all right in front of me: that mysterious union, that indecipherable enigma, that terrible encounter of two worlds facing each other across the corridor as Cortés and his troops faced the Aztec warriors centuries ago. There was Quetzalcóatl, symbolized by a large stone-carved image of a plumed serpent with Huitzilopochtli's eagle-feathered warriors in the background, ready to supply their monstrous deity with fresh victims for human sacrifice. Farther along the wall this scene was mirrored by the arrival of the conquistadors (*The Prophecy*) carrying a huge armored cross soon to be anointed with the blood of thousands of Aztecs, slain in the name of another god. In the next panel, their mutilated bodies were piled up at the feet of the triumphant Cortés, standing proudly and self-assuredly in front of a tall, dark cross rising amidst the ruins of Tenochtitlán against the luminous background of the conqueror's burning fleet. The towering, dark figure of Cortés on the eastern wall was poised against the gleaming white image of Quetzalcóatl as the Great White Father, hovering majestically over the twin pyramids of Teotihuacán in the midst of an awesome pantheon of Aztec deities. The Great White Father had indeed returned in the twin shapes of Quetzalcóatl and Cortés. The panel to the right of *The Coming of Quetzalcóatl* offered images of the cultural achievements of pre-Columbian civilization—agriculture, sculpture, astronomy—images that, in the corresponding panel on the eastern wall, had been replaced by a gigantic, impersonal machine that, appropriately, seemed to feed on the bodies of the dead Aztecs. Farther to the right of that monstrous vision of modern technology were juxtaposed images of Anglo-America and Hispano-America. The first one could have been an illustration of Williams's "Voyage of the Mayflower," whose images of Puritan sterility were reflected in the expressionless, pale faces of the stiff, lifeless crowd.

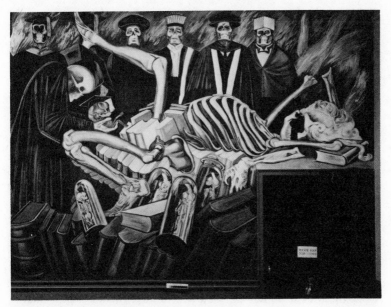

Figure 3.
José Clemente Orozco, *Gods of the Modern World*

In contrast, *Hispano-America* evoked Guillén's portrait of Havana, a chaotic amalgam of images of violence, greed, and corruption surrounding the solitary figure of a Mexican revolutionary in the center.

But of all those images, which began to proliferate and multiply in my mind and to which my imagination added others that Orozco did not actually paint, the panel I found most striking was the one on the far right of the eastern wall: *Gods of the Modern World* (fig. 3), curiously related to the Cortés panel at the opposite end of that part of the wall, depicts the scene of a birth—the birth of modern America. The painting is dominated by the figure of a human skeleton sprawled, with awkwardly raised legs, across a tombstone-like array of books. In this grotesque position, it delivers its stillborn offspring into the meticulous hands of an equally skeletal obstetrician in an academic gown, who diligently places each of the dead newborns into a transparent glass tube. Presiding over the grueling reproduction of dead knowledge are the "gods of the modern world," posing in academic costumes of various European and American universities. They oddly recall the parade of Aztec deities dispersed by the arrival of Quetzalcóatl and now reassembled, in somewhat different shapes, by Cortés and his descendants. The ruins Cortés left behind are

241

now imaged as ponderous tomes commemorating, like tombstones, the spiritual death of modern civilization. As in the Cortés panel, all these gruesome figures of death are set off against a lurid background of flames. The painting's extraordinary appeal is due to the fact that it brings together a number of now familiar images employed by Williams, Wright, and Guillén in their respective critiques of the myth of Literature and the institution Culture. Both structures are, as we have seen in numerous instances, embodied in the trope of the Library, which represents traditional Western ideas of order and knowledge perceived as confining rather than liberating. The Library represents the conditions that presumably make (self)-knowledge possible, but Williams, Wright, and Guillén experience these conditions—formal literary conventions and criteria for canonization, as well as the very concept of Literature itself—as ideological strictures that imprison the imagination and render it illiterate. For them, the Library is a conceptual construct that impedes self-knowledge rather than facilitating it. A figure for available forms of literary representation and, in fact, for the myth of representation itself, the Library becomes a voided presence in the work of these three poets: Once the texts it houses are subjected to the rigors of critical (that is, historical) interpretation instead of being sheltered from it, once their truth-value is questioned rather than being confirmed, the entire structure collapses. Divested of everything that gave it strength and authority, it is reduced to a mere skeleton, whose bleached bones uncomfortably, but appropriately, recall Williams's white ink. Ironically, as in Orozco's painting, this grotesque skeletal structure and the kind of knowledge it continues to generate are preserved by those Guardians of Culture, those modern "gods" in their somber academic attire, who silently worship death, stillborn knowledge that is perceived as a fetish rather than as an intellectual tool.

In contrast to the scene it depicts, Orozco's painting itself is extremely fertile. It lends visible (and visual) resonance to some of the principal tropological clusters we have encountered in the writing of Williams, Wright, and Guillén. We see, through Orozco's vision of the gods of the modern world, images not only of the burning library in *Paterson*—the painting's fire motif is particularly suggestive in this case—but also of the crumbling body of García Márquez's galleon in *One Hundred Years of Solitude*. In addition, we surmise shapes of other, more representationally elusive figures: Like *In the American Grain*, *Dimensions of History*, and *El diario*, Orozco's *Gods of the Modern World* is an allegory of undoing conceptual strictures that render historical knowledge meaningless by imprisoning it in dead metaphors. What Orozco's painting puts on display are the lifeless remains of the same structures of authority our three poets set out to dismantle in their respective texts. Like those texts, Orozco's mural in its entirety is an impressive play of contrasting structures and antistructures, attempting to give shape to the peculiarities of the New World's cultural texture. It is a pictorial Archive situated symbolically within the structure of an actual library. Precisely because of that suggestive location, one cannot help but wonder whether Orozco's mural is really, as the voice offering the visitor an interpretation of the *Epic of American Civilization* claims, a demonstration of his faith in our academic institutions or whether it is a warning.[2]

It is worth noting in this context that none of the three writers whose work we have been exploring is (or, in Williams's case, was) a professional academic. Williams, as is known, did not hide his profound distrust in and even hostility toward universities. Jay Wright, as Hollander has put it, is a "studious recluse," who only occasionally transplants himself from his New Hampshire residence into an academic setting (he has taught at Yale, Boston University, and the universities of Utah, Kentucky, and most recently, North Carolina). Guillén's academic career was largely confined to the study of law in his early years, and although he holds an *honoris causa* doctorate from the University of Havana, he never taught at that or any other institution. In short, Williams, Wright, and Guillén have been, quite deliberately for the most part, as marginal to academic circles in the United States and Latin America as their texts are to established literary canons. While this particular kind of marginality vis-à-vis the traditional centers of ideological dissemination—the university communities in the United States and various literary groups in Latin America[3]—is perhaps not all that unusual, it is, I believe, telling that it should coincide with each writer's awareness of, and insistence on, his mixed cultural background and heritage.

For Williams, for instance, to be an American writer did not mean to pledge allegiance to, and establish some sort of continuity with, the so-called classics of nineteenth-century United States literature, or any other classics for that matter, but to explore and cultivate areas of uncertainty created by cultural contact. Those areas, according to him, made the New World different from Europe or from whatever image of European culture American intellectuals cherished, and owing to that actual or potential difference, they were apt to compromise the efforts of those guardians of culture who were attempting to legitimize American Culture (and Literature) by making it conform to European patterns (and pretenses) of cultural purity and national unity. Such delusions of cultural purity, Williams recognized, can only be maintained as long as those uncertain and uncomfortable areas of cultural contact are ignored, that is, as long as each culture is kept safely in its place. That "place" may be an urban or a suburban ghetto, or it may be a literary canon. "What a farce!" he exclaims in *In the American Grain*, "But what a tragedy. It rests upon false values and fear to discover them. Do not serve another for you might have to TOUCH him and he might be a JEW or a NIGGER" (*IAG*, 176–77).

Canonization, as it is practiced today in the United States and elsewhere, is a form of intellectual and academic ghettoization. Rather than admitting a work written by an Afro-American or a Latin American author (or by a woman) into the canon of American Literature, we create a separate category for each, thus hoping to have solved the problem such texts pose without endangering the entire system of classification. By doing so, we make assumptions about cultural and literary differences (and similarities) based, for the most part, on purely biological criteria. We assert the existence of such differences and similarities without knowing exactly what they are. As a result, we confuse canonization with literary history.

In a letter to the *New York Times Book Review,* Henry Louis Gates, Jr., insists that "[the Afro-American] literary tradition exists *only* because black writers read other black writers, and *ground* their representations of experience in models of language provided to a significant degree by other black writers."[4] While Gates's language may be different from that employed by more traditional critics of Afro-American literature, his argument nevertheless has a familiar ring. Despite the focus on textual (rather than racial) relationships, and even despite the disclaimer that "this is not to deny the crucial role of other formal influences" such as "Frederick Douglass's revisions of Emerson and Carlyle; Jean Toomer's revision of Sherwood Anderson; James Baldwin's revisions of Henry James," Gates's pronouncement appears to be based on assumptions similar to the ones underlying Irving Howe's 1963 *Dissent* article entitled "Black Boys and Native Sons," in which he identified Ralph Ellison as a direct literary descendant of Richard Wright. Ellison's indignant response to Howe is well known, and while there is no doubt, despite Ellison's claims to the contrary, that his *Invisible Man* is, at least in part, a recasting of Wright's *Black Boy,* his angry refusal to submit to Howe's implicit assumptions about what constitutes Afro-American literary history is a statement of considerable importance.[5]

It would be relatively easy to dismiss Ellison's remarks on his literary relationship with Richard Wright as yet another instance of the Bloomian paradigm of the "anxiety of influence" by appealing to the unreliability of an author's assessment of his own work. But to do so would detract from the larger issues Ellison raises, namely that the category *Afro-American Literature*, even when it is not explicitly based on the supposedly irremediable condition of racial identity, still serves to reduce the complexity of the literary relationships a text encodes to patterns of cultural unity rather than allowing for a comparative perspective. Like all literary canons, it is a system of power that controls which texts are read and taught as well as *how* they are to be read and taught: in this case, in relation to other Afro-American texts. What Ellison demands, and justly so, is that *Invisible Man* be read not only in relation to *Black Boy* and other Afro-American texts but also, at the same time, in relation to the work of Eliot, Pound, Stein, Hemingway, Malraux, and Dostoievsky. He insists that his text is a product of *all* those readings, not simply of one. Similarly, if we place James Baldwin next to Jean Toomer and Frederick Douglass, we get one set of literary relationships; if we place him beside Henry James, we get another. Either approach yields an interpretation, but not a *reading* of Baldwin's texts, for a reading would require that we examine the specific formal relationships Baldwin establishes between all of those different precursor texts. While each of these precursor or "ancestral" texts may belong to different literary canons, all are part of the literary history of the text that brings them together through formal echoes and recast metaphors.

Ellison's refusal of the label *Afro-American* for his work is not an unusual or exceptional occurrence. Other prominent examples are Jean Toomer and Robert Hayden, not to mention Jay Wright and Nicolás Guillén. What they acknowledge is the incontrovertible fact that their works exist in a problematic relationship not only to the traditional ("American") literary canon but to the politics of and, in fact, the very idea of canonization. Their texts question the modes of literary (as well as social and cultural) authority that underlie the traditional idea of a canon. This approach or challenge to established forms of authority, fictional and real, is very different from the desire to demonstrate the existence of another canon, which, although composed of a different set of texts, would rely on similar modes of authority. What we witness in the texts of those and other New World authors from various cultural backgrounds are profound transformations of the concept of authority, which signal the impact of formerly silenced or "marginalized" voices on the political economy of a literary canon. This process is something very different from canon formation in any traditional sense. It is a strategic development of "inner correctives" to the principles of canonization, correctives that also challenge and subvert the social authority that institutes the canon(s) and, on that basis, designs models of literary history.

If the point of canonization is to underwrite the authority of a text, then in order for a text to be accepted into the fold of a given literary canon, the modes of textual authority it enshrines have to be in conformity with the forms of authority the canon itself embodies, that is, with the conventions from which it derives its authority and legitimacy. Put differently, the ideology of literary production has to conform to the ideology of canonization. There is no room for discrepancies. The most basic of those conventions, of course, are the ones that define the concept of "literariness," or what I have called the myth of Literature. Implicit in the definition of Literature as an ordered system of signs that, unlike other ("nonliterary") forms of written discourse, gives total representation to human experience and history is the assumption of a universal predesign according to which human experience and history unfold. It is that preexisting, universal order that literature can presumably represent. Even the existence of different modes or forms of representation matters but little as long as they do not question the validity of such an underlying order.

None of the texts I have analyzed in this book make it possible for us to maintain those traditional ideas of literary unity and canonical order. Their main goal is to challenge our dependency on those constructs and with it our faith in the kind of writing that conceals its own conventionality and thus the fact that what it presents as truth derives its truth-value only from a set of unquestioned assumptions, that is, myths. We have seen, for instance, that the idea of a universal pattern of historical and cultural development is a myth derived from the fiction of European cultural supremacy and centrality, which was used to legitimize imperialistic ventures of various kinds. We have also seen that the myth of America, which ascribed to New World civilizations the potential to duplicate the European model(s) rather than acknowledging the existence of cultural differences, ensured the persistence of a cultural inferiority complex that prevented most American writers and intellectuals from attributing any significance to their countries' own, allegedly nonexistent, history. This, in turn, has resulted in the systematic marginalization or suppression of non-European cultural influences whose historical presence in the New World would testify to the existence of profound cultural differences vis-à-vis Europe and thus would question, among other things, the legitimacy of the United States' continued practice of both internal and external cultural imperialism. Those historical differences, as Williams, Wright, and Guillén insist, constitute a more meaningful and reliable basis for the formulation of the New World's complex cultural identity than the patriotic clichés used in both the United States and Latin America to evoke some sort of nationally unifying revolutionary heritage.

For all three writers, literature is a forum for bringing into focus those marginalized or silenced voices and texts in New World history and for exposing as fictions the structures of authority upon which the traditional concept of American Culture is predicated: the presumed universality of European cultural models. In the texts of Williams, Wright, and Guillén, the imaginative processes that retrieve those silences accentuate, rather than conceal, their artifices by removing things from their expected symbolic places, that is, by decentering existing forms of cultural and literary authority. The clearings that are created as a result of this displacement are new semantic openings that perforate the protective shell (or "dead layer") of convention and conceit, the "sealed mausoleums" in which North American society enshrines its national myths. We are reminded here of the glass tubes, those containers of stillborn knowledge, in Orozco's painting, which clearly recall Carpentier's splendid image of Henri Christophe's finger, preserved in a glass crystal bottle filled with alcohol. Once the container is opened and the fluid drained, its contents decompose. The same thing happens to myth once we penetrate its protective ideological enclosure and expose it to history and thus to interpretation: It decomposes into a multitude of fragments, which can be arranged into new, different shapes, but whose original form cannot be recovered, no matter how hard we try.

This illustration best characterizes the nature of that "rich, regenerative violence" we encounter in *In the American Grain, Dimensions of History,* and *El diario.* For Williams, Wright, and Guillén, writing is an act of violence, whose radical historicity makes it impossible for it to signify a static cultural origin. The only thing writing can do is to create a fiction of that origin, a fiction that is founded not on historical fact—or whatever interpretation of history we accord the status of a "fact"—but on readings of texts whose own fictional status has been forgotten and which are allowed, consequently, to parade as truths. These readings, or unreadings, as I have called them, create room for doubt as well as for change. Above all, they urge us to heed Williams's warning that "aesthetically, morally, we are deformed unless we read."

The texts of Williams, Wright, and Guillén, in short, teach us to read. They teach us to be attentive not only to what is being said but also to what is not being said, to what is *also* being said without being named.

More specifically, they teach us that reading is an imaginative reconstitution of a text and not a semiscientific dissection of a finished product. To read *In the American Grain*, *Dimensions of History*, and *El diario* is an imaginative reconstitution of the shape of New World writing from the scattered fragments of several American literary canons. Those readings, like the texts themselves, are experiments in disorder that ultimately reveal a kinship much more significant than the genealogies they destroy: an order, or an idea of order, that is based on the knowledge that, no matter what our ethnic or national origins, we are all, as Octavio Paz put it, "living on the margin because there is no longer any center" (*Labyrinth*, 170).

The consequences of this knowledge for the future study of American literatures and cultures are profound. The realization that the established ideas of historical and cultural centrality, which authorize fictions of cultural homogeneity and literary unity, are no longer valid assumptions helps us grasp the complex and problematic canonical standing of those so-called marginal texts. That the rhetorical strategies that mark William Carlos Williams's texts have, in final analysis, more in common with those employed by Jay Wright and Nicolás Guillén than with the poetic configurations of a T. S. Eliot and a Hart Crane[6] shows that the traditional canons of American Literature not only have to be opened, they have to be reworked from the ground up.

I have shown that any revitalization of the study of American literatures is not just a matter of shifting our focus from one canon to another while maintaining the same critical perspective. That the problems and challenges so-called marginal texts pose to existing forms of cultural and literary theory are not that easily solved becomes particularly evident when we examine the works that have been assigned to the Afro-American literary canon, in this case *Dimensions of History* and, to a lesser extent, *El diario*. These texts do not, contrary perhaps to most readers' expectations, proclaim that Africa should replace Europe as history's paradigm. What they demonstrate is that there is no one cultural tradition that can legitimately claim such centrality and assert its superiority over another. This former kind of historical revisionism would be nothing but a gratuitous power play and a form of self-aggrandizement that does not bring us any closer to the dynamics of cultural interaction. Nor does it help us read Afro-American texts, because it fails to explain why Afro-American writers from the United States and Latin America insist on laying claim to a wide variety of different cultural and literary traditions. It also does not acknowledge that Afro-American writers are not the only ones to do so; Williams's *In the American Grain*, Carpentier's *The Kingdom of This World*, *¡Ecue Yamba-O!*, and *Concierto barroco*, and Cabrera Infante's *Tres tristes tigres* demonstrate this quite well.

The literary and cultural revisionism of *Dimensions of History* and *El diario* is rooted not in the politics of Pan-Africanism or black nationalism but in an attitude toward and perception of history and of language that emphasizes change, transformation, and discontinuity. This perception of cultural and literary history as inherently metamorphic processes, as ritualistic designs that invite freeplay rather than attempting to stifle it, that create openings rather than closures, inextricably links Wright and Guillén with Williams. The figurative activities in their respective texts generate what I have termed historical, as well as mythological, fields, dense tropological clusters that contract (*dichten*, after all, does means *to condense*, if we care to remember Pound) into a set of ideogrammatic master tropes: (1) that of the contrapuntal dance in *In the American Grain*, which represents the same kinds of transformations or unreadings inscribed in the figure of the burning Library in *Paterson*; (2) that of the *limbo* in *Dimensions of History*, which signals the presence of a ritualistic grammar in Wright's language as well as charts the historico-cultural relationships embodied in the trope of the city; (3) that of *algarabía* in *El diario*, Guillén's version of the Latin American Neobaroque that culminates in the figure of the carnival as associated with the "Día de Reyes" celebrations in colonial Havana.

Insofar as these compound tropes or poetic ideograms translate cultural and historical relationships into new spatial arrangements, they are also figures of writing. Writing is, as well as represents, a process of measuring cultural relationships by transposing them into semantic ones. In each case, these new measures—a trope that refers to the kind of spacing (or measuring) that makes contrapuntal structures (the three ritualistic dance forms) possible—configure into cities, which are both mythical *genii loci* and actual historical sites. These cities are, at the same time, configurations of the Archive. They are not only structures that house founding texts, they are themselves founding texts inscribed upon the New World landscape. Like their historical populations, the cities that Williams, Wright, and Guillén reconstruct are marvelous admixtures of fragments from many cultures and historical periods. They are multilayered hybrids that cannot be deciphered unless we know *all* their ingredients, that is, the different forms, styles, and grammars they combine. And until we do, until we realize that it is impossible to read poets like Williams, Wright, and Guillén without knowing all the cultural and literary traditions they interlace in their texts, we confine ourselves to the ghetto(s) of our own biases and our own ignorance. Walls, real or imaginary, may be places of communion; but they may also be formidable barriers.

Notes

Part I. Writing against the American Grain: William Carlos Williams's New Language

1. For a thorough historical record of critical responses to *In the American Grain* see Paul L. Mariani, *William Carlos Williams: The Poet and His Critics* (Chicago: American Library Association, 1975). Five early reviews are reprinted in *William Carlos Williams: The Critical Heritage*, ed. Charles Doyle (London: Routledge & Kegan Paul, 1980), 84–108.

2. Burke's review ("Subjective History," *New York Herald Tribune* Books, 14 March 1926) praised Williams for endeavoring "to see beyond the label" but at the same time criticized *In the American Grain*, particularly the final section on Abraham Lincoln, for its tendency toward "a maximum of 'interpretation' and a minimum of research." Munson's "William Carlos Williams, a United States Poet" (*Destinations: A Canvass of American Literature since 1900* [1928]) de-

scribes Williams as a "primitive." Lawrence ("American Heroes," *Nation*, 14 April 1926) is "only too thankful" that Williams wrote *In the American Grain* but finds his modernist style "sometimes irritating" (Doyle, *William Carlos Williams*, 87, 91, 102). Yet, given his condemning remarks about Poe in *Studies in Classic American Literature* (1923), Lawrence could have hardly been enthusiastic about Williams's choice of Poe as a literary ancestor.

3. Williams's ambiguous relationship with Pound is too complex a matter to be considered in the context of this study. Lazlo Géfin, in *Ideogram: History of a Poetic Method* (Austin: University of Texas Press, 1982), provides a good summary: "While never denying Pound's singular position as *the* pioneer of modernism, at the same time [Williams] resented both Pound's living outside of America and his Provençal, Italian and Chinese 'archeology.' Only late in life did he acknowledge that Pound's 'digging' was not a snob's way of filling his poems with quaint subject matter, but that in his own way . . . , Pound had enriched American poetry just as he had done" (68–69). For further details see also Louis Simpson's excellent biographical-critical work *Three on the Tower: The Lives and Works of Ezra Pound, T. S. Eliot, and William Carlos Williams* (New York: Morrow, 1975).

Brooks's programmatic essay "On Creating a Usable Past" was first printed in the *Dial* in 1918. It was later included in his *Three Essays on America* (New York: Dutton, 1934).

4. E. P. Bollier, "Against the American Grain: William Carlos Williams between Whitman and Poe," *Tulane Studies in English* 23 (1978): 126.

5. Randolph Bourne, "The History of a Literary Radical," *Yale Review* 8 (1919): 484. Reprinted in *History of a Literary Radical and Other Essays* (New York: Huebsch, 1920).

6. Bollier, "Against the American Grain," 127.

7. Harold Bloom puts the matter in slightly different terms by claiming that Poe, because of his negativity with regard to Emerson, "is central to the American canon, both for us and for the rest of the world" ("Inescapable Poe," *New York Review of Books*, 11 October 1984, 36). One may well quibble with Bloom's choice of language: If anything, Poe's presence de-centers, rather than being central to, the American literary canon, at least as it was conceived by Williams's contemporaries.

8. William Carlos Williams, *In the American Grain* (1925; reprint, New York: New Directions, 1956), 212. All further references to this edition are identified in the text as *IAG*.

9. Bollier, "Against the American Grain," 128.

10. Williams, *The Autobiography of William Carlos Williams* (1951; reprint, New York: New Directions, 1967), 174.

11. Olson even criticized *Paterson* for its attachment to eighteenth- and nineteenth-century America, that is, for not going back far enough into history. Robert von Hallberg points out that the same criticism could be made of *The Maximus Poems* (1960), which are preoccupied with seventeenth-century New England (*Charles Olson: The Scholar's Art* [Cambridge: Harvard University

Press, 1978], 52). Despite such criticisms of both Williams and Pound, however, there is no question about Olson's indebtedness to their poetic theories (see Géfin, *Ideogram*, 85–98).

12. Joseph N. Riddel, *The Inverted Bell: Modernism and the Counterpoetics of William Carlos Williams* (Baton Rouge: Louisiana State University Press, 1974), 45.

13. The most prominent critical studies of those myths as canonizing mechanisms are R. W. B. Lewis's *The American Adam: Innocence, Tragedy, and Tradition in the Nineteenth Century* (Chicago: University of Chicago Press, 1955) and Henry Nash Smith's *Virgin Land: The American West as Symbol and Myth* (Cambridge: Harvard University Press, 1950). For the misuse of the founders' ideals, see Alan Trachtenberg, *The Incorporation of America: Culture and Society in the Gilded Age* (New York: Hill & Wang, 1982).

14. Van Wyck Brooks, *America's Coming of Age* (New York: Huebsch, 1915, 178; reprint, New York: Octagon Books, 1975).

15. Perry Miller, *Errand into the Wilderness* (Cambridge: Harvard University Press, Belknap Press, 1956); Brooks, *America's Coming of Age*, 53.

16. Sacvan Bercovitch, "The Rites of Assent: Rhetoric, Ritual, and the Ideology of American Consensus," in *The American Self: Myth, Ideology, and Popular Culture*, ed. Sam B. Girgus (Albuquerque: University of New Mexico Press, 1981), 29.

17. Theodor Adorno and Max Horkheimer, *Die Dialektik der Aufklärung: Philosophische Fragmente* (1944; reprint, Frankfurt am Main: Fischer Verlag, 1969), 139; trans. John Cummings as *Dialectic of Enlightenment* (New York: Herder & Herder, 1972).

18. Roland Barthes, *Mythologies*, trans. Annette Lavers (1957; New York: Hill & Wang, 1979), 142–43.

19. Ibid., 129.

20. Ibid., 143.

21. My discussion of the rhetoric of myth is indebted to Roberto González Echevarría's *The Voice of the Masters: Writing and Authority in Modern Latin American Literature* (Austin: University of Texas Press, 1985).

22. Riddel, *Inverted Bell*, 16; see also Barthes, *Mythologies*, 134.

23. Barthes, *Mythologies*, 135.

24. Bercovitch, "Rites of Assent," 15, 29.

25. See Barthes, *Mythologies*, 110, 122.

26. Wilson Harris, *The Womb of Space: The Cross-Cultural Imagination* (Westport, Conn.: Greenwood Press, 1983).

27. The phrase is Octavio Paz's. It is used to describe the nature of the *fiesta* in *The Labyrinth of Solitude* (1950), which I discuss at the end of this section.

28. Charles Olson, *Letters for Origin: 1950–1955*, ed. Albert Clover (London: Goliard, Grossman, 1969), 29.

29. *Dimensions of History* was not reviewed at all. To my knowledge, the only reviews of *El diario* are Luce López-Baralt's "El más reciente experimento poético de Nicolás Guillén: *El diario que a diario*," *Avance* (San Juan, Puerto Rico), 9

November 1972, 16–18; Raúl Hernández Novás's "La más reciente poesía de Nicolás Guillén," *Casa de las Américas* 13 (November-December 1972): 156–58, which is mostly devoted to *La rueda dentada;* and Hernán Lavín Cerda's "Historia de Cuba en prosa y verso," *Puente Final* (Santiago de Chile), 22 May 1973, 14–15.

30. A notable example of such confusion is the controversy over Danny Santiago's (alias Daniel James) award-winning novel, *Famous All Over Town* (1984). *Famous All Over Town,* which won the 1983 American Academy and Institute of Arts and Letters Rosenthal Foundation Award, was hailed as "a book about Mexican-American culture from the inside but for outsiders" until it was discovered that its author was not a Chicano but a white American writing under a pseudonym. The controversy created by this belated revelation centered on the question of whether or not the author's presumed ethnic identity had any bearing on the novel's receiving the prize. For details see John Gregory Dunne's "The Secret of Danny Santiago," *New York Review of Books,* 16 August 1984, 17–18, 20, 22, 24–27, as well as *New Journal* (Yale University), 7 September 1984, 34–37. See also Anthony Appiah, "The Uncompleted Argument: Du Bois and the Illusion of Race," *Critical Inquiry* 12 (Autumn 1985): 21–37. Appiah declares, "Talk of 'race' is particularly distressing for those of us who take culture seriously" (36).

31. John Hollander, "Poetry in Review," *Yale Review* 74 (November 1984), xix.

32. See Ralph Ellison's response to Irving Howe in "The World and the Jug," in *Shadow and Act* (New York: New American Library, 1964), 115–47.

33. Several months before embarking on his first voyage, Columbus presented the Spanish kings with a legal document granting him the title of viceroy and governor of the territories he was to discover. See "Articles of Agreement between the Lords the Catholic Sovereigns and Cristóbal Colón," 17 April 1492, reprinted in *Original Narratives of Early American History: The Northmen, Columbus, and Cabot, 985–1503,* ed. Julius Olson and Edward Gaylord Bourne (New York: Scribner, 1906), 77–78. Williams's use of this and other related documents in *In the American Grain* will be discussed below.

34. Edmundo O'Gorman, *The Invention of America: An Inquiry into the Historical Nature of the New World and the Meaning of Its History* (1958; reprint, Westport, Conn.: Greenwood Press, 1972), 4; my italics.

35. Ibid., 137.

36. Ibid., 133.

37. Octavio Paz, *The Labyrinth of Solitude: Life and Thought in Mexico,* trans. Lysander Kemp (1950; New York: Grove Press, 1961; reprint, 1978), 170; my italics.

38. *The Collected Poems of Wallace Stevens* (1954; reprint, New York: Knopf, 1980), 46. See also Joseph Riddel's remarks on "The Comedian" in "Reading America/American Readers," *MLN* (French Issue) 99 (September 1984), 903–4.

39. Géfin emphasizes that Eliot's poems, as well as Pound's early works, are not ideogrammatic or synthetic. He cites *The Waste Land* as an exception, calling

attention to Pound's editing of that poem (*Ideogram*, xviii). Despite Pound's editing, however, Eliot's text still reveals just how different his poetics were from Pound's, and Williams's, for that matter.

40. Eugenio Donato contends that "Romantic poetry is constantly preoccupied with the problems of how to pass from the fragmentation of perception to a totality" ("The Ruins of Memory: Archeological Fragments and Textual Artifacts," *MLN* [French Issue] 93 [May 1978], 581).

41. See Jorge Luis Borges's story "The Library of Babel" (1956) in *Labyrinths: Selected Stories and Other Writings*, ed. Donald A. Yates and James E. Irby (New York: New Directions, 1964), 51–58, which begins with the words, "The universe (which others call the library). . . ." Also relevant here is Eugenio Donato's distinction between the Library and the Museum in "The Museum's Furnace: Notes toward a Contextual Reading of *Bouvard and Pécuchet*," in *Textual Strategies: Perspectives in Post-Structuralist Criticism*, ed. Josué V. Harari (Ithaca: Cornell University Press, 1979), 213–38.

42. My discussion of the Archive here and elsewhere is indebted to Roberto González Echevarría's "*Cien años de soledad*: The Novel as Myth and Archive," *MLN* (Hispanic Issue) 99 (March 1984): 358–80.

43. Hart Crane, *The Bridge* (1930; reprint, New York: Liveright, 1970), 67. Future references to this text will be identified as *B*.

44. Williams, *The Great American Novel* (1923), reprinted in *Imaginations*, ed. Webster Schott (New York: New Directions, 1971), 196. Future references to this edition will be identified in the text as *Imag*.

45. "Inner correctives" is Wilson Harris's phrase. See "History, Fable, and Myth in the Caribbean and Guianas," in *Explorations: A Selection of Talks and Articles, 1966–1981*, ed. Hena Maes-Jelinek (Mundelstrup, Denmark: Dangaroo Press, 1981), 28.

46. Carlos Fuentes, *Terra Nostra*, trans. Margaret Sayers Peden (1975; New York: Farrar, Straus & Giroux, 1976), 470; my italics.

47. *Collected Poems of Wallace Stevens*, 30.

48. Derek Walcott, "What the Twilight Says: An Overture," in *Dream on Monkey Mountain and Other Plays* (New York: Farrar, Straus & Giroux, 1970), 9.

49. One of the few texts of that period in which the failure of unity becomes a literary success is Jean Toomer's *Cane* (1924), a work whose internal fragmentation, represented visually by the broken circle, parallels that of *In the American Grain*. It is also interesting to note in this context that *Cane* and Williams's *The Great American Novel* were reviewed together by Matthew Josephson in the October 1923 issue of *Broom*. See Mariani, *William Carlos Williams*, 17.

50. Riddel, *Inverted Bell*, 20.

51. Williams, "The Modern Primer," in *The Embodiment of Knowledge*, ed. Ron Loewinsohn (New York: New Directions, 1974), 17.

52. See Jean Garrigue, "America Revisited," *Poetry* 90 (1957): 316–17, who writes, "Out of these parts and pieces, from documents, letters, Williams constructed, by carefully chosen data, this montage of the stream of past events that

he would relate to the stream of our own unconsciousness and consciousness."

53. Riddel, *Inverted Bell*, 14.

54. The original lines read: "I measure my song,/measure the sources of my song,/measure me, measure/my forces." ("Letter 9," in *The Maximus Poems* [1960; reprint, Berkeley and Los Angeles: University of California Press, 1983], 48).

55. Williams, *Paterson* (New York: New Directions, 1963), 176. All further references to this edition are identified in the text as *P*.

56. Barbara Lanati, *L'avanguardia americana: Tre esperimenti: Faulkner, Stein, W. C. Williams* (Turin: Giulio Einaudi, 1977), 127–38; my translation.

57. My use of this term here and elsewhere is indebted to Jacques Derrida's concept of the "supplement" as elaborated in *Of Grammatology*.

58. Both are reproduced in translation in Olson and Bourne, *Original Narratives of Early American History*, 14–66.

59. See "Freydis Causes the Brothers to Be Put to Death," in ibid., 62–65.

60. Williams, "The Modern Primer," *The Embodiment of Knowledge*, 19.

61. Alejo Carpentier, *El arpa y la sombra* (Mexico: Siglo Veintiuno, 1979), 16; my translation. All subsequent translations of this text will be accompanied by parenthetical page numbers that refer to this edition. Tzvetan Todorov has commented at length on Columbus's religious zeal. See *The Conquest of America: The Question of the Other*, trans. Richard Howard (1982; New York: Harper & Row, 1985 [1984]), 3–50. Regrettably, Todorov's decidedly moralistic posture and his reductive approach to Europe's dealings with the "others" add, as Roberto González Echevarría states in his review of that book, "little to our understanding of such a complex historical process" ("America Conquered," *Yale Review* 74:2 [1985]: 281–87). Nor do his theories about the exchange of signs within and between each culture illuminate Williams's and Carpentier's literary endeavors.

62. For further details see L. A. Vigneras's foreword to *The Journal of Christopher Columbus*, trans. Cecil Jane with an appendix by R. A. Skelton (London: Anthony Blond, 1968).

63. Von Hallberg, *Charles Olson*, 180.

64. Jean-François Lyotard tellingly defines postmodernism as "incredulity toward metanarratives" in *The Postmodern Condition: A Report on Knowledge*, trans. Geoff Bennington and Brian Massumi (1979; Minneapolis: University of Minnesota Press, 1984), xxiv.

65. For a more detailed discussion of various aspects of canonization see *Canons*, ed. Robert von Hallberg (Chicago: University of Chicago Press, 1984). This collection of essays approaches canons from three perspectives: "how artists determine canons by selecting certain styles and masters to emulate; how poet-critics and academic critics, through the institutions of literary study, construct canons; and how institutionalized canons effectively govern literary study and instruction" (Introduction, 1–2). My own comments are based on the assumption of differences and tensions between institutionalized canons and the "canons" determined by writers and texts themselves through processes of selection that are not primarily concerned with literary merit. As those latter canons are not

simply a matter of emulating certain styles and masters, but of exploring differences and discontinuities, I have found it more useful to call them traditions of writing.

66. Joseph Riddel, in his above-mentioned essay, "Reading America/ American Readers," argues that "from its earliest problematic formulations, the notion of 'American literature' has always been *post*-modern, indeed the *beyond* of modernism, a literature burdened with producing a past it never had, except in the figure of revolution, in order to mime that past into a future it lagged behind" (906). No matter how attractive this formulation may be otherwise, given one of Riddel's earlier essays on the subject, one cannot help but wonder exactly what his distinction between modernism and postmodernism might be. In "Decentering the Image," in *Textual Strategies* (1979), he wrote: "'American literature' has always been modern . . . is always an event that is logically anterior yet historically posterior to that literature we call traditional or classical" (322). Are we to understand from this that "American literature" is both modern and postmodern at the same time? Riddel's persistent use of the phrase "has always been" in both essays makes me suspect that this is not his intention. My idea of simultaneity is one possible solution to this terminological dilemma.

67. Letter to Horace Gregory, 22 July 1939, in *The Selected Letters of William Carlos Williams*, ed. John C. Thirlwall (New York: McDowell, Obolensky, 1957), 185.

68. In a letter to the editors of the *Liberator*, Toomer insists: "Racially, I seem to have (who knows for sure) seven blood mixtures: French, Dutch, Welsh, Negro, German, Jewish, and Indian. Because of these, my position in America has been a curious one. I have lived equally amid the two race groups. Now white, now colored. From my own point of view I am naturally and inevitably an American. I have strived for a spiritual fusion analogous to the fact of racial intermingling." Quoted in Arna Bontemps's 1968 introduction to *Cane* (New York: Harper & Row, 1969), viii.

69. For an extensive discussion of modern Latin American poetry in the context of European and Anglo–North American poetry, see Octavio Paz, *Children of the Mire: Modern Poetry from Romanticism to the Avant-Garde*, trans. Rachel Phillips (Cambridge: Harvard University Press, 1974).

70. In 1930 Waldo Frank traveled all over Latin America, giving forty lectures in various countries with the intention of remedying Latin American intellectuals' "misconceptions" of the United States and the kind of hostility kindled by Enrique Rodó's *Ariel* (1900) on the one hand and the poetry of Rubén Darío on the other. An editorial in the *Revista de Avance* called Frank's position "a vast plan for the spiritual *reconquest* of the continent" (my italics; reprinted in *Waldo Frank in Latin America* [New York: Instituto de las Españas, 1930], 45). See also Frank's *Primer mensaje a la América Hispana* (Madrid: Revista de Occidente, 1930) and *America Hispana: A Portrait and a Prospect* (New York: Scribner, 1931).

The Paz quotation appears in "A Literature of Foundations," *Triquarterly Anthology of Latin American Literature*, ed. José Donoso and William A. Henkin (New York: Dutton, 1969), 3–8.

71. Williams, *Autobiography*, 349. Williams's lifelong interest in Spanish and Latin American literatures and the ways in which this concern entered his own writing, not only in *In the American Grain*, but also in *Al Que Quiere!* and later on in "The Desert Music," as well as the translations he undertook at various points throughout his literary career, no doubt helped shape his conception of New World writing. It set his work apart from that of most of his Anglo–North American contemporaries, again, with the possible exception of Stevens, whose interest in Latin America is also well known. For further commentary on some of Williams's translations and his relations to Latin America—Mexico in particular—see Steven Weiland, "Where Shall We Unearth the Word? William Carlos Williams and the Aztecs," *Arizona Quarterly* 35 (1979): 42–48; and especially John Felstiner, "Through a Spanish Looking Glass: Williams's Poetry in Translation," *Américas* 29 (November-December 1977): 5–8.

72. See Felstiner, "Through a Spanish Looking Glass," 7–8.

73. Paz, *Labyrinth of Solitude*, 166. All further references to this edition will appear in textual parentheses.

74. Harris, *Womb of Space*, especially chaps. 3 and 4.

75. *Collected Poems of Wallace Stevens*, 165.

76. Williams, *Pictures from Brueghel and Other Poems* (1949; reprint, New York: New Directions, 1949), 109.

77. Williams, *Autobiography*, 183.

78. For a more detailed reading of "The Kingfishers" see Don Byrd, *Charles Olson's Maximus* (Urbana: University of Illinois Press, 1980), 9–15.

79. Another notable disciple of Williams's (and Olson's) in this respect is Allen Ginsberg. See particularly *The Fall of America: Poems of These States, 1965–1971* (San Francisco: City Lights Books, 1972).

80. *Selected Writings of Charles Olson*, ed. Robert Creeley (New York: New Directions, 1966), 172.

81. In his second letter to the emperor (30 October 1520), Cortés casually dismisses La Malinche as "a native Indian girl." No reference is made to the fact that she was invaluable to him as an interpreter and that her services greatly contributed to his victory over the Aztecs. For further details compare *Hernando Cortés: Five Letters, 1519–1526*, trans. Bayard Morris (New York: Norton, n.d.), 56–57, 382 (note 11); and Francisco López de Gómara, *Cortés: The Life of the Conqueror by His Secretary*, trans. and ed. Lesley Byrd Simpson from the *Istoria de la conquista de Mexico* (1552; Berkeley and Los Angeles: University of California Press, 1964), 56–57.

82. For an etymology of this verb and a list of its possible meanings, see *Labyrinth*, 75–79.

83. *Collected Poems of Wallace Stevens*, 10.

84. See Pt. 2, Sec. 2.

85. The influence of Williams's method can be traced, for instance, in Robert Duncan's idea of *"grand collage"* and in the perhaps even more precariously interrelated fragments of both "The Structure of Rime" (1968–1973) and "Pas-

sages" (1968–1970), serial poems that are scattered across several books of poetry. See also Robert Creeley's *Pieces* (New York: Scribner, 1969).

Part II. The Black Limbo: Jay Wright's Mythology of Writing

1. Wilson Harris, *Explorations: A Selection of Talks and Articles, 1966–1981*, ed. Hena Maes-Jelinek (Mundelstrup, Denmark: Dangaroo Press, 1981), 5.

2. John Hollander, "Poetry in Review," *Yale Review* 74 (November 1984): xvi.

3. Charles H. Rowell, "The Unravelling of the Egg: An Interview with Jay Wright," *Jay Wright: A Special Issue*, *Callaloo* 19 6 (Fall 1983): 6–7. Wright has also published several plays, among them "Love's Equation," *Callaloo* 19: 39–75, and "The Death and Return of Paul Batuta: A Play in One Act," *Hambone* 4 (Fall 1984): 61–110. Given its focus on Wright's poetry, this study will not consider these plays.

4. The term is Michael S. Harper's; see "High Modes: Vision as Ritual: Confirmation," in *Images of Kin: New and Selected Poems* (Urbana: University of Illinois Press, 1977), 177–78.

5. Included in my definition of cultural groups of a non-European origin are not only Afro-Americans, Asian-Americans, and Native Americans but also Latin Americans. The rather ambiguous position Spain has occupied in European cultural history since the Middle Ages because of her intense contact with the Arabic world justifies this inclusion. See Américo Castro, *The Structure of Spanish History*, trans. Edmundo L. King (Princeton: Princeton University Press, 1954), which was first published in 1948 as *España en su historia*.

6. Erich Auerbach, *Gesammelte Aufsätze zur Romanischen Philologie* (Bern: Francke Verlag, 1967), 223.

7. Auerbach, "Philologie der Weltliteratur," in ibid., 310.

8. Jay Wright, Afterword, *The Double Invention of Komo* (Austin: University of Texas Press, 1980), 114. All further references to this edition are identified in the text as *DI*.

9. Jay Wright, "Desire's Design, Vision's Resonance: Black Poetry's Ritual and Historical Voice," *Callaloo* 30 (Winter 1987). Page numbers refer to the manuscript.

10. Harris, "The Native Phenomenon," in *Explorations*, 52–53.

11. Williams, "The Poem as a Field of Action," in *Selected Essays of William Carlos Williams* (New York: New Directions, 1969), 285.

12. Robert B. Stepto, *From Behind the Veil: A Study of Afro-American Narrative* (Urbana: University of Illinois Press, 1979).

13. My use of the term *origin* is indebted to Walter Benjamin's comments in *Der Ursprung des deutschen Trauerspiels* (1963), where he writes: "Origin [*Ursprung*], although an entirely historical category, has, nevertheless, nothing to do with genesis [*Entstehung*]. The term 'origin' is not intended to describe the process by which the existent came into being, but rather to describe that which

emerges from the process of becoming and disappearance. Origin is an eddy in the stream of becoming, and in its current it swallows the material involved in the process of genesis. . . . Origin is not, therefore, discovered by the examination of actual findings, but it is related to their history and their subsequent development." (*The Origin of German Tragic Drama*, trans. John Osborne [London: NLB, 1977], 45–46.)

14. See Melvin Dixon, "Singing a Deep Song: Language as Evidence in the Novels of Gayl Jones," in *Black Women Writers (1950–1980): A Critical Evaluation*, ed. Mari Evans (Garden City, N.Y.: Doubleday-Anchor, 1984), 236.

15. For a discussion of the extent to which African slaves in the Americas refused to abandon their linguistic ties with their homeland see John W. Blassingame, *The Slave Community: Plantation Life in the Antebellum South*, rev. and enl. ed. (New York: Oxford University Press, 1979), 24–30.

John Blassingame and Mary Berry cite a 1740 South Carolina state law as a representative example of the early institution in North America of a pattern of compulsory ignorance designed to ensure the continuation of slavery: "That all and every person and persons whatsoever, who shall hereafter teach, or cause any slave or slaves to be taught to write, or shall use or employ any slave as a scribe in any manner of writing whatsoever, hereafter taught to write; every such person or persons shall, for every offense, forfeit the sum of one hundred pounds current money" (*The Long Memory: The Black Experience in America* [New York: Oxford University Press, 1982], 261–62). No such legal restrictions on the education of slaves were found in the *Recopilación de las leyes de los reynos de las Indias* (1680) or in the Spanish slave codes of 1789 and 1842. See Franklin W. Knight, *Slave Society in Cuba during the Nineteenth Century* (Madison: University of Wisconsin Press, 1974), 121–36.

16. See, for instance, Stepto's discussion of such "passes" in connection with Frederick Douglass's 1845 *Narrative* and Ralph Ellison's *Invisible Man* (1952); *From Behind the Veil*, 172–73. For an extensive bibliography of Afro-American slave narratives see John W. Blassingame, ed., *Slave Testimony: Two Centuries of Letters, Speeches, Interviews, and Autobiographies* (Baton Rouge: Louisiana State University Press, 1977).

17. See Lawrence W. Levine, *Black Culture and Black Consciousness: Afro-American Folk Thought from Slavery to Freedom* (New York: Oxford University Press, 1977), and Stephen Henderson, *Understanding the New Black Poetry: Black Speech and Black Music as Poetic References* (New York: Morrow, 1973).

18. See Jacques Derrida's critique of Saussure in *Of Grammatology*, trans. Gayatri Chakravorty Spivak (1967; Baltimore: Johns Hopkins University Press, 1976), especially pt. 1, "Writing before the Letter."

19. The splendid contradictions in a passage from Charles Olson's "Human Universe" corroborate this: "Logos, or discourse," he writes, "so worked its abstractions into our concept and use of language that language's other function, *speech*, seems so in need of restoration that several of us *go back to hieroglyphics or to ideograms to right the balance*" (quoted in Lazlo Géfin, *Ideogram: History of a Poetic Method* [Austin: University of Texas Press, 1982], 92; my italics).

20. Baraka is quoted in Kimberly W. Benston, *Baraka: The Renegade and the Mask* (New Haven: Yale University Press, 1976), 110.

21. Jay Wright, *The Homecoming Singer* (New York: Corinth Books, 1971), 75. All further references to this edition are identified in the text as *HS*.

22. Ralph Ellison, *Shadow and Act* (New York: New American Library, 1964), 147. Also Robert Stepto, "Study and Experience: An Interview with Ralph Ellison," in *Chant of Saints: A Gathering of Afro-American Literature, Art, and Scholarship*, ed. Michael S. Harper and Robert B. Stepto (Urbana: University of Illinois Press, 1979), 453.

23. See *Christopher Columbus: Four Voyages to the New World: Letters and Selected Documents*, bilingual ed., trans. and ed. R. H. Major (Gloucester: Peter Smith, 1978), 49–50; also *Hernando Cortés: Five Letters, 1519–1526*, trans. Bayard Morris (New York: Norton, n.d.), 17–18.

24. See Juan Rodríguez Freyle, *El carnero* (1638; Bogota: Editorial Bedout, 1976). Parts of this book have been translated by William C. Atkinson as *The Conquest of New Granada* (London: Folio Society, 1961). See also Kutzinski, "The Logic of Wings: Gabriel García Márquez and Afro-American Literature," *Latin American Literary Review* 13 (January–June 1985):133–46.

25. For details see Perry Miller, *Errand into the Wilderness* (Cambridge: Harvard University Press, Belknap Press, 1956), and Sacvan Bercovitch, *The American Jeremiad* (Madison: University of Wisconsin Press, 1978).

26. Silvio Bedini, *The Life of Benjamin Banneker* (New York: Scribner, 1972), 104–5. Banneker's letter is reprinted on 152–56.

27. One of the most prominent examples is Aimé Césaire's *Cahier d'un retour au pays natal* [*Notebook of a Return to the Native Land*] (1939). The most recent translation of this poem is included in *The Collected Poetry of Aimé Césaire*, trans. Clayton Eshleman and Annette Smith (Berkeley and Los Angeles: University of California Press, 1983), 34–85.

28. Afro-Americans, that is, those who were United States citizens, were excluded from the Exposition: Frederick Douglass, ironically enough, attended the fair as a representative of Haiti. Despite a petition, signed by Douglass, Dunbar, and others, no exhibit was arranged to show the contributions of blacks to American life. A compromise was reached by setting aside 25 August 1893 as Colored Americans' Day. See Benjamin Quarles, *Frederick Douglass* (New York: Atheneum, 1968), 346–47. Details on Douglass as Haiti's representative can be found in Frederick May Holland, *Frederick Douglass: The Colored Orator*, rev. ed. (New York: Haskell House, 1969), 398; Philip S. Foner, *Frederick Douglass* (New York: Citadel Press, 1969), 360; and Nathan Irving Huggins, *Slave and Citizen: The Life of Frederick Douglass* (Boston: Little, Brown, 1980), 168. For details on the Exposition itself see Alan Trachtenberg, *The Incorporation of America: Culture and Society in the Gilded Age*, especially chap. 7, "White City," 208–34.

29. More detailed references to the Haitian Revolution can be found in *Dimensions of History* (Santa Cruz: Kayak, 1976), 20–22. All further references to this edition are identified in the text as *DH*. See also C. L. R. James's *The Black*

Jacobins: Toussaint L'Ouverture and the San Domingo Revolution, 2d ed., rev. (New York: Random House, 1963 [1938]).

30. Alejo Carpentier, *The Kingdom of This World*, trans. Harriet de Onís (1949; New York: Collier Books, 1970 [1957]), 178.

31. *Selected Poetry of Amiri Baraka/LeRoi Jones* (New York: Morrow, 1979), 23.

32. Jay Wright, *Soothsayers and Omens* (New York: Seven Woods Press, 1976), 27. All further references to this edition are identified in the text as *SO*.

33. Bedini, *Life of Benjamin Banneker*, 158–201.

34. Joseph N. Riddel, "Decentering the Image: The 'Project' of 'American' Poetics?" in Josué Harari, ed., *Textual Strategies: Perspectives in Post-Structuralist Criticism* (Ithaca: Cornell University Press, 1979), 357.

35. Charles Olson, "Projective Verse," in *Selected Writings of Charles Olson*, ed. Robert Creeley (New York: New Directions, 1966), 15–26.

36. Riddel, "Decentering the Image," 344–45.

37. See Olson, *Human Universe and Other Essays*, ed. Donald Allen (New York: New Directions, 1967), 19.

38. See Germaine Dieterlen and Marcel Griaule, *Le renard pâle*, vol. 1, *Le mythe cosmogonique* (Paris: Institut d'Ethnologie, Université de Paris, 1965).

39. Paul de Man, *Blindness and Insight: Essays in the Rhetoric of Contemporary Criticism*, 2d ed., rev. (Minneapolis: University of Minnesota Press, 1983), 185. See also Eugenio Donato's insightful comments on memory and representation in "The Ruins of Memory: Archeological Fragments and Textual Artifacts," *MLN* (French Issue) 93 (May 1978), especially 579–80.

40. See my discussion of the Seventh Nommo in Pt. 2, Sec. 3. Compare this to Allen Ginsberg's notion of "basketweaving" in connection with *The Fall of America* (quoted in Géfin, *Ideogram*, 124).

41. D. T. Niane, *Sundiata: An Epic of Old Mali* (London: Longman Drumbeat, 1979), 1; my italics.

42. R. G. Collingwood, *The Idea of History* (1956; reprint, London: Oxford University Press, 1982), 113.

43. de Man, *Blindness and Insight*, 165.

44. Roland Barthes, *Mythologies*, trans. Annette Lavers (1957; New York: Hill & Wang, 1979), 112.

45. Jacques Derrida, "Structure, Sign, and Play in the Discourse of the Human Sciences," in *The Structuralist Controversy: The Languages of Criticism and the Sciences of Man*, ed. Eugenio Donato and Richard Macksey (Baltimore: Johns Hopkins University Press, 1972), 260.

46. Rowell, "Unravelling of the Egg," p. 12.

47. See, for instance, Vladimir Nabokov's *Ada or Ardor: A Family Chronicle* (New York: McGraw-Hill, 1969) and *Pale Fire* (1962; reprint, New York: Putnam, 1980); Ishmael Reed's *Mumbo Jumbo* (New York: Avon Books, 1972); and Augusto Roa Bastos's *Yo el supremo* (Buenos Aires: Siglo Veintiuno, 1974).

48. Mikhail Bakhtin, *The Dialogic Imagination: Four Essays*, ed. Michael

Holquist, trans. Caryl Emerson and Michael Holquist (Austin: University of Texas Press, 1982).

49. One of Wright's earlier poems entitled "The Neighborhood House" (*HS*, 36–37) was in part inspired by Guillén's "El apellido" [My Last Name], a poem preoccupied with this process of effacement. I shall return to this text, as well as to the literary relationship between Wright and Guillén, in Pt. 3, Sec. 1.

50. See Wande Abimbola, *Ifa Divination Poetry* (New York: NOK Publishers, 1977); L. O. Sanneh, *The Jakhanke: A History of an Islamic Clerical People of the Senegambia* (London: International African Institute, 1979); also Franz Rosenthal, *A History of Muslim Historiography* (Leiden: E. J. Brill, 1968); J. B. Danquah, *The Akan Doctrine of God: A Fragment of Gold Coast Ethics and Religion*, 2d ed., rev. (London: Frank Cass, 1968 [1944]).

51. Derrida, "Structure, Sign, and Play," 251.

52. Roberto González Echevarría, "*Cien años de soledad:* The Novel as Myth and Archive," *MLN* (Hispanic Issue) 99 (March 1984): 364.

53. The term "ideogrammatic writing" has not been adopted here to suggest an indebtedness of Wright to Pound's poetics. It has to be noted, however, that while Wright is hardly a self-confessed Poundian, Pound's notion of the ideogram is relevant to Wright's poetics, an influence that could possibly be traced through Olson. See Géfin, *Ideogram*, for a lucid analysis of Pound's method.

54. Claude Lévi-Strauss, *The Savage Mind* (1962; Chicago: University of Chicago Press, 1968), 264.

55. Michael Houseman, "Les artifices de la logique initiatique," *Journal des Africanistes* 54:1 (1984): 41–65.

56. See W. E. B. Du Bois, *The Souls of Black Folk* (1903; reprint, New York: New American Library, 1969), 45.

57. Harris, "History, Fable and Myth in the Caribbean and the Guianas," in *Explorations*, 25–28.

58. Octavio Paz, "A Literature of Foundations," in *Triquarterly Anthology of Latin American Literature*, ed. José Donoso and William A. Henkin (New York: Dutton, 1969), 4.

59. See Dieterlen and Griaule, *Le renard pâle*, 252–53.

60. See Germaine Dieterlen, *Les âmes des Dogons* (Paris: Institut d'Ethnologie, 1941); Geneviève Calame-Griaule, *Ethnologie et langage: La parole chez les Dogons* (Paris: Gallimard, 1965).

61. See Dieterlen and Griaule, *Le renard pâle*, 253, 475–76; also Wright's notes in *Dimensions of History*, 105.

62. These underlying connections may be effectively compared to Esteban's meditations on celestial constellations in the epigraph of Carpentier's *El siglo de la luces* [Explosion in a Cathedral], trans. John Sturrock (1962; New York: Harper & Row, 1979), 7–8. Carpentier's double image of the guillotine as "a doorway opening on to the immense sky" and as "a gigantic instrument of navigation," which is suggestive of Wright's "gates" in the quotation below, accentuates the dangers and ambiguities involved in the passage toward self-knowledge on which both Esteban and Wright's poet embark.

63. See Césaire's poem "Le verbe marronner/a René Depestre poète haitien" (*Noria*) in *Collected Poetry*, 368–71. The poem was initially entitled "Réponse à Depestre poète haitien" and first appeared in *Présence Africaine* (April–July 1955). See also A. James Arnold's comments on that exchange between Césaire and Depestre in *Modernism and Negritude: The Poetry and Poetics of Aimé Césaire* (Cambridge: Harvard University Press, 1981), 181–83.

64. John Deredita, "Vallejo Interpreted, Vallejo Traduced," *Diacritics* 8 (Winter 1978): 17.

65. See Wright, "Desire's Design, Vision's Resonance"; also Stepto, *From Behind the Veil*, to which this part of my discussion owes much.

66. Robert Hayden, *Angle of Ascent: New and Selected Poems* (New York: Liveright, 1975), 10.

67. Gabriel García Márquez, "Un señor muy viejo con unas alas enormes," in *La increíble y triste historia de la cándida Eréndira y de su abuela desalmada: Siete cuentas.* (Caracas: Monte Avila, 1972), 11–20. A translation of this story by Gregory Rabassa is included in *Leaf Storm and Other Stories* (1972; New York: Harper & Row, 1979), 105–12. See Kutzinski, "Logic of Wings," 143–44.

68. See Calame-Griaule, *Ethnologie et langage*, 32.

69. W. B. Yeats, "Among School Children," in *The Variorum Edition of the Poems of W. B. Yeats*, ed. Peter Allt and Russell K. Alspach (New York: Macmillan, 1977), 446.

70. Calame-Griaule, *Ethnologie et langage*, 25.

71. Frederick Douglass, *The Narrative of the Life of Frederick Douglass, An American Slave: Written by Himself* (1845; New York: reprint, New American Library, 1968), 43.

72. See Du Bois, *Souls of Black Folk*, 45.

73. This is quoted from the *Egyptian Book of the Dead*: "I am the great Bennu [Phoenix] in Annu [Heliopolis]. I am the Former of Beings and Existences." See Charles H. S. Davis, ed., *The Egyptian Book of the Dead: The Most Ancient and Most Important of the Extant Religious Texts of Ancient Egypt* (New York: Putnam, 1894), 54.

74. Wright's fire images here also evoke the ancient Arawak/Macusi creation myth of "The Tree of Life in Flames," which is discussed in connection with Guillén's inner geography in "El apellido" in Pt. 3, Sec. 1.

75. See Griaule and Dieterlen, *Le renard pâle*, chap. 3.

76. Danquah, *Akan Doctrine of God*, 75–76.

77. Ralph Ellison, *Invisible Man* (New York: Random House, 1952), 432.

78. Ibid., 5.

79. *Republic*, 514–21. References are to *The Dialogues of Plato*, vol. 2, trans. B. Jovett (Oxford: Clarendon Press, 1953).

80. See also Ellison's second epigraph in *Invisible Man*, which is from Melville's *Benito Cereno*: " 'You are saved,' cried Captain Delano, more and more astonished and pained, 'you are saved: *what has cast such a shadow upon you?*' " (my italics).

81. The phrase is Robert Stepto's; see "After Modernism, After Hibernation: Michael Harper, Robert Hayden, and Jay Wright," in *Chant of Saints*, 470–86.
82. Ellison, *Invisible Man*, 11.
83. Stepto, "After Modernism, After Hibernation," 470.
84. Robert Stepto, " 'The Aching Prodigal': Jay Wright's Dutiful Poet," *Callaloo 19* (Fall 1983): 82.
85. See Frederick Turner, *Beyond Geography: The Western Spirit against the Wilderness* (New York: Viking Press, 1980).
86. Nicolás Guillén, *Obra Poética, 1920–1970*, ed. Ángel Augier (Havana: Instituto Cubano del Libro, 1974), 1: 395; my translation.
87. See Lydia Cabrera, *El monte: Igbo finda ewe orisha, vititi nfinda: Notas sobre las religiones, la magia, las supersticiones y el folklore de los negros criollos y del pueblo de Cuba.* (Havana: Ediciones C.R., 1954; reprint, Miami: Colección del Chichereku, 1971).
88. Castro, *Structure of Spanish History*, 234.
89. Ibid., chap. 2.
90. Octavio Paz, *Piedra de sol* (Mexico: Tezontle, 1957), 39–40; my italics. *Sun Stone*, trans. Muriel Rukeyser (New York: World Poets Series, New Directions, n.d.), 45.
91. Jay Wright, *Explications/Interpretations* (Lexington: University of Kentucky Press, Callaloo Poetry Series, 1984), 1.
92. Roberto González Echevarría, "Literature of the Hispanic Caribbean," *Latin American Literary Review* 8 (Spring-Summer 1980): 10.
93. Fernando Ortiz, *La antigua fiesta afrocubana del "Día de Reyes"* (1925; reprint, Havana: Ministerio de Relaciones Exteriores Departamento de Asuntos Culturales, División de Publicaciones, 1960).
94. For further details about the "Día de Reyes" see my discussion of Guillén's "Sensemayá" in Pt. 3, Sec. 1.
95. Roberto González Echevarría, "Socrates among the Weeds: Blacks and History in Carpentier's *Explosion in a Cathedral*," in *Voices from Under: Black Narrative in Latin America and the Caribbean*, ed. William Luis (Westport, Conn.: Greenwood Press, 1984), 51.
96. See Germaine Dieterlen and Youssouf Tata Cissé, *Les fondements de la societée d'initiation du Komô* (Paris: Mouton, 1972), 91.
97. See Todorov, *Conquest of America*, 79–81.
98. For further details see *DH*, 108–9.
99. Nicolás Guillén was the first to develop the *son* into a distinctive literary form, the *poema-son*. See Pt. 3, Sec. 1.
100. See Alejo Carpentier, "América Latina en la confluencia de coordenadas históricas y su repercusión en la música" (1977); reprinted in *Ese músico que llevo dentro*, Selección de Zoila Gómez (Havana: Editorial Letras Cubanas, 1980), 3:336.
101. Du Bois, *Souls of Black Folk*, 209.
102. Quoted by González Echevarría in "Literature of the Hispanic Caribbean," 7.

103. Ibid., 8.
104. See Lydia Cabrera, *Yemayá y Ochún* (Madrid: Colección del Chichereku en el exilio, 1974).
105. Rodríguez Freyle, *El carnero*, 143.
106. See Kutzinski, "Logic of Wings," 137-38.
107. Fernando Ortiz, *Hampa afrocubana: Los negros brujos: Apuntes para un estudio de etnología criminal* (Madrid: Editorial América, 1917). See also Cirilo Villaverde's novel *Cecilia Valdés, or Angel's Hill*, trans. Sydney G. Gest (1882; New York: Vantage Press, 1962), and Nicolás Guillén, *Prosa de Prisa, 1929-1972* (Havana: Arte y Literatura, 1976), 3:288-89.
108. Albert William Levi, "Culture: A Guess at the Riddle," *Critical Inquiry* 4 (Winter 1977): 315.
109. *The New Science of Giambattista Vico*, 3d ed., abr., trans. Thomas Goddard Bergin and Max Harold Fisch (1744; Ithaca: Cornell University Press, 1961; reprint, 1970), 149.
110. Ibid., 138 and 241.
111. Marcel Griaule, *Conversations with Ogotemmêli: An Introduction to Dogon Religious Ideas*, intro. Germaine Dieterlen. This is a translation of *Dieu d'eau* (1948). (New York: Oxford University Press, 1975), 131-37.
112. Ibid., 158.
113. Wright, "Desire's Design, Vision's Resonance," 11.
114. Paz, "A Literature of Foundations," 5.
115. Ibid., 3.
116. See Alejo Carpentier's concept of the Baroque and of the "stylelessness" of Latin American reality in "De lo real maravilloso américano," in *Tientos y diferencias* (Montevideo: ARCA, 1967), 102-20; also relevant to this is my later discussion of Guillén's recasting of the Latin American Neobaroque as "algarabía en lengua de piratas y bozales" (*El diario*) in Pt. 3, Sec. 2.
117. See Frederick Webb Hodge, *History of Hawikúh, New Mexico, One of the so-called Cities of Cíbola* (Los Angeles: Southwest Museum, 1937), 3-4.
118. See *Cabeza de Vaca's Adventures in the Unknown Interior of America*, trans. Cyclone Covey (Albuquerque: University of New Mexico Press, 1983). An earlier translation of the original *relación* by Frederick Hodge ("The Narrative of Alvar Núñez Cabeca de Vaca") is included in the *Original Narratives of Early American History: Spanish Explorers in the United States, 1528-1543* (New York: Scribner, 1907), 3-126.
119. "Narrative of Fray Marcos," in Cleve Hallenbeck, *The Journey of Fray Marcos de Niza* (Dallas: University Press in Dallas, 1949), 18. Other translations of that narrative are included in *Discovery of the Seven Cities of Cíbola*, trans. and ed. Percy M. Baldwin (Albuquerque: Historical Society of New Mexico Publications, vol. I, 1926), 3-59, which also has the Spanish text; Henry W. Haynes, "Early Explorations of New Mexico," in *Narrative and Critical History of America*, ed. Justin Winsor (New York: Houghton Mifflin, 1887), 2:473-503; A. F. Bandelier, *The Gilded Man (El Dorado) and Other Pictures of the Spanish Occupancy of America* (New York: Appleton, 1893), 125-257.

120. Quoted in Hodge, *History of Hawikúh*, 25–26. See also John Upton Terrell, *Estevanico the Black* (Los Angeles: Westernlore Press, 1968), 144.

121. For details see Hodge, *History of Hawikúh*, 28, 112; Cleve Hallenbeck is convinced that the friar was a liar (*The Journey of Fray Marcos de Niza*); so is John Upton Terrell, who gives Estevan full credit for discovering Hawikúh (*Estevanico the Black*, 144).

122. See George P. Hammond, *Coronado's Seven Cities* (Albuquerque: U.S. Coronado Exposition Commission, 1940); "Coronado's Letter to Mendoza," (3 August 1540), in *Old South Leaflets* (n.p., n.d.), 1:20; J. H. Simpson, *Coronado's March in Search of the Seven Cities of Cibola and Discussion of their Probable Location* (Washington, D.C.: U.S. Government Printing Office, 1871).

123. See Hodge, *History of Hawikúh*, 1–2; also Terrell, *Estevanico the Black*, 64; Stephen Clissold, *The Seven Cities of Cibola* (London: Eyre & Spottiswoode, 1961), 24–33. Aileen Nusbaum, *The Seven Cities of Cibola* (New York: Putnam, 1926), a collection of Zuñi folktales, presents a slightly different version (3–8).

124. See Garcilaso de la Vega, el Inca, *Royal Commentaries of the Incas and General History of Peru*, trans. Harold V. Livermore (Austin: University of Texas Press, 1966; reprint, 1970), 1:27–30.

125. Todorov's portrait of Cabeza de Vaca is somewhat different. It is perplexing that he ignores Estevan's presence (*Conquest of America*, 196–200).

126. Danquah, *Akan Doctrine of God*, 53.

127. Jacques Derrida, *Dissemination*, trans. Barbara Johnson (Chicago: University of Chicago Press, 1981), 92–93.

128. James Joyce, *A Portrait of the Artist as a Young Man: Text, Criticism, and Notes*, ed. Chester G. Anderson (1916; reprint, New York: Viking Press, 1974), 225.

129. See also Janheinz Jahn, "Nommo: The Magic Power of the Word," in *Muntu: An Outline of New African Culture*, trans. Marjorie Greene (1958; New York: Grove Press, 1961), 121–55.

130. Griaule, *Conversations with Ogotemmêli*, 27.

131. See Derrida, *Dissemination*, 88.

132. Griaule, *Conversations with Ogotemmêli*, 27–28.

133. Ibid., 77.

134. Harris, *Explorations*, 53; my italics; for further details on this Carib ritual see Harris, *The Womb of Space: The Cross-Cultural Imagination* (Westport, Conn.: Greenwood Press, 1983), 24–26.

135. Danquah, *Akan Doctrine of God*, 131.

136. Du Bois, *Souls of Black Folk*, 139.

137. José María Arguedas, *Deep Rivers*, trans. Frances Horning Barraclough (1958; Austin: University of Texas Press, 1981), 6–7.

138. See José Lezama Lima, "Imagen de América Latina," in *América Latina en su literatura*, ed. César Fernández Moreno (Paris and Mexico: Siglo Veintiuno for UNESCO, 1972).

139. A translation of the ancient Náhuatl text narrating the "Legend of the Suns" is provided by Miguel León-Portilla in *Aztec Thought and Culture: A*

Study of the Ancient Náhuatl Mind, trans. Jack Emory Davis (1963; Norman: University of Oklahoma Press, 1975), 38–39.

140. See ibid., 51; also Hans Helfritz, *Mexican Cities of the Gods: An Archeological Guide* (New York: Praeger, 1968; reprint, 1970), 43–44.

141. It is worth recalling here the previous discussion of "anochecímos enfermo amanecímos bueno." Venus, as Octavio Paz points out in his notes to *Piedra de sol* (43–44), appears in the sky twice every day: at dusk and at dawn. It is both the Evening Star and the Morning Star, and therefore embodies the universe's essential ambiguity and duality. Fuentes clarifies this in *Terra Nostra:* "Quetzalcóatl, Venus, Hesperia, Spain, identical stars, dawn and dusk, mysterious union, indecipherable enigma, but cipher for two bodies, two lands, cipher for a terrible encounter" (485).

142. León-Portilla, *Aztec Thought,* 51, and Helfritz, *Mexican Cities,* 44.

143. Rodríguez Freyle, *El carnero,* 93.

144. Pablo Neruda, *Canto General* (Buenos Aires: Editorial Losada, 1955), 1:36. The translations are from John Felstiner, *Translating Neruda: The Way to Macchu Picchu* (Stanford: Stanford University Press, 1980), 231. Felstiner's translation is, in many respects, superior to the standard translation by Nathaniel Tarn (1966; New York: Farrar, Straus & Giroux, 1983).

145. *Canto General,* 32–33; *Translating Neruda,* 219.

146. Ángel María Garibay Kintana, *Llave de Náhuatl: Collección de trozos clasicos, con gramática y vocabulario,* 2d ed., rev. and enl. (Mexico: Porrúa, 1961), 115.

147. Harris, *Explorations,* 99; my italics.

148. Ibid.

Part III. The Carnivalization of Poetry: Nicolás Guillén's Chronicles

1. For a list of available translations see "Guillén en otros idiomas," in *Bibliografía de Nicolás Guillén: Biblioteca Nacional José Martí* (Havana: Instituto Cubano del Libro, 1975), 160–84; also "Bibliografía sumaria de Nicolás Guillén," *Revista de Literatura Cubana* 1 (July 1982): 94–103.

2. Keith Ellis, *Cuba's Nicolás Guillén: Poetry and Ideology* (Toronto: University of Toronto Press, 1983), ix. See also Ángel Augier's two-volume critical biography, *Nicolás Guillén: Notas para un estudio biográfico-crítico* (Santa Clara, Cuba: Universidad Central de las Villas, 1964); Nancy Morejón's *Recopilación de textos sobre Nicolás Guillén* (Havana: Casa de las Américas, 1974) and her more recent *Nación y mestizaje en Nicolás Guillén* (Havana: UNEAC, 1982); Dennis Sardinha's monograph *The Poetry of Nicolás Guillén* (London: New Beacon Books, 1976); Lorna Williams's *Self and Society in the Poetry of Nicolás Guillén* (Baltimore: Johns Hopkins University Press, 1982).

3. See my reviews of Nancy Morejón's *Nación y mestizaje en Nicolás Guillén* and Williams's *Self and Society in the Poetry of Nicolás Guillén* ("Poetry and

Politics: Two Books on Nicolás Guillén," *MLN* (Hispanic Issue) 98 [March 1983]: 275–84) and Ellis's *Cuba's Nicolás Guillén* ("The Miraculous Weapons of Nicolás Guillén and Aimé Césaire," *Callaloo* 22 7 (Fall 1984): 141–50. Other recent examples of Marxist approaches to Guillén are Alfred Melon, "El poeta de la síntesis," in *Recopilación de textos sobre Nicolás Guillén*, 199–242; Hans-Otto Dill, "Valor revolucionario y valor estético-artístico de la poesía de Nicolás Guillén," *Casa de las Américas* 22 (May-June 1982): 54–62; and José Antonio Portuondo, "Canta la revolución con toda la voz que tiene," *Revista de Literatura Cubana* 1 (July 1982): 53–58.

4. Ellis, *Cuba's Nicolás Guillén*, 196.

5. Lydia Cabrera, *El monte: Igbo finda ewe orisha, vititi nfinda: Notas sobre las religiones, la magia, las supersticiones y el folklore de los negros criollos y del pueblo de Cuba* (Havana: Ediciones C.R., 1954; reprint, Miami: Colección del Chichereku, 1971), 9; my translation.

6. Guillén, *Obra poética* (Havana: Instituto Cubano del Libro, 1974), 1:114. All further references to this standard edition are identified in the text as *OP*. Unless otherwise indicated, all translations of Guillén's prose and poetry are mine.

7. See "Conversación con Nicolás Guillén" in *Recopilación de textos sobre Nicolás Guillén*, 44–45.

8. René Depestre, "Orfeo negro," in *Recopilación de textos sobre Nicolás Guillén*, 122; my translation.

9. "Sensemayá" was put to music in 1937 by the Mexican composer Silvestre Revueltas, as Ángel Augier notes in *Nicolás Guillén: Notas para un estudio biográfico-crítico*, 1:213.

10. See Morejón, "Prólogo," in *Recopilación de textos sobre Nicolás Guillén*, 20.

11. See, for instance, Lorna Williams, *Self and Society in the Poetry of Nicolás Guillén*, 17–18; Ángel Augier, *Nicolás Guillén* (Havana: Instituto Cubano del Libro, Contemporáneos, 1971), 141–42; Janheinz Jahn, *Neo-African Culture: A History of Black Writing*, trans. Oliver Coburn and Ursula Lehrburger (1968; New York: Grove Press, 1969), 222–25.

12. Ellis, *Cuba's Nicolás Guillén*, 83–84.

13. Ibid., 85.

14. See Jacques Derrida, "Plato's Pharmacy," in *Dissemination*, trans. Barbara Johnson (Chicago: University of Chicago Press, 1981), 95–117.

15. See Fernando Ortiz, *Nuevo catauro de cubanismos* (Havana: Editorial de Ciencias Sociales, 1974), 351.

16. Ibid., 349. See also *La antigua fiesta afrocubana del "Día de Reyes"* (1925; reprint, Havana: Ministerio de Relaciones Exteriores Departamento de Asuntos Culturales, División de Publicaciones, 1960) and *Hampa afrocubana: Los negros brujos: Apuntes para un estudio de etnología criminal* (Madrid: Editorial América, 1917), 48–49.

17. See Ellis, *Cuba's Nicolás Guillén*, 83.

18. Quoted in Augier, *Nicolás Guillén: Notas para un estudio*, 1:212–13; my translation.

19. Alejo Carpentier, *El reino de este mundo* (1949; reprint, Seix Barral, 1981 [1969]), 40–41, trans. Harriet de Onís as *The Kingdom of This World* (New York: Collier Books, 1957; reprint, 1970). I have adjusted de Onís's translation. Future references to *El reino* will be included in the text.

20. Kay Boulware-Miller mentions Mackandal in connection with Guillén's "Balada del güije" in "La 'Balada del güije' de Nicolás Guillén, un experimento en el folclor," *Casa de las Américas* 22 (May–June 1982): 101–2.

21. See Kutzinski, "The Logic of Wings: Gabriel García Márquez and Afro-American Literature," *Latin American Literary Review* 13 (January–June 1985): 141.

22. Depestre, "Orfeo negro," 123; my translation.

23. In the original, these lines appear in a footnote.

24. *The Complete Poems of Paul Laurence Dunbar* (New York: Dodd, Mead, 1896), 71. Morejón argues that Guillén's anguish is comparable to that of North American black poets such as Dunbar and Langston Hughes (*Nación y mestizaje*, 300). See also David Arthur MacMurray, "Dos negros en el Nuevo Mundo: Notas sobre el 'americanismo' de Langston Hughes y la cubanía de Nicolás Guillén," *Casa de las Américas* 14 (January–February 1974): 122–28; Enrique Noble, "Nicolás Guillén y Langston Hughes," *Nueva Revista Cubana* (1961–62): 41–85; Cathy Gilmore, "Towards an Understanding and Application of the Folk Poetry of Nicolás Guillén and Langston Hughes," M.A. thesis, Cornell University, 1975. Langston Hughes, in collaboration with Ben Frederic Carruthers, translated some of Guillén's early poems in *Cuba Libre: Poems by Nicolás Guillén* (Los Angeles: Ward Ritchie Press, 1948).

25. Morejón, *Nación y mestizaje*, 328; my translation.

26. Ortiz, *Nuevo cauturo de cubanismos*, 336–37.

27. Ezequiel Martínez Estrada, *La poesía de Nicolás Guillén* (Buenos Aires: Calicanto, 1977), 8.

28. Other relevant examples of documentary poetry are Robert Hayden's "Middle Passage" (*Angle of Ascent: New and Selected Poems* [New York: Liveright, 1975], 118–23) and Ernesto Cardenal's *Zero Hour and Other Documentary Poems*, ed. Donald D. Walsh (New York: New Directions, 1980), which includes translations of poems written between 1954 and 1979. Cardenal's indebtedness to Pound's *Cantos* and particularly to Guillén's *Elegías* is obvious in this collection. For an account of Cardenal's relations with postrevolutionary Cuba see *In Cuba*, trans. Donald D. Walsh (1972; New York: New Directions, 1974).

29. Gabriel García Márquez, *Cien años de soledad* (Buenos Aires: Editorial Sudamericana, 1967); trans. Gregory Rabassa as *One Hundred Years of Solitude* (1970; reprint, New York: Avon Books, 1971), 20–21.

30. Harold V. Livermore, introduction to Garcilaso de la Vega, el Inca, *Royal Commentaries of the Incas and General History of Peru* (Austin: University of Texas Press, 1966; reprint, 1970), 1:xxvi.

31. Morejón, *Nación y mestizaje*, 329; my translation.

32. Wilson Harris, *The Womb of Space: The Cross-Cultural Imagination* (Westport, Conn.: Greenwood Press, 1983), 50. See also Mercedes López-Baralt, *El mito taíno: Raíz y producciones en el Amazonia continental* (Río Piedras, Puerto Rico: Ediciones Huracán, 1976).

33. See Fernando Ortiz, *Contrapunteo cubano del tabaco y el azúcar*, trans. Harriet de Onís as *Cuban Counterpoint: Tobacco and Sugar* (1947; New York: Random House, 1970).

34. Wilson Harris, *Explorations: A Selection of Talks and Articles, 1966–1981*, ed. Hena Maes-Jelinek (Mundelstrup, Denmark: Dangaroo Press, 1981), 44–45.

35. Hayden, "Middle Passage," 121.

36. See José Lezama Lima, "Imagen de América Latina," in *América Latina en su literatura*, ed. César Fernández Moreno (Paris and Mexico: Siglo Veintiuno for UNESCO, 1972), 465; Garcilaso de la Vega, *Royal Commentaries of the Incas*, 1:280–81.

37. See H. R. Hays, "Nicolás Guillén y la poesía afrocubana," in *Recopilación de textos sobre Nicolás Guillén*, 98.

38. Richard Wright, *American Hunger* (1944; New York: Harper & Row, 1979), 135.

39. See Claude Lévi-Strauss, "Introduction a l'oeuvre de Marcel Mauss," in Marcel Mauss, *Sociologie et anthropologie* (1950; reprint, Paris: Presses Universitaires de France, 1968), l; my translation.

40. See also William Carlos Williams's figure of the *radium* in *Paterson*: "The radiant gist that/resists final crystallization" (109).

41. Quoted in Morejón, *Nación y mestizaje*, 314–15; my translation.

42. Roberto González Echevarría, "Criticism and Literature in Revolutionary Cuba," *Cuban Studies/Estudios Cubanos* 11 (January 1981): 15–16.

43. Ibid., 16.

44. *Unión* (1982); *Casa de las Américas* 22 (May–June 1982); *Revista de Literatura Cubana* 1 (July 1982).

45. Nancy Morejón is so far the only Cuban writer who has given some critical recognition to the achievement of *El diario* (*Nación y mestizaje*, 312–24). From within Latin America, the only reviews of *El diario* are the aforementioned brief essays by Luce López-Baralt, Hernán Lavín Cerda, and Raúl Hernández Novás.

46. Mikhail Bakhtin, *The Dialogic Imagination: Four Essays*, ed. Michael Holquist; trans. Caryl Emerson and Michael Holquist (Austin: University of Texas Press, 1982), 11.

47. Ibid., 5.

48. Mikhail Bakhtin, *Problems of Dostoevsky's Poetics*, trans. R. W. Rotsel (Ann Arbor, Mich.: Ardis, 1973), 165.

49. Bakhtin, *Dialogic Imagination*, 7.

50. Stephanie Davis-Lett, "Literary Games in the Works of Nicolás Guillén," *Perspectives on Contemporary Literature* 6 (1980): 136, and her dissertation, "Development of Poetic Techniques in the Works of Nicolás Guillén," Princeton University, 1976, especially chap. 3: "Post-Vanguardism: The Playful Spirit,"

187–275. Davis-Lett deserves credit for being the first to recognize the significance of humor in Guillén's work. Another essay on the same topic is José Prats Sariol, "Del humor en la poesía de Nicolás Guillén," *Unión* (1982): 181–87. See also Jorge A. Marbán, "Innovaciones formales en la última poesía política de Nicolás Guillén," *Crítica Hispánica* 6 (Fall 1984): 145–53.

51. Theodor Adorno and Max Horkheimer, *Dialektik der Aufklärung: Philosophische Fragmente* (1944; reprint, Frankfurt am Main: Fischer Verlag, 1972), 139; my italics; my translation.

52. Martínez Estrada, *La poesía de Nicolás Guillén*, 70.

53. See Bakhtin, *Dialogic Imagination*, 280–83.

54. See, for instance, Gabriel García Márquez in *El olor de la guayaba: Conversaciones con Plinio Apuleyo Mendoza* (Bogota: Editorial la Oveja Negra, 1982), 55.

55. Severo Sarduy, "El barroco y el neobarroco," in *América Latina en su literatura*, ed. César Fernández Moreno (Paris and Mexico: Siglo Veintiuno for UNESCO, 1972), 170; my translation.

56. Octavio Paz's comments on the differences between Romanticism and the Baroque are relevant here: "Although the Baroque and Romanticism are two mannerisms, their similarities reveal very profound differences. Both proclaim, vis-à-vis classicism, an aesthetic of the irregular and the singular; both present themselves as transgressions of standard norms. But in the Romantic transgression, the main thrust of the action is the subject, whereas the baroque transgression concentrates on the object. Romanticism liberates the subject; the Baroque is the art of the metamorphosis of the object. Romanticism is passionate and passive; the Baroque is intellectual and active. The Romantic transgression culminates in the apotheosis of the subject or in its fall; the baroque transgression ends with the appearance of an unusual object. Romantic poetry negates the object through passion or irony; in the Baroque the subject disappears in the object. Romanticism is expansion; the Baroque is implosion. The Romantic poem is time overflowing; the Baroque is time congealed. . . . The Baroque seeks to dominate the object, but not by creating an equilibrium but by accentuating contradictions" (*Sor Juana Inés de la Cruz, o las trampas de la fe* (Barcelona: Seix Barral, 1982), 79–80.

57. *Concierto barroco* is also the title of one of Alejo Carpentier's novels (1974; reprint, Madrid: Siglo Veintiuno, 1981).

58. Ellis, *Cuba's Nicolás Guillén*, 187.

59. See Octavio Paz, *Children of the Mire: Modern Poetry from Romanticism to the Avant-Garde* (Cambridge, Mass.: Harvard University Press, 1974), 29.

60. Roberto González Echevarría has noted that Oriente Province is commonly regarded as the cradle of Cuban culture; see "Son de la loma," *Enlace* 1 (September 1984): 14. The English version of this essay appeared in the *New England Review/Breadloaf Quarterly*, 8:4 (1985): 566–75.

61. See Roberto González Echevarría, "The Life and Adventures of Cipión: Cervantes and the Picaresque," *Diacritics* 10 (September 1980): 20–21.

62. For a similar posture see Antonio Benítez Rojo's Jorge Emilio Lacoste in the short story "La tijera" [The Scissors] in *Estatuas sepultadas y otros relatos* (Hanover: Ediciones del Norte, 1984), 191–205.

63. Ellis, *Cuba's Nicolás Guillén*, 187.

64. The work of Góngora (1561–1627) reached Guillén indirectly through his contact with the "nueva poesía" of the so-called Group of '27, a generation of young Spanish poets including, among others, Jorge Guillén, Pedro Salinas, Rafael Alberti, and Federico García Lorca, who were engaged in restoring Gongorine poetry to twentieth-century Spanish letters. The influence particularly of García Lorca on Guillén is explicit in *España: Poema de cuatro angustias y una esperanza* (1937) [Spain: Poem in Four Anxieties and One Hope]. The final part of the "Angustia cuarta," subtitled "Momento en García Lorca," is, interestingly enough, written in the same tercets as "Epístola" (*OP*, 1:214).

65. According to the *Diccionario histórico de la lengua española* (Madrid, 1977), the word first appeared in the thirteenth century as *algaravía* or *algarauía* (315).

66. Ibid.; my translation.

67. *Croquis et fantaisies* (1830), quoted in Leo Spitzer, *Lingüística e historia literaria*, 2d ed. (Madrid: Gredos, 1974), 260.

68. Quoted in Hugh Thomas, *Cuba, or the Pursuit of Freedom* (London: Eyre & Spottiswoode, 1971), 12.

69. García Márquez, *El olor de la guayaba*, 55; my translation.

70. Roberto González Echevarría, *Alejo Carpentier: The Pilgrim at Home* (Ithaca: Cornell University Press, 1977), 223–24. As mentioned above, Carpentier's discussion of the Baroque is part of an essay entitled "De lo real maravilloso americano," which appeared in the collection *Tientos y diferencias* (Montevideo: ARCA, 1967).

71. Stephanie Merrim, "A Secret Idiom: The Grammar and Role of Language in *Tres tristes tigres*," *Latin American Literary Review* 8 (Spring–Summer 1980): 97. See also William Siemens, "Guillermo Cabrera Infante: Language and Creativity," Ph.D. diss., University of Kansas, 1971.

72. *OP*, 1:416–36. An illustrated anniversary edition of the "Elegía a Jesús Menéndez" was published by Editorial Letras Cubanas in 1982. For a discussion of that poem see Mirta Aguirre, "En torno a la 'Elegía a Jesús Menéndez,'" *Revista de Literatura Cubana* 1 (July 1982): 25–33.

73. Roberto González Echevarría, "*Cien años de soledad*: The Novel as Myth and Archive," *MLN* (Hispanic Issue) 99 (March 1984): 374–75.

74. For further details see Max Henríquez Ureña, *Panorama histórico de la literatura cubana* (New York: Las Américas, 1963), 1:41–48.

75. The only prior American poem in which a black character appeared was the Renaissance epic *La araucana* (1569–1594) by Alonso de Ercilla y Zúñiga, whom Guillén mentions in a footnote later on in *El diario*. This poem describes the war between the Spaniards and the Arauca Indians during the conquest of Peru. See Ángel del Río, *Historia de la literatura española* (New York: Dryden

Press, 1948), 1:145; also, William Luis, "History and Fiction: Black Narrative in Latin America," in *Voices from Under* (Westport, Conn.: Greenwood Press, 1984), 4.

76. See Franklin Knight, *Slave Society in Cuba during the Nineteenth Century* (1970; reprint, Madison: University of Wisconsin Press, 1974), 122.

77. See Thomas, *Cuba*, who quotes one of those original advertisements (37); other sources are Fernando Ortiz, *Los negros esclavos* (Havana: Editorial de Ciencias Sociales, 1975), 170–71, and Manuel Moreno Fraginals, *El ingenio: Complejo económico social cubano del azúcar* (Havana: Editorial de Ciencias Sociales, 1978), 2:80.

78. See "Ayer en el puerto" [Yesterday in the Harbor] (*OP*, 2:398).

79. See Ellis, *Cuba's Nicolás Guillén*, 190.

80. See, for instance, "Dos niños" [Two Children], "Balada de los dos abuelos" [Ballad of the Two Grandfathers], and "Elegía cubana" [Cuban Elegy].

81. Guillén refers here to the rebel leaders Guillermón, usually described as a gigantic ex-slave, the mulatto general Antonio Maceo, and Maceo's supporter Flor Crombet, who protested the Peace of Zanjón, signed in 1878, on the grounds that it provided neither for the abolition of slavery nor for Cuban independence. This famous Protest of Baraguá led to the renewal of hostilities. See Thomas, *Cuba*, 254, 266–67, 300.

82. As Thomas notes (ibid., 323), it was estimated that about 80 percent of the rebels in the war of 1895 were black, and they themselves claimed afterwards to have constituted 85 percent of the rebel army. These percentages, however, were probably exaggerated for propagandistic purposes.

83. See Joseph P. Pereira, "Raza en la obra de Nicolás Guillén después de 1959," *Sin nombre* 13 (April–June 1983), who argues that this particular item shows the connection between racism and class (35).

84. Alejo Carpentier, *Explosion in a Cathedral*, trans. John Sturrock (1963; reprint, New York: Harper & Row, 1979), 7–8. It is worth adding that the cover of this paperback edition is adorned with a gigantic guillotine.

85. Leo Spitzer, "La enumeración caótica en la poesía moderna," in *Lingüística e historia literaria*, 247–300. This essay is, curiously enough, not included in the English edition, *Linguistics and Literary History* (London: Russell & Russell, 1962); neither is the one on Pedro Salinas, which is also relevant to my topic. Both seem to be available only in Spanish.

86. See Stephanie Davis-Lett, "Literary Games in the Works of Nicolás Guillén."

87. José de Espronceda, *Poesías completas*, ed. Juan Alcina Franch (Barcelona: Editorial Bruguera, 1968), 102.

88. Guillermo Cabrera Infante, *Tres tristes tigres* (Barcelona: Seix Barral, 1968), 212.

89. Sarduy, "El barroco y el neobarroco," 121.

90. See Thomas, *Cuba*, 6–11.

91. Morell de Santa Cruz (1694–1768) was the author of the *Historia de la isla*

y catedral de Cuba, the island's first history, which included Silvestre de Balboa's "Espejo de paciencia." The bishop was also known for his encouragement of African brotherhoods (*cofradías*). See Thomas, *Cuba*, 39–40, and Henríquez Ureña, *Panorama*, 57–58.

92. Juan Prado had recruited many free blacks and mulattoes as well as slaves for the defense of Havana against the English. The slaves were to receive their freedom in exchange for military service, a promise that was kept. See Thomas, *Cuba*, 7.

93. "En tan breve intervalo cerca de un millar de embarcaciones comerciales." [In so brief a period, about a thousand commercial vessels entered the port (385).] Thomas notes that over seven hundred merchant ships entered Havana during the time of the English occupation, as compared to no more than fifteen vessels a year before, that is, apart from the royal treasure fleet (*Cuba*, 51).

94. Ibid., 61.

95. See "Gobierno y Capitanía General de la siempre fiel isla de Cuba" [The Government and Captaincy-General of the Always Loyal Island of Cuba], *OP*, 2:405. The phrase "la siempre fiel isla" was used in the nineteenth century by Spain when referring to Cuba.

96. The original is entitled *Etudes sur la littérature et les moeurs angloaméricains au XIX siècle*. The fact that this change was not corrected in the second (1979) edition of *El diario* indicates that it must have been an intentional distortion.

97. Guillén appears to conflate the French influence in the east of Cuba, especially in Santiago, which was derived mainly from the coffee boom sponsored by immigrants from Saint Domingue (1823–1830), with the fashionable "Frenchification" of Havana during the 1860s, supported in this case by the sugar boom.

98. Quoted in Thomas, *Cuba*, 102.

99. Tacón was a Spanish patriot who ascended to power in 1834. He was the one to expel the writer José Antonio Saco for spreading abolitionist doctrines, an act curiously contradictory to Tacón's tolerance of African cultural activities such as the Abakuá cult. See ibid., 194–99.

100. The British consul reported in 1825 that "transactions of this nature are now public and notorious." Even the 1835 Equipment Treaty between Spain and England did not stop illicit slave imports into Cuba. In addition, orders from Madrid to free all slaves brought to the island after 1820 were systematically ignored. See ibid., 200–203.

101. At the time, almost all Cuban vessels were built in the United States.

102. The importation of Chinese labor to Cuba started in 1840. Thomas notes that between September 1866 and April 1868, over 17,000 Chinese arrived in Havana, bringing the total of Chinese imported to the island to almost 100,000 (186, 240). Guillén's reference to the Chinese may also be compared to Severo Sarduy's emphasis on oriental culture in Cuba at the beginning of *De donde son los cantantes* [From Cuba with a Song] (1967). See González Echevarría, "Son de la loma," 15–16.

103. Gonzalo de Berceo, *Obras completas* (Logroño: Excma. Diputación Provincial, 1971), 494.

104. See Enrique Pupo-Walker's discussion of the indebtedness of Juana García to Celestina in his *"El carnero y una forma seminal del relato afrohispanico,"* in *Homenaje a Lydia Cabrera,* ed. Reinaldo Sánchez and José A. Madrigal (Barcelona: Ediciones Universal, 1977), 251–57; also *La vocación literaria del pensamiento histórico en América: Desarrollo de la prosa de ficción, siglos 16, 17, 18, y 19* (Madrid: Gredos, 1982), 123–55.

105. Fernando de Rojas, *The Celestina: A Novel in Dialogue,* trans. Lesley Byrd Simpson (Berkeley and Los Angeles: University of California Press, 1974), 100–101.

106. Carlos Fuentes, *Terra Nostra,* trans. Margaret Sayers Peden (1975; New York: Farrar, Straus & Giroux, 1976), 27.

107. For further details see González Echevarría, "Life and Adventures of Cipión," 15–26.

108. Guillén's bibliographical information here is precise. The first (1860) edition of Mendive's *Poesías* included a prologue by Manuel Cañete, and the second (1883) edition also contained biographical notes by Vidal Morales y Morales.

109. For details of the Pacto del Zanjón and the Protest of Baraguá see Philip S. Foner, *A History of Cuba and Its Relations with the United States* (New York: International Publishers, 1963), 2:265–75.

110. *The America of José Martí: Selected Writings of José Martí,* trans. Juan de Onís (1954; New York: Minerva Press, 1968), 143; my italics.

111. See Henríquez-Ureña, *Panorama,* 1:260–69.

112. For details see ibid., 2:65–85, and Juan J. Remos, *Los poetas de "Arpas amigas"* (Havana: Cardenas, 1943), 136–72.

113. See Remos, *Los poetas de "Arpas amigas,"* and Henríquez Ureña, *Panorama,* 2:157.

114. Loló de la Torriente, "Landaluze: El pintor más cubano de su época," *Cuadernos Americanos* 26 (March–April 1967): 217.

115. Alejo Carpentier's short story "Los fugitivos" [The Fugitives (1946)] is based on Landaluze's "El cimarrón," which is reproduced in Moreno Fraginals, *El ingenio,* vol. 1.

116. Several of Landaluze's paintings are included in Ortiz's *Los negros esclavos* (1916)—plates 36, 37, and 64—and in his *La antigua fiesta del "Día de Reyes."*

117. In 1895, United States investments in Cuba were estimated at $50,000,000. See Foner, *History of Cuba,* 2:297.

118. Martí is quoted in ibid., 359.

119. See Thomas, *Cuba,* 378–79.

120. The historical reference is to the mysterious sinking of the USS *Maine* in 1898 in the Havana harbor, an incident used as an excuse for the active involvement of the United States in Cuba's Second Independence War.

121. See Oscar Rivero-Rodas, "La imagen de los Estados Unidos en la poesía

de Nicolás Guillén," *Casa de las Américas* 20 (May–June 1980): 154–60. Curiously enough, this essay does not mention *El diario*.

122. Walter Benjamin, *Der Ursprung des deutschen Trauerspiels*, rev. ed. (Frankfurt am Main: Suhrkamp, 1963), 233–34; my translation.

123. Leo Spitzer, "American Advertising," *Essays on English and American Literature*, ed. Anna Hatcher (Princeton: Princeton University Press, 1962), 266.

124. This pun appears in "Meta-Final," initially conceived as the final part of *Tres tristes tigres*, but published separately in 1970. Roberto González Echevarría translates Cabrera Infante's play on "casinos" as "quasinots, or casi-nots, cacasinaughts, quasinos." See "Meta-End," *Latin American Literary Review* 8 (Spring–Summer 1980): 89.

125. Cabrera Infante, *Tres tristes tigres*, 15.

126. See "La muerte de Trotsky referida por varios escritores cubanos, años después—o antes" [The Death of Trotsky Described by Various Cuban Writers, Before—and After], ibid., 235–37, 241–58.

127. Ibid., 17–18.

128. Coolidge went to Havana for the Sixth Pan-American Conference in 1927, declaring that Cuba's people were "independent, free, prosperous, peaceful, and enjoying the advantages of self-government. . . . They have reached a position of stability of their government in the genuine expression of their public opinion at the ballot box." Quoted in Thomas, *Cuba*, 587. Of course, the "stable" government to which Coolidge refers so naively was the Machado regime, which encouraged the "genuine expression of public opinion" by brutally killing four students who had been accused of being Communists, only a few months after Coolidge's visit.

129. Merrim, "Language in *Tres tristes tigres*," 99.

130. Benjamin, *Der Ursprung des deutschen Trauerspiels*, 9 (29 in the translation).

131. Ortiz, *Nuevo cauturo de cubanismos*, 375.

132. Alejo Carpentier, "Lettre des Antilles," *Bifur* (Paris), no. 3 (1929), trans. Frederick M. Murray as "Cuban Magic," *Transition: An International Workshop for Orphic Creation*, no. 22 (1933), 386.

133. Miguel Barnet, "The Culture That Sugar Created," *Latin American Literary Review* 8 (Spring–Summer 1980): 43. The Spanish version of this essay is included in Barnet's *La fuente viva* (Havana: Editorial Letras Cubanas, 1983), 140–53.

134. See Ortiz, *Hampa afrocubana*, 28–29.

135. Carpentier, "Cuban Magic," 385–86. A slightly different version of this prayer appears in ¡*Ecue-Yamba-O!* (1933; Barcelona: Editorial Bruguera, 1979), where it is employed to heal young Menegildo Cué's crab bite (29–30).

136. Carpentier, "Two Cuban Negro Prayers," *Transition*, no. 23 (1935): 53–54. Carpentier also includes a copy of this prayer, in the form of a leaflet for sale at a Havana bookstore, in the first edition of ¡*Ecue-Yamba-O!* (Madrid: Editorial España, 1933) between pp. 116 and 117. This, as well as all the other plates, has been removed from subsequent editions of the novel.

137. See Ortiz, *Hampa afrocubana*, 39.

138. See José Piedra's notes to Carpentier's "Tale of Moons," *Latin American Literary Review* 8 (Spring–Summer 1980), especially n. 28, p. 79.

139. Carpentier, *¡Ecue-Yamba-O!*, 28.

140. See Piedra, n. 37, p. 81; also Carpentier, "Cuban Magic," 386, and Barnet's "Divinidades yorubas en la santería cubana," in *La fuente viva*, 191–92.

141. Barnet, "The Culture That Sugar Created," 41.

142. Ortiz, *La antigua fiesta del "Día de Reyes,"* 37; my translation.

143. See Martí, quoted in Thomas, *Cuba*, 310.

144. See Fidel Castro, *History Will Absolve Me* (1961; reprint, Secaucus, N.J.: Lyle Stuart, 1984).

145. Castro is quoted in Thomas, *Cuba*, 829.

146. Ibid., 855.

147. It is worth noting that Castro's use of this *personalismo* in that particular speech was met with considerable resentment by his supporters; see ibid., 847.

148. See ibid., 835.

149. See ibid., 851.

Part IV. The Writing on the Wall

1. Carlos Fuentes, *Terra Nostra*, trans. Margaret Sayers Peden (1975; New York: Farrar, Straus & Giroux, 1976), 485.

2. For a transcript of that lecture see Churchill P. Lathrop, "An Interpretation of the Orozco Frescoes at Dartmouth" (1980).

3. While Guillén emphasizes in a 1972 interview that "although most people do not know this, I have been a collaborator in most of the Cuban journals both before and after the triumph of the Revolution," he was hardly ever directly involved in any of the literary groups that published journals such as *Orígenes* or the *Revista de Avance*. See "Conversaciones con Nicolás Guillén," in Nancy Morejón, ed., *Recopilación de textos sobre Nicolás Guillén* (Havana: Casa de las Américas, 1974), 55. This interview was originally printed in *Casa de las Américas* 73 (1972).

4. *New York Times Book Review*, 10 February 1985, 37; first italics mine.

5. See Ralph Ellison, *Shadow and Act* (New York: Random House, 1964), 144–45.

6. See also Kutzinski, "The Distant Closeness of Dancing Doubles: Sterling Brown and William Carlos Williams," *BALF* 16 (Spring 1982): 19–25.

Select Bibliography

William Carlos Williams

Works

The Autobiography of William Carlos Williams. 1951. Reprint. New York: New Directions, 1967.

The Collected Earlier Poems of William Carlos Williams. New York: New Directions, 1951.

The Collected Later Poems of William Carlos Williams. Rev. ed. New York: New Directions, 1967.

Collected Poems, 1921–1931. Preface by Wallace Stevens. New York: Objectivist Press, 1934.

The Desert Music. New York: Random House, 1954.

The Embodiment of Knowledge. Edited by Ron Loewinsohn. New York: New Directions, 1974.

Select Bibliography

The Great American Novel. Paris: Three Mountains Press, 1923. Reprinted in *Imaginations,* 1970.
Imaginations. Edited by Webster Schott. New York: New Directions, 1970.
In the American Grain. 1925. Reprint, with introduction by Horace Gregory. New York: New Directions, 1956.
I Wanted to Write a Poem: The Autobiography of the Works of a Poet. Edited by Edith Heal. 1958. Reprint. New York: New Directions, 1978.
Kora in Hell: Improvisations. 1920. Reprint. San Francisco: City Lights Books, 1957. Reprinted in *Imaginations,* 1970.
A Novelette and Other Prose, 1921–1931. Toulon, France: Impr. F. Cabasson, 1932. Reprinted in *Imaginations,* 1970.
Paterson. New York: New Directions, 1963. Originally published in single volumes by New Directions in 1946, 1948, 1949, 1951, and 1958.
Pictures from Brueghel and Other Poems. 1949. Reprint. New York: New Directions, 1962.
Selected Essays of William Carlos Williams. New York: New Directions, 1954.
The Selected Letters of William Carlos Williams. Edited by John C. Thirlwall. New York: McDowell, Obolensky, 1957.
Selected Poems of William Carlos Williams. Edited by Randall Jarrell. New York: New Directions, 1949.
Spring and All. Paris: Contact, 1923. Reprint. New York: Frontier Press, 1970. Reprinted in *Imaginations,* 1970.

Critical Studies

Bollard, Margaret Lloyd. "The Newspaper Landscape of Williams's *Paterson.*" *Contemporary Literature* 16 (1975): 317–27.
Bollier, E. P. "Against the American Grain: William Carlos Williams between Whitman and Poe." *Tulane Studies in English* 23 (1978): 123–42.
Brosman, Catharine S. "A Source and Parallel of Michel Butor's *Mobile: In the American Grain.*" *MLR* 66 (April 1971): 315–21.
Conarroe, Joel. *William Carlos Williams' "Paterson": Language and Landscape.* Philadelphia: University of Pennsylvania Press, 1970.
Doyle, Charles, ed. *William Carlos Williams: The Critical Heritage.* London: Routledge & Kegan Paul, 1980.
Felstiner, John. "Through a Spanish Looking Glass: Williams's Poetry in Translation." *Américas* 29 (November–December 1977): 5–8.
Garrigue, Jean. "America Revisited." *Poetry* 90 (1957): 316–17.
Guimond, James. *The Art of William Carlos Williams: A Discovery and Possession of America.* Urbana: University of Illinois Press, 1968.
Holder, Alan. "*In the American Grain:* William Carlos Williams on the American Past." *American Quarterly* 19 (Fall 1967): 499–515.
Jay, Paul L. "American Modernism and the Uses of History: The Case of William Carlos Williams." *New Orleans Review* 9 (Winter 1982): 16–25.
Kenner, Hugh. "Columbus' Log-Book." *Poetry* 92 (June 1958): 174–78.

Select Bibliography

Koch, Vivienne. *William Carlos Williams*. New York: New Directions, 1950.

Kutzinski, Vera M. "The Distant Closeness of Dancing Doubles: Sterling Brown and William Carlos Williams." *BALF* 16 (Spring 1982): 19–25.

Lanati, Barbara. *L'avanguardia americana: Tre esperimenti: Faulkner, Stein, W. C. Williams*. Turin: Giulio Einaudi, 1977.

Mariani, Paul L. *William Carlos Williams: The Poet and His Critics*. Chicago: American Library Association, 1975.

Nash, Ralph. "The Use of Prose in *Paterson*." *Perspective* 6 (Autumn–Winter 1953): 191–99.

Neussendorfer, Sister Macaria. "William Carlos Williams's Idea of a City." *Thought* 40 (Summer 1965): 242–74.

Noland, Richard. "A Failure of Contact: William Carlos Williams on America." *Emory University Quarterly* 20 (Winter 1964): 248–60.

Riddel, Joseph N. *The Inverted Bell: Modernism and the Counterpoetics of William Carlos Williams*. Baton Rouge: Louisiana State University Press, 1974.

Sienicka, Marta. "Poetry in the Prose of *In the American Grain*." *Studia Anglia Posnaniensia* 1-2 (1968): 109–16.

Simpson, Louis. *Three on the Tower: The Lives and Works of Ezra Pound, T. S. Eliot, and William Carlos Williams*. New York: Morrow, 1975.

Spencer, Benjamin T. "Doctor Williams' *In the American Grain*." *Tennessee Studies in Literature* 8 (1963): 1–16.

Wagner, Linda Welshimer. *The Prose of William Carlos Williams*. Middletown, Conn.: Wesleyan University Press, 1970.

Weatherhead, A. Kingsley. "William Carlos Williams: Prose, Form, and Measure." *ELH* 33 (1966): 118–31.

Weaver, Mike. *William Carlos Williams: The American Background*. Cambridge: Cambridge University Press, 1971.

Weiland, Steven. "Where Shall We Unearth the Word? William Carlos Williams and the Aztecs." *Arizona Quarterly* 35 (1979): 42–48.

Whitaker, Thomas. *William Carlos Williams*. New York: Twayne United States Authors Series, 1968.

Jay Wright

Works

Death as History. New York: Poet's Press, 1967.

"The Death and Return of Paul Batuta: A Play in One Act." *Hambone* 4 (Fall 1984): 61–110.

"Desire's Design, Vision's Resonance: Black Poetry's Ritual and Historical Voice." *Callaloo* 30 (Winter 1987).

Dimensions of History. Santa Cruz: Kayak, 1976.

The Double Invention of Komo. Austin: University of Texas Press, 1980.

Select Bibliography

Explications/Interpretations. Lexington: University of Kentucky Press, Callaloo
Poetry Series, 1984.
The Homecoming Singer. New York: Corinth Books, 1971.
"Love's Emblem Lost: LeRoi Jones's 'Hymn for Lanie Poo.'" *Boundary 2* 6
(Winter 1978): 415–34.
"Love's Equation: A Play." *Callaloo* 19 6 (Fall 1983): 39–75.
Soothsayers and Omens. New York: Seven Woods Press, 1976.

Critical Studies

Barrax, Gerald. "The Early Poetry of Jay Wright." *Jay Wright: A Special Issue.*
Callaloo 19 6 (Fall 1983): 85–101.
Benston, Kimberly W. "'I Yam What I Am': Naming and Unnaming in Afro-
American Literature." *BALF* 16 (Spring 1982): 3–11.
Hollander, John. "Tremors of Exactitude" [on *The Double Invention of Komo*].
TLS, 30 January 1981, 115.
———. "Poetry in Review." *Yale Review* 74 (November 1984): 301–14.
Kutzinski, Vera M. "The Descent of Nommo: Literacy as Method in Jay Wright's
'Benjamin Banneker Helps to Build a City.'" *Jay Wright: A Special Issue.*
Callaloo 19 6 (Fall 1983): 103–19.
———. Something Strange and Miraculous and Transforming." *Hambone* 2
(Fall 1982): 129–34.
Pinckney, Darryl. "You're in the Army Now." *Parnassus: Poetry in Review* 9
(Spring–Summer 1981): 301–14.
Rowell, Charles. "The Unravelling of the Egg: An Interview with Jay Wright." *Jay
Wright: A Special Issue. Callaloo* 19 6 (Fall 1983): 3–15.
Stepto, Robert B. "After Modernism, After Hibernation: Michael Harper, Robert
Hayden, and Jay Wright." In *Chant of Saints: A Gathering of Afro-American
Art, Literature, and Scholarship,* edited by Michael S. Harper and Robert B.
Stepto. Urbana: University of Illinois Press, 1979): 470–86.
———. "'The Aching Prodigal': Jay Wright's Dutiful Poet." *Jay Wright: A Spe-
cial Issue. Callaloo* 19 6 (Fall 1983): 76–84.

Nicolás Guillén
Works

Cantos para soldados y sones para turistas. Mexico: Editorial Masas, 1937.
Cantos para soldados y sones para turistas: El son entero. Buenos Aires: Editorial
Losada, 1952 (1957).
El diario que a diario. Havana: UNEAC, 1972. 2d ed. Editorial Letras Cubanas,
1979.
Elegía a Jacques Roumain en el cielo de Haití. Havana: Imp. Ayón, 1948.
Elegía a Jesús Menéndez. Havana: Editorial Páginas, 1951.

Select Bibliography

Elegía a Jesús Menéndez. Prologue by Blas Roca. Havana: Imp. Nacional de Cuba, 1962. Reprint. Introduction by Ángel Augier. Havana: Editorial Letras Cubanas, 1982.

Elegía cubana. Havana: Mujeres y Obreros Unificadores, 1952.

El gran zoo. Havana: Ediciones Unión, 1967. Reprint. Madrid: Editorial Ciencia Nueva, 1969. 2d ed. Havana: UNEAC, 1971.

El son entero: Suma poética, 1929–1946. Buenos Aires: Editorial Pleamar, 1947.

España: Poema en cuatro angustias y una esperanza. Mexico: Editorial México Nuevo, 1937.

Motivos de son. Havana: Imp. Rambla, Bouza, 1930.

Obra poética: 1920–1972. Prologue by Ángel Augier. 2 vols. Havana: Instituto Cubano del Libro, 1972–73. 2d ed. Havana: UNEAC, 1974.

Páginas vueltas: Memorias. Havana: UNEAC, 1982.

La paloma de vuelo popular: Elegías. 1958. Reprint. Buenos Aires: Editorial Losada, 1959. 2d. ed. 1965.

Prosa de prisa, 1929–1972. Compiled with a prologue by Ángel Augier. 3 vols. Havana: Instituto Cubano del Libro, Editorial Arte y Literatura, 1975–76.

La rueda dentada. Havana: UNEAC, 1972.

Sóngoro cosongo: Poemas mulatos. Havana: Úcar, García, 1931.

Sóngoro cosongo, Motivos de son, West Indies Ltd., España: Poema en cuatro angustias y una esperanza. 1952. Reprint. Buenos Aires: Editorial Losada, 1957, 1967.

Sóngoro cosongo y otros poemas: Con una carta de Miguel de Unamuno. Havana: Le Verónica, 1942. 2d ed. Havana: Editorial Páginas, 1943.

Tengo. Prologue by José Antonio Portuondo. Havana: Editorial del Consejo Nacional de Universidades, Universidad Central de las Villas, 1964.

Versos negros. Selected with a prologue by José Luis Varela. Madrid: Edinter, 1950.

West Indies, Ltd.: Poemas. Havana: Úcar, García, 1934.

English Translations

Cuba Libre: Poems by Nicolás Guillén. Translated by Langston Hughes and Ben Frederic Carruthers. Los Angeles: Ward Ritchie Press, 1948.

Man-Making Words: Selected Poems of Nicolás Guillén. Translated and annotated, with an introduction by Robert Marquez and David Arthur McMurray. Amherst: University of Massachusetts Press, 1972.

¡Patria o muerte! The Great Zoo and Other Poems by Nicolás Guillén. Translated by Robert Marquez. New York: Monthly Review Press, 1972.

Tengo. Translated by Richard J. Carr. Detroit: Broadside Press, 1974.

Critical Studies

Aguirre, Mirta. "En torno a la 'Elegía a Jesús Menéndez.'" *Revista de Literatura Cubana* 1 (July 1982): 25–33.

Select Bibliography

Augier, Ángel. "The Cuban Poetry of Nicolás Guillén." Translated by Joseph M. Bernstein. *Phylon* 12 (1951): 29–36.

———. "Hallazgo y apoteosis del poema-son de Nicolás Guillén." *Casa de las Américas* 22 (May–June 1982): 36–53.

———. *Nicolás Guillén: Notas para un estudio biográfico-crítico.* 2 vols. Santa Clara, Cuba: Universidad Central de las Villas, 1964.

———. *Nicolás Guillén.* Havana: Instituto del Libro, 1971.

———. "La revolución cubana en la poesía de Nicolás Guillén." *Plural* 59 (August 1976): 47–61.

Bottiglieri, Nicola. "Consideraciones y apuntes sobre 'El gran zoo' de Nicolás Guillén." *Casa de las Américas* 22 (May–June 1982): 108–16.

Boulware-Miller, Kay. "La 'Balada del güije' de Nicolás Guillén, un experimento en el folclor." *Casa de las Américas* 22 (May–June 1982): 99–107.

Boyd, Antonio Olliz. "The Concept of Black Esthetics as Seen in Selected Works of Three Latin American Writers: Machado de Assis, Nicolás Guillén, and Adalberto Ortiz." Ph.D. diss., Stanford University, 1974.

Brathwaite, Edward Kamau. "The African Presence in Caribbean Literature." In *Slavery, Colonialism, and Racism,* edited by Sidney W. Mintz. New York: Norton, 1974.

Cartey, Wilfred G. *Black Images.* New York: Teachers College Press, Columbia University, 1970.

Cobb, Martha K. "Concepts of Blackness in the Poetry of Nicolás Guillén, Jacques Roumain, and Langston Hughes." *CLA Journal* 18 (December 1974): 262–72.

———. *Harlem, Haiti, and Havana: A Comparative Critical Study of Langston Hughes, Jacques Roumain, and Nicolás Guillén.* Washington, D.C.: Three Continents Press, 1979.

Costán de Pontrelli, María. "The Criollo Poetry of Nicolás Guillén." Ph.D. diss., Yale University, 1958.

Coulthard, Gabriel R. "Nicolás Guillén and West Indian Negritude." *Caribbean Quarterly* 16 (1970): 52–57.

———. *Race and Colour in Caribbean Literature.* London: Oxford University Press, 1962.

Davis, Paul A. "The Black Man and the Caribbean Sea as Seen By Nicolás Guillén and Luis Palés Matos." *Caribbean Quarterly* 25 (May–June): 72–79.

Davis-Lett, Stephanie. "Development of Poetic Techniques in the Works of Nicolás Guillén." Ph.D. diss., Princeton University, 1976.

———. "Literary Games in the Works of Nicolás Guillén." *Perspectives on Contemporary Literature* 6 (1980): 135–42.

Depestre, René. *Poète à Cuba.* Paris: Eds. Pierre Jean Oswald, 1976.

Ellis, Keith. "El americanismo literario y la más reciente poesía de Nicolás Guillén." *Unión* 14 (December 1975): 4–21.

———. "Conversation with Nicolás Guillén." *Jamaica Journal* 7 (March–June 1973): 77–79.

Select Bibliography

———. *Cuba's Nicolás Guillén: Poetry and Ideology.* Toronto: University of Toronto Press, 1983.

Fernández Retamar, Roberto. "El son de vuelo popular." *Revista de Literatura Cubana* 1 (July 1982): 34–52.

Fitz, Earl E. "The Black Poetry of Nicolás Guillén and Jorge de Lima: A Comparative Study." *INTI* 4 (Fall 1976): 76–84.

García Barrio, Constance Sparrow de. "The Black in Cuban Literature and the Poetry of Nicolás Guillén." Ph.D. diss., University of Pennsylvania, 1972.

González Echevarría, Roberto. "Literature of the Hispanic Caribbean." *Latin American Literary Review* (Special Issue on Hispanic Caribbean Literature) 8 (Spring–Summer 1980): 1–20.

Hernández Novás, Raúl. "La más reciente poesía de Nicolás Guillén." *Casa de las Américas* 13 (November–December 1972): 156–58.

Irish, E. A. George. "Nicolás Guillén's Position on Race: A Reappraisal." *Revista Interamericana* 6 (Fall 1976): 335–47.

Jackson, Richard. *Black Writers in Latin America.* Albuquerque: University of New Mexico Press, 1979.

Kutzinski, Vera M. "The Miraculous Weapons of Nicolás Guillén and Aimé Césaire." *Callaloo* 22 7 (Fall 1984): 141–50.

———. "Poetry and Politics: Two Books on Nicolás Guillén." *MLN* (Hispanic Issue) 98 (March 1983): 275–84.

Liddell, Janice Lu. "The Whip's Corolla: Myth and Politics in the Literature of the Black Diaspora: Aimé Césaire, Nicolás Guillén, Langston Hughes." Ph.D. diss., University of Michigan, 1978.

López-Baralt, Luce. "El más reciente experimento poético de Nicolás Guillén: *El diario que a diario.*" *Avance* (San Juan, Puerto Rico), 9 November 1972, 16–18.

Lowery, Dellita Martin. "Selected Poems of Nicolás Guillén and Langston Hughes: Their Use of Afro-Western Folk Music Genres." Ph.D. diss., Ohio State University, 1975.

MacMurray, David Arthur. "Dos negros en el Nuevo Mundo: Notas sobre el 'americanismo' de Langston Hughes y la cubanía de Nicolás Guillén." *Casa de las Américas* 14 (January–February 1974): 122–28.

Mansour, Mónica. "Transformaciones en la poesía de Nicolás Guillén." *Plural* 11 (July 1982): 4–11.

Marbán, Jorge A. "Innovaciones formales en la última poesía política de Nicolás Guillén." *Crítica Hispánica* 6 (Fall 1984): 145–53.

Marinello, Juan. "Hazaña y triunfo americanos de Nicolás Guillén." *Revista de Literatura Cubana* 1 (July 1982): 17–24.

Martínez Estrada, Ezequiel. *La poesía afrocubana de Nicolás Guillén.* Montevideo: ARCA, 1966.

———. *La poesía de Nicolás Guillén.* Buenos Aires: Calicanto, 1977.

Morejón, Nancy. *Nación y mestizaje en Nicolás Guillén.* Havana: UNEAC, 1982.

Select Bibliography

————, ed. *Recopilación de textos sobre Nicolás Guillén*. Havana: Casa de las Américas, 1974.

Mullen, E. J. "Nicolás Guillén and Carlos Pellicer: A Case of Literary Parallels." *Latin American Literary Review* 3 (Spring–Summer 1975): 77–88.

Noble, Enrique. "Nicolás Guillén y Langston Hughes." *Nueva Revista Cubana* (1961–62): 41–85.

Olchyk, Martha K. "Historical Approach to Afro-Cuban Poetry." Ph.D. diss., Texas Christian University, 1972.

Pereira, Joseph R. "Raza en la obra de Nicolás Guillén después de 1959." *Sin nombre* 13 (April–June 1983): 30–48.

Piedra, José. "From Monkey Tales to Cuban Songs: On Signification." *MLN* (Hispanic Issue) 100 (March 1985): 361–90 (on "Balada del güije").

Prats Sariol, José. "Del humor en la poesía de Nicolás Guillén." *Unión* (1982): 181–87.

Rivero-Rodas, Oscar. "La imagen de los Estados Unidos en la poesía de Nicolás Guillén." *Casa de las Américas* 20 (May–June 1980): 154–60.

Rodríguez Rivera, Guillermo. "Nicolás Guillén y el vanguardismo." *Revista de Literatura Cubana* 1 (July 1982): 59–70.

Ruscalleda Bercedóniz, Jorge M. *La poesía de Nicolás Guillén*. Rio Piedras: University of Puerto Rico, 1975.

Sabourin Fronaris, Jesús. "De 'Negro bembón' a 'El apellido' (lectura de un poema de Nicolás Guillén)." *Casa de las Américas* 22 (May–June 1982): 91–98.

Sardinha, Dennis. *The Poetry of Nicolás Guillén*. London: New Beacon Books, 1976.

Smart, Ian. "The Creative Dialogue in the Poetry of Nicolás Guillén: Europe and Africa." Ph.D. diss., University of California at Los Angeles, 1975.

Vitier, Cintio. *Lo cubano en la poesía*. Havana: Instituto del Libro, 1958.

White, Florence E. "Poesía negra in the Works of Jorge de Lima, Nicolás Guillén, and Jacques Roumain, 1927–1947." Ph.D. diss., University of Wisconsin, 1952.

Williams, Lorna V. *Self and Society in the Poetry of Nicolás Guillén*. Baltimore: Johns Hopkins University Press, 1982.

Acknowledgments

Acknowledgments

The lines from "The Kingfishers" are reprinted by permission of New Directions Publishing Corporation.

From *The Collected Poems of Wallace Stevens:* Copyright © 1923, 1931, 1935, 1936, 1937, 1938, 1942, 1944, 1945, 1946, 1947, 1948, 1950, 1951, 1952, 1954 by Wallace Stevens. The lines from "The Comedian as the Letter C," "The Man with the Blue Guitar" and "The Snow Man" are reprinted with the permission of Alfred A. Knopf, Inc.

From *The Maximus Poems*, by Charles Olson: Copyright © 1960, 1968, 1975 by Charles Olson and the Estate of Charles Olson. © 1983 by the Regents of the University of California. Reprinted with the permission of the University of California Press.

From *Explications/Interpretations*, by Jay Wright: Copyright © 1985 by Jay Wright. From *Dimensions of History*, by Jay Wright: Copyright © 1976 by Jay Wright. From *The Homecoming Singer*, by Jay Wright: Copyright © 1971 by Jay Wright. From *The Double Invention of Komo*, by Jay Wright: Copyright © 1980 by Jay Wright. From *Soothsayers and Omens*, by Jay Wright: Copyright © 1976 by Jay Wright. Reprinted with the permission of Jay Wright.

From *Sun Stone*, by Octavio Paz. In *Configurations*, translated by Muriel Rukeyser. Copyright © 1971 by New Directions Publishing Corporation. Reprinted with the permission of New Directions Publishing Corporation.

The photograph of Jose Clemente Orozco's *Gods of the Modern World* (Panel 17 of *The Epic of American Civilization*) is reproduced courtesy of the Trustees of Dartmouth College, Hanover, N.H.

Index

Index

Index

Brown, Sterling, 53
Burke, Kenneth, 3, 109, 251n2
Byrd, Don, 258n78

Cabeza de Vaca, Alvar Núñez, 113, 116, 266n118, 267n125; in "The Kingfishers," 42–43
Cabrera, Lydia, 134, 177, 220, 265n87, 266n104, 269n5
Cabrera Infante, Guillermo, 136, 183, 195–96, 206, 209, 219–25, 227, 249, 274n88, 277nn124–27
Calame-Griaule, Geneviève, 263n60, 264nn68,70
Canon, 13–14, 28, 34–35, 149, 234, 242–50, 256n65. See also Library; Modernism
Caotismo (chaotic enumeration), 192–93, 213–15, 230, 274n85. See also Algarabía; Baroque; Fragmentation; Freeplay
Cardenal, Ernesto, 270n28
Carlyle, Thomas, 244
Carnival, 41, 183, 196, 231–34, 249. See also "Día de Reyes"; Limbo
Carpentier, Alejo, 45, 72, 73, 157, 208, 228, 265n100, 276n115, 277n132, 278n140; El arpa y la sombra, 26–32, 34, 35, 59, 94, 151, 265n61; Concierto barroco, 201, 249, 272n57; ¡Ecue Yamba-O!, 36, 229–30, 249, 277nn135–36, 278n139; Explosion in a Cathedral, 101, 117, 263n62, 274n84; The Kingdom of This World, 57–58, 141–43, 146, 247, 249, 262n30, 270n19; on "lo real maravilloso," 145, 182, 220–21, 226–27, 266n116, 273n70; Reasons of State, 166. See also Baroque
Cartagena de Indias, 125, 130, 239
Castro, Américo, 98, 115, 259n5, 265nn88–89
Castro, Fidel, 164, 176, 233–34, 278nn144–49
Catholicism, 31, 41, 42, 125, 187, 200, 203, 228–30
Cervantes, Miguel de, 206
Césaire, Aimé, 81, 261n27, 264n63

Céspedes, Manuel de, 206
Charles V (Carlos I, Spanish emperor), 124
Christianity, critiques of, 19, 41, 58–59, 62. See also Catholicism
Christophe, Henri, 57, 58, 247
Cíbola (Hawikúh, or Granada). See Seven Cities
Circumcision, and writing, 77, 79, 85, 90–91, 107–9. See also Excision; Ritual; Wounding
City, 56, 64, 97, 139–40, 181–82, 185, 239, 241; in Benjamin Banneker poems, 49, 55–64; and origins of culture, 107–9; as structure of freedom and authority, 106–30, 249. See also Cartagena de Indias; Columbian Exposition; Cuzco; Havana; Labná; Macchu Picchu; Rome; Santafé de Bogota; Seven Cities; Tenochtitlán
Class, 135, 189–90. See also Race
Clearings, textual, 97–101, 117–21, 129, 140, 143, 151, 153, 159, 161, 173, 209, 247. See also "El monte"; Silences; Wounding
Clissold, Stephen, 267n123
Closure, 69–71, 83, 85, 95, 139, 143, 162–63, 173–74. See also Authority; Epilogue; Supplement
Collingwood, R. G., 262n42
Columbian Exposition (Chicago), 57, 261n28
Columbus, Christopher, 4, 30, 56, 57, 254n33, 256nn61–62, 261n23; in El arpa y la sombra, 26–32, 34; in The Bridge, 33–34; in "The Discovery of the Indies," 26–33, 39, 41; Journal of the First Voyage, 30, 149, 151, 156, 172, 182
Consensus ideology, x, 6, 8–9, 15, 152, 246. See also Canon; Culture
Coolidge, Calvin, 224, 277n128
Cortés, Hernando, 4, 261n23; and Cabeza de Vaca, in "The Kingfishers," 42–43; in "The Destruction of Tenochtitlan," 41–43, 123; and La Malinche, 43–45, 258n81; in Orozco frescoes, 240–42; and Père Sebastian Rasles, 42–43

291

Index

Index

Index

Index

reception of, 3, 12; "De Soto and the New World," 43, 46; "The Destruction of Tenochtitlan," 31, 41–43, 123; "The Discovery of the Indies," 26–33, 39, 44; "The May-Pole at Merry Mount," 39, 41; "Père Sebastian Rasles," 38, 41, 42–43; as poetic montage, 22, 255n52; "Red Eric," 23–26; "Voyage of the Mayflower," 38, 240

Jahn, Janheinz, 267n129, 269n11
James, C. L. R., 261n29
James, Daniel. See Santiago, Danny
James, Henry, 244–45
Jefferson, Thomas, 56, 59–60, 65. See also Banneker
Johnson, James Weldon, 36, 53
Journey, 76–79, 81–85, 90. See also Ritual
Joyce, James, 117–18, 206, 267n128

Knight, Franklin W., 260n15, 274n76
Kutzinski, Vera M., 261n24, 264n67, 266n106, 268n3, 270n21, 278n6

Labná, 64, 129–30, 239
La Chingada (La Malinche, or Doña Marina), 43–45, 46, 258n81. See also Cortés
Lanati, Barbara, 23, 256n56
Landaluze, Victor Patricio de, 207–8, 276nn115–16
Larsen, Nella, 36
Las Casas, Bartolomé de, 30
Lavin Cerda, Hernán, 254n29, 271n45
Lawrence, D. H., 3, 4, 251n2
Leante, César, 136
León-Portilla, Miguel, 267n139, 268n142
Lersundi, Francisco (Captain-General), 201, 206–7, 208, 209
Levi, Albert William, 107, 109, 266n108
Lévi-Strauss, Claude, 72, 75, 163, 263n54, 271n39
Lezama Lima, José, 122, 152, 172, 178, 267n138, 271n36
Library: in El arpa y la sombra, 27–32; burning of, in Paterson, 26, 28, 32, 41, 249; as homogeneous representa-

tional space, 18–19, 45, 127–28, 239–43, 255n41. See also Archive
Limbo, 76–79, 87, 97, 100, 105, 129, 142, 249
Lincoln, Abraham, 4, 23, 45–46
Literacy: and freedom, 51, 54, 61, 81–82, 89–90, 121, 142, 152, 234; and social control, 52–53, 260n15
Literature: of the Cuban Revolution, 165–68; myth of, 5, 9–10, 18, 242, 246; as propaganda, 149. See also Representation
Locke, Alain, 37
López-Baralt, Luce, 253n29, 271n45
López-Baralt, Mercedes, 271n32
López Prieto, Antonio, 207
Luis, William, 274n75
Lyotard, Jean-François, 256n64

Macchu Picchu, 126, 130
Maceo, Antonio, 207, 210, 219, 221, 274n81
Machado, Gerardo, 232, 277n128
McKay, Claude, 36
MacMurray, David Arthur, 270n24
Marban, Jorge A., 272n50
Marginality, 36–37, 46, 166–68, 242–48. See also Hyphenation
Mariani, Paul, 251n1, 255n49
Martí, José, 147, 172, 207–8, 210, 232–33, 276nn110,118, 278n143
Martínez Estrada, Ezequiel, 147–50, 164, 170–71, 270n27, 272n52
Mayas, 64, 129–30
Mellon, Alfred, 269n3
Melville, Herman, 4, 264n80
Mendive, Rafael María, 206–7, 276n108
Merrim, Stephanie, 225, 273n71, 277n129
Metaphysics, 69, 72, 76, 82
Miller, Perry, 253n15, 261n25
Modernism, 86, 252nn2–3; and postmodernism, x, 11, 34–35, 93–95, 257n66. See also Epilogue
Moncada Barracks, attack on, 233–34
"El monte," 96–97, 161, 229
Morejón, Nancy, 147, 156, 268nn2–3, 269n10, 270nn24–25,31, 271nn41,45, 278n3

295

Index

Index

Race, 187, 192, 227, 274nn80–83; and
  canon formation, 14, 111, 254n30,
  257n68; and class, 189–90
Remos, Juan, 276nn112–13
Representation, 63–64, 87, 242, 262n39.
  See also Literature
Revueltas, Silvestre, 269n9
Riddel, Joseph, 5, 21, 22, 60, 61,
  253nn12,22, 254n38, 255n50,
  256n53, 257n66, 262nn34,36
Ritual, as poetic grammar, 50, 59, 64–
  65, 74–79, 85, 87, 90–92, 107–30,
  138–40, 230–31, 249. *See also* Ide-
  ograms; Sacrifice
Rivero-Rodas, Oscar, 276n121
Rodríguez Freyle, Juan, 105–6, 124–25,
  205, 261n24, 268n143, 276n104
Romantic poetry, 255n40, 272n56
Rome, 64, 107–8, 110, 121, 124
Rosenthal, Franz, 263n50
Rowell, Charles H., 259n3, 262n46

Sacrifice, 65, 85, 90–91, 108–9. *See
  also* Culture; Ritual
Sanneh, L. O., 71, 263n50
Santafé de Bogota, 105, 124–25, 130
Santiago, Danny, 254n30
Sardinha, Dennis, 268n2
Sarduy, Severo, 136, 173, 216, 272n55,
  274n121, 275n102
Self, 40–41, 81, 87–91; effacement of,
  73, 83–86, 100, 140, 143, 163, 170.
  See also Identity; Otherness
"Sensemayá" (Guillén), 136–46, 150,
  155, 163–64, 170, 183, 196, 205,
  228, 265n94, 269n9
"Separation of the Twins, The," 79–82,
  89
Seven Cities, legend of, 111–21, 239,
  266nn117–19, 267nn120–23,124. *See
  also* Alarcón; Cabeza de Vaca; Es-
  tevan; Guzmán; Niza; Vásquez de
  Coronado
Siemens, William, 273n71
Silences, as cultural subtexts, 43–44, 59,
  151. *See also* Clearings
Simpson, J. H., 267n122
Slave insurrections, 140–42, 203

Slave narratives, 53, 260n16
Slavery, 27, 52, 61–62, 65, 81–82, 101,
  105, 139–42, 144, 148, 150, 155,
  159, 188–90, 260nn15–17, 274nn76–
  78; abolition of, 57, 59, 65, 207, 210,
  274n81
Slave trade: Equipment Treaty, 275n100;
  illegal, 189, 203; transatlantic, 57,
  157, 188
Son, 104–6, 265n99
"Son de la Ma' Teodora," 103–6, 110,
  121, 140, 221, 229
Spain, 16, 31, 56, 124–25, 145, 152,
  155, 162, 187, 260n15; and Arabic
  world, 98, 115, 181, 230, 259n5. *See
  also* Cuba; Imperialism
Spitzer, Leo, 193, 214–15, 273n67,
  274n85, 277n123
Stepto, Robert B., 51, 95–96, 259n12,
  260n16, 261n22, 265nn81,83–84
Stevens, Wallace, 17, 18, 20, 35, 39,
  44, 121, 254n38, 255n47,
  258nn71,75,83
Sundiata (Sun Dyata) (King of Mali),
  66–67, 262n41
Supplement, 23, 69–71, 78, 95, 109–
  10, 127, 148–49, 153, 158–59, 162–
  63, 173–74, 209, 256n57. *See also*
  Clearings; Epilogue

Tejera, Diego Vicente, 208
Tenochtitlán, 42, 64, 123–24, 126, 130,
  239–40. *See also* Cortés
Ten Years' War, 174, 190, 201, 206–8
Terrell, John Upton, 276nn120–21
Thomas, Hugh, 273n68, 274nn77,81–
  82,90–91, 275nn92–96,98–102,
  276n119, 277n128, 278nn143,145–49
Thoth, 116–18, 121. *See also* Death
Todorov, Tzvetan, 256n61, 265n97,
  267n125
Toomer, Jean, 36, 244–45, 255n49,
  257n68
Trachtenberg, Alan, 253n13, 261n28
Translation, 25, 30, 98–99, 258n71,
  268n1; and deculturation, 218, 220–
  21; of ideograms, 80–82

Index

Varela Zequeira, José, 208
Vargas Llosa, Mario, 223
"Variation on a Theme by LeRoi Jones" (Wright), 58–59
Varona, José Enrique, 207–8
Vásquez de Coronado, Francisco, 115
Vico, Giambattista, 107–9, 266nn109–10
Villaverde, Cirilo, 208, 266n107
Violence, and writing, 19, 22–23, 44–45, 247. *See also* Wounding
Voice, figures of, 54, 74–78, 88, 130, 171. *See also* Orality; Phonocentrism
Von Hallberg, Robert, 34, 35, 252n11, 256nn63,65

Walcott, Derek, 20, 95, 255n48
Weaving, 64, 118–19, 262n40. *See also* Nommo; Writing
Weiland, Steven, 258n71
"West Indies, Ltd." (Guillén), 143–47, 150
Whitman, Walt, 3, 5, 7, 8, 18, 46, 81, 193
Williams, Lorna, 268nn2–3, 269n11
Williams, William Carlos, x, xi, 4, 60, 73, 94, 134, 172, 176, 239, 241–44, 255n51, 258nn77,85, 259n11; *Al Que Quiere!* 258n71; *The Desert Music*, 39, 258n71; and Eliot, 5, 51, 255n39; *The Great American Novel*, 19, 20, 255nn44,49; *In the American Grain*, 3–46, 59, 62, 123, 130, 150, 151, 152, 167, 173, 240, 244, 247–49; on mixed ancestry, 36–37, 257n67; on new mythology, 25, 256n60; *Paterson*, 3, 5, 21–22, 26, 28–29, 39, 49, 70, 91, 242, 249, 252n11, 256n55,

271n40; on poetry and prose, 21–22; and Pound, 5, 252nn3,11; on Spanish and Latin American literature, 37, 258n71; *Spring and All*, 20–21; as translator of Octavio Paz, 37, 258nn71–72. *See also individual titles*
Wounding, and writing, 89–91, 94, 96, 97, 108–9. *See also* Clearings; "El monte"; Violence
Wright, Jay, x, xi, 15, 41, 52, 53, 54, 134, 135, 138, 143, 145, 152, 153, 155, 160, 163, 167, 170, 176, 209, 234–35, 239, 245, 259n9, 263n53, 264nn65,74, 266n113; *Dimensions of History*, 11, 12, 14, 17, 28, 37, 38, 49, 58, 67, 68, 70–75, 77–130, 133, 149, 151, 162, 173, 177, 229, 242, 247–49, 261n29, 263nn61–62; *The Double Invention of Komo*, 9, 50, 69–78, 90–91, 102, 128, 161, 177, 259n8; *Explications/Interpretations*, 49, 73, 99, 128, 265n91; *The Homecoming Singer*, 49, 58–59, 71, 261n21; plays, 259n3, 263n49; on *poiêsis*, 109; *Soothsayers and Omens*, 45, 49, 55–65, 69, 71, 73, 74, 75–76, 91, 94, 119, 262n32. *See also titles of poems*
Wright, Richard, 161, 244, 271n38
Writing: as unwriting, 39, 76–78, 155, 209; figures of, 64, 74–78, 76–79, 89, 109, 127–28, 172–73, 180–82, 249. *See also* Algarabía; Baroque; Journey; Orality; Weaving; Wounding

Zanjón, Peace of, 207, 210, 274n81, 276n109
Zequeira, Manuel de, 186

298

Against the American Grain

Designed by Chris L. Smith.
Composed by the Composing Room of Michigan, Inc.
in Electra with display lines in Gill Sans Bold.
Printed by Thomson-Shore, Inc.
on 50-lb. S. D. Warren's Olde Style and
bound by John H. Dekker and Sons, Inc.
in Holliston's Kingston Natural and stamped in AP Glossy #45.